"HOW THE DOMINOES FELL"

SOUTHEAST ASIA IN PERSPECTIVE

Second Edition

John H. Esterline
California State Polytechnic University, Pomona
and
Mae H. Esterline
Ramon Magsaysay Award Foundation

UNIVERSITY
PRESS OF
AMERICA

Lanham • New York • London

Copyright © 1990 by
University Press of America®, Inc.
4720 Boston Way
Lanham, Maryland 20706

3 Henrietta Street
London WC2E 8LU England

Library of Congress Cataloging-in-Publication Data

Esterline, John H.
How the dominoes fell : Southeast Asia in perspective / John H.
Esterline and Mae H. Esterline.—2nd ed.
p.   cm.
Includes bibliographical references (p.   ) and index.
1. Asia, Southeastern—Politics and government.
I. Esterline, Mae H.   II. Title.
DS525.7.E84   1990   959—dc20   90–12914 CIP

ISBN 0–8191–7971–X (cloth : alk. paper)
ISBN 0-8191-7972-8 (pbk. : alk. paper)

The paper used in this publication meets the minimum requirements of
American National Standard for Information Sciences—Permanence
of Paper for Printed Library Materials, ANSI Z39.48–1984.

To our grandson
John Herschel Esterline

FOREWORD

If there is such a thing as an Asian Mind, John and Mae Esterline have encountered it in all its varied nuances and have gotten to know not only what happened, but why things happen the way they do. Few historians and analysts of current affairs or diplomats in the field are able to do this because they lack the sort of empathy which the Esterlines have—the ability to enter another country's personality and to imaginatively and correctly appreciate it to the full.

As Asia Director of the International Press Institute and as a foreign correspondent for many years, I was able to observe the Esterlines' work in the Philippines, Egypt and in my own country, Sri Lanka, when John Esterline was Public Affairs Officer of the United States Information Service. They had many intimate friends in the national governments, the media and in the universities whose trust and affection they had earned because of that empathy. Not an easy thing to do in those nervous years of the Cold War.

Later, after his retirement from the United States Foreign Service when Esterline re-entered academia, the United Nations Population Fund assigned the Esterlines to make a qualitative survey of how the Asian media reported and commented upon the population problems of a region which was home to half the world's peoples. This enabled them to study many other Asian countries and to take a second look at the countries in which they had served before. The Esterline Report became the basis of the planning of the UNFPA's information system in the ensuing years of the decade.

To write studiously on Asia beyond and beneath the stereotypes, to find the relevant connections between seemingly discrete events, to relate ancient history and current affairs, to touch the deep vein of values which underlie social and political behavior in a highly complex and complicated region is a mammoth undertaking. This is what Dr. and Mrs. Esterline have achieved.

Varindra Tarzie Vittachi
Deputy Executive Director,
External Relations, UNICEF

v

TABLE OF CONTENTS

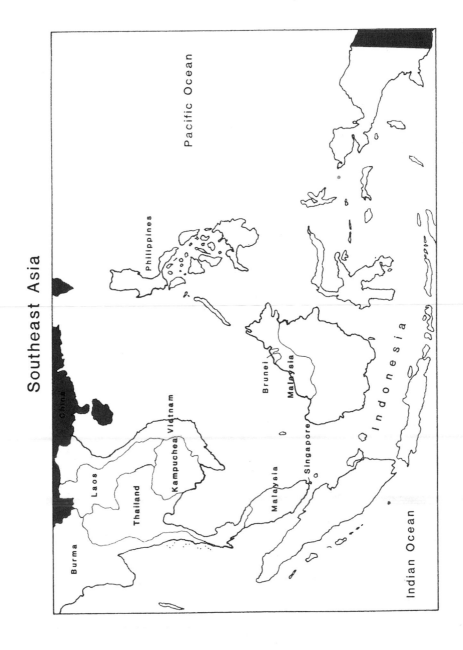

CHAPTER 1
INTRODUCTION

Southeast Asia as an entity entered the consciousness of most western peoples during World War II when the term was used to identify the heterogeneous areas of mainland and insular Asia east of India and south of China as a theatre of military operations. The war was followed by the decline and gradual demise of the colonial era and the release of nationalist energies on an unprecedented scale. Eight newly independent nations—Vietnam, Kampuchea, Laos, Burma, Indonesia, Malaysia, Singapore and the Philippines—emerged during subsequent years; only Thailand enjoyed pre-war independence. Brunei became independent January 1, 1984, thus ending the last vestige of traditional European colonialism in the region.

As the peoples of Southeast Asia, acting within separate national political frameworks, sought to achieve political and economic expectations, namely responsible governments, material well being, and the benefits of modernization, they encountered severe problems. Ideological conflict, intra-regional and domestic ethnic, religious and cultural differences, and the inability to assimilate western political institutions, combined to destabilize the new political entities. Political and military conflict, intensified by superpower intervention in the region, assumed such proportions that within a decade after 1945 Southeast Asia had shifted from the wings to center stage in world politics.

The ensuing war in Vietnam involved, in addition to the indigenous combatants, some 50 countries that provided economic, military and medical assistance, and in some cases military contingents. It enmeshed the United States in the longest armed conflict in its history, and the third most costly in terms of lives lost. The war divided Southeast Asia anew—into an ideologically rigid bloc of Indochinese communist-governed states on one hand, and the pragmatic five-party Association of Southeast Asian Nations (ASEAN) on the other. In its wake came tragedy (new conflicts, brutal regimes, floods of refugees, invasions) as well as progress (rapid economic development, move-

1

ment toward bloc integration), and the rise of the region to major international political, economic and strategic importance.

The clock cannot be turned back. The new importance of the Southeast Asian nations is permanent, as are the new complexities in their relations with each other, with the western world, and especially with China, the United States and the Soviet Union. Some of their new problems appear almost intractable in the short run. Refugees, lack of jobs, rapid population growth, overcrowded cities, ethnic and religious tensions and the difficulties of evolving workable and responsible governmental mechanisms are challenges which are not likely to disappear. Indeed, they may become more difficult to resolve. Thus familarity with the political culture (i.e., the patterns of orientations of societies toward politics and government) of Southeast Asia is a prerequisite for the student or general reader who seeks a perspective on international politics and comparative governments.

COMPARATIVE POLITICS: ANALYTICAL APPROACHES

A number of theoretical and analytical approaches are used by scholars for studying comparative politics. The *political culture* approach seeks "an explicit and systematic understanding of political orientations and behavior" through analysis of the cultural environment within which political behavior takes place.[1] The *group politics* concept suggests that the study of interaction among collectivities of individuals, acting in pursuance of common political goals, is the appropriate area of focus; the collectivity is considered to have a greater role than the individual in shaping political processes.[2] *Systems analysis* applies the concept of system, as in biology, to politics. Thus a political system experiences inputs in the form of expectations, demands and supports which it must convert into outputs, namely policy and behavior that will enable the system to survive as a political entity. *Structural-functionalism,* a variation of systems analysis, theorizes that predictable patterns of interaction (structure) within the political system are necessary for function accomplishment, the chief function being system survival. *Elite analysis* attempts to identify those who wield real political power and who make the important decisions within or without the formal political apparatus. The theory posits, in the words of Harold Lasswell, that the "few who get the most of any value are the elite; the rest are the rank and file."[3]

These and other theoretical approaches seek to discern and to describe patterns of decision making, power and authority relationships within political entities. While this volume focuses upon exposition rather than theory, leaving to others the application of their ideas to events and developments, the work is most compatible with the *political culture* approach.

"Political culture is the product of the historical experience of the whole society."[4] Moreover, as Professor Benjamin Schwartz observes, it appears questionable whether *strictly political data* can "be treated in isolation from the historical and cultural context from which they are extracted."[5] Building upon the concept, scholars emphasize that contemporary politics in Southeast Asia must be viewed within the context of precolonial antipathies among disparate ethnic and religious groups, and that the countries of Southeast Asia differ from those of any other part of the world.[6]

IDEOLOGY

Aspirations of peoples took a quantum leap forward in the wake of World War II as decolonization proceeded and as new independent, national, political entities emerged under varying circumstances to supplant colonial regimes. The goal of political independence was universally portrayed as the first step toward achieving a better life. But the bountiful life is not achievable unless economic and human resources (land, capital, labor, technology, natural resources and management) are available and *are utilized* and unless societies are organized for production and for effective distribution of goods and services.

Both satisfactory means and the desired ends have eluded political leadership in many parts of the world. Indeed large numbers of people within national political cultures are worse off than in former times. Therefore decision-makers, i.e., the political elites within societies, have widely invoked ideology—the articulation of basic values held by a party, class or group—to defuse threats to their leadership as well as to promote enthusiasm for their programs.

The major ideological conflict of this century is between political systems founded upon an already mature ideology of individualistic capitalism that emphasizes individual rights of political choice and property, and the Marxist-Leninist doctrine of communism which advocates centralism and emphasizes collective rather than individual rights. The contest between the two systems produced ideological warfare whereby "each side seeks to achieve ideological conformity among its own people while trying to convert the large masses of mankind outside its borders to its basic values and 'way of life.' "[7]

While neither the communists nor the non-communists have been able fully to meet human expectations, the non-communist world of developed states has been by far the more successful. This is so in large measure because the developed non-communist world has reacted to the Marxist-Leninist challenge by inaugurating reforms that have substantially modified the capitalist philosophy of unfettered individual property rights while retaining and expanding other individual rights, and by sanctioning broad government intervention in the social process. Mixed economies and "welfare states" are the results. The communists adhered rigidly to communist orthodoxy until the mid-1980s, despite their inability to meet the economic and political expectations of the one and a half billion persons governed by their regimes. Political leaders in China and the Soviet Union have since initiated dramatic social change. Nevertheless they and their allies continued to oppose perceived inequalities and injustices which they attributed to norms imposed upon them by industrialized, non-communist western nations. Posited in these terms, both communist and non-communist state behavior after World War II is more readily understandable.

In the immediate postwar period decolonization in Southeast Asia was embraced both by the international communist movement and by the principal western leader, the United States—which pushed its subordinate allies toward acceptance. Decolonialization provided Marxist-Leninists opportunity to pursue their goal of achieving fundamental social change in Southeast Asia to reflect their political/economic values; for the victorious western allies it was an opportunity to create social value systems that would mirror their political and economic mores. Conflict became inevitable.

How the Dominoes Fell   The domino theory, which was accepted by President John F. Kennedy among others, "assumes that if some key nation or geographical region falls into Communist control, a string of other nations will subsequently topple 'like a row of dominoes'."[8] The theory was elevated to prominence in a National Security Council paper of January 1954, approved by President Dwight D. Eisenhower, which predicted that the loss of any single country in Southeast Asia would lead to the loss of all of Southeast Asia, with eventual broader political implications.[9]

Although widely criticized, the "domino" concept helped explain events in Southeast Asia which followed the military victory of the Democratic Republic of Vietnam over the forces of the Republic of Vietnam in 1975. China and the Soviet Union, both patrons of the victorious communist leaders in their successful struggle against the non-communist south and its U.S. ally, each sought political influence in Indochina. The Vietnamese sided with the Soviets, who offered them direct military assistance. The Kampucheans established a pro-Chinese communist government in 1975 which was driven out by a Soviet-Vietnamese-supported regime in 1978–79. Earlier Laos had been subjugated by Vietnam.

The validity of the domino theory became evident as Vietnam consolidated its control over all of Indochina. If the concept is broadened to include societal dominoes—democratic values, individual rights, the rule of law—then indeed many dominoes have been toppled in Indochina. Genocide, expulsion of peoples and shattered economies have resulted. Moreover, Indochina has experienced armed conflict in each of the succeeding years.

Nevertheless, the domino theory can only partially explain post- 1975 events in Southeast Asia. The political histories of the peoples of the region offer further clues to understanding contemporary politics. Their precolonial institutions and ethnic rivalries, as well as their colonial experiences, have helped shape their societies.

GEO-ETHNIC SETTING

Contemporary scholars and governments identify Southeast Asia as the area of the Asian continent and the offshore archipelagos and islands which lie roughly between the Tropic of Cancer and 12 degrees south latitude, and comprise the mainland states of Burma, Kampuchea, Laos, Thailand and Vietnam; peninsular Malaysia; insular Brunei and Singapore; and archipelagic Indonesia and the Philippines.

All lie within the great wind-rain systems known as the southwest and northeast monsoons. Winds blowing from the southwest across the Indian Ocean or South China Sea at a steady speed of 14 to 25 knots per hour bring heavy rains to most of Southeast Asia during the summer months. The strength, speed and regularity of these winds made possible the early voyages to the region from India and the Arabian peninsula. The northeast monsoon, with considerably less strength and regularity, blows down from central Asia and brings dry winds to most of mainland Southeast Asia during the winter, but brings rain to the east coasts and islands when it blows across water. The northeast winds permitted the return trips of the early voyagers. Most coastal areas except those of Singapore and Indonesia, which lie in the doldrums (a belt of calms and light variable winds), are threatened seasonally by typhoons. All the states are characterized by a hot tropical climate, with tropical forests (jungles) in the low lying areas, deciduous forests at medium altitudes and evergreen rain forests at the higher elevations.

Mainland Southeast Asia is separated from the great plains of central China by heavily dissected high plateaus and lower mountains running roughly west to east. South of these peaks and plateaus the mountain ranges of mainland Southeast Asia run parallel north to south and channel the river systems of the area in a north-south pattern.

The major rivers of mainland Southeast Asia originate in the highlands of Tibet or the Yunnan plateau of southeastern China. The Mekong, one of the great river systems of the world, rises in the Tibetan Himalayas and empties some 2,500 miles away in the South China Sea. It flows through or forms the borders of Burma, Laos, Thailand, Kampuchea and Vietnam. Luang Prabang, the former royal capital of Laos, is situated at the upper navigational limit of the Mekong; Phnom Penh, the capital of Kampuchea, is at the apex of its delta which, encompassing most of southeast Kampuchea and Vietnam below Saigon, is one of the major rice growing regions of Southeast Asia.

In north Vietnam the Red River (so called because of the amount of red silt it carries to the sea) rises in Yunnan and flows a brief 311 miles into the Gulf of Tongking, again forming a rich agricultural delta which has long been a center of human settlement.

The great river system of Thailand, the Chao Phraya, is formed by four major tributaries in the north—Ping, Wang, Yom and Nan—and the Pa Sak which drains the eastern portion of the country. Often called the Menam, which simply signifies river, it empties into the Gulf of Siam 25 miles below Bangkok, Thailand's capital. The delta and the central basin are also major rice growing regions.

The third large river system of Southeast Asia is the Irrawaddy of Burma. Rising in all probability in the extreme southeastern corner of Tibet, the river flows entirely within Burma. It is made up of many tributaries and empties through nine channels into the Andaman Sea, the eastern portion of the Bay of Bengal. The Irrawaddy delta begins 180 miles from the sea, is 150 miles at its widest point and has historically been a great rice basket.

The Malay peninsula and the islands which make up archipelagic Southeast Asia lack major river systems, but the short, sometimes navigable streams, have been foci for human settlement since prehistoric times.

Human settlements have existed in Southeast Asia for millenia. Cave dwellings on the Philippine island of Palawan date back 30,000 to 40,000 years, and recent discoveries in Borneo indicate a pottery-using people lived in what is now the modern Malaysian state of Sabah some 18,000 years ago. Findings in Thailand (Non Nok Tha) show evidence of rice planting, domestication of cattle and use of bronze in the 5th millenium B.C. The oldest known people still extant in Southeast Asia are the Negritos, a small dark race with a primitive social structure, who are found mainly in the mountains and jungles of Malaysia, Thailand, the Philippines, and certain Indonesian islands; their origins are uncertain.

The major group of the present day peoples, the Malays, apparently migrated into the region from Yunnan and Tibet within the past 4,000–

5,000 years. They have traditionally been divided into two branches, the Proto-Malay, the earliest Malay who brought with them a neolithic (polished stone) culture, and the later Deutero-Malay, who either had already developed a bronze and iron culture, or who readily absorbed it from contact with Chinese traders in the area.

The Proto-Malay are thought to have moved into mainland Southeast Asia by 2500 B.C., pushing on to the islands of the east and south by 1500 B.C., and the Deutero-Malay by about 300 B.C. The migrations of these two related peoples are considered to have been slow, continuing movements rather than two waves. Although much assimilation took place over the centuries, the Deutero-Malay, with their greater ability or willingness to adopt superior cultures and techniques, eventually pushed the Proto-Malay into less desirable mountain and jungle regions.

When Indian cultural expansion into Southeast Asia began the peoples of the region already had well developed but less sophisticated social systems. These had, in many cases, been influenced by the Chinese, either before the Malays left Yunnan, or by contact with traders after their migrations. The social structure was based upon rice culture and domestication of the water buffalo and ox. Many of the peoples had developed a high artistic tradition in wood carving, in the practical and artistic use of bronze and to a limited extent of iron, and they had mastered the arts of navigation, even though their ancestral roots were in the highlands of central Asia.

Women were important in this society and the male-dominated religions introduced from India never completely destroyed their role. Lineage continued to be traced through the female line, as did often succession to leadership. Religion was a combination of animism and ancestor worship, both of which have persisted to the present in various forms.

When Southeast Asia first appears in recorded history, about the beginning of the Christian era and primarily in Chinese annals, four peoples were *in situ:* the Viet in north Vietnam; the Cham in central Vietnam; a Khmer-type people in the Mekong River valley and delta of Kampuchea and south Vietnam; and the Mon, cousins of the Khmer, in the Irrawaddy (and Salween) of southern Burma. The Pyu, a Tibeto-Burman race which has disappeared as an ethnic entity, also lived in the central plain of Burma. The Tai were to appear on the scene shortly, first in Burma (as the Shan) and subsequently in Laos (as the Lao) and Thailand (as the Thai). Malays, in today's understanding of the term as primarily the Deutero-Malays of Malaysia, Indonesia and the Philippines, were settled in riverine communities throughout those areas.

In the ensuing centuries a sinicization of Southeast Asia took place.

As cities and opportunities for trade developed, Chinese merchants and traders entered the region. The movement greatly accelerated during the last two hundred years as business and investment expanded and Chinese coolie labor was imported into the region to work the new plantations and mines, particularly in the area under British control—Burma and the Malay peninsula. Heavy migration into Vietnam also occurred.

Impact of Religion   Although the major early population movements came from the perimeters of the Chinese empire, influences from India determined the religious, political and cultural orientations of the states and empires that developed subsequently. The first penetration of Indian culture was achieved by sea traders before the Christian era and the first empire in Southeast Asia, Funan (100–600 A.D.), was founded upon an already developed Hinduized political base. The Shaivite form of Hinduism exerted the greatest influence since Shaivism exalted the ruler as *devaraja*—god and king. The *devaraja,* who recognized no superior on earth, could thus legitimize his claim to be *chakravartin,* or universal monarch. Although Hinduism remains evident in literature, the arts, and popular religion throughout Southeast Asia, it is practiced today, in mutated form, only on the Indonesian island of Bali.

The next great religious-political wave from India was Buddhism. Mahayana (Greater Vehicle) Buddhism came primarily from western and south India via seamen as early as the 5th century. For Mahayanists the ideal is the *bodhisattva,* one who has achieved enlightenment but has pledged not to enter Nirvana until all living creatures can enter as well. But by attributing god-like qualities to *bodhisattvas,* the Mahayanists paved the way for the deification of the king as a *buddha-* or *bodhisattva-raja,* paralleling the Hindu concept of *devaraja.* Mahayana Buddhism played a major role during the great empires of Kampuchea and Indonesia, but it can be found today only in Vietnam and there in a sinicized form, influenced heavily by Taoism.

Hinayana (Lesser Vehicle), or preferably Theravada (School of Elders), Buddhism was exported from eastern India and Sri Lanka, primarily under the Pala dynasty of India (750–1200 A.D.). It "reformed" the Buddhism of much of mainland Southeast Asia without essentially changing the political culture that had developed under Hinduism and Mahayana Buddhism. Theravada, which holds to the doctrine of the historical Buddha, requires one to work out his own salvation, independent of celestial help. Since Theravada doctrine is taught, rather than divined, it developed a concept of hierarchy which could easily be translated into a political structure of power. Theravada Buddhism has traditionally been the religion of Burma, and since roughly the 13th–14th centuries, of Kampuchea, Laos and Thailand.

The third major religious influence in Southeast Asia was Islam, which arrived via Indian as well as Arab traders. For the most part, it was an Islam that had been Indianized. Its appeal was perhaps its forthright theology, a contrast to the complexities of the earlier religions, and like the latter, it represented a total way of life. It was quickly accepted in Malaya, Indonesia, Brunei and the southern Philippines where its expansion was halted in the early 16th century by aggressive Spanish Catholicism.

Christianity is the only major religion (except for Confucianism and Taoism which entered the region with the Chinese and for the most part have remained beliefs of the Chinese communities) that did not have Indian roots. Unlike Indian religions, Christianity achieved its greatest penetration as a consequence of conquest and vigorous government-supported proselytization. Protestant Christianity had less impact than Catholic Christianity. Protestant Dutch and English colonial governments did not play an active role in religious matters as did Catholic Portuguese, Spanish, and French colonial authorities. Christianity is practiced today primarily in the Philippines.

Underlying all the great Indian and Middle Eastern religions was animism, the popular beliefs of the Malay peoples who settled Southeast Asia. It maintained a continuous hold on the common people despite the adoption of more sophisticated religions by the courts.

HISTORICAL EMPIRES

Southeast Asian political histories usually deal with the region as a whole, chronologically recounting broad sweeps of empire. In this volume the authors have chosen to trace the development of individual modern states. While recognizing that the peoples living within these geographic perimeters have been influenced by the beliefs, feelings, and values of nearby cultures, the authors also believe that the particularity of each socio-political culture has produced specific and different orientations over the centuries and that these should be addressed individually. As a prelude to observing individual political systems, a brief mention of the major empires of the region and a broad chronology of their periods of influence is appropriate to help the reader identify historic periods.

Funan (1st–6th centuries, A.D.) was the first empire in Southeast Asia. Founded upon Hindu religious and political concepts, the state was centered in the Mekong delta, in what is today Kampuchea and the southern tip of Vietnam. It controlled most of southern mainland Southeast Asia and the trade routes between China and the Bay of Bengal. Funan was succeeded in the heartland of Southeast Asia (Kampuchea, Thailand, Laos) by the Hinduized empire of Chenla

(7th–9th) and the Hindu/Mahayana Buddhist state of Angkor (9th–15th). At its apogee Angkor was the greatest empire in size and in cultural influence known to Southeast Asia, extending from its center in Kampuchea to the tip of the Malay peninsula and to northern Thailand and Laos.

Other mainland empires, more or less coincident with the empires centered in Kampuchea, were Champa (2nd–15th) in central and southern Vietnam, and the Mon states of Dvaravati (Thailand), and Thaton and Pegu (lower Burma), which existed in some form from at least the beginning of the Christian era until the final subjugation of the Mon peoples by the Thai (14th) and Burmese (18th). The Mon were apparently the first peoples to be exposed to the Indian religions of Hinduism and Theravada Buddhism, and they passed on these culture systems to their successive conquerors.

Three empires arose in Burma between the 11th and 19th centuries—Pagan (11th–13th), Toungoo (15th–18th) and Alaungpaya (18th–19th). They came into conflict with the growing Thai empire of Ayutthia (14th–18th) and the Chakri dynasty (18th–20th) which sought to expand Thai territory both east and west. On the east the Thai collided with the 19th century empire of Annam (Vietnam).

Maritime empires developed on the perimeter islands, sometimes coincident with those of the heartland, but more often arising when mainland empires were weak. They controlled the sea lanes and entrepots between China and India and had their greatest political impact on the Malay peninsula and the Indonesian and Philippine archipelagos, although at times they were strong enough to dictate policies on the mainland. The Sumatran empire of Srivijaya (7th–13th) was superseded briefly by the Sailendra dynasty (8th–9th) on Java. The Sailendras built the great Buddhist temple-mountain at Borobudur which marked the high point in Javanese culture. It was followed on Java by the Majapahit (14th–15th).

The period of European empire building in Southeast Asia began in the early 16th century when the Portuguese took Malacca from its Muslim Malay sultan, and ended essentially with the Japanese conquest of the area during World War II. Portugal (1511–1641) controlled the trade and trade routes between Europe and the Far East. Spain (1565–1898) seized the Philippines and control of the trade between the Far East and the Americas. The Dutch (1596–1949) replaced the Portuguese in the monopoly of European-Asian trade and ushered in the era of European settlement and the plantation economy. The British (1761–1957) eventually broke the Dutch monopoly and unintentionally opened up Southeast Asia to other European powers—the French (1858–1954) who seized Indochina for church and trade, and the Americans (1898–1946) who took the Philippines from Spain because they were available.

The brief Japanese military empire of 1941–1945 superseded the European colonial governments in Southeast Asia and gave rise in the immediate post-World War II period to the area-wide movement for political indepencence.

PLAN OF BOOK

This volume briefly addresses Southeast Asia's political history from earliest times, becoming a more detailed account of events and developments within the nations and within the region from the close of World War II through 1989. It underscores characteristics of indigenous and colonial political cultures, the influence of nationalism, and the impact of the Vietnam War on the region. A watershed in Southeast Asian and world affairs, the war in Vietnam is addressed at length in the chapter on Vietnam.

FOOTNOTES

1. James A. Bill and Robert L. Hardgrave, Jr., *Comparative Politics: The Quest for Theory* (Columbus, Ohio: Charles E. Merriam Publishing Co., 1973. Reprinted by University Press of America, Lanham, Maryland, 1982), p. 85.

2. *Ibid.*, p. 119.

3. Harold D. Lasswell, *World Politics and Personal Insecurity* (New York: Free Press, 1965), p. 3.

4. Jack C. Plano, *et al., Political Science Dictionary* (Hinsdale, Illinois: Dryden press, 1973), p. 287.

5. Benjamin I. Schwartz, "Presidential Address: Area Studies as a Critical Discipline," *Journal of Asian Studies,* November 1980, p. 17.

6. See Donald K. Emmerson, "Issues in Southeast Asian History: Room for Interpretation—A Review Article," *Journal of Asian Studies,* November 1980, p. 45.

7. Plano *et al., op. cit.,* p. 27.

8. Murray Marder, "Our Longest War's Tortuous History," in *A Short History of the Vietnam War,* Millett, Allan R. (ed.) (Bloomington, Indiana: Indiana University Press, 1978), p. 126.

9. *Pentagon Papers* (New York: Bantam Books, Inc., 1979), p. 7.

Vietnam

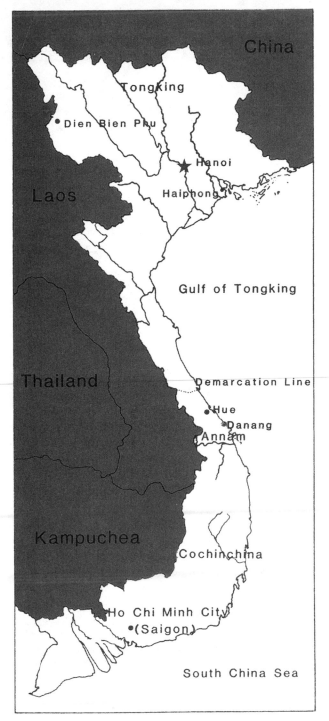

CHAPTER 2
VIETNAM

Vietnam extends 1,000 miles along the eastern rim of mainland Southeast Asia, from southern China to the Gulf of Siam. It is washed on the east by the South China Sea; on the west mountains paralleling the coast form its border with Laos and Kampuchea. It is tropical, monsoonal and subject to devastating typhoons.

Northern Vietnam, known when it appeared on the historical scene as Nam Viet—land of the southern people, that is, those living south of China proper—and in colonial times as Tongking, is drained by the Red River system whose delta forms the bulk of the alluvial land suitable for cultivation. Its traditional capital, Hanoi, is at the head of the delta. The central portion, originally known as Champa and later as Annam, is narrow and lodged between mountains and sea. Its capital is Hue. The south, called during French rule Cochinchina, extends from a mountain plateau to the vast lowlying delta of the Mekong River which drains most of central Southeast Asia. Its modern capital has been Saigon. Vietnam can thus be thought of as two rich rice-growing deltas—that of the Red River in the north and of the Mekong in the south—which are linked by a long narrow littoral.

The Nam Viet, who gave their name to the state, were heavily influenced by the Chinese. But while their political culture reflects an unbroken line and predominates today, civilizations of quite different ethnic, religious and political cultures developed early in south and central Vietnam. These two regions, ethnically Malay, were most affected by India and the Hinduized states of Southeast Asia.

INDIANIZED STATES

In the 1st century A.D. southern Vietnam was part of the Funan empire, the first great power in Southeast Asia. Centered in what is today the Ca Mau Peninsula of Vietnam and Kampuchea, Funan spread across all of southern mainland Southeast Asia and controlled the major trade routes from China to the Bay of Bengal. It was highly

15

Indianized, adopting both Hindu and Mahayana Buddhist religious and court practices, and reached its peak in the 4th and 5th centuries, coincident with the brilliant Gupta period of India. South Vietnam was successively part of the Kampuchean-based empires of Chenla and Angkor (see Kampuchea).

Champa: 192–1471 The people of central Vietnam, the Cham, because of their narrow, rocky coastline and mountainous interior, were a maritime people, preying upon shipping along the coast, and trading as far away as Java and China. They exploited their natural resources and exported camphor, sandalwood and lacquer from their forests, and lead and tin from their mines.

Champa had direct contact with India by sea and was in turn heavily influenced by Hinduism, which permeated religious and social customs and dictated government administration. Champa adopted the Hindu concept of the divine king *(devaraja)* but did not carry the idea as far as did the courts of Funan or the later empires of Kampuchea. Peak Indianization occurred in Champa, as in Funan, during the Gupta period of India when Indian culture was at its brightest and Chinese influence was at a low ebb because of internal political disarray. In 503 Funan conquered Champa but by 540 Champa had turned the tables and absorbed all the territories of Funan above the Mekong delta; these continued to be occupied by Champa and its successor states.

The history of the relationship between the Cham and the Nam Viet of the north was that of constant probing for advantage by one at the expense of the other, with the strength of China at any particular time often determining the outcome. At the beginning of the 5th century Champa took advantage of a dynastic change in China to attack the north, which was at that time a province of China known as Giao Chi. In 446 Giao Chi reversed the situation, invading Champa and carrying off a huge booty—reportedly 100,000 pounds of pure gold; for some time thereafter Champa sent tribute to the Chinese court. However, at the end of the century Champa again began to raid the north. In 605 China retaliated, once more extracting a large booty. Throughout the strong Chinese Tang dynasty (618–906) Champa paid regular tribute to the Chinese emperor. From the 8th to the 11th centuries attacks by the north caused Champa to move its capital further and further south, and during that period the Nam Viet permanently occupied the three northernmost provinces of Champa.

The 12th and early 13th centuries saw the struggle for power swing to the west and the Cham were engaged in constant conflict with the Khmer empire of Kampuchea. The politico-military contest during the last half of the 13th century shifted once again to the north. The Mongol invasion of China, which spread into Vietnam, brought a temporary cessation to inter-state strife.

During the 14th century Champa enjoyed a flash of renewed military might. Its forces invaded and sacked Hanoi in 1371 and then attacked Kampuchea, forcing the Khmer to call on China for aid. A period of civil war followed and exactly one hundred years after the sack of Hanoi, the Nam Viet conquered Champa, taking 30,000 prisoners, including the royal family. All of Cham territory except for one small state in the far south now came under the north. After 1471 Champa, as such, never rose again, but the tensions between central-southern Vietnam and northern Vietnam have continued to surface in other guises, most recently in the Vietnam War of the 20th century.

Although Indian influence predominated in central and south Vietnam for over 1,000 years, it was dissipated during the last 500 as the Nam Viet replaced the Cham in central and south Vietnam and Chinese refugees migrated to the Mekong delta. Indian place names and court names disappeared; Hindu religious practices gave way to the Chinese form of Buddhism (mixed with Taoism and Confucianism); the administrative system was modeled on the Chinese, with civil and military appointments based upon examination, and Sanskrit became a lost language. Even the ethnic characteristics of the people have largely disappeared although some 50,000 now-Islamicized Cham remain in pockets in the central coastal mountain area.

SINICIZED NORTH

The Kingdom of Nam Viet emerged in the millenium before Christ in South China and along the Red River delta of northern Vietnam. It was peopled by a mixture of Malays and Chinese Mongoloids. In 111 B.C. the Han dynasty of China overthrew the Kingdom of Nam Viet and incorporated the Red River valley and a coastal strip as far south as Hue as the southernmost province of China, calling it Giao Chi. By the 3rd century A.D. the Nam Viet had come under firm Chinese imperial administration. Chinese values and Chinese culture were absorbed but the Viet continued to resist Chinese political control.

In 679 the Tang dynasty made the province of Giao Chi a protectorate and renamed it Annam (Pacified South)—a term resented by the Vietnamese. The Tang administered the protectorate as an integral part of imperial China. In the opinion of some historians the long exposure to Chinese administration, ideas and techniques of social organization overcame parochialism and gave the Nam Viet a cohesion and headstart in developing a sense of national identity.[1] Thus, when the Tang dynasty weakened and opportunity arose to break direct Chinese rule, the Nam Viet were better equipped to assert autonomy than were other peoples on the fringes of empire.

In order to break the feudal power of the Nam Viet aristocracy the

Chinese had introduced the concept of the commune, which became the basic administrative and social unit of the village. The commune councils, chosen by the villagers, enjoyed substantial freedom to manage local affairs as long as they met Chinese tax and corvée demands. As a result the communes became foci for preserving traditional language and customs. When they were occasionally subjected to Chinese bureaucratic pressure, the peasants resisted by rallying around their communes. Cohesion was reinforced by the religious tradition of animism or spirit worship, each village having its own guardian spirit which reposed in a communal house, a symbol of village unity. Even the venality of the council members who dealt with the Chinese had a unifying effect: these notables habitually falsified the village rolls to minimize tax and manpower obligations.

The importance of the village to Vietnamese society is central to an understanding of Vietnam's subsequent political history. Organizational and social characteristics of the traditional village became hallmarks of new settlements which were formed in the process of southward migration following military conquests which nearly doubled the size of Vietnam between 939 and the final defeat of Champa in 1471. Each Vietnamese dynasty recognized the village as the linchpin of political and social organization and took pains to preserve its autonomy. In time the village rather than the state came to have the greater executive role in Vietnamese politics, its position being well expressed in the age-old saying, "the laws of the emperor yield to the customs of the village."[2] When the French centuries later compromised village autonomy, their control faltered.

In addition to village autonomy Chinese contributions to Vietnamese political culture included the Confucian system of administration, based upon a scholar-bureaucracy theoretically open to all educable persons, and perhaps more importantly, the tradition of social order which promoted harmony between man and nature as well as man and man. In an extension of Confucian logic, the role of the emperor as Son of Heaven, was to harmonize man's activities with the unchanging cycles of nature. Failure to do so, it was believed, brought calamity, either natural (flood, famine, drought) or human (breakdown of administration, incapacity to maintain public order). Such catastrophes were clear signs that the central authority was no longer fit to govern—it had lost the "mandate of heaven." These attitudes can help explain the failure of south Vietnam to maintain village allegiance during the civil war of the 20th century. The villagers may have concluded that the mandate had passed to the communists.

Vietnamese Dynasties The demise of the Tang dynasty in China in 906 and the ensuing disorders provided the Vietnamese with the opportunity under Ngo Quyen to drive the Chinese out of the Red

River delta. By 946 the state of Vietnam had become a reality, although a special relationship with China was acknowledged by regular tributary missions to the Chinese court, a practice that continued until the French absorption of Vietnam in 1885. The tributary system both minimized Chinese interest in reasserting direct control and legitimized the rulers of Vietnam.

The Ly dynasty (1009–1225) was the first of the great Vietnamese dynasties. In 1069 the third emperor, Ly Thanh Tong, inflicted a severe defeat on the Hinduized southern kingdom of Champa, the first of many. He also gained territory at the expense of the Khmer kingdom of Kampuchea in the west and renamed his state Dai Viet (Greater Viet), a name retained until 1802 when Emperor Gia Long changed it to Vietnam.

The Ly achieved more than merely expanded territorial control based on military might. By providing access to power through the examination process, and by regularizing recruitment for civil administration—both hallmarks of the Confucian system in China—they brought about political stability. The bureaucracy, or mandarinate, maintained relative stability and order for almost 400 years. Buddhism became the state religion but Confucianism and Taoism were tolerated. Taoism, with its accent on nature and spirits, was especially popular in the countryside where it intermixed with animism and an adulterated form of Buddhism.

The Tran dynasty (1225–1400) came to power in consequence of a marriage arrangement between the Ly and Tran families. The period was marked by further territorial expansion at the expense of the Cham and Khmer kingdoms to the south and west; by three invasions from China by the Mongol armies (1257, 1284 and 1287); by eventual reestablishment of peaceful relations with the Chinese Mongol (Yuan) dynasty, and by a reemphasis on Confucianism rather than Buddhism.

The political system remained essentially intact until the late 14th century when a military leader who proclaimed himself Emperor Ho Quy Ly usurped the throne and precipitated Chinese reoccupation of the country. Autonomy was restored in 1428 by Le Loi. The greatest achievements of the Le emperors were on the battlefield. Champa was destroyed as a political entity in 1471 and all Cham territory to about the 13th parallel was annexed. The remaining southern territory became a vassal state to the kingdom of Dai Viet.

However, within the next forty years regional rebellion displaced the central authority. By 1516 three families—Mac, Trinh and Nguyen—had emerged in the north, central and southern regions respectively, each wielding significant military power. They reduced the Le dynasty to figurehead status, yet upheld its legitimacy. The defeat of the Mac by the Trinh in 1592 brought the Trinh in the north and the Nguyen south of the 17th parallel into conflict over control of the puppet Le rulers whom both sides regarded as the only legitimate authority. In many respects the Nguyen-Trinh conflict was the Champa-Dai Viet feud in new guise. After more than a half century of war a truce was concluded which was to last 100 years. The country was divided north and south, a fact underscored by the double wall across the plain erected by the Nguyen at the 18th parallel just north of Hue.

Trinh-Nguyen Dualism   The division of Vietnam after 1673 enabled the Trinh to consolidate their hold on the northern kingdom—called Tongking by the Europeans who had appeared on the scene. The Nguyen at Hue, in what was now known as Annam, accelerated their southern expansion at the expense of the Cham, as well as of the Khmer who occupied the Mekong River delta and most of the south-central portion of the Indochinese peninsula. By the mid-18th century the Nguyen kingdom of Annam extended to the limits of contemporary Vietnam in the south. This expansion brought the Nguyen into competition with Thailand for control of Kampuchea and bitter fighting continued between the two until 1847. They were also frequently at war with Laos during the 17th to 19th centuries. During this period a large number of Ming dynasty refugees from Manchu (Ching) China settled in the Mekong delta, populating and sinicizing the previously lightly inhabited Cham-Kampuchean areas. While Annam was involved in the mainstream of Southeastern Asian politics, Tongking was primarily concerned with its relationship with China.

ARRIVAL OF THE EUROPEANS

The Portuguese, following the seminal voyage to India of Vasco da Gama in 1498, were the first Europeans in Vietnam. By 1540 they had begun to visit Annam regularly and Tongking occasionally. The objective of the Portuguese was to expand their trade routes and missionary network, which by 1550 extended from Goa (India), through Malacca (Malaya), Indonesia, and Macao (South China), to Nagasaki in Japan. But Portuguese dreams of buying raw silk in Vietnam to sell in Nagasaki were thwarted by the Japanese who at that time maintained highly successful economic relations with Southeast Asia. Thus, although trade with the Nguyen was nominal, Portugal kept a permanent resident in Annam, and Portuguese missionaries were active in various parts of the country.

The Dutch, whose commercial fortunes in Asia rose as those of the Portuguese declined, set up a factory (trading establishment) in Tongking in 1640, and the English established one there in 1672. However, by 1700 both the Dutch and the English had abandoned their commercial interests. They learned, as had the Portuguese, that trading and shipping facilities were allotted by the Vietnamese on a selective basis and that the Japanese and Chinese were favored over Europeans.

The place of the Dutch and the English was soon taken by the French who pursued both religious and trading goals, vigorously supported by the Foreign Missionary Society and the French East India Company both founded in 1664. By the 18th century the Society had converted significant numbers of Vietnamese, and Christian influence was an important factor at the Annamese court in Hue. The French East India Company, however, failed to achieve economic penetration. It attempted a number of unsuccessful ventures in the first half of the 18th century and was finally disbanded by the French government in 1769.

In 1777 the French saw another opportunity to gain a foothold in Vietnam. The Tay-son rebellion, named after the home district of three brothers—Van-Nhac, Van-Lu and Van-Hue—who led a coalition of merchants and peasants against Nguyen repression, broke out in 1771. Van-Nhac and Van-Lu captured Saigon in 1777, killing all leading members of the Nguyen family except young Prince Nguyen Anh who, with the help of the French missionary Pigneau de Behaine, escaped to an island in the Gulf of Siam where he was able to rally supporters. Pigneau aided Nguyen Anh, hoping that in an alliance with France the Nguyen ruler would champion Christianity.

For the next six years Nguyen Anh fought the rebels for possession of Saigon—one of the few southern strongholds not securely in Tay-son hands. In 1784, his army shattered, the prince commissioned Pigneau to approach Paris concerning a formal alliance, which resulted in the Versailles Treaty of November 28, 1787. The treaty called for substantial Vietnamese concessions to France in return for French military and naval aid to the Nguyen forces.

In the meantime the tide of war turned and French help was of only subsidiary importance to Nguyen Anh's increasingly successful campaigns against Saigon—which were aided also by the Thai. Nevertheless, only the French Revolution, which erupted in mid-1789, diverted France from its preoccupation with obtaining political leverage in Southeast Asia.

By 1793 Nguyen Anh defeated Van-Lu and began to move north against Van-Nhac. He captured Hue in 1801 and Hanoi in 1802. Proclaiming himself Emperor of Vietnam at Hue the same year, he assumed the name Gia Long, a contraction of the names of the capitals at the extremes of his empire, Gia Dinh (Saigon) and Thanh Long (Hanoi). He made Hue into a strong fortress, established firm central governmental control, revived the Confucian examination system, permitted Christianity and founded the united Vietnamese state which persisted until the French conquest in the latter half of the century.

The Nguyen dynasty remained nominally in place until the abdication of the last emperor, Bao Dai, at the end of World War II.

POLITICAL INDICATORS

Vietnamese political history prior to the mid-19th century underscores characteristics of Vietnamese society which help explain its subsequent political development.

1. Vietnam's long association with China produced a deep-rooted internal sinification which led to absorption of Chinese ideas and values (the Confucian model) and to Chinese social and political organization (the scholar-bureaucracy).
2. Vietnamese religious beliefs were based on Chinese models of Confucianism, Taoism and Buddhism and owed little to Indian religious/cultural values as found in the rest of Southeast Asia. Sinification, however, diminished as one moved south.
3. The tradition of village autonomy assured the continuity of Vietnamese society despite long periods of extreme disequilibrium beyond village walls.
4. The "mandate of heaven," and thus the legitimacy of power, was seen to pass from one ruler to another in times of natural or human catastrophe.
5. The Nam Viet of the north and the Cham of the south both historically exhibited military prowess and expansionist tendencies. The history of Vietnam, therefore, has been one of internal division and inter-area struggle, and a brief one of union; division has traditionally been between the north and south at a line slightly north of Hue.
6. The European states failed to achieve significant economic or political penetration of Vietnam prior to the French conquest in the mid-19th century, a period late in the history of European colonial exploitation.

FRENCH COLONIALISM

Mid-19th century French imperialism in Vietnam was advanced by an alliance of French religious zealots and French naval forces. The religious, smarting under the anti-Catholic policy of Gia Long's successors, played upon the expansionist desires of the naval commanders whose ships plied the China seas to protect French political and commercial interests in coastal Asia. Three times during the 1840s French warships showed the flag to protect French nationals.

In 1857 a decision was made to intervene in Vietnam on the domestic political grounds that France had to obtain further Asian possessions or accept second-power status among European nations. A French naval expedition accordingly captured Danang September 2, 1858 and Saigon on February 17, 1859. Lack of reinforcements and outbreak of tropical diseases caused abandonment of Danang early in 1860, but the faltering French garrison at Saigon was heavily reinforced early in 1861 and by June three southern provinces were in French hands. On July 1 the French announced to the world that Saigon had become a French city.

A year later Emperor Tu Duc (1848–1883) sued for peace. The Saigon Treaty of June 6, 1862 granted the French possession of the three Mekong delta provinces. Tu Duc's capitulation was a tradeoff with the French for their assurance that they would not actively support the rebellion in his northern province, Tongking. In 1867 a French admiral occupied the remainder of the Mekong delta and simultaneously secured French protectorate status over Kampuchea. The Vietnamese territories became the French colony of Cochinchina.

Five years later a French trader precipitated French involvement in Hanoi by seizing a portion of the city and obtaining support of the governor of Cochinchina. The adventure came to an end in 1874 when France signed a treaty securing formal Vietnamese recognition of all French conquests in Cochinchina, the right to post a resident (adviser) in Hue, and access to Red River commerce. For their part the French agreed to relinquish the fortifications seized in Hanoi. Nevertheless within the decade a French expeditionary force took Hanoi and a French fleet bombarded Hue which capitulated; the treaty making Tongking and Annam French protectorates was signed August 25, 1883. Thereafter, the Nguyen dynasty, confined to its court in Hue, was virtually powerless. The designation of the country as Vietnam was forbidden and France proceeded to divide and rule the area as three states: Tongking, Annam and Cochinchina. The Indochinese Federation, which included Kampuchea, and after 1893 Laos, was formed to consolidate the French acquisitions.

Colonial Administration   French management of Indochina from the 1880s to World War II mirrors the classic administrative pattern employed by European colonial powers during that period. Throughout Southeast Asia the empire builders were challenged to meld traditional values, social organizations and economies, with modernized western ones. In part they were successful; in part they failed ignominiously. The result was to produce in Indochina, as elsewhere, a halfway house which satisfied neither the governors nor the governed.

French residents general were in place after 1884 and the office of Governor General of French Indochina was established that year. Separate policies and programs were promulgated for each of the three major administrative regions. Cochinchina, an outright colony, was administered directly by a governor and a colonial council which sent a representative to the Chamber of Deputies in Paris. The council had legislative functions and both French and Vietnamese members. The French recruited and trained civil servants without regard for the traditional Confucian examination system—initially because the mandarins fled north—and instituted the French judicial system.

Annam and Tongking, technically protectorates rather than colonies, were administered indirectly through the existing political and administrative structures under the supervision of advisory councils. The extremely punitive traditional judicial system was retained in both regions. However, French and French-trained technocrats and bureaucrats gradually replaced the mandarins as the examination system, unsuitable to a modernizing society, was phased out. Overall, French rule was more liberal in Cochinchina than in the protectorates.

Social and economic change in Vietnam produced problems similar to those of other modernizing colonial societies in Southeast Asia. The French, after a cursory study of Vietnamese landholding, decided all land belonged to the emperor, and thus to them as his de facto successor. Land that was temporarily unoccupied, but which by custom belonged to a peasant because his ancestor had cleared it, was given to Frenchmen who established plantations and hired the peasant as laborer on his own land. New areas in the south which had been drained were sold cheaply to French *colons* rather than to the landless Vietnamese. By 1930 the average peasant holding was smaller than before 1880, although the amount of land under cultivation had quadrupled.[3] Moreover, the mercantilist economic system—based upon Vietnam supplying raw materials to France and absorbing French industrial production—inhibited a broadening of the economic base and thus of opportunity.

In the social sphere the French practiced a policy of assimilation, turning the peoples of their overseas possessions into *français de couleur* (Frenchmen of color). Rooted in both humanitarianism and an assumption of white superiority, French policy ignored the values and vitality of the indigenous culture. Therefore, as the Vietnamese elite (administrative cadres, naturalized French citizens, western educated persons, entrepreneurs, and members of the traditional ruling class) moved away from traditionalism it was difficult for them to find a place for themselves in society since they were neither French nor truly Vietnamese.

Civil government was dominated by the French so positions of real authority for Vietnamese were few. The industrializing north was controlled by a limited number of French proprietors and the agricultural south by an equally small number of French landowners. Urban migration caused severe unemployment. Worse, the French were reluctant to share political power. They suppressed newly forming and broadly based political organizations and failed to develop a community of interest with the Vietnamese.

This situation was not unique. Each of the other colonial societies of Southeast Asia also reflected a basic disequilibrium. The same kinds of elites in other countries faced similar problems concerning personal identity and frustration over unfulfilled expectations resulting from conflict between traditional and modern values. In the economic sphere mercantilism was the rule and colonial policy and programs favored the metropolitan powers. Alien legal norms produced limited numbers of wealthy indigenous entrepreneurs and landowners and the consequence was the same: the rise of nationalism. But only in Indochina was nationalism captured by the communist movement.

NATIONALISM

The phenomenon of nationalism—a sense of allegiance that exalts one nation above all others—emerged at the close of the 19th century, particularly in Vietnam, Indonesia and the Philippines. Its first tangible targets were the colonial administrations whose bureaucracies appeared to indigenous scholars, journalists and politicians as symbols of alien, self-anointed and self-alleged superior cultures. The power, privileges and even the very presence of colonial administrators became catalysts that drew together heretofore disparate groups, creating among them a sense of nationhood.

An initial goal of the nationalists was to achieve reform of colonial administrative structures to an extent that would enable the indigenous populations to enter them and to participate in administrative decision making. The goal, although technically achieved, was insufficient because indigenous personnel admitted to the colonial civil services were often coopted by the authorities, becoming themselves members of the elite and thus indistinguishable from the foreign rulers, Nationalists then turned to political action. They demanded lawmaking bodies and electoral representation in them. In response the metropolitan powers permitted indigenous advisory bodies. The ensuing frustration accelerated growing demands for complete political independence.

Ironically, political independence and full nationhood have underscored the continuing economic and cultural dependence of the developing Southeast Asian nations on their former political masters. Nationalism therefore persists as a vital force, manifested in the world of 1990 by demands for reforms in international economic, technological, financial, legal—and even information—systems.

Rise of Vietnamese Nationalism   The tortuous course of nationalism in Vietnam is usually considered to have begun with the scholar Phan Boi Chau (1867–1940) of central Nghe An province (also the birthplace of Ho Chi Minh), who participated in the first "Scholars Revolt" against French occupation during the years 1893–1895. Self-exiling himself to Japan in 1906, he founded the Viet Nam Duy Tan Hoi (Association for the Modernization of Vietnam). Shortly after the outbreak of the 1911 Chinese revolution Chau arrived in Canton where he inaugurated the Viet Nam Quang Phuc Hoi (Association for the Restoration of Vietnam) with the support of Chinese revolutionary leaders. Both organizations were able to exert some influence within Vietnam by communicating with members of internal Vietnamese secret societies that substituted for political cadres. In 1916 the Quang Phuc Hoi, operating from Canton, was able to coordinate simultaneous rebellions throughout most of Cochinchina. Chau eventually took a more favorable view of the French but not before he had spread Chinese revolutionary ideas among his countrymen and promoted Japan as a constitutional model. Two main political currents sprang from Chau's activities: moderate nationalism which sought a meaningful protectorate, and revolutionary nationalism which sought independence and basic political change.

The Constitutionalist Party, the first indigenous political organization sanctioned by the French, was organized in Saigon in 1923. Although it advocated reform within the framework of Franco-Vietnamese collaboration, the French showed little enthusiasm for, or understanding of, the movement. In the early 1930s Emperor Bao Dai drew up proposals for reform, assisted by young Ngo Dinh Diem (later to become prime minister and president of South Vietnam), who was minister of the interior and head of the secretariat of a Vietnamese-French commission formed to carry out the proposals. When the French declined to make meaningful concessions, the emperor's enthusiasm evaporated and Diem resigned, disillusioned with both the emperor and the French. The failure of the moderate section to secure reform or to develop a strong economic and social platform to raise the status of the—for the most part—landless peasantry, precipitated the rise of revolutionary nationalism.

Revolutionary nationalist agitation in the 1920s centered in Canton, China, where the Kuomintang (KMT), the Chinese Nationalist Party, was in power. Having overthrown the Manchu dynasty, the KMT—then supported by the Soviet Union—welcomed the numerous political exiles from Vietnam. Among them was Nguyen Sinh Cung, or Ho Chi Minh as he later chose to be called, apparently to conceal his earlier communist affiliation.

In Paris in 1920 Ho had become a charter member of the French Communist Party and had gone to Moscow to study Marxist doctrine.

In 1925 he went to Canton where, with fellow exiles from his native province of Nhge An, he established the Viet Nam Cach Menh Thanh Nien Chi Hoi (Vietnam Revolutionary Youth League) commonly known as Thanh Nien. In 1927 the Viet Nam Quoc Dan Dang (Vietnam Nationalist Party), or VNQDD, was organized in opposition to the Thanh Nien. Operating from Hanoi, it was led by Nguyen Thai Hoc who chose the organization, programs and methods of the KMT as the party's model. In 1930 the VNQDD sponsored mutinies and demonstrations which the French repressed so severely that the VNQDD was driven underground and did not resurface until World War II.

In the meantime Ho Chi Minh was forced to leave Canton in 1927 when the KMT turned against the Communist Party. He fled to the Soviet Union and subsequently went to Hong Kong where in 1930 he established the Dong Duong Cong San Dang (Indochinese Communist party) on instructions from the Moscow-based Communist International. With suppression of the VNQDD, revolutionary momentum shifted to the communists who brought the factions in exile together, announced a program for revolution and freedom, and dispatched agents to establish revolutionary village governments in Vietnam. The French reacted with severe "pacification" measures, demolishing the "soviets" and jailing much of the communist leadership; Ho was imprisoned by the British in Hong Kong and the Indochinese Communist Party was suppressed.

Rise of the Vietminh   Ho was freed by the British in 1933, and in 1936 the French released his colleagues in Vietnam. An Indochinese Democratic Front, made up of both communist and non-communist groups, was organized and functioned briefly, mainly as a vehicle for the communists. It was led by Pham Van Dong who was to become premier of the Democratic Republic of Vietnam (DRV) and by Vo Nguyen Giap, the general who would defeat the French at Dien Bien Phu in 1954.

The Front found itself in disarray in the face of swiftly changing international alignments as World War II began. The Stalin-Hitler pact of September 1939 caused Paris to outlaw the Communist Party and all communists who could be found in Vietnam were arrested; others fled to China. After the defeat of the French by the Germans in June 1940 and the creation of the Vichy collaborationist government, the Japanese, who were allied with the Germans, imposed their demands on the French in Indochina. In return for Japan's recognition of Vichy sovereignty in Indochina, French authorities agreed to accept large numbers of Japanese troops in the region and to permit Japan to establish naval and air bases there. A further exodus to China of Vietnamese communists took place as these events unfolded.

Nevertheless Ho, in May 1941, convened in northern Vietnam the eighth session of the Central Committee of the Indochinese Communist Party to create the Viet Nam Doc Lap Dong Minh Hoi (Vietnam Independence League), better known as the Vietminh. It was ostensibly a coalition of all anti-French Vietnamese groups: in practice it became indistinguishable from the Communist Party.

The third external event that changed the situation was the sudden German invasion of the Soviet Union in June 1941. This action turned the Vietminh overnight into a pro-Allied, pro-French force; following the Japanese attack on Pearl Harbor in December it became pro-American as well.

The Chinese nationalist government, fighting the Chinese communists as well as the Japanese, became suspicious of Ho. They traced his communist connections back to the early 1920s and arrested him in 1942. They then turned to the non-communist Vietnamese exiles and provided them with financial support to create a new political coalition, the Dong Minh Hoi (Revolutionary League) which included both the VNQDD and the Vietminh. In this way the Chinese hoped to dilute communist influence in Vietnamese exile politics and to make use of the exiles to gather intelligence for them on Japanese activities in Vietnam.

The Vietminh continued, however, to pursue its own course. It successfully employed guerrillas in Vietnam to harass the Japanese and the French and it established its own intelligence network. Faced with the fact that the Vietminh was the only effective Vietnamese force working against the Japanese, the Chinese released the ostensibly reformed Ho in September 1943 in exchange for his offer of assistance. Ho instead strengthened the Vietminh at the expense of the other parties in the coalition. Alarmed, the Chinese in March 1944 prompted the VNQDD, acting under the banner of the Dong Minh Hoi, to establish in southern China the Provisional Government of Vietnam in which Ho Chi Minh was permitted to fill a minor post. Chang Fa-kwei, the south China warlord, became its leader. Vietminh association with the Provisional Government lasted only a few months.

Vietminh guerrilla operations and intelligence reports proved useful enough to the war effort that the U.S. flew Ho into Vietnam in October 1944 to join his associate, Vo Nguyen Giap, and establish a headquarters there. Ho's emphasis on nationalism at this time gave him legitimacy in American eyes, and his and Giap's political-military skills drew praise from other allies who also chose to look on them as anti-Japanese patriots.

Operating from mountain areas north of Hanoi the Vietminh, however, remained only a localized force until a Japanese move on March 9, 1945 provided an opportunity of which they took quick advantage. The Japanese—sensing impending defeat, and unnerved by evidence of munitions and agents from newly liberated France being air dropped into northern Vietnam—demanded that the French military be placed under Japanese command. When the French rejected the ultimatum, the Japanese quickly disarmed and interned most French units and Cochinchina was placed under direct Japanese military occupation.

Two days later Emperor Bao Dai, at Japanese insistence, proclaimed the independence of Annam and attempted to form an administration to replace French civil authority; Cochinchina, entirely in Japanese hands, was not mentioned in the proclamation. In Tongking Ho Chi Minh refused to support the Bao Dai initiative and began to refer to Vietminh units as the "National Liberation Army." Not strong enough to rise frontally, the Vietminh mounted strikes and demonstrations against the Japanese and expanded their guerrilla operations.

French and Americans operating from China assisted the Vietminh with air drops of arms and a Franco-American liaison team. Japanese authority began to disintegrate and the Vietminh began to achieve acceptance by its ability to maintain a semblance of civil order in the wake of the Japanese breakdown. By June 1945 six mountain provinces were under Vietminh control.

In April the Japanese had sought to bring the nationalist groups into the Bao Dai regime. Tran Trong Kim, a prominent educator, agreed to form a government which eventually established itself in Saigon, Hanoi and Hue. Some administrative progress was achieved and in July the government declared "Vietnam" the name of the country. On August 8 the Japanese returned sovereignty over Cochinchina to the imperial government at Hue.

On July 27, 1945 the Allied chiefs of state, meeting in Potsdam, Germany, had issued an ultimatum for Japan's immediate and unconditional surrender which the Japanese rejected. August 10, following the American atomic bomb attacks on Hiroshima and Nagasaki, Japan accepted the ultimatum. Six days later the Vietminh, under the direction of Ho Chi Minh, formed the nucleus of a provisional government and formally severed its ties with the Dong Minh Hoi-sponsored government-in exile.

On August 17 the Hue government called a mass meeting in Hanoi to enlist support, but Vietminh propagandists took over the assemblage of 150,000 persons and turned the gathering into a repudiation of the Bao Dai government. On August 19 some 1,000 armed Vietminh entered Hanoi and occupied government buildings without resistance. The emperor gave up the throne August 25 and expressed his support for the Vietminh—believing it to be a pro-Allied force—and in effect gave it legitimacy. On August 30 Ho entered Hanoi. Two days later, before 500,000 people, he proclaimed the Democratic Republic of

Vietnam (DRV) and declared September 2, 1945—the Feast of Vietnamese Martyrs—as Vietnam Independence Day.

Democratic Republic of Vietnam Ho Chi Minh perpetuated the
nationalist theme in his first government, choosing half his ministers
from outside the Vietminh, three from the affiliated Democratic Party
and three from non-party groups. In November 1945 he officially
dissolved the Indochinese Communist Party. Meanwhile the regime
consolidated its position by means of political indoctrination and by
impressive mobilization of labor to cope with widespread famine and
economic breakdown. The multi-party posture was maintained during
the six months Chinese troops remained in the north, under the
Potsdam agreement, to see to Japanese withdrawal.

With the signing of the Sino-French accord of February 1946, which
provided for the withdrawal of Chinese troops from Tongking and the
entry of French forces, it became imperative for Ho to obtain as
favorable as possible an agreement with the French. General Philippe
Leclerc, commander of French reoccupation forces and acting High
Commissioner of Indochina, offered to recognize the Democratic
Republic of Vietnam as a "free state" in the Indochinese Federation
proposed by the French government. Ho reluctantly acquiesced because French warships were in the act of entering Haiphong harbor.
The agreement of March 6, 1946 provided for the presence of 15,000
French troops north of the 16th parallel to be withdrawn in five years,
and provided that the DRV would have its own parliament and army
and manage its own finances. It also committed both parties to negotiations in France to determine whether the three states of Vietnam
should be united under one national government.

With the departure of the Chinese, the Dong Minh Hoi and VNQDD
concluded that they could maintain an identity separate from the
Vietminh only by a fierce anti-French stance. They therefore engaged
in violence to such a degree that the French and Vietminh military
forces combined to attack their strongholds which, when conquered,
were taken over by the Vietminh. In May 1946 the Vietminh, now
tantamount to the previously dissolved Communist Party, developed
the Lien Viet (Popular Front) encompassing all legal political organizations—including remnants of the VNQDD and the Dong Minh Hoi—
and all cultural religious and professional groups. Non-joiners were
stigmatized as being hostile to independence and democracy. The Lien
Viet thus became the vehicle through which the Vietnamese communists, emulating their fellow ideologues in China, embarked upon total
mobilization of the population under their control.

As agreed in March, a conference was held at Fontainebleau,
France, in July. Ho, who led the Vietnamese delegation, acquiesced in
a *modus vivendi* that left the unity question unresolved but set October

30, 1946 as the date for a ceasefire in the guerrilla war which was raging in the south.

When Ho and his delegation returned from France great gains in Vietminh strength were evident. At the National Assembly meeting, October 28 to November 14, a new, more openly communist government was chosen. A new, but never promulgated, constitution was also announced proclaiming the Democratic Republic of Vietnam to be an indivisible nation of three parts—Bac Bo (Tongking), Trung Bo (Annam) and Nam Bo (Cochinchina)—and a Permanent Committee was installed to administer the government. By the end of 1946 non-communist nationalist elements in the north had been neutralized.

Republic of Cochinchina The Potsdam Conference had provided that the British would accept the surrender of Japanese forces south of the 16th parallel and British troops arrived in Saigon on September 12, 1945. At the time Saigon was in chaos because of the continued presence of large numbers of Japanese soldiers and the contending claims of various Vietnamese nationalist organizations. When French troops there encountered severe difficulties the British general, Douglas D. Gracey, commanded Japanese forces to assist the French against the nationalists. Taken aback by the actions of Gracey and Jean Cédile—the newly appointed Commissioner of the Republic for the South—Admiral Lord Louis Mountbatten, Supreme Allied Commander for Southeast Asia, summoned both men to Singapore to insist they reopen negotiations with the nationalists. However when General Leclerc, accompanied by large French units, arrived in Saigon in October he drove the various Vietnamese nationalist forces from the city's outskirts and began the task of reasserting French control to the 16th parallel.

On March 24, 1945 France had proclaimed its intention to create an Indochinese Federation with limited self government within a French Union. A year later a reconstituted version of the pre-war Constitutional Council elected Nguyen Van Thinh as president of the Provisional Government of the Republic of Cochinchina. At the same time France reluctantly recognized the Democratic Republic of Vietnam in the north as a free state within the Federation. On June 1, 1946 France proclaimed the Republic of Cochinchina as a counterbalance free state in the south. By so doing the French secured the support of most of the political elite south of the 16th parallel, as well as recruited over 6,000 Vietnamese for service with the French military forces to be used against both Vietminh guerrillas in the south and Vietminh military forces in the north.

The French now turned to uniting anti-Vietminh nationalists in the south. Their objective was to create a government whose nationalist aspirations would be temperate enough that it would be satisfied with

French Union status rather than full independence. The French theo-
rized that the communist-controlled Vietminh reflected only a small
segment of the nationalist movement, and that with establishment of a
broadly based government the influence of the Vietminh would be
diluted. The Vietminh would then have to accept the situation or be
defeated by the combined forces of the French and the new government of Cochinchina.

But the French badly misjudged the depth and strength of Vietnamese feeling. They could not find a leader for a less than thoroughly
nationalist government. The prominent Catholic, Ngo Dinh Diem, who
had declined in 1945 to associate himself with the Japanese-sponsored
"free Vietnam," declined, as did initially Emperor Bao Dai, self-exiled
in Hong Kong. However in 1949, upon French agreement to dismantle
the Cochinchina government, Bao Dai finally agreed to head a unified
Vietnam, one in which the French—at their insistence—would retain
control of defense and foreign affairs. The four Bao Dai governments,
each headed by a prime minister of his choice, achieved little progress
toward further independence and Bao Dai steadily lost credibility.

PREVIEW: FOUR PHASES OF WAR IN VIETNAM

Next to the revolution which culminated in the creation of the
People's Republic of China (PRC), conflict involving Vietnam has
influenced the post-war political history of Southeast Asia more than
any other phenomenon. Hostilities involving Vietnam occurred every
year since French reoccupation of the area in 1945 through 1989. In
1945 the armed struggle between the French, and the Vietnamese
communists and nationalists, began; in 1984 France was long gone but
some 180,000 Vietnamese troops were occupying Kampuchea and
50,000 others were in Laos.

The protracted nature of the conflict within Vietnam itself can be
divided into four phases as the different adversaries emerged. The first
phase, the war of liberation or the French colonial war, ended in 1954
with partition of the country at the 17th parallel, de facto recognition
of the independent Democratic Republic of Vietnam (DRV) in the
north and of the emerging Republic of Vietnam (RVN) in the south.
The French relinquished all claims to sovereignty over the area. This
first phase was fought primarily in the north. The next three phases
were fought in the south as the DRV tried to unify the country by
force.

The second phase, 1954 to 1961, may be termed a period of civil
war. During phase two the states of north and south Vietnam became
clients, respectively, of the People's Republic of China and the Soviet
Union, and of the United States.

The third phase, beginning in 1961, but accelerating in 1964 and extending through 1973, was a period of international intervention. In the south the massive and extended American military build-up was augmented by military contingents from Korea, New Zealand and Australia; economic, educational and medical assistance were provided by more than 40 other nations. The DRV was supplied by China and the Soviet Union. The conflict was unaccompanied by a declaration of war by any of the participants.

The last phase, 1973 to 1975, was again a period of civil war as DRV forces overran the south after the ceasefire was in place and American troops had withdrawn.

WAR OF LIBERATION

The 1945–1954 period is identified as the war of liberation or the French colonial war in Indochina. Certainly it was the former, since during the period Vietnam achieved complete independence. And it was also the latter because it was a major French effort to perpetuate the entity Indochina—the French creation which had united the Vietnamese states of Cochinchina, Annam and Tongking with the nations of Laos and Kampuchea. However, by 1954 not only was Vietnam divided into basically the historic regions of Tongking and Annam, and lost to the French, but Indochina in the French sense had ceased to be.

The Fontainebleau agreement of July 1946 had done little to settle the problems between the DRV and the French. The latter continued to refuse to negotiate a ceasefire with the guerrillas of the Vietminh-sponsored Committee of the South. For its part the DRV refused to become part of the Indochinese Federation and the French Union. The French in turn promulgated a constitution for the French Union without consulting any of the Indochinese states.

A showdown between France and the DRV arose over questions of customs collections and the currency to be used in the north. On November 20, 1946 a series of incidents occurred in Haiphong, the port for Hanoi, and fighting between French and Vietminh forces erupted in the city. A two day pause in the fighting was succeeded by an ultimatum from the French demanding complete military control of Haiphong. The Vietminh vacillated and the French navy bombarded the town which fell on November 28.

Another French-Vietminh militia incident in Hanoi in mid-December led to the French demand that security in Hanoi be turned over to them. Instead of acceding, the Vietminh under General Giap began to attack French garrisons throughout the country. The French responded to the uprisings with force. They quickly overcame the

Vietminh in Hanoi and Ho Chi Minh and his chief aides fled. The French then mounted a full military campaign which in three months extended their control from Hanoi to the urban centers of most of Tongking and Annam. Unrealized by them, however, a war had begun.

Vietminh forces retreated into the northern mountains where they concentrated on training and building up troop strength, while harassing the extended French garrisons. Gradually the French were forced to abandon vulnerable positions. By 1950 Vietminh hit-and run tactics had given them control over about half of Tongking and they began to conduct frontal offensives. Although they were recipients of external aid from the People's Republic of China and the Soviet Union, this was not the critical factor in their mounting success. Their fundamental strength was their appeal to national pride. Such strength, however, was not sufficient for them to take a major town, thus through 1952 the conflict continued, with the French holding the cities and the Vietminh holding the countryside.

When the Vietminh widened the war to Laos the die was cast for a crucial test of wills. Giap invaded Laos at several points in the first half of the year, at one time surrounding the royal capital at Luang Prabang, although the real prize was the administrative capital of Vientiane in the south. The border town of Dien Bien Phu—on the road to Luang Prabang—was taken by the Vietminh in November 1952. A year later, November 20, 1953, the French recaptured Dien Bien Phu as part of a major effort to prevent further Vietminh incursions into Laos. The little town, ten miles from the Laotian border, was built into a fortress. Meanwhile, aided by massive Chinese military assistance following the Korean War armistice of July 7, 1953, Giap began an intensive military build-up in the hills around the town.

The Vietminh siege of Dien Bien Phu lasted from early March 1954 until the French capitulated on May 8—as the Geneva Conference was debating the future of Vietnam. This was the turning point for France in its involvement in Indochina. On July 21 France signed an armistice with the DRV.

Geneva Conference: 1954 France, the United Kingdom, the Soviet Union and the United States convened the Geneva Conference in April 1954 in an effort to achieve political solutions in Korea, which proved impossible, and Indochina, which proved little more successful. The PRC was represented by its prime minister and foreign minister, Chou En-lai. In May France invited the "Associated States of Vietnam, Cambodia [Kampuchea] and Laos," and the Soviets invited the Ho Chi Minh regime, to the conference table.

The U.S. was not pleased when the conference sought to achieve ceasefire agreements which would temporarily divide Vietnam into two zones near the 17th parallel, with reunification by elections scheduled for two years later. In return for accepting partition, Washington insisted that the state of Vietnam in the south, as well as Kampuchea and Laos, remain free to arm themselves against aggression, and that no elections would be held until internal conditions were stable enough to permit genuinely free choice.

The DRV representatives were also displeased with partition. The French had capitulated at Dien Bien Phu on May 8 and the Vietminh were confident that, with Chinese aid, they could overrun the entire country. Their reluctant acceptance of partition is attributed to pressure on them by the USSR (which feared Vietminh-Chinese collaboration) and the PRC which was still a client of the Soviet Union.

France's policy toward Vietnam at the conference, ambivalent at first, shifted in the wake of the disastrous Dien Bien Phu defeat which occurred 24 hours before the first plenary session on Indochina. Dien Bien Phu convinced the French National Assembly that a ceasefire was improbable without substantial compromise, especially after French Premier Joseph Laniel's request for American military intervention in Indochina came to naught. The Laniel government in France fell on June 12 on a no-confidence motion concerning the pace toward accommodation. The new premier lost no time in testing the already announced willingness of the DRV to compromise.

Three armistice agreements were signed at Geneva on July 21 covering Vietnam, Laos and Kampuchea. The one between the Commander in Chief of the French Union Forces in Indochina and the Commander in Chief of the People's Army of Vietnam set up the provisional partition line and a demilitarized zone. The agreements concerning Laos and Kampuchea specified that Vietminh troops would be withdrawn from those countries. According to U.S. Secretary of State Henry A. Kissinger only 40 of the 6,000 Vietnamese troops left Laos.[4] By Kampuchean government estimate 4,000 to 5,000 Vietnamese military remained in Kampuchea after 2,500 to 4,000 were evacuated.[5]

The Final Declaration of the Geneva Conference on July 21 was an unsigned document which "took note" of the ceasefire agreements and provided that general elections concerning unification of the divided country would be held in July 1956 under supervision of the international commission—comprising representatives of Poland, Canada and India—created by the agreements to monitor them. Seven of the nine conferee states verbally assented, some with reservations. The foreign minister of the State of Vietnam declined to assent, as earlier he had declined to associate his government with the ceasefire which partitioned his country, but he informed the French prime minister that the State of Vietnam would not oppose the armistice. The U.S. also declined to associate itself with the declaration on the ground that the United Nations, rather than the three-member commission, should supervise the elections in order to ensure fairness; it noted however that it would not interfere with the agreements and would view any violation of them with "grave concern."

Comment   The French attempt of 1945–1954 to unite non-communist Vietnamese nationalists as a counterforce to the DRV was destined to fail because the French were patently dishonest concerning decolonization. Their conception of "free states" within a French federation satisfied neither the communist-dominated "free state" in the north, communists elsewhere, nor non-communist nationalists whether of the north or south. Rather, French tactics reinforced the determination of the communist-led DRV to prevail in all of Vietnam, thus precipitating French, and later American, intervention to thwart DRV aspirations. Moreover, as France's perfidy concerning true independence became evident, the position of non-communist nationalists who had relied on French assurances was weakened. Without French and subsequent American help the nationalist government in the south could not survive. Even with such help survival was achieved only by employing draconian measures.

United States policy on the eve of the 1954 Geneva Conference was that of vigorous reaction to continued communist expansion in Asia. The conference had been called to resolve the problems arising from the attempt by communist North Korea, with the aid of the communist Chinese, to conquer the non-communist Republic of Korea. But the problems of Indochina were more immediate as the French military defeat showed. French agreement at Geneva to full independence for all of Vietnam thus left a non-communist power vacuum which the U.S. stepped in to fill. The United States took over the French role, not in the service of empire, but rather as the protector of a post-colonial emerging state. The move was quite logical under the circumstances; it not only supported the longheld American value of political independence, but also the post-World War II-acquired value of anti-communism.

The conduct of the Soviet Union at the 1954 Geneva Conference suggests that the Soviets did not relish a united Vietnam under a regime whose leaders were closely associated with the Chinese.

CIVIL WAR: RVN VS. DRV

Republic of Vietnam: 1954–1956   On June 4, 1954 a treaty was initialed by France and the State of Vietnam, although never actually signed or ratified, recognizing the state as "fully independent and sovereign" and providing for its continuing assocation with the French Union. The Bao Dai-designated prime minister and his government resigned on June 19, stating that its mission had been completed with the initialing of the treaty, and Bao Dai asked Ngo Dinh Diem, then in Paris, to form a new government. Diem agreed only after assurance that he would have full military and police power. The fledgling state, beset by factions, was in physical control of little more than the main cities of the south. French Union forces, still some 200,000 strong despite Dien Bien Phu, helped the government survive.

Diem, a mandarin-like Catholic, eschewed popularity for respect which he gradually achieved by consolidating government operations, inaugurating some reforms, resettling—with French and American help—the 900,000 refugees who had fled from the north, and most importantly, improving the quality of the armed forces. In August 1954 the United States decided to provide direct military assistance to build Diem's forces so they would be able to provide internal security; heretofore U.S. aid had been extended through the French.

Diem's success hastened transformation of the State of Vietnam into an entity entirely independent of France, although France tried, as the Geneva conferees expected, to maintain a military and political position. The French intrigued with the Cao Dai and Hoa Hao religious sects during Diem's struggle with them in 1955, but Diem won the loyalty of enough army battalions to crush the armed units of the religious groups, as well as the Binh Xuyen, a political and racketeering organization which also conspired against him. After their defeat, and with his army growing stronger in consequence of American assistance, he successfully demanded that France withdraw its armed forces in accordance with the terms of the Geneva Conference. In October 1955 Diem initiated a popular referendum which resulted in the deposition of Bao Dai as chief of state and in the establishment of the Republic of Vietnam (RVN) with himself as the first president. He withdrew Vietnamese representation from the High Council of the French Union, and France recognized this final severance of political ties by designating its representative in Saigon "ambassador" rather than "high commissioner."

Within six months the Diem government was stable enough to hold elections for a constituent assembly. While the goverment won a large majority in the new assembly, a number of non-government candidates were also successful, even though most of the opposition parties had refused to campaign because the government severely restricted public expression. The constitution drafted by the constituent assembly—under the close supervision of Diem—provided for an extremely strong presidential system rather than the traditional parliamentary form. The document was proclaimed as the supreme law of the land on October 26, 1956, with Diem continuing as president for a five–year term.

DRV-Supported Insurgency in the South   In the north leaders of the

Lao Dong (Workers' Party, which succeeded the Communist Party and technically at least, the Vietminh) had returned to Hanoi under terms of the Geneva Conference. They were faced with the tasks of setting up an orderly administration, achieving economic reconstruction and putting down a serious rebellion in Nghe An province. Despite Chinese and Soviet aid, essential technicians were scarce, capital needed for industrialization was lacking and food was in short supply. Worse, the United States had been drawn into the conflict on the side of the south, and the hated Diem regime not only survived but had begun to prosper. Instead of the victory they had foreseen, the communists were confined to the north and the goal of reunification of the country under DRV control appeared more distant than before. Moreover, the Diem government rebuffed overtures from Hanoi for elections on reunification as specified at the Geneva meeting. Diem insisted that "nothing constructive" could be achieved toward reunifying the country through free elections "as long as the communist regime in North Vietnam does not allow each Vietnamese citizen to enjoy the democratic freedoms and fundamental rights of man".[6] The United States and the United Kingdom supported his position, in retrospect probably a political mistake inasmuch as it suggested indifference.

It was against this backdrop of political and economic frustration that Ho Chi Minh and his lieutenants decided to mount a protracted effort to exploit insurgency in the south where communist agents and guerrilla units had remained after main units withdrew to the north in compliance with the Geneva agreements. The effort diverted attention from the regime's inability to provide the better life it had promised, and the goal of reunification reinforced ideological fervor.

The southern communist cadres, popularly called the Vietcong (abbreviation of Viet Nam Cong San for Vietnamese Communists), controlled some southern areas where they had confiscated private land holdings, often distributing them free to peasants. This radical move served to popularize them in areas they controlled and upstaged Diem's more conventional land reform efforts which limited private holdings to 100 hectares, imposed rent reduction and facilitated purchase of public land by the landless. Diem's employment of civic action teams to rally the rural population, and the army to root out the Vietcong, were not successful; the civil action teams lacked coordination and sometimes integrity, and the French-trained army knew conventional warfare rather than the hit-and-run tactics of the guerrillas.

In 1956 the DRV established a Central Reunification Department whose purpose was to retrain in politico-military techniques the communists from the south who had fled north, and facilitate their return to the south to assist and instruct indigenous guerrilla units. By 1957 their tactics of terrorism and subversion had begun to paralyze RVN programs for economic development, land reform and social welfare.

In 1960 the Third Congress of the ruling Lao Dong party adopted a program of official political and military support for the southern insurgency. The strategy was to unite dissident political and religious groups in the south against the Diem regime. "Advisers" were sent southward who depicted Diem's benefactor, the United States, as the enemy of reunification and the fount of imperialism. The General-Secretary of the Lao Dong, Le Duan, directed the program. His efforts produced the National Front for the Liberation of the South (NLF) which was formed in December. The communists, as they had done previously in the north, presented themselves as only one faction within the NLF. When the NLF, reflecting views of its non-communist elements, began to display "bourgeois" tendencies, Hanoi convened the First Congress of the NLF in January 1962 to sanction formation of the People's Revolutionary Party as the "vanguard" of the NLF. Meanwhile, in February 1961 the People's Liberation Armed Forces was established to serve as the central vehicle through which military support by Hanoi could be effected.

Scholars differ on the source of the violence which engulfed the southern Vietnam countryside by 1959–60. Some insist that the insurgency was of local origin and directed against a perceived repressive Diem regime. Others conclude that it was precipitated by large-scale infiltration of armed cadres who raised and led insurgent forces, and a third view is that the uprising was instigated by the southern communists and quickly attracted popular support, but would not have achieved its remarkable success without the guidance and backing of the DRV regime.

Whichever version more nearly reflects the facts, it is clear that political and military resources had been marshalled by north and south to a degree which made escalation of conflict inevitable. And of equal importance in the longer term, by the end of 1961 United States military personnel in the RVN totaled 3,164.

At the same time the Diem regime in Saigon had survived only with great difficulty the three years of steady decline which followed its initial successes in 1954–1956. Military operations had been adversely affected by infiltration of armed communist cadres and military advisers from the DRV, and deterioration in internal security had reached serious proportions. Vietcong strength continued to increase even though U.S. forces engaged in air and naval combat support missions throughout 1962. As economic and social programs were derailed by the rising insurgency, and security problems escalated, Diem turned increasingly to one-man rule and barely outwitted a military coup against him in November 1960.

Overthrow of Diem   The origins of the downfall of the Diem regime in November 1963 can be traced to a number of developments: 1) conflict between Diem and the Buddhists, long resentful of Diem's favoritism to Catholics over the Buddhist majority, 2) widespread dissatisfaction with Diem's family which increasingly concentrated authority in its own hands, 3) long standing disagreement between Diem and the military leaders over the conduct of military operations, and 4) lack of appreciable economic progress.

In late summer 1963 several army generals who were planning a coup against Diem sounded out the Americans. Ambassador Heny Cabot Lodge, about the same time, informed the Department of State that the struggle could not be won with Diem in power. Lodge argued that the U.S. should support Diem's ouster. Washington's response was to pressure Diem to undertake reforms by selectively suspending U.S. aid and by conveying the message to alternative leaders that while the U.S. would not actively encourage a coup, it nevertheless would not thwart one or deny assistance to a new regime.[7] On November 1 Vietnamese army, navy, and air force units that supported the coup moved into Saigon. There General Duong Van Minh explained to them the aims of the conspiracy and the same afternoon the generals called on Diem to surrender. The president and his brother fled the palace through an underground passage, but the following day telephoned the conspirators and agreed to surrender. In the car sent to pick them up, they were shot to death, apparently on the order of the chief conspirators.

Seven RVN governments succeeded one another during 1964. As each failed, and as the communists gained further control over the rural south, the U.S. was drawn deeper into military action against the north, which was perceived as the root cause of the instability in the south. The United States was impelled to major intercession in 1965 for an additional reason. The instability of RVN governments in 1964–65 coincided with abandonment by Indonesia's Sukarno of his non-aligned posture in favor of a Peking-Jakarta axis.[8] As British support for Malaysia and American support for the RVN increased, the axis concept was expanded to include North Korea and Kampuchea, and the United States was warned to withdraw from Southeast Asia as "victory would surely be won by this new Asian axis."[9] The stakes had escalated and a critical question had emerged: would Vietnam be added to the axis, thus completing a cordon of communist-dominated nations extending from Korea to Indonesia?[10]

In this context increased American armed intervention was inevitable. After March 1965 massive U.S. military aid slowed the communist advance and equally massive economic aid and assistance to civil authorities kept the state afloat despite the succession of governments. Some observers conclude that the unexpected survival of the RVN propelled the communists in Indonesia to the precipitate, and therefore unsuccessful, takeover attempt of September 30, 1965.[11]

U.S. MILITARY INVOLVEMENT

The rationale for American military involvement in Vietnam has come under intense scrutiny by scholars, politicians and others and their views should be summarized before tracing the course of U.S. action.

The majority position is that the American phase of the war in Vietnam can be explained as a consequence, albeit the most dramatic and expensive, of decolonization and nationalism which followed World War II. The thesis maintains that political leaders in the United States, which itself had spurred decolonization, badly misread the phenomenon. By adopting the domino theory—which held that if Indochina fell to the communists the remainder of Southeast Asia would fall like a set of dominoes—the United States proceeded to make decisions concerning Vietnam that were tragically wrong, as well as in some cases deliberately concealed until long after the fact.

A small but distinguised minority of Southeast Asian scholars, who had given American participation in the war in Vietnam unqualified support from the beginning, have continued to defend the basic United States decision to intervene in Vietnam on moral grounds. Their premise indeed employs a logical consistency. From a moral standpoint, if the 1946 Truman Doctrine to prevent communist domination of Greece and Turkey was warranted, and if the 1948–49 Berlin airlift and the 1950 US-UN military action in Korea were justifiable on similar grounds, then American intervention in Vietnam should enjoy the same encomium.

A second minority analysis, popularly called the "new revisionism," holds that although intervention in Vietnam did not warrant its costs in lives and money, and was a failure, nevertheless American decisions were made in good faith by intelligent and reasonable men and their judgment takes on validity in light of developments in Southeast Asia since 1975. [12]

U.S. Air and Ground War: 1964–1966   A program of covert operations against the DRV was approved by President Lyndon B. Johnson in January 1964. It included authorization of U.S. combat support of RVN commando raids from the sea and RVN bombardment of DRV coastal military installations. On August 2 and 4 DRV torpedo boats attacked two American naval vessels, engaged in intelligence activities off the coast of Vietnam, under circumstances that remain unexplained. Johnson ordered reprisal air attacks from carriers in the vicinity and 25 patrol aircraft on the ground in the DRV were destroyed. Johnson met with congressional leaders to explain the reprisals and to request congressional support for his policy. On August 7 the House unanimously, and the Senate by a vote of 88 to 2, adopted the so-called Gulf of Tongking Resolution in support of his actions and authorized him "to take all necessary measures to repel any armed attack against the forces of the United States and to prevent further aggression."

As the American commitment to the RVN grew it tended to reinforce the already privileged position of the military and urban elite in Vietnamese society, since these were the people with whom the Americans interacted. The elites, not surprisingly, were more interested in maintaining the status quo than in promoting the social revolution promised in government declarations.

As governments continued to fall and military factions intrigued against each other to succeed to political power, President Johnson became cautious and equivocal about waging war against the DRV unless there were reforms within the RVN government. Others in the U.S. government, however, urged continuing and stronger action regardless of conditions, on the grounds that otherwise the Saigon regime might capitulate to the NLF, that American allies such as Thailand would be vulnerable to communist expansion if the RVN fell, and that air strikes would help "contain China."

Following a Vietcong attack on the American military advisers' compound at the town of Pleiku on February 6, 1965—which killed 9 Americans and injured 76—Johnson ordered aerial bombardment of DRV military installations in the north as well as in the south. This decision "transformed the character of the Vietnam War and the U.S. role in it" according to the *Pentagon Papers*.[13] The air war became a sustained assault by March but its main consequence appeared to be a stiffening of DRV resolve rather than the expected compromise. The U.S. was then left with the options of unilaterally withdrawing from Vietnam or of committing ground forces in the south to achieve its objectives. A third option of heavily increasing the scope and scale of the bombing was rejected for fear it would cause Chinese intervention.

The decision to commit American troops to offensive action was contained in National Security Action Memorandum 328 of April 6, 1965. Under its terms the mission of the 3,500 marines who had landed at Danang on March 8 was changed from simple defense of the Danang airfield to offensive operations in south Vietnam. These "search and destroy" actions were carried out in cooperation with RVN and Australian units. In rapid succession additional combat units were dispatched to Vietnam at the request of General William C. Westmoreland, the U.S. commander. American forces rose from 27,000 in March 1965 to 184,314 in December. Massive American military intervention achieved the immediate objective of preventing the collapse of the Saigon government.

Air Vice Marshall Nguyen Cao Ky, one of the Young Turks in the internecine squabbling, emerged as prime minister of the RVN in June 1965; General Nguyen Van Thieu, as head of the newly formed National Leadership Committee, became in effect chief of state. The Ky-Thieu team brought authoritarian, military-oriented rule to the troubled RVN, as well as a modicum of stability. With the internal governmental situation more stabilized and after 10 months of air warfare, President Johnson on Christmas Eve 1965 ordered a bombing halt in an effort to elicit peace feelers from Hanoi. None were forthcoming.

Bombing was resumed by presidential order January 31 after a 39-day pause, even though the administration recognized that the air war had not successfully interdicted infiltration of troops and supplies to the south. In June Johnson ordered strikes against oil depots and within a month 70 percent of the DRV oil storage capacity was demolished. But the flow of men and materials to the south continued undiminished because of the DRV's "adaptability and resourcefulness in switching to small, dispersed sites, almost impossible to bomb."[14]

General Westmoreland continued to request more ground troops throughout 1966 and 1967 even though Secretary of Defense Robert McNamara began to show disenchantment. In November 1966 McNamara for the first time recommended substantially fewer additional troops than Westmoreland requested. A decision announced on November 11 set a limit of 469,000 men in the field by June 30, 1968.[15]

Peace Offensives: 1967–1968 Ho rejected President Johnson's proposal of early 1967 for "direct talks," causing Johnson to step up attacks in a spring offensive. Meanwhile Westmoreland reported large enemy buildups in sanctuaries in Laos and Kampuchea, in parts of the RVN, and just north of the demilitarized zone (DMZ) which had been agreed to at the Geneva Conference of 1954. Because Johnson was reluctant to "break the political sound barrier" by mobilizing U.S. reserve forces, he widened the air war in August. Simultaneously he attempted to obtain from Hanoi a guarantee not to use a pause in the northern bombing—a possibility under consideration—to increase its infiltration of the south; he hoped productive talks could take place. This "San Antonio Formula" was flatly turned down by the DRV.

General Westmoreland reported at the end of 1967 that "the year ended with the enemy increasingly resorting to desperation tactics in attempting to achieve military/psychological victory; and he has experienced only failure in these attempts."[16] Yet on the Vietnamese lunar

new year (Tet), January 31, 1968, the communists broke into the
American embassy in Saigon and attacked 34 of the 44 provincial
capitals and five of the six major cities. They held Hue and the Imperial
Citadel there for 26 days. The RVN army and the Americans counter-
attacked, no cities were permanently lost and at the beginning of
March the communists were back where they had been at the end of
January. Nevertheless the psychological effect of the Tet offensive on
the American people was devastating.

In April 1968 American military involvement in Vietnam reached its
true climax when the authorized—as distinct from the actual—level of
troops reached a peak of 549,000. Actual U.S. troop strength in
Vietnam reached the level of 543,000 in April 1969.[17] In March 1968
Secretary of State Dean Rusk suggested to Johnson that providing
military equipment to the Vietnamese and assisting them in building
up their own troop strength would be a better investment than raising
the U.S. troop level. Rusk's suggestion was to emerge as "Vietnamization" in the succeeding Nixon administration. He identified the crux
of the Vietnam problem, from the point of view of the American
people, as doubt whether the South Vietnamese would be able to do
their full share and could survive "when we leave."[18] He also advocated a bombing halt, to let the action speak for itself and to await
Hanoi's reaction. Within the month Rusk's idea of suspending bombing
became policy and was announced in President Johnson's speech of
March 31 when he also announced his withdrawal from the 1968
presidential election to devote his full attention to achieving an "hon-
orable peace."

On April 3, three days after Johnson's dramatic announcement on
suspension of bombing "except in the area north of the demilitarized
zone where the continuing enemy build up directly threatens allied
forward positions,"[19] Hanoi stated that "the DRV government declares
its readiness to send its representatives to make contact with U.S.
representatives to decide with the U.S. side the unconditional cessation of bombing and all other war acts against the DRV so that talks
could begin."[20] The Central Intelligence Agency had accurately concluded in March that the DRV "would probably respond to an offer to
negotiate," but that the communists "would not modify their terms
for a final settlement or stop fighting in the south."[21] The next four
years were to prove the accuracy of these estimates.

RVN AND DRV: 1966–1969

In Saigon elections had been held in September 1966 to select a
constituent assembly of the RVN. The successful candidates were a
reasonable cross-section of the electorate and the election was reason-

ably honest. The assembly completed a draft constitution in March 1967 which was approved April 1. The document provided for an elected, four-year, strong president; a prime minister appointed by the president; an elected bicameral National Assembly; a bill of rights; and an assembly veto by majority vote over the powerful Armed Forces Council. Elections in September 1967 produced victory for the government party candidates for president and vice president—Thieu and Ky respectively.

The 1966 and 1967 elections partially legitimized the regime in the south and served as a rationale for its support by allies of the United States, but problems abounded. The elections had taken place with many politicians in exile while others had been disqualified for pro-neutralist or compromise sentiments. Universities were crowded with frustrated, idealistic students. The Buddhists were alienated and began to blame the U.S. for the country's plight. Intellectuals safe in Paris decried the decline of social and cultural values. Inflation and under-employment exacted their toll on the middle class and many thoughtful people were concerned with the regime's inability to formulate and carry out coherent planning.

The government increasingly was viewed as a jumble of cliques, mostly military, competing for power. Vice President Ky, tempermental, ambitious and seriously immature (he once made the ill-considered admission that he admired Adolph Hitler) was a hindrance to President Thieu and subsequently became his bitter political rival. Thieu—who controlled the police, selected the premier and appointed the cabinet—relegated Ky to a minor role and removed his supporters from policy-making positions. In May 1968 Thieu replaced the pro-Ky premier, Nguyen Van Loc, with Tran Van Huong, a former chief of state.

The DRV fared hardly better. It suffered from inflation, shortages, and from its increasing dependency on the PRC and the USSR. The latter became a particular problem as the Sino-Soviet quarrel deepened and mixed signals emanated from Peking and Moscow. The NLF in the south began to veer from Hanoi's orthodox Marxist line: some NLF leaders spoke in favor of private ownership of land, private initiative in economic development and amnesty for the RVN bureaucracy to lure it into the NLF. Adding to these unorthodox tendencies, the NLF proceeded to consider international neutrality for the south, instead of unification with the north. After the failure of the Tet offensive the DRV, prodded by Truong Chinh, the regime's chief ideologue, engaged in introspection to "conserve resources and gain time to revolutionize the masses more thoroughly."[22]

A new program emerged in June 1969 when the NLF announced it had organized "somewhere in the south" the Provisional Revolutionary Government of the Republic of South Vietnam (PRG). The NLF said it had transferred its authority in domestic and foreign affairs as "sovereign agent of the South Vietnamese people" to the PRG, although retaining its role as the "leader of the liberation struggle."[23]

FIVE YEARS OF NEGOTIATION

Ambassadorial meetings began in Paris May 13, 1968. DRV representatives demanded the end of all bombing in the DMZ area and withdrawal of all U.S. forces so that the Vietnamese could make their own political decisions. American conditions for cessation of the remaining interdictive bombing in the DMZ area called for prompt and serious talks which would include the RVN, and demanded that the DRV not send troops into the DMZ nor put it under fire and not attack RVN cities with rockets or artillery.

The American conditions were finally accepted in October and both sides agreed that both the RVN and NLF could attend the substantive meetings which were to begin immediately after the cessation of all U.S. bombing of the north—a condition that was met on October 31. Another three months of procedural haggling took place over the shape of the conference table in Paris and the status of the NLF at the table. When Richard M. Nixon became president of the U.S. on January 20, 1969 not a single substantive negotiating session had taken place.

Fruitless Peace Talks   The immediate task facing U.S. negotiators when the meetings finally began in January 1969 was to persuade DRV representatives to negotiate with those of the RVN and to persuade the RVN to talk directly with the NLF. The U.S. sought to conduct two-track negotiations—military issues to be discussed between the U.S. and the DRV, with political issues left to the Vietnamese parties.

Meanwhile in Vietnam DRV armed units infiltrated the south in ever greater numbers through corridors in Kampuchea rather than through the DMZ as formerly; the DRV continued its supply services to the southern Vietcong; the American troop commitment increased to its in-country peak of 543,000; and the communists in the south launched a broad new offensive in late February. Nixon in March authorized the subsequently widely controversial "secret" bombing of the Kampuchean sanctuaries (these bombing sorties continued and became "public" in May 1970 when they were used to support a US-RVN incursion into Kampuchea). Prospects for substantive public negotiations in such an environment were dim so private meetings among the participants began in addition to the plenary sessions. These were equally unfruitful.

On May 8, 1969 the DRV, at the 16th plenary session, set forth steps which "must be taken" to end the war: unilateral and complete U.S. withdrawal from Vietnam, abolition of the RVN's government and its replacement by a coalition of all political groups in the south "that stand for peace, independence and neutrality," and U.S. reparations for war damage. Nixon responded May 14 by advocating simultaneous rather than unilateral troop withdrawal (DRV withdrawal could be de facto rather than explicit), participation of the NLF in the political process, and elections under international supervision.

Nixon also accepted the concept of beginning phased U.S. troop withdrawals to provide the DRV an incentive to negotiate, a follow-on to the emerging policy of Vietnamization. He met Thieu at Midway Island in June to gain his support for an immediate limited (25,000 man) U.S. troop withdrawal and for NLF political participation in the south. Under U.S. pressure Thieu announced, in July, land reforms and elections to be supervised by international observers in which the communists would be allowed to participate.

By mid-September Nixon and the new secretary of defense, Melvin Laird, could claim that 60,000 Americans had been withdrawn from Vietnam. On November 3, in a major policy speech designed to allay widespread popular dissatisfaction and protest in the U.S. and to spur response by the DRV, Nixon spelled out the new policy of Vietnamization: "the complete withdrawal of U.S. combat troops and their replacement by South Vietnamese forces on an orderly scheduled timetable."[24]

RVN Internal Politics In the RVN internal political rivalries increased. The cabinet resigned in August and General Tran Thien Khiem, a Thieu supporter, became premier. The Thieu-Khiem team pledged cooperation with the U.S. plan of Vietnamization, but Thieu continued to face serious opposition in both houses of the Assembly from various front groups, most of whom advocated a policy of neutralization. In his annual address to the nation on January 9, 1970 Thieu pointed to substantial progress in pacification and reconstruction, in large part due to an unique American civil/military agency called Civil Operations and Revolutionary Development Support (CORDS). At its peak in 1969 CORDS, operating directly with the appropriate RVN ministries, employed some 6,500 military and 1,100 civilian personnel to coordinate the US-RVN pacification effort which included an "Open Arms" program for Vietnamese who voluntarily returned to RVN control. Some 500,000 persons were resettled, village security was improved, 50,000 houses were rebuilt, road transport was expanded, rice shipments to cities were increased and water supply and electric services were upgraded.

Secret Negotiations in Paris With formal negotiations stalled, the U.S. requested informal secret meetings which began in Paris in February 1970 between Le Duc Tho of the DRV's Politburo and Henry Kissinger. Tho set forth the same terms at the first as at all subsequent meetings until October 1972: political and military problems must be dealt with simultaneously; the sole military issue was unconditional U.S. withdrawal with a six month deadline; cessation of fighting by the DRV depended upon replacement of the Saigon regime by a coalition government to include neutralists and the NLF. All the Paris talks, public and private, languished when RVN and U.S. troops combined for an "incursion" into Kampuchea in May–June 1970 to destroy communist border sanctuaries.

In the U.S., Nixon and Kissinger were under ever increasing pressure to end the war. The DRV recognized the fact and in September raised the ante. *"Our unilateral exit was not enough,"* Kissinger has written, "we had to engineer a political turnover before we left, or else the war could not end, we would have no assurance of a safe withdrawal of our remaining forces, and we would not regain our prisoners."[25]

On October 7, 1970 Nixon took the initiative and offered a standstill ceasefire, a halt in U.S. bombing throughout all of Indochina, a negotiated mutual withdrawal timetable, and political settlement based upon the wishes of the Vietnamese people. In his speech Nixon rejected the DRV demand for dismantlement of the RVN government. The Nixon proposals were immediately rejected and formal sterile sessions of the Paris talks dragged on into 1971. In February 1971 the talks suffered another breakdown when the RVN, with U.S. air and artillery support, attempted to interdict the "Ho Chi Minh supply trail" in Laos.

The secret talks resumed in May and Kissinger added to previous U.S. proposals an offer to set a date for total U.S. withdrawal and a ceasefire throughout Indochina to become effective when U.S. withdrawals began—rescinding demands for mutual withdrawal, provided infiltration into the Indochinese countries ended and all American prisoners of war were released during the withdrawal period. The U.S. was apparently willing to negotiate all points except the DRV demand for the replacement of the Thieu government. The talks ended in an impasse in September.

Internal Politics, DRV and RVN: 1970–1971 The Hanoi political leadership continued to be plagued, especially after Ho Chi Minh's death in September 1969, by conflicting views on how to conduct the war. Questions of the degree of communist orthodoxy to be maintained arose, and differences in view emerged between the DRV and the NLF on this point. Widening the war by using Kampuchea as an infiltration route to the south had provoked "secret" American bombing in Kampuchea throughout 1969 and the bombing had intensified with the May 1970 U.S.-RVN ground incursion into the area. Heavy DRV losses had to be absorbed. In February 1971 the U.S.-supported RVN foray into Laos had disrupted operations there and more manpower losses occurred. Complicating matters for the DRV, the quarrel between its patrons—China which supplied it with small arms, consumer goods and food, and the Soviet Union which provided sophisticated weaponry and industrial equipment—had erupted into border warfare in 1969, endangering the DRV's supply routes.

In the south the RVN leadership was beset by continued and increasing demands for everything from a ceasefire, through neutralization, to reunification with the north. General elections, called for by the constitution, were held for the Senate in August 1970 and for the House of Representatives a year later. In both elections Buddhist elements won the majority of the seats.

The second presidential election under the 1967 constitution was scheduled for October 3, 1971. Thieu's rivals were strongly anticommunist Vice President Ky, and General Duong Van Minh who courted the Buddhists and the peace advocates. Thieu rendered the candidacies of his rivals difficult by various legal maneuvers and both Ky and Minh disgustedly withdrew. Eighty-seven percent of the eligible electorate voted to give the unopposed Thieu 94 percent of the ballots cast.

Resumption of Negotiations   When Hanoi declined to set a date for resumption of the private talks in early 1972, and instead began a large military offensive across the DMZ, Nixon decided to respond in kind. He ordered massive air and naval strikes against the DRV and at the same time applied diplomatic pressure on both the PRC and the USSR to bring the DRV back to the talks. Peking was susceptible to pressure because it valued its new relationship—the so-called "China Opening" Nixon achieved in February 1972—as an advantage in its quarrel with the Soviets. Moscow was susceptible because of the scheduled and desired spring 1972 summit meeting with the U.S. in Moscow. In consequence the Soviets secured DRV consent to a private meeting May 2, considered by Kissinger to be of "showdown" importance.

When at the May 2 meeting Le Duc Tho remained intractable because the DRV military offensive was proving so successful, Kissinger recommended the intensification of bombing in the north and the blockade of DRV ports by mining them. He feared that the RVN might collapse in the face of the offensive and that the DRV would neither halt the offensive nor resume negotiations on any acceptable basis.

On May 8 Nixon announced U.S. plans to mine DRV ports to prevent the delivery of war supplies, and to continue the northern bombing; one day later U.S. planes dropped mines in Haiphong and six other harbors. Nixon promised to end the blockade and the bombing if the DRV would end its military offensive and agree to an internationally supervised ceasefire in place. Under those conditions he offered to withdraw all American forces from Vietnam within four months.

The American moves were successful. By mid-June the DRV was stopped and RVN forces recovered ground and morale. In July, once more, both plenary and private meetings were resumed. By this time U.S. congressional supporters and opponents of administration policy had narrowed their differences mainly to the question of whether a ceasefire was necessary, or whether the return of American prisoners in conjunction with withdrawal of U.S. forces was sufficient. Meanwhile the Paris talks moved toward actual negotiation. The DRV dropped its demand for Thieu's immediate removal; accepted participation of the RVN government in a three-part coalition in which the communists and the RVN would each appoint their own third and one-half of the neutral third; and gave up demand for an unconditional deadline for U.S. withdrawal. Kissinger's proposal in response was to accept the tripartite formula, making it applicable to a joint electoral commission which the U.S. had often proposed, rather than to a coalition government.

Thieu, however, objected to any tripartite arrangement. The U.S. decided to proceed with negotiations, apprising the DRV of the objections of the Thieu government, and in November talks resumed again. The DRV procrastinated by adding many new demands, as did Thieu. Time was running out for Nixon and Kissinger because U.S. congressional threats to vote the United States out of the war became increasingly strident. On December 13 Le Duc Tho, exploiting the American distaste for continuing the war and the public split which had developed between the Nixon administration and the Thieu government, reintroduced earlier demands.

Christmas Bombing: 1972   The DRV's apparent "determination *not to allow the agreement to be completed*" was, according to Kissinger, the root cause behind President Nixon's decision to attack the DRV with heavy U.S. bombers during the period December 18–30, 1972.[26] The administration took the view that the only alternatives were an endless war, or a peace which would "wreck" the RVN. General Alexander M. Haig, Jr., Kissinger's military assistant, was apparently the leading proponent of the use of B-52 bombers, on a sustained basis for the first time north of the DMZ, on the ground that "only a massive shock could bring Hanoi back to the conference table."[27] The sustained bombings provoked a storm of U.S. congressional and editorial outrage and popular moral indignation.

The DRV had been warned repeatedly of massive U.S. military steps should the talks break down and on December 18, as the bombing began, the U.S. proposed to the DRV a negotiating solution and a date for resuming the talks. The DRV replied affirmatively on December 26 and private meetings were resumed in Paris between Le Duc Tho and Kissinger on January 8, 1973. On January 13 an agreement was reached in Paris satisfactory to the United States. Nixon then told Thieu he had "irrevocably" decided to accept the agreement; he halted all U.S. air and naval operations against the DRV on January 15. On January 20, the day of Nixon's second inauguration, Thieu acquiesced. Kissinger and Le Duc Tho initialed the agreement in Paris January 23 and the agreement and a ceasefire throughout Vietnam went into effect.

RENEWED CIVIL WAR AND COLLAPSE OF THE RVN

The Paris Agreement on Ending the War and Restoring Peace in Vietnam, with its four accompanying protocols concerning a ceasefire, the International Commission of Control and Supervision, return of prisoners, and mine clearance, "resolved" the military questions while leaving the political problems to be worked out peacefully by the Vietnamese parties themselves. The agreement also called for the UN Secretary General to convene a conference within 30 days to acknowledge the agreement and guarantee the ending of the war. On March 2 the Act of the International Conference on Vietnam was signed in Paris by the U.S., France, the DRV, RVN, NLF, PRC, UK, Poland, Canada, Indonesia, Hungary and the UN Secretary General. The parties to the Act called "on all countries to strictly respect . . . the right of the South Vietnamese people to self-determination and to strictly respect the Agreement and Protocols by refraining from any action at variance with their provisions."[28]

Withdrawal of all American forces was accomplished within the prescribed period of 60 days and U.S. mine-sweeping operations cleared Haiphong and other DRV ports. Political talks began between the RVN and the DRV to form a National Council of National Reconciliation and Concord, to be followed by elections. In February, during a Kissinger visit to Hanoi, a US-DRV Joint Economic Commission was formed to discuss reconstruction aid, and Kissinger and Le Duc Tho met twice during 1973 in Paris to review implementation of the ceasefire. But these constituted the sum total of positive consequences of the agreement and the international conference which drew it up.

Instead, throughout 1973 war materiel and sophisticated offensive weaponry went south along with DRV troops. By May 1974, according to U.S. Department of State estimates, DRV troops in the south had increased from 160,000 at the time of the ceasefire to 210,000. DRV forces carried out numerous attacks against communications facilities and occasionally population centers, and RVN forces counterattacked; the fighting produced significant casualties and the RVN began to suffer territorial losses. The RVN informed the NLF in April that

Saigon would break off further talks unless the communists demonstrated a willingness to compromise, and in May walked out of the meetings.

Thieu meanwhile moved further toward consolidation and authoritarianism. A constitutional amendment of January 1974 allowed him to run for a third term and extended the term of office from four to five years. Legal requirements were promulgated which forced most parties except Thieu's Democratic Party off the political stage. At the same time the government exerted special efforts to rally support, pointing out that one million Vietnamese had become landowners in the preceding five years as a result of the "Land to the Tiller" program whereby virtually all privately owned riceland not actually cultivated by owners had been distributed free to tenants. On the adverse side the RVN currency was devalued ten times that year.

Opposition mounted steadily. By September Catholic, Buddhist and press elements declared their united opposition to Thieu who, in response, dramatized his efforts to sanitize his administration. He dismissed nearly 400 army officers on charges of corruption and announced a comprehensive economic policy to stimulate foreign investment, concentrate on labor-intensive production and control prices and supplies.

The year 1975 started badly with another monetary devaluation and the announcement in January that 250,000 Vietnamese had died in the fighting since the Paris accords of early 1973. A communist military offensive resulted in the capture of the provincial capital of Phouc Binh on January 4, the first provincial capital to fall to the communists since May 1974. Eighteen additional cities fell between January and March; Danang, the linchpin city of 1,500,000 inhabitants in central Vietnam, was captured March 30, in the worst defeat of the entire war. By early April the communist offensive had engulfed three-fourths of the RVN. Thieu made a final desperate appeal to the United Nations to halt Hanoi's offensive and on April 21 he resigned. Vice President Tran Van Huong assumed the presidency until the National Assembly elected General Duong Van Minh as president on April 27, with a mandate to negotiate with the Provisional Revolutionary Government of the Republic of South Vietnam (PRG)—surrogate of the DRV in the south—and the DRV.

On April 28 communist forces entered Saigon and bombed the airfield, setting off huge explosions which shook the city. Saigon surrendered on April 30. With the surrender came the end of American aid. During the period 1950–1975 the U.S. had provided the Republic of Vietnam with US$14.75 billion in military equipment and related services alone.[29]

ESTABLISHMENT OF THE SOCIALIST REPUBLIC OF VIETNAM: 1975

When the RVN surrendered it was to the forces of the PRG, but a Military Management Committee, staffed by political and economic experts from the DRV, was established to preside over Saigon until civil government could be reinstituted. DRV forces rather than PRG troops policed the city. While the PRG had a government on paper that included a head of state and a cabinet, its role was played down by the DRV which desired speedy unification of the two states. However a dilemma arose. By mid-May, 78 nations had already extended diplomatic recognition to the PRG. On June 6, sixth anniversary of its formation, the PRG officially took over the government from the Military Management Committee, but without public ceremony, and the Military Management Committee was not dissolved. It was announced that Saigon, which had been renamed Ho Chi Minh City, would be a free-market city within a socialized south and that political unification of the two Vietnams was five years distant. However, on June 8 the DRV National Assembly designated Hanoi as the capital of both north and south Vietnam.

DRV government officials and communist party workers continued to flood into the south, taking control of local administration, and reunification talks began on August 1. Nevertheless the PRG and the DRV both applied for membership in the United Nations. Their applications were vetoed by the United States on the basis that they could not be admitted until South Korea was admitted.

By November it became clear that Sino-Soviet rivalry was involved in the contest over when reunification would take place. Soviet naval expansion in the Pacific and Indian oceans alarmed China which thus supported the PRG's desire for an independent south in the hope that the PRG might, temporarily at least, deny its economic and strategic assets to the Soviet Union. The DRV, no longer dependent on the Chinese railways for transportation of military supplies, increasingly turned to the USSR because the kind of rehabilitative assistance it offered was much more attractive than anything China could provide.

On November 21 the DRV and the PRG agreed on the "ultimate merger of the two countries" and on Vietnam-wide general elections. The National Electoral Council announced in February 1976 that candidates must be approved by the NLF and the PRG. The elections, held April 25, elected a 492-member Vietnam National Assembly—243 of whom were from the south—and consummated the merger of the two states.

State and Party   The new National Assembly met on June 24 to set up the administrative machinery to govern a united Vietnam, and the

Socialist Republic of Vietnam (SRV) was proclaimed July 2, 1976. Octegenerian Ton Duc Thang, president of the DRV, was elected president of the SRV. Pham Van Dong, the tireless revolutionary who with Ho Chi Minh and Vo Nguyen Giap comprised the "iron triangle" of original Vietnamese communist leaders, continued as prime minister.

The National Assembly agreed to use the 1960 DRV constitution as the basis for organization of the state, pending adoption of a new document. The 1960 constitution specified that the highest organ of state authority was the unicameral National Assembly which was charged with electing the president and vice presidents for four year terms of office, choosing a prime minister on the recommendation of the president, and selecting a council of ministers on the recommendation of the prime minister. It described Vietnam as a "people's democratic state" advancing toward socialism, and established a framework for *full political control* by the Vietnam Workers' Party, i.e. the communist party.

On July 6 the north's umbrella political organization—the Fatherland Front controlled by the Workers' Party—and its counterparts in the south—the heretofore vague Vietnamese Front for Democracy and Peace of South Vietnam and the NLF—were combined. Meanwhile Le Duan, longtime general secretary of the Workers' Party, continued in that role. On December 20, 1976 the Workers' Party changed its name to the Communist Party of Vietnam (CPV).

The communist party, in its various guises, had been born and come to maturity within a highly favorable revolutionary setting. Its goals of independence and socialism attracted the masses and sustained the party during the many years of war. At the end of the war the party lost the unifying and stimulating influence of revolutionary struggle and was confronted with an economically and politically unassimilated south. Its problem therefore was to produce a transformation to a collectivized economy throughout Vietnam while retaining party control of the process. Administrative machinery had to be created to carry out collectivization of property and commerce and to manage both. Although the administrative units responsible to the State Council of Ministers and to committees and teams at various levels were fashioned to be joint party—state organs, party control was diluted as the state administrators—already in extremely short supply—tended to place more emphasis on expertise than on ideology.

ECONOMIC POLICY AND PROBLEMS

The forced demise of the Republic of Vietnam and subsequent emergence of the Socialist Republic of Vietnam in 1975 enabled the communist regime in Hanoi to commence the long promised transformation to strict, orthodox "scientific socialism" founded upon Marxist-Leninist principles. In the words of Douglas Pike, the goal was to achieve radical restructure of the thousand-year old Vietnamese farm-village system by relocating agricultural production into district-sized agro production units or giant "farm factories" and by creating a heavy industry sector.[30]

In June 1976 the Fourth Party Congress adopted a Five Year Plan (1976–1980). The plan focused on overall economic development with primary emphasis on agriculture, but it also allocated considerable resources to industrial activity on the premise that foreign assistance would be forthcoming. Export-import firms and banks were nationalized. Collective agriculture was mandated for the south but private property was tolerated in the southern cities. Individuals deemed in need of "attitude change" were sent to "reeducation centers" to prepare them for participation in the new economic society, and some 1.5 million persons in the south, most of them commercial, business and RVN government personnel, were moved to "new economic zones" and resettled as farmers.

These moves precipitated wholesale flight from south Vietnam as individuals and families sought to escape economic hardship, discipine, heavy labor in forced land clearing and agricultural production, and loss of personal freedoms. From mid-1975 to late 1977 some 1,500 persons per month fled in small boats to Malaysian, Thai and other Southeast Asian ports. The economic exodus followed on the heels of the political exodus which had occurred immediately after the fall of the RVN when 240,000 persons fled, including 135,000 who were evacuated to the United States.

Meanwhile, economic recovery nationwide eluded Vietnam and massive western aid was not forthcoming. The U.S. did not consider itself bound by the Paris agreement of 1973 to aid in rehabilitation since the DRV had observed none of its promises concerning the ceasefire, the right of the South Vietnamese to self-determination, or the return of American prisoners of war.

Despite the wholesale resettlement of people in the new economic zones, resistance to collectivization, frequently faulty management, and widespread crop failures due to natural disasters and to the fact that much of the land in the new zones was unsuitable for cultivation, resulted in a grain deficit of an estimated two million tons in 1977, equal to almost 20 percent of the normal rice crop. Nearly one million tons of grain had to be imported to keep the people from starving. In consequence a major reorganization of agriculture in the southern provinces was undertaken and urgent appeals were made for internnational assistance.

In March 1978 the state nationalized all commerical and industrial enterprises to unify the economic policy of the country and to bring the south in line with the already long-collectivized north. Private trading in rice and other commodities was abolished and 30,000 businesses, mostly owned by ethnic Chinese, were closed in Ho Chi Minh City alone. A sudden currency switch in May practically wiped out these dispossessed Sino-Vietnamese who had owned some 60 percent of the rice mills, river transport and textile and other industries of the south. The new currency was issued at a premium in exchange for the old, with a maximum exchange per individual of 100 units of currency. The displaced Chinese (as well as Vietnamese) entrepreneurs were given a choice of either participating in joint state-private enterprises or embarking on an "economically productive" life in new economic zones in remote areas. Instead of accepting either alternative they chose to flee by the thousands, overland or in unseaworthy boats or aboard several dilapidated ships provided hastily by the PRC government.

In the north the ethnic Chinese became alarmed at the possibility of the invasion of Vietnam by the PRC in retaliation for these actions and of probable Vietnamese reprisals, and another mass exodus occurred, deliberately spurred by Vietnam government harassment. From April through June 1978 some 160,000 ethnic Chinese (mostly from the north) fled to China before that country closed its borders.

The drastic measures against commerce and business and the currency restrictions failed to solve the economic problems of scarcity and lack of production and led instead to a quantum jump in the volume of black market transactions in the south. These actions also resulted in curtailment by the PRC of its US$556.6 million assistance program.

Economic growth was further impeded by the fact that the Soviet contribution of US$2.9 billion to the Five Year Plan was a loan rather than a grant and had the effect of forcing Vietnam into substantial economic bondage. Thus after it joined the Soviet-sponsored Council for Mutual Economic Assistance (COMECON) in mid-1978, Vietnam became a source of cheap labor for the Soviet bloc. Factories in Vietnam began to produce cloth for the Soviet market from Soviet-supplied material, and plastic products for Eastern Europe from chemicals supplied by East Germany. The production of medicine, rugs, textiles, beer and handicrafts for the Soviet bloc had the effect of denying consumer goods to the Vietnamese. These developments, reflecting the movement toward integrating the Vietnamese economy with those of the COMECON countries, recalled Douglas Pike's prophetic remark that, although Vietnam survived French conquest and

American hostility, surviving Soviet friendship would be more difficult.

To ease pressures, the government in mid-1979 suddenly reversed
itself and announced a policy of providing loans for "sideline" private
production, stating ironically that "under socialism, the national collective and private economies are closely interrelated." Enterprises
and individuals were invited to develop products from local raw or
discarded materials not under state management, and to sell them
directly to others with prices determined by supply and demand. State
enterprises were also encouraged to produce beyond planned targets
by allowing them to profit directly from proceeds derived from supplementary production. In September the Council of Ministers decreed
that arable lands not being exploited by state farms and cooperatives
should be turned over to peasants for personal cultivation and profit,
with loans to be made to farmers under the program.

Nevertheless the agricultural crisis continued unabated. Food production was two million tons short of estimated requirements again in
1979. Officials blamed 30 years of war, droughts, floods and crop
diseases, and pointed to bad management and general lack of enthusiasm as reasons for failure of 63 percent of the agricultural cooperatives
in the north to achieve their production targets.

The crisis worsened in 1980 when typhoons destroyed 40 percent of
the rice crop in the north. The 2 million ton food shortfall at the end of
1979 increased to 3.2 million at the end of 1980 and the Soviet Union,
itself a grain importer, was the only major foreign supplier. Aid from
the European Economic Community and other western countries had
been suspended in 1979 after Vietnam invaded Kampuchea, although
in December 1981 France resumed food aid which it described as a
token amount to keep communication lines open.

The acute food supply problem eased in 1981, with a four percent
rise in production and a further rise in 1982. According to the government the increase was due mainly to introduction in the north of a new
"contract system" that permitted families on collective farms to sell
to the state or on the open market all produce in excess of contract
quotas. The opportunity to supplement incomes led to greater efficiency and to an increased yield.

In mid-1985 the Eighth Plenum of the Fifth Party Congress sought
to decentralize decision making by mandating the elimination of "bureaucratic centralism," cessation of the wartime system of economic
subsidies and adoption of the "socialist mode of enterprise." Disappointed and embarrassed because the economy continued to decline
even more rapidly in the succeeding year despite directives and guide-
lines, the CPV chose new leaders at the Sixth Party Congress in
December 1986. Designated as "reformers," the new leaders during

the first half of 1987 attributed the failed economy to a "simplistic and unrealistic conception of socialism."[31] They called for "rejuvenation" or "renovation" (doi moi) under the direction of the reformers who would bestow their imprimatur on temporary economic liberalization while retaining the longer term commitment to orthodox socialism.

Throughout 1987 the hard liners resisted reform and continued to do so through 1988, frequently forcing the reformers to compromise as the latter did in June by acquiescing in the formers' choice of conservative Du Muoi as Chairman of the Council of Ministers (premier) to succeed Vo Van Kiet, a reformer. Nonetheless, by mid-1988 significant policy changes including the following were in place: a liberal investment code to attract foreign companies, encouragement of market forces, down grading of collective agriculture, creation of the nation's first commerical bank, and insistence that state enterprises conduct operations on a profit-loss basis.[32] But foreign debt had risen to US $8 Billion.[33]

POLITICAL DEVELOPMENTS

By 1978 jurisdictional disputes between the bureaucracy and party had adversely affected party control; economic deterioration had sapped ideological fervor; the Chinese were perceived as threatening to invade Vietnam over the latter's treatment of the ethnic Chinese; and the masses were uprooted and restless. A major corrective political action appeared necessary. The device chosen was "mass mobilization," a technique perfected earlier by the Chinese communists. Mobilization of the people in the service of the state is more feasible in times of perceived danger and China was presented as a threat.

The mass mobilization drive which ensued took several forms. First, the already large army was further increased to serve as a defense against the Chinese and to use as a massive conscript labor force. The army numbered 600,000 in 1978; by February 1979 the figure had increased to 920,000 with the ultimate goal one million.[34]

Second, large segments of the civilian population were mobilized in semi-military fashion, both to transform the people into a more productive labor force and to condition them for further war. In February 1979 Vietnamese workers were admonished by Communist Party Secretary Le Duan to undergo two hours of military training daily and to make every factory an "impregnable fortress." In the same announcement Le Duan said, "the three million workers and public employees in the country must be three million fighters."[35] By 1981 some 1.5 million men and women were serving in local armed militia units. And third, the party attempted to reassert its control over the bureaucracy and the administration. Premier Pham Van Dong lashed out at "bureaucratism, conservatism, authoritarianism, waste, misappropriation, inertia, irresponsibility and indiscipline.''[36]

The December 1978 Vietnamese invasion of Kampuchea and the February 1979 Chinese invasion of Vietnam served as rationales for maintaining both the massive standing army and the military-type mobilization of the masses.

Government A new constitution was drafted in August 1979 and was approved by the party's central committee in September; it was promulgated in December 1980. Unlike the 1960 constitution, the new document concentrated administrative authority in a powerful new body—the State Presidium of Collective Chairmanship, or Council of State—rather than in the Council of Ministers. Its chairman is head of the state and commander-in-chief of the armed forces, giving the head of state real political power for the first time.

The Council of State is supposed to decide policy and supervise its execution by the Council of Ministers. In practice, policy is adopted at periodic party congresses, but is actually determined through consensus achieved within the party's Politburo and Central Committee. On April 1981 Vietnam held elections for the 496-seat National Assembly, the first election in five years and the first nationwide elections since reunification. All candidates were chosen by the Vietnam Fatherland Front, the umbrella organization of the CPV. Elections to the Eighth National Assembly in April 1987, conducted under similar circumstances, were considered, even by foreign observers, as examples of broader political participation.

In 1986 the benchmark Sixth Party Congress had called for "renovation" of the economic system, but doctrinaire ideology continued to dominate politics through 1989, regardless of specific liberalizing decrees and regulations.

FOREIGN RELATIONS

The Provisional Revolutionary Government of the Republic of South Vietnam was speedily accepted by the international community after the 1975 communist victory. Eighty of the world's states—non-communist as well as communist—recognized the new government in the south and extended that recognition to the Socialist Republic of Vietnam when the country became unified. France was in the vanguard in initiating diplomatic and assistance talks. Only the United States and some of its allies demurred. The ASEAN (Association of Southeast Asian Nations) states, except temporarily the regime's former enemy Thailand, extended the "hand of friendship," only to be rebuffed when the SRV branded ASEAN as a tool of U.S. imperialism. However by mid-1976 Hanoi itself was successfully courting ASEAN members. In

1977, after the U.S. ceased its opposition, the SRV succeeded the RVN in the United Nations as it had already done in other international bodies.

Contacts with the United States during the early postwar years were confined to exchanges of messages concerning American servicemen missing in action. Hanoi refused to undertake a search or tabulation unless the U.S. contributed to Vietnam's reconstruction as promised in the 1973 agreements. Humanitarian needs of both sides arising from the conflict were gradually addressed however. By 1989 U.S. voluntary agencies were assisting war-disabled Vietnamese, and Washington and Hanoi were collaborating in identifying remains of Americans missing in action (MIAs).

In 1978, recognizing that its economy was on the verge of disaster, Hanoi had dropped its demand for war damage reparations from the United States and proposed to the Carter administration the establishment of diplomatic relations without any conditions, hoping apparently that such a development would bring in its wake large-scale economic assistance from the western world. Moreover it sent signals to the U.S. by declining Soviet offers to assist in searching for offshore petroleum and by initially refusing to join COMECON.[37] However, Chinese impatience over the slow pace of US-PRC "normalization" placed the Carter administration in a difficult position. Preferring to placate the Chinese, the Americans declined to extend diplomatic recognition. Vietnam thereupon became the first East Asian member of COMECON and on November 3, 1978 signed a Treaty of Friendship and Cooperation with the Soviet Union which included agreements on economic aid, science, technology and cultural exchanges, and committed the signatories to "take appropriate and effective measures" in the event "either party is attacked or threatened with attack."[38]

Japan, Denmark, Italy, West Germany, and especially Sweden, emerged as significant aid donors in 1977; the same year Vietnam signed a 25-year friendship pact with East Germany which included a promise of US$260 million in assistance. Malaysia pledged US$1 million in aid in 1978 and India offered Hanoi loans. However the exodus of the ethnic Chinese in the spring of 1978 as the result of overt Vietnamese government action proved to be the beginning of a general deterioration in Vietnam's international relations.

Sino-Soviet Rivalry and Vietnam The key to understanding post-1975 political events in Indochina and Vietnamese actions is the rivalry between the Soviet Union and China which had its roots in earlier years. Geopolitical problems, experienced by many states with common borders, intensified beginning about 1960 when China's Mao Tse-tung sought to establish an ideological position independent of the Soviet Union to complement China's evolving political independence.

The conflict was fought in communist terms, Mao claiming that the Chinese personified communist orthodoxy and that the Soviets had become "revisionists." The ideological quarrel, which was in reality a struggle for influence in communist and emerging "third world" countries, escalated to the point of termination by the Soviet Union of military cooperation with, and assistance to, the PRC.

For many years Vietnamese communists were successful in manipulating Sino-Soviet differences to their advantage, obtaining substantial military and economic assistance from both. Between the years 1952 and 1975 Hanoi received US$1.675 billion in economic aid from the PRC, primarily in the nature of foodstuffs, and grants and interest-free or low interest loans for modernizing infrastructure and basic industries. Soviet economic aid in the same period (1955–1975) totaled US$2.218 billion in interest free or low interest loans, raw materials and complete plants.[39]

Until 1978 when the PRC cut off aid, Vietnam was the major recipient of Chinese assistance even though Hanoi favored the Soviet position of a united front of communist parties in Asia under the leadership of the "Father Party" of the Soviet Union, rather than under Chinese tutelage. Outbreak of the Cultural Revolution in China in 1966, which elevated PRC perceptions of its ideological purity to new heights and exacerbated tensions between it and the Soviet Union, had not interfered with rail transport of Soviet military shipments through China to Vietnam. China did, however, perceive the danger of permanent Soviet influence on its southern border in the event of American withdrawal, and undertook a series of moves designed to delay if not prevent that possibility. First it deliberately stalled regarding united political action in Vietnam and in the timing of a general offensive against the RVN; Chinese strategy apparently was to perpetuate a divided Vietnam until China could shore up its position in Laos and Kampuchea, particularly in the latter which had been its staunchest ally since 1954.

In a second related move the Chinese began to show relative tolerance of the American military presence in Southeast Asia, in response to, or at the same time as, the American enunciation of the policy of "Vietnamization" of the war effort. These actions led to the Sino-American rapprochment of 1971–72, an anathema to the Vietnamese communist leadership which reacted by drawing closer to the USSR. Communist victories in 1975 resulted in capitulation of the RVN to the Vietnamese clients of the Soviet Union and the surrender of the Lon Nol regime in Kampuchea to the Kampuchean clients of the PRC (see Kampuchea). The stage was thus set for a Soviet-and-Chinese-backed struggle between these two new communist states.

Kampuchea Border clashes between the PRC-supported Pol Pot regime in Kampuchea and the Soviet-supported government in Vietnam began early in May 1975, literally within days of the respective communist takeovers. Extreme internal repression from the beginning by the Pol Pot government caused the chronically unstable border area between the two states to become even more destabilized as thousands of Kampucheans fled into Vietnam and as the Kampuchean regime tested the Vietnamese response by military incursions.

Military conflict increased throughout 1977 and diplomatic relations between the two states were terminated in December. As early as February 1978 the Central Committee of the Vietnamese Communist Party, with Soviet encouragement, began to consider employment of a large-scale military force to break the "Peking-Phnom Penh Axis."[40] Although both the PRC and the Soviets stepped up military assistance to their respective clients, the quality and quantity of Chinese arms to Kampuchea stood "in sharp contrast to large-scale deliveries [by the Soviets] of tanks, aircraft and munitions to Vietnamese ports in the six months before Vietnam's December–January 1979 final assault."[41]

In December 1978 the Vietnamese army, according to General Vo Nguyen Giap, prepared to fulfill its "historic mission" to defeat the "aggressive war of the reactionary clique in Phnom Penh."[42] By January 7, 1979 some 120,000 Vietnamese troops, armored cars and aircraft had moved against Phnom Penh, securing the city and setting up the pro-Vietnamese Revolutionary Council headed by Heng Samrin. On April 13 Vietnam and Kampuchea ratified a Treaty of Peace, Friendship and Cooperation which provided the legal basis for the presence of Vietnamese troops in that country.

Repercussions of the Invasion of Kampuchea   A major result of the Vietnamese invasion of Kampuchea was loss of international support for the Vietnamese regime, particularly in Southeast Asia. During 1978 Hanoi had undertaken well publicized efforts to defuse ASEAN dismay over the flood of refugees it had loosed on the area, and in visits to ASEAN capitals in the fall Premier Pham Van Dong exuded goodwill and was warmly welcomed. Nevertheless, following the invasion, the ASEAN states announced their united opposition to the action and attacked Vietnam at the September 1979 Summit of Non-Aligned Nations in Havana. Vietnam responded by accusing ASEAN of "toeing the Peking and Washington line." European nations and Australia terminated their aid programs and Sweden demanded troop withdrawal. Of greater impact were the subsequent actions by China.

The fall of Kampuchea created a dilemma for China. Non-response to the defeat of an ally would further reduce the credibility of the PRC as regional leader of the communist movement; military action risked direct confrontation with the Soviet Union. Despite Soviet admonition against use of force and the presence of Soviet warships in the Gulf of

Tongking, the Chinese opted to "punish" the Vietnamese. Therefore on February 17, 1979 Chinese forces crossed the border into Vietnam, penetrating 25 miles and destroying two dozen towns, railways and bridges. They withdrew after three weeks claiming they had accomplished their purpose.

Although the Chinese action did not result in a diplomatic break between the two nations, each intensified its propaganda war against the other and China reemphasized its territorial claims to the disputed Paracel and Spratly islands in the South China Sea, strategically important as possible sources of oil and as naval bases. Hanoi responded by instituting a massive military buildup in the north and inviting an increased Soviet presence.

The only winner in the Chinese-Vietnamese conflict of 1979 was the Soviet Union, which won credence as a dependable ally and champion of Vietnam against a "Sino-American alliance." The Soviet presence and its influence in Vietnam dramatically expanded. The core of the Moscow-Hanoi relationship is the bilateral treaty of 1978 which afforded legitimacy for Soviet use of former U.S. bases at Danang and Camranh Bay. The Soviets provided direct military assistance, capital resources, and the technical help of thousands of advisers in an annual aid package totaling US$2 billion.

Vietnam's military occupation of Kampuchea continued unabated during the following years. By 1987, however, international opposition forced Hanoi to a token troop withdrawal as precondition for relaxation of the political isolation the ASEAN states had successfully imposed. Warming Sino-Soviet relations in 1988 produced further Vietnamese policy modification and a verified reduction of the occupying forces. Finally, on the eve of the spring 1989 Sino-Soviet summit which normalized their relationship, Hanoi suddenly announced that a complete troop withdrawal would occur within the year. Although unverified, Vietnam's declaration in September that total troop withdrawal had been achieved was generally accepted by the international community.

Laos   Vietnamese troop presence in Laos dates back to 1953 when the Vietminh joined forces with Pathet Lao (Laotian communist) units against the French and the newly established independent Laotian government. They were not withdrawn but merely disbanded in 1954 in spite of the fact that the Geneva Conference of that year called for full foreign troop withdrawal. The 1962 Geneva Agreement on the neutralization of Laos called again for withdrawal of foreign military personnel, but Vietnamese compliance was minimal and Vietnamese units were backing the Pathet Lao in the fighting that resumed the following year.

According to Kissinger the total number of DRV troops in Laos rose

from 6,000 in 1953 to 67,000 by 1970 and "southern Laos was in effect
annexed by the North Vietnamese army, which constructed there an
intricate system of infiltration routes into South Vietnam."[43] It continued to be used as such throughout the war. When the Laotian monarchy collapsed in April 1975 and was succeeded by the communist Lao
People's Democratic Republic, Vietnamese troops remained.

In mid-July 1977 comprehensive economic and military agreements
were reached between Vietnam and Laos and a 25-year treaty of
cooperation was inaugurated in September. Hanoi claimed that Chinese threats necessitated continued deployment of Vietnamese troops
in Laos. These numbered about 20,000 in early 1989, down from 50,000
a decade earlier.

WHITHER VIETNAM?

In the final decade of the 20th century Vietnam faces daunting tasks.
Decades of economic failure, attributed by the political leadership to a
"simplistic and unrealistic conception of socialism," must be reversed.
Vietnam's human rights record and the quality of the lives of its
citizens must be improved in tandem with reforms being undertaken
by its superpower patron, the Soviet Union. Vietnam must cooperate
with the international community to resolve the dispute over Kampuchea which has precipitated armed conflict every year since Vietnam's
invasion of that nation in 1978–79. The problems are formidable but
not insurmountable.

Vietnam's economic disasters have forced it to recognize that the
only alternative to even deeper economic malaise is to decentralize
decision making and to encourage development of market forces.
Circumstances elsewhere in the socialist world have compelled political leaderships, notably in Moscow and Peking, to bestow their impri-
maturs upon fledgling capitalist-like, market oriented segments of
economies. However, as the pragmatists among Vietnam's leaders put
into place incrementally less rigid economic policies ("renovation"),
they have been opposed by the hard line Marxist-Leninists among the
leadership. Market socialism, as it might be termed, has led the
country in one direction, orthodox communist ideology in a very
different one. Unfettered, the Vietnamese display entrepreneurial in-
stincts and abilities similar to those of the Chinese.

In the event the pragmatists eventually prevail, foreign firms and
investment could invigorate Vietnam's economy, as has occurred in
China. In 1988 Vietnam began to reduce its decades-old economic
dependency on the Soviet Union and regained eligibility for International Monetary Fund concessional loans. A liberal investment code
to attract foreign companies was in place and about 30 percent of the

country's trade was with non-communist nations. Member states of the Association of Southeast Asian Nations informally began to hedge concerning their professed trade embargo against Vietnam occasioned by its invasion and occupation of Kampuchea. Much of the new trading, however, was limited, as was trade with the Soviet Union, to barter deals and export processing rather than significant investment for capital construction. Non-communist investment capital appeared to be awaiting a definitive "renovation" of Vietnam's ideology to parallel the new openness policy.

The decade-long conflict over Hanoi's domination of Kampuchea, often characterized as "Vietnam's Vietnam," appeared to be partially resolved when the remaining Vietnamese troops were apparently withdrawn in late 1989 as promised. Nevertheless, obsessed by security concerns, Vietnam will not tolerate border regimes which might be vulnerable to control by external forces (read China). Despite apparent USSR-PRC rapprochement, the two giant powers will continue to compete for influence in Indochina and the Soviets are unlikely to give up the political gain they have achieved in Vietnam since 1975. A similar Chinese investment in Indochina dates back more than a thousand years. Conflict resolution in Southeast Asia will fail unless these realities are addressed by the parties involved and by the world community.

FOOTNOTES

1. John T. McAlister, *Viet Nam: The Origins of Revolution* (N.Y.: Knopf, 1969), p. 19.

2. *Ibid.*, p. 34.

3. Joseph Buttinger, *Vietnam: A Political History* (N.Y.: Praeger, 1968), p. 163.

4. Henry A. Kissinger, *The White House Years* (Boston, Little, Brown and Co., 1979), p. 450.

5. David J. Steinberg, *Cambodia* (New Haven: Human Relations Area Files, 1957), p. 112.

6. Quoted by Wesley R. Fishel, *Vietnam: Anatomy of a Conflict* (Itasca, Illinois: Peacock Publishers, 1968), p. 205–206.

7. *The Pentagon Papers* (N.Y.: Bantam Books, Inc., 1971), p. 250.

8. Guy J. Pauker, "Indonesia in 1964: Toward a 'People's Democracy'?", *Asian Survey*, February 1965, p. 88.

9. "Asia Chooses Sides," *Los Angeles Times*, September 22, 1965, p. 5.

10. See Arnold C. Brackman, *The Communist Collapse in Indonesia* (N.Y.: Norton, 1969), p. 196–197.

11. Albert Ravenholt, a veteran of the World War II press corps in China and longtime resident and writer in Southeast Asia, told the authors in a June 24, 1982 interview, that Chinese Defense Minister Lin Piao's September 2, 1965 speech rejecting direct Chinese intervention in Vietnam was in effect recognition that the RVN's survival had upset the time frame envisaged to consolidate the axis. The speech, according to this view, was a signal to the Indonesian communists that they would have to conduct a "People's War" on their own and the Indonesian communists decided to strike. See also Richard C. Thornton, *China: The Struggle for Power, 1917–1972* (Bloomington, Indiana: Indiana University Press, 1973).

12. See Barry Siegel, "Revisionism: A New Look at Vietnam," *Los Angeles Times*, features analysis, November 16, 1980, p. 1.

13. *Pentagon Papers, op. cit.*, p. 343.

14. *Ibid.*, p. 461.

15. *Ibid.*, p. 521.

16. *Ibid.*, p. 593.

17. Kissinger, *op. cit.*, p. 235.

18. Lyndon B. Johnson, *The Vantage Point* (N.Y.: Holt, Rinehart and Winston, 1971), p. 398.

19. *Ibid.*, p. 420.

20. *Ibid.*, p. 495.

21. *Pentagon Papers, op. cit.*, p. 599.

22. John F. Cady, *The History of Post-War Southeast Asia* (Athens, Ohio: Ohio University Press, 1974), p. 588.

23. Quoted in Department of State *Background Notes (North) VietNam*, April 1974, p. 8.

24. Kissinger, *op. cit.*, p. 306–307.

25. *Ibid.*, p. 979.

26. *Ibid.*, p. 1444.

27. *Ibid.*, p. 1448.

28. Text of the Act of the International Conference on Vietnam, Department of State Press Release 55, March 5, 1973.

29. "Military Assistance Program," *GAO Report ID-82-40*, June 1, 1982.

30. Douglas Pike, "The Vietnamese Economy," unpublished Department of State Study, March, 1987.

31. Foreign Minister Nguyen Co Thach, personal interview, March 17, 1987.

32. See *Foreign Broadcast Information Service (FBIS) Daily Reports*, EAS, 1986–88.

33. *FBIS*, EAS, June 9, 1988, p. 16–17.

34. *Data Asia* (Manila: Press Foundation of Asia), 1979, p. 6041.

35. *Ibid.*, p. 6104.

36. *Asia Yearbook* (Hong Kong: Far Eastern Economic Review Ltd.), 1980, p. 299.

37. Robert C. Horn, "Soviet-Vietnamese Relations and the Future of Southeast Asia," *Pacific Affairs*, Winter 1978–79, p. 590–604.

38. Douglas Pike, "The USSR and Vietnam," *Asian Survey*, December 1979, p. 1162.

39. *Data Asia, op. cit.*, 1977, p. 4984.

40. Huynh Kim Khanh, "Into the Third Indochina War," *Southeast Asian Affairs*, 1980, p. 333.

41. Sheldon W. Simon, "Kampuchea: Vietnam's Vietnam," *Current History*, December 1979, p. 197.

42. *Asia Yearbook, op. cit.*, p. 301.

43. Kissinger, *op. cit.*, p. 450.

Kampuchea
(Cambodia)

Thailand

Laos

Siemreap

Battambang

Angkor

Tonle Sap

Mekong
River

Phnom Penh ★

Vietnam

Gulf of Siam

CHAPTER 3
KAMPUCHEA
(CAMBODIA)

The term "Kampuchea" (or Kambuja) for identifying the Khmer region was in use by the 9th century. During the 19th century colonial era, and until the communist victories in Indochina in 1975, the French term "Cambodge," or the English "Cambodia" was used. The revolutionary Khmer Rouge government revived the designation "Kampuchea" upon its accesession to power in 1975. Upon overthrow of the Khmer Rouge regime in 1979, its successor revolutionary government adopted the term "People's Republic of Kampuchea." In 1989 Prince Sihanouk, leader of the resistance forces, insisted upon reinstatement of the term "Cambodia" as one precondition for beginning reconciliation discussions with the Phnom Penh regime. Cognizant of the impermanence of titles, the authors have chosen to retain the term "Kampuchea."

Contemporary Kampuchea consists of a large, rich, low-lying plain surrounding the seasonally, fluctuating Tonle Sap (Great Lake). To the north the plain is broken by the Dangrek escarpment, and in the southwest by the Elephant and Cardamon mountains which form a barrier between the plain and Kampuchea's southern seacoast on the Gulf of Siam. About the size of the state of Missouri, the nation is bordered by Thailand on the west and northwest, Laos on the northeast and Vietnam on the east and southeast.

The Tonle Sap is the natural flood reservoir of the Mekong River, which enters Kampuchea from the north through the low hills east of the Dangrek range. The river rises in Tibet and drains the eastern third of mainland Southeast Asia, finding its way to the sea through many delta channels in southern Vietnam. Monsoonal rains regularly cause the river to flood large areas of Kampuchea's central plain; at flood stage in mid-summer the Tonle Sap expands from roughly 1,000 square miles to three times that extent. Kampuchean civilization has traditionally centered on this plain.

EARLY EMPIRES

Funan   Funan was not only the first Kampuchean empire, but the first great empire in Southeast Asia, and therefore, as Rome in Europe, lived on in men's memories long after its fall. According to Chinese annals Funan was founded in the 1st century A.D. by an Indian Brahman named Kaundinya, which is the name of a Brahman class of north India. The dynasty linked itself with Indian myths of divinity by declaring Kaundinya's consort—in all likelihood a local princess—to be a snake goddess. The reenactment of this legend was an integral part of court ceremony for over a thousand years.

Funan's first capital was on the Mekong River about 120 miles above the major port of Oc Eo on the Gulf of Siam in what is now southern Vietnam. The people were Malay with a mixture of aboriginal Negrito. Funan culture was heavily influenced by Indian traders and missionaries who, from earliest times, had sailed around the Bay of Bengal and portaged across the Malay peninsula into the Gulf of Siam. By the 1st century Indian ships, capable of carrying 700 passengers and a thousand tons of cargo, were sailing through the Strait of Malacca, into the South China Sea, and to the southern coast of China. The delta of the Mekong was a convenient stopping point on these voyages and Indian influence became both more direct and more intense during this period. Hinduism soon overlay the indigenous animism of Kampuchea. Brahmans were prominent in court functions and ritual. Sanskrit became the court language, and a north Indian script was adopted for writing the local language.

Almost all we know of Funan is from Chinese chronicles of the time. The names of the rulers as well as the name Funan itself—which came from the title of the ruler, Kurung Phnom (King of the Mountain)—were sinicized. The first great warrior-emperor was Fan Shih-man, who died in the first quarter of the 3rd century and is thought to have conquered southern Vietnam to Camranh Bay, and possibly the northern part of the Malay peninsula. During this century Funan, whose wealth depended largely on trade, was known to be in direct contact with both India and China. When Funan was mentioned by Chinese chroniclers in the middle of the 4th century it was associated with Pallavan (south Indian) culture and customs; the Pallava script from which modern Kampuchean letters evolved had been adopted.

There was a reinfusion of Indian culture in the early part of the 5th century when another Kaundinya—perhaps from an Indianized state or city in the south—became king. The greatest king of this dynasty, Jayavarman I, ruled from 470 to 514. His powerful fleets engaged in both trade and piracy. Although Buddhism had become widespread, especially among the common people, the worship of Shiva and the cult of the *devaraja* continued to be the religion of the court and a mechanism for controlling the state.

The *devaraja* cult played a more important political role in Kampuchea than elsewhere in Southeast Asia, although all courts in the area adopted the concept. The king was considered a manifestation or incarnation of Shiva, and his power was worshipped in the form of a lingam which was enshrined on a "sacred mountain" in the center of his capital city. At its peak Funan extended from the South China Sea to the Bay of Bengal and from Laos to the southern part of the Malay peninsula.

Chenla: 627–820 To the north of Funan proper was Chenla, inhabited by a Khmer people, and one of the vassal states of the empire whose power rose as that of Funan fell. Funan itself was fully incorporated into Chenla in 627 by Isanavarman who built his capital at what is today Kompong Thom, where the most impressive ruins of pre-Angkor are to be found. He conquered western Kampuchea and a successor, Jayavarman I, conquered central and upper Laos.

The civil wars which followed the death of Jayavarman I left Chenla divided into "Chenla of the Land" in the north (Chenla proper), and "Chenla of the Water" in the south, former Funan including the Mekong delta. Land Chenla seems to have had a more stable government and continued to be noted in Chinese annals, but Water Chenla appears to have broken into two or more units, and was attacked by Malays, probably the Sailendra dynasty of Java, between 774 and 787. Indeed, the last king of Water Chenla, Jayavarman II (802–850), seems to have come from Java, probably chosen by the Javanese from among possible dynastic successors. Jayavarman II successfully reunited Water Chenla by force, established a new capital at the head of Tonle Sap near the site where Angkor would later be built, and revived the *devaraja* cult. In a ceremony performed in 819 or 820 he was officially transformed into a god-king and universal ruler. By this ceremony he announced his rejection of Javanese overlordship. Thus he is both the last king of the vassal state of Chenla and the first of the sovereign kingdom of Angkor.

During the Chenla period the name Kambuja (Kampuchea) came into use for the area. It undoubtedly came from the Indian word for "sons of Kambu"—the mythical ascetic ancestor of the Chenla Khmer who wed a heavenly nymph and founded the Chenla dynasty.

Angkor Empire: 820–1500 The *devaraja* ceremony by which Jayavarman II asserted the independence of himself and his kingdom also reestablished the power of the priestly Brahman families who performed the royal rituals and with whom the royal family intermarried. The narrow oligarchy so created ruled over the vast body of commoners and slaves. Consumption laws which prevented the common man from aping the court in extravagance of personal adornment and living accouterments permitted the court to appropriate surplus "capital" for its elaborate rituals and ceremonies and for its great building projects. The king as god was the legal possessor of all the lands, products and people thereof, the divine source of law, the protector of religion and the defender of the state from outside threats. The strengthened religious base and the administrative organization established by Jayavarman II were to be two of the three pillars of the state for the next four centuries. The third was the great irrigation system undertaken by a successor.

Jayavarman's choice for his capital was astute. By locating it at the head of the Great Lake, on the rich alluvial flood plain, the economic basis for the state was secure. The land was ideal for rice cultivation and the lake teemed with fish which could be scooped from the mud as the lake shrank in the dry season. It was near the mountains where sandstone could easily be quarried and where iron supplies were sufficient for the needs of a pre-industrial civilization.

Indravarman (877–889) built the first great temple of classical Khmer style, expanded the empire and began the first irrigation project, constructing a huge catchment basin to save the monsoon rains. He was succeeded by his son Yasovarman I (889–900) who founded Angkor, naming the city in his own honor, Yasodharapura; Angkor means simply capital city. His greatest accomplishment, however, was to change the course of the Siemreap River and to build an intricate system of reservoirs, moats and irrigation channels which advanced the agricultural base upon which the economy of the country depended. Irrigation of the extremely fertile soil of the flood basin made possible three or even four rice crops per year and the surplus wealth created permitted the great architectural and artistic accomplishments of the Angkor period. Angkor was built at the furthest navigable point from the sea and was deemed safe from surprise attack—an assumption proved false in later years.

Rajendravarman II who ruled during the middle of the 10th century incorporated Land Chenla into the empire, defeated the Cham with whom Angkor was to be intermittently at war over the next four centuries and undertook major rebuilding projects. In the 11th century Angkor conquered the Mon confederacy that extended across the southwestern sector of mainland Southeast Asia, and added most of present day Thailand to its domains.

Suryavarman II (1113–1150) is credited by most scholars with building the masterpiece of Khmer architecture, Angkor Wat. This great temple to Vishnu, located outside the capital city, is a stupendous architectural feat; the main temple covers an area equal to that of the Great Pyramid in Egypt and is covered with sculptural design of extremely high quality. This was the golden age of Khmer civilization, the country reached its widest territorial extent to date, Suryavarman was an able ruler and statesman and Angkor was the greatest state, politically and culturally, in Southeast Asia.

However, a host of problems beset the empire after his death. Among them were: 1) a series of rebellions by the peasantry against demands levied upon them for war and temple building, 2) neglect by subsequent rulers of the all-important irrigation system, 3) repeated outbreaks of malaria, the plague and other diseases, 4) the impact of the Mongol invasions on Southeast Asia and 5) finally and most importantly, the rise of new competing empires, as well as the revival of Champa.

· The next three kings expended much of their energy defending themselves against the Cham, who in 1177 sailed up the Mekong, pillaged Angkor and killed the king. In 1181 Jayavarman VII (1181–1218) defeated the Cham and ascended the throne. Under his rule the empire reached its greatest physical extent. He subjugated Champa and made it a province, and parts of contemporary Thailand, Burma, Laos and Malaya were forced to become vassal states.

Jayavarman VII can be considered the first Buddhist ruler of the Khmer. The king embraced Mahayana Buddhism, which had appeared as early as the Funan period. The carved heads of the Bayon Temple portray Jayavarman VII as the Bodhisattva Lokesevara to whom Mahayanists attributed godlike qualities that were probably indistinguishable in the popular mind from those of the *devaraja*. Nevertheless a different philosophy—one which took account of the individual—was being expressed. During the next century Theravada Buddhism, which deemphasized court ritual and renounced the notion of a kingly *bodhisattva,* spread from Ceylon. As Theravada Buddhism gradually displaced the Mahayana variety it undermined both the supermundane and the temporal power of the Khmer rulers.

Even as Jayavarman VII was extending the perimeters of the Khmer empire, seeds of decline were taking root. Under his son and immediate successor the Sukhothai province in the Chao Phraya valley of Thailand broke away. As the Mongolian empire pushed down into Southeast Asia from China, Thai tribes were forced south and east against the Khmer frontiers. Before the end of the century Thai authority had replaced that of Angkor throughout the Chao Phraya River area in the west, the upper Mekong River centers of Vientiane and Luang Prabang in the northeast (Laos), and Ligor in Malaya to the south. The dwindling state of Angkor survived mainly because Mongol pressures on Southeast Asia ceased.

By this time reduced to kingdom rather than empire status, the Angkor state entered another long and further debilitating period caused by succession problems. The Hindu-Mahayana Buddhist concept of the god-king, still essentially in place, exacerbated the problem; divine incarnation was a ready-made device for usurpers because the successful claimant automatically became the new *devaraja*.

By 1359 armies of a newly risen Thai kingdom, removed from Sukhothai to Ayutthia, had invaded the Angkor state to begin a long struggle between the Thai and Khmer people. The Khmer stubbornly resisted for more than 70 years until Angkor was captured and sacked by Thai forces in 1430–31. Although Angkor was retaken by the Khmer the following year, it ceased to be their capital because of its proximity to Ayutthia. With the abandonment of Angkor it is useful for the sake of clarity to refer henceforth to the Khmer state as Kampuchea.

THAI-VIETNAMESE COMPETITION FOR HEGEMONY

Continuing wars with the Thai preoccupied succeeding Kampuchean kings during the 15th century, obscuring the rise of a new threat in the east. The Vietnamese of the north absorbed Champa in 1471 and began to push south into the underpopulated southeastern provinces of Kampuchea. The danger went largely unrecognized as Kampuchea stumbled through the 16th century, still preoccupied by its wars with the Thai. However by the beginning of the next century the Thai were determining the successors to the Kampuchean throne, a situation which set the stage for clashes for the next two and a half centuries between the Thai and the Vietnamese dynasty of the Nguyen in Annam for the control of Khmer territories.

In consequence of an intermarriage between the Vietnamese and Kampuchean royal families in the early 17th century the Annamese secured permission to establish a customs house, trading center and settlements at Saigon—Water Chenla of the old Khmer empire—thus establishing a formal Vietnamese foothold in Kampuchea. In mid-century the Nguyen sought to expand, using the pretext that the Khmer had violated the frontier in 1658. They occupied a border area, defeated the king and forced him to pay homage as vassal to Annam.

During the 18th and 19th centuries the see-saw conflict between the Thai and the Annamese for control of Kampuchea intensified, and the two nations fought each other on Kampuchean soil, the Thai moving southeast along the Cardamon mountains and coming into conflict with the Vietnamese moving south into the Ca Mau peninsula of southernmost Vietnam. In the course of their military contest each forced Kampuchea to cede its provinces. By 1749 Kampuchea had relinquished to the Nguyen all of today's southern Vietnam, including the entire Ca Mau peninsula. Throughout the rest of the century the two nations intrigued to influence the succession to the Kampuchean throne. The contest came to a climax during the period of the Tay-son rebellion in Vietnam when the Thai obtained control of the infant king, Ang Eng, and spirited him to Bangkok, their new capital. When he reached majority he was crowned, and in the company of a Thai army, returned to his own country as king. The price exacted by the Thai "for their service" was the ceding to Thailand of the fertile western provinces of Battambang and Siemreap.

By 1802 the situation in Vietnam had changed. Nguyen Anh had united the country and proclaimed himself Gia Long, Emperor of Annam. Alarmed anew, the Thai quickly recognized the new heir, Kampuchean Ang Chan, and crowned him in Bangkok in 1806.

Confronted by two expansionist neighbors whose aggrandizement had already seriously compromised Kampuchea's territorial integrity, the young king attempted to placate both by paying double allegiance, a traditional practice of weak states in Southeast Asia. The Thai ruler was displeased and in 1812 supported one of Ang Chan's brothers, Ang Snguon, against the king. Chan fled to Saigon for help and Emperor Gia Long responded with a large Vietnamese army. The Thai, supporting Snguon, retreated with him before the superior Vietnamese force which reinstalled the king and left a permanent Vietnamese garrison there to protect him. Now embroiled in a continuous war with Burma, the Thai tacitly acknowledged Vietnamese domination of Kampuchea but nevertheless gained possession of additional provinces around Tonle Sap.

In 1833 a combination of international developments led the Thai to move again to gain control of Kampuchea. The harsh Vietnamese occupation and a severe economic depression had precipitated a number of revolts by the Kampucheans against their Vietnamese overlords; the British had defeated Burma in 1825–26, erasing the threat to Thailand's western frontier and freeing its military forces for a campaign in the east; and the Vietnamese were preoccupied with revolts in the southern delta. Thus the Thai swept across Kampuchea, overcoming Ang Chan's army on the way and forcing him to flee to the safety of Vietnam. They then drove southeastward toward the provinces held by Vietnam but were forced by the latter to withdraw.

In 1834 Ang Chan died and the Vietnamese seized direct control of the Kampuchean government. They installed his 20-year-old daughter as queen and proceeded with a policy of Vietnamization, changing the name of the capital to Nam Viang, introducing Vietnamese administrative procedures, installing Vietnamese residents to whom provincial Kampuchean governors were responsible, requiring Vietnamese names and customs, and engaging in the suppression of Buddhism.[1] In 1840 they removed the queen's ministers, and then the queen herself, to their capital at Hue.

These actions, and intense Khmer resentment of the Vietnamese administrative procedures of census taking and land registration (disliked in any circumstances since census taking was traditionally identified with labor service—corvée—and land registration with taxes), led to a countrywide revolt. At the same time elements of the nobility petitioned the Thai king for help. The Thai responded, sending two armies into the Tonle Sap region. Rebuffed by opposing Vietnamese forces, the Thai retreated south to the town of Banang which they fortified.

War between the Thai and the Vietnamese continued on Kampuchean soil for the next six years. A peace settlement between them was achieved in 1846 and Ang Duong (1847–1860) was recognized by both countries as the king of Kampuchea. He agreed to pay tribute to each and was forced to accept permanent occupation by the Thai of two more of his provinces. Ang Duong made strenuous efforts to rebuild the devastated economy: neglected paddy land was retilled, the deplorable condition of the people was eased by regular rice distribution, roads were repaired and extended, and taxes and corvée requirements were reduced.

POLITICAL INDICATORS

The foregoing sketch of Kampuchea's political history to the eve of the establishment of the French protectorate in the 19th century underlines long-term characteristics of Kampuchean society which are helpful to an understanding of later politics.

1. The monarchical tradition was extremely strong throughout Kampuchean political history and the *devaraja* concept of the god-king, which spurred both empire and temple building, was a source of state stability; it could also be viewed as a source of instability since in the word's of a leading scholar: "the theory of divine incarnation could be used not only as a means to exalt the position of the legitimate king, but equally well as justification for the usurpation of the throne."[2]
2. The two-tiered Angkor-Kampuchean society—king and Brahman nobility comprising the upper tier, and the common people and slaves the lower—singularly impeded individual upward mobility.
3. The society achieved extraordinary military and artistic achievements based upon an economy of rice cultivation and trade.
4. Beginning with the 14th century Thai invasion, the country became the pawn of, and battleground for, her two powerful neighbors—Thailand and Vietnam, a situation obtaining to the present.

FRENCH PROTECTORATE

Ang Duong's assumption of the Kampuchean throne, under the auspices of both the Thai and the Vietnamese, left him at the mercy of both in this strange "condominium." Fearful that further conflict would obliterate Kampuchea entirely, the king looked to the French for protection.

Traditionally at odds with the British, the French were attempting to establish a presence in Indochina to counterbalance British expansion in Burma and Malaysia, and British influence in Thailand. Ang Duong appealed to Napoleon III in 1855 for a guarantee of independence in return for trade concessions. The Thai, hearing of his initiative, threatened war should Kampuchea sign a treaty with France. Failing to achieve his goal of European protection, Duong abdicated a few years later in favor of his eldest son, Norodom, who was a protégé of Thailand.

Norodom was faced with an internal revolt in 1860, after he ascended the throne but before he was recognized by other states, and fled to Bangkok with the royal insignia—crown, sacred sword and seal. The Thai restored him to his throne two years later, but declined to return the royal regalia which signified kingly authority. The French, meanwhile, had occupied southern Vietnam (which they named Cochinchina) and claimed co-suzerainty over Kampuchea with Thailand as heir to the rights of Vietnam. Although they had provided refuge for the instigator of the revolt, they now offered Norodom French protectorate status as a shield against the Thai. The proposition, quite different from Ang Duong's earlier request, offered a guarantee against external attack and support of Norodom's kingship in return of Kampuchean acceptance of a French adviser to the king, extraterritorial courts for French residents, and free entry of French goods. Norodom accepted since in the absence of French help Thailand would certainly have completed the subjugation of his kingdom.

But Norodom's troubles were not over. While he awaited ratification of the treaty by the French government, the Thai again threatened war. To buy them off, Norodom secretly acknowledged Thai suzerainty anew and again ceded them the western provinces of Battambang and Siemreap. He then prepared to journey to Bangkok to retrieve the royal insignia, but was prevented from so doing by the French. Later, when the protectorate treaty was approved (1863), the French pressured Thailand to return the insignia in exchange for French recognition of Thai suzerainty over Battambang and Siemreap. Thai officials brought the regalia to Kampuchea and in June 1864, in their presence, Norodom was officially crowned by the new French resident.

During the following 20 years France consolidated its hold over

Kampuchea, quelling Thai-supported rebellions and in 1867 negotiating a treaty under which Thailand abandoned all claims to Kampuchea in return for a French promise not to incorporate Kampuchea into Cochinchina which had become an outright French colony. However, when in 1884 Norodom refused to enter a customs union with Annam and Cochinchina, the French attacked Phnom Penh—the Kampuchean capital on the Mekong River—with naval forces dispatched from Saigon. Norodom was forced to sign a document which gave France full control of internal Kampuchean administration. The same year Kampuchea became part of France's Indochina Federation which comprised Laos and the three Vietnamese states—Cochinchina, Annam and Tongking.

Administration   French control was exercised through strategically located residents (local governors) who maintained order and internal security so that Kampuchea would be a buffer against Thailand and British influence there. France's primary objective was to protect her valuable new acquisition—Vietnam. Subordinate objectives were to promote the economic development of Kampuchea for the benefit of France and to develop loyalty to the French regime. The status of the common man was improved by the abolition of debt slavery, an onerous system which bound debtors to masters. Corn and rubber cultivation was encouraged, the former bringing benefits to local consumers and the latter to French industry. The resident's task of maintaining law and order was simplified by reform of the penal code, modernization of the police system and training of the Kampuchean armed forces in the French tradition.

The French left in place the centralized Kampuchean bureaucracy, permitting it little power, and took pains to perpetuate the prestige of the monarchy. Royal ceremony and ritual were emphasized and traditional social customs and institutions were left intact. The monarchy shared its prestige and nominal authority with the aristocracy and at times demonstrated considerable skill in dealing with both the French and the Thai.

French archeologists began restoring the jungle-covered temples at Angkor which had been completely forgotten by the Kampucheans in a brief four hundred years, and French historians painstakingly assembled the story of the Khmer people. The symbols and saga of the glorious Khmer empire strengthened the monarchy and at the same time linked it with a rising nationalism. These esteem-building measures produced, by the time of Norodom's death in 1904, a faithful, stable and prosperous state in the French Union, though it lacked real authority or control of its destiny.

The French displayed their influence and political acumen when they successfully proposed as Norodom's successor his brother Sisowath

(1904–1927). In bypassing Norodom's sons and rewarding Sisowath for his help in putting down the rebellions of 1885–1886, they strengthened the fealty of the throne to France to such a degree that Kampucheans fought in French armies on European battlefields during World War I. Sisowath's son, Sisowath Monivong, succeeded him in 1927.

The next accession to the throne, 1941, took place in an environment of worldwide crisis. The Germans had defeated the French in Europe, setting up the Vichy French government, and French representatives of the Vichy regime in Indochina were beset by pressures from Germany's ally, Japan. Needing a weak and pliable monarch, they passed over Monivong's son whom they considered too independent, in favor of his nephew, Prince Norodom Sihanouk. The prince, then completing high school in Saigon, was the great grandson of King Norodom, and his mother was a Sisowath. Since Sihanouk had ties to both royal lines, his choice quelled a dispute over the throne and, supposedly, provided a malleable monarch for Vichy France. In the latter the French were badly mistaken.

MILESTONES TO INDEPENDENCE

Japanese forces entered Kampuchea in mid-1941. A 1942 agreement between Japan and vichy France left French administration in nominal control except in the provinces of Battambang and Siemreap. These provinces had been returned to Kampuchea in 1907 and Japan now forced the Vichy regime to cede them once more to Thailand which was a formal belligerent on the side of the Japanese.

By the early part of 1945 it became increasingly evident that Japan was losing the war and that a new political order would ensue. Within this setting conflict arose which shaped the course of developing Kampuchean nationalism, demonstrated the strength of the Kampuchean monarchical tradition and helps explain communist success in securing a foothold in that nation. Sihanouk and the Kampuchean nationalist leader, Son Ngoc Thanh, were the initial protagonists.

Thanh, in 1936, had founded the first Kampuchean language newspaper, *Nagaravatta* (Angkor Wat) to appeal to traditional sympathies by reviving memories of the glorious Khmer past. His anti-French stance was exploited during the war by the Japanese who had encouraged him to launch a revolt against Sihanouk and the French in 1942. When expected Japanese support failed to materialize and the French broke up the rebellion, Thanh had sought refuge in Japan.

On March 9, 1945 the Japanese, their defeats mounting in the broader war, embarked upon a desperate gamble. They suddenly interned the French garrisons throughout Indochina, dissolved the entire French colonial administration and encouraged the Vietnamese, the Laotians and the Kampucheans to declare their independence within the Greater East Asia Co-Prosperity Sphere of Japan. Independence, it was reasoned, would pose difficulties for now-liberated France and would stave off final Japanese defeat. Sihanouk declared Kampuchea's independence on March 12th, but resisted further actions under the Japanese "independence plan" because he wanted to maintain ties with France.

Unlike in Vietnam, where monarchy was a relatively weak political force, in Kampuchea the monarchy was strong. To counter Sihanouk's influence, the Japanese returned Thanh to Phnom Penh and arranged his appointment, first as foreign minister and then in August, on the eve of Japan's surrender, as Kampuchea's first premier.

Thanh's declaration of his intention to maintain independence from the French provoked serious street fighting between pro and anti monarchical nationalist groups in the capital. The returning French forces reoccupied Phnom Penh in September 1945, arrested Thanh for collaboration with the enemy and sent him into exile in France, even though his government had been "overwhelmingly" supported by the people in a plebiscite.[3] Sihanouk immediately denounced Thanh and affirmed Kampuchea's loyalty, but not necessarily suzerainty, to France.

Eight years of negotiations with the French over the issues of political autonomy and legal independence began. Admiral Thierry d'Argenlieu, the French High Commissioner to Indochina (the title replaced the prewar designation of governor-general) invited Sihanouk to Saigon to negotiate new formal relations with France. Sihanouk agreed provided Kampuchean negotiators were accepted as "delegates from an independent country" and that the negotiations would not "impinge upon the independence of our Fatherland."[4] The resulting *modus vivendi* of January 7, 1946 satisfied neither condition; it recognized Kampuchea as "an autonomous kingdom within the French Union" but essentially restored the prewar relationship. Sihanouk, however, was convinced by French expressions of readiness to negotiate further that progress would be forthcoming. To make the arrangement less unpalatable, France secured return of the provinces ceded to Thailand in 1941.

A French—Kampuchean commission drafted a constitution and a Constituent Assembly was elected in September 1946 to consider it. The Democratic Party, favoring the end of French rule and a ceremonial king, was opposed by the Liberal Party which favored prolongation of French control and a strong monarchy. The Democratic Party elected the majority of the delegates to the Constituent Assembly and was supported therein by a faction holding similar strong anti-French nationalist ideas, the Khmer Issarak (Khmer for Independence), consisting of followers of Thanh who had been granted amnesty. However, Thanh himself and some of his followers opposed the entire electoral process; they became known as the Khmer Serai or Free Khmer.

The Constituent Assembly's revised version of the draft constitution was promulgated by King Sihanouk on May 6, 1947, although he did not favor it because it drastically reduced his authority. The Democratic Party won a large majority of the seats to the new National Assembly which was convened a year later. The party's amalgam of political groups enabled the disciplined Khmer Issarak subsequently to achieve control of the party.

In a treaty of November 9, 1949 the French recognized Kampuchean sovereignty over most of its internal affairs and obtained international recognition for the country as one of the "associated states" of Indochina within the French Union. The United States and most noncommunist powers accorded Kampuchea diplomatic recognition in 1950.

The king's acceptance of "associated state" status provoked party leaders to repudiate Prime Minister Yem Sambaur, who retaliated by dissolving the assembly with the king's approval. The treaty was thus never approved by the assembly; it was agreed to by an exchange of letters between the two governments.

For the next two years Sihanouk ruled through a provisional government which he appointed and which was headed by Yem Sambaur. The king justified his authoritarian rule as necessary in the face of the attacks on the French presence in the western portion of the country by the Khmer Issarak and in the eastern by communist-dominated forces from southern Vietnam. In some instances the two movements collaborated.

Pressed by nationalists on the French issue, Sihanouk gambled. Advancing the notion that anti-government hostility was playing into the hands of the communists—both the indigenous Khmer Rouge (Red Khmer) and those infiltrating from Vietnam—and was thus prolonging the French military presence. Sihanouk appealed for unity and called for new elections in September 1951.

The Democrats again won heavily and the new government requested the French to offer Thanh amnesty again and to urge his return to Phnom Penh. The French agreed, to their later regret, since Thanh was widely acclaimed upon his return and immediately undertook a strong campaign to oust the French and to fight for complete independence. When the French moved to arrest him, Thanh escaped to the jungle to join the Khmer Serai. In June 1952 Sihanouk dismissed the cabinet, branded Thanh a traitor, assumed control of the state as prime minister and asked the assembly for a three year period of emergency powers during which he would try to gain full independence for the country. In January 1953 he suddenly dissolved the legislature and declared marital law.

SIHANOUK YEARS: 1953–1970

Sihanouk, who was expected to be a titular king in a fading monarchical era, displayed instead a political astuteness which propelled him into the front ranks of Asian statesmen in the post World War II period. He not only achieved full independence for Kampuchea, but also played external powers against each other with consummate skill for 17 years.

In March 1953 he made a dramatic move. Appointing his father regent and leaving national affairs in the hands of an advisory council, Sihanouk personally took his case for independence to the world. From Bangkok he announced he would not return to Kampuchea without French assurance of full independence. His move evoked the desired response. On July 3, 1953 the French declared their intention to grant full independence to all three of the Associated States of Indochina, and Sihanouk returned home. By a simple exchange of letters in February 1954 all political ties were severed and Kampuchean secession from the French Union was completed.

Sihanouk next turned his attention to achieving integration of dissident elements into a national political structure, a task which would be complicated by the Khmer Serai, the Khmer Rouge and the Vietcong (Vietnamese Communists). By April 1954 several Vietnamese communist battalions were operating on Kampuchean soil.

Balancing Act In May 1954 France invited Kampuchean participation in the Geneva Conference to negotiate a settlement among the states of Indochina. At the conference Kampuchea obtained agreement from the French and the Vietnamese communists to withdraw all forces from Kampuchea by October 1954, at the same time retaining the right to permit establishment on its soil of foreign military bases for defense against aggression. Sihanouk wanted to keep his options open since, at that time, he considered the United States the only effective power that could counterbalance the rising communist influence in Southeast Asia. Sihanouk's security position was further buttressed in September 1954 when a protocol to the 1954 SEATO (Southeast Asia Treaty Organization comprising the U.S., U.K., France, Australia, New Zealand, Philippines, Thailand and Pakistan) Treaty included Kampuchea, along with Laos and Vietnam, within the treaty's area of protection.

In December Kampuchea formally announced political neutrality as the basis of its foreign policy, anticipating the Bandung Conference of April 1955 when many of Asia's leaders adopted the same stance.

Sihanouk participated at Bandung where he publicly expressed fear of the aggressive intent of the Democratic Republic of Vietnam (DRV) and the People's Republic of China (PRC). Only after he was assured of their peaceful intentions by DRV Foreign Minister Pham Van Dong and PRC Premier Chou En-lai, would he associate himself with the Bandung declarations.

In May the same year he negotiated a security agreement with the United States wherein the latter pledged to provide military aid to help Kampuchea cope with internal subversion and external aggression, but which included a specific provision that U.S. aid would not be utilized in any way to compromise Kampuchea's neutralism. Reaffirming Kampuchean neutrality, he visited Peking in February 1956. In 1957 the Kampuchean National Assembly made political neutrality the law of the land.

Personalization of Politics   The 1954 Geneva Conference called for national elections in the Indochinese states. Sihanouk in February 1955 upstaged the elections by announcing a nationwide referendum to ascertain the people's judgment as to whether or not he had fulfilled his three-year "mandate" of achieving national independence and security. The campaign slogan was: "If you love the king, vote white; if you do not love the king, vote black." The king obtained 99.8 percent of the total ballots cast.

Sihanouk next proposed that major constitutional changes be submitted to a popular referendum. These changes were designed to eliminate the party system, allow Sihanouk to appoint a cabinet directly responsible to him and create a powerless assembly. Opposition to the plan developed and the long-building polarization between the king and his entourage on the one hand, and the Democratic party on the other, became increasingly apparent. Sihanouk once again chose a dramatic and personal solution. On March 2, 1955 he abdicated in favor of his father, Norodom Suramarit. "If I have abdicted," he said, "it is not to abandon the people but to save them and to obtain the triumph of the new reforms which I have worked out."[5] His objective was to reinforce his image as the ultimate symbol of nationalism and to come back stronger than ever. The ploy was eminently successful. The prince, as he was subsequently known, was now free to engage in partisan politics and he immediately employed his prestige in forming a new political organization, the People's Socialist Community, or Sangkum. The Sangkum reflected elements of populism and fascism, and emphasized patriotism, the Khmer nation, opposition to injustice, loyalty to the monarchy and Buddhism. In the national elections which were finally held on September 11, 1955 the Sangkum won 83 percent of the votes cast and all of the assembly seats. The

Democratic Party secured only 3 percent of the vote. In October a new government was formed and Sihanouk became prime minister.

Sihanouk's authority, exercised through the Sangkum as well as through the National Assembly, soon became complete. In 1957 he institutionalized the Sangkum as the principal government organization for expressing the voice of the people. However, one-party rule did not eliminate factionalism. Cabinets lasted a year or less—usually less during the periods when Sihanouk chose not to serve as prime minister. Nevertheless Kampuchea weathered the decade 1955–1966 with relative internal stability (the Sangkum easily won assembly elections in 1958, 1962 and 1966), despite Sihanouk's authoritarian proclivities and mounting tensions exacerbated by external sources.

Ideological Somersault   The byzantine international politics pursued by Norodom Sihanouk in the decade 1955–1965 and his ideological somersault from anti-communist to neutralist to communist collaborator can be explained within the context of five interrelated factors: 1) Sihanouk's conviction that close relationship with China would insure Kampuchea's national identity and enhance its external security, 2) his distrust of his traditionally expansionist neighbors, Thailand and Vietnam, 3) his growing perception that the principal threat to his personal regime lay with the pro-American Khmer Serai, operating for the most part from Bangkok and in coordination with the Saigon-based Republic of Vietnam (RVN), both clients of the United States, 4) his recognition of the failure of neutrality in Laos, and 5) his prescience that the war in Vietnam would be won by the communists.

Sihanouk's interest in a close relationship with China dates from his favorable impression of Chou En-lai at the 1955 Bandung Conference when the Chinese premier reportedly hinted at Chinese support if Sihanouk were to diassociate Kampuchea from SEATO protection or involvement. Sihanouk promptly did so on his first visit to Peking in February 1956. In 1958 Kampuchea established full diplomatic relations with China and in 1960 Sihanouk visited Peking to sign a treaty of friendship and non-aggression. Close relations with China became, in Sihanouk's mind, his best hope for shielding his nation from: 1) pressures by Vietnam and Thailand, 2) internal communism, 3) the United States which was urging him to adhere to its anti-communist coalition, and 4) China itself.

The new relations with China perhaps emboldened Sihanouk in 1956 to revive Kampuchea's claim to the Angkor empire's provinces in south Vietnam. As a consequence the RVN curtailed all trade with Kampuchea and denied it access to the port of Saigon—its major link, along with Bangkok, to foreign trade. Thailand announced closure of its border with Kampuchea and the RVN followed suit. Sihanouk viewed their behavior as a conspiracy, instigated by the U.S., to overthrow him, and claimed they were supporting the Khmer Serai whom he described as misguided agents of the West. His distrust increased in June 1958 when RVN troops pursued Vietcong forces across the Kampuchean border.

Vietnamese communist troops had been in Kampuchea since 1945 when they had collaborated on occasion with the Khmer Issarak against the French. In 1946 Vietminh agents had infiltrated the country and had been able by 1950 to establish a headquarters in the south; at the same time the Kampuchean communists announced the formation of a "free, provisional government of Cambodia," and a "Khmer People's Liberation Army" to conduct joint guerrilla warfare against the royal government. The Vietnamese sought to utilize Kampuchean territory to safeguard supply and communication lines to the battle- fields of southern Vietnam. Their longer range objective was to install in Kampuchea a Khmer Rouge (communist) government which they hoped to dominate through a protectorate similar to the former French arrangement.

In 1954, as the war in Vietnam widened, DRV regular troops invaded the northeast province of Stung Treng, a move which had impelled Sihanouk to seek direct military aid from the United States. However most of the DRV regular forces were withdrawn in conformity with the mandate of the Geneva Conference. Thus by 1955, and for some years thereafter, the Liberation Army amounted to little more than armed bands of dissidents in the hilly northeastern provinces who were supported by the communist-dominated National Liberation Front (NLF) of South Vietnam and were used as a communication link when the Vietcong made forays into Kampuchea. Khmer Serai and Khmer Rouge guerrillas operated from the jungle and the NLF tried con- stantly, and with some success, to persuade the two groups to join ranks. Sihanouk's ire, however, continued to be directed primarily at the Khmer Serai, some of whom had crossed over into South Vietnam and were being trained by the United States. He consciously down- played the significance of the Khmer Rouge.

During the early 1960s, while he was still receiving American assis- tance to preserve his political neutralism, Sihanouk watched with dismay the comparative failure of the 1962 Geneva Conference on the neutrality of Laos. He recognized that the conference's prescription regarding the nature of a neutralist Lao government produced only a temporary solution. He therefore intensified his efforts in 1964 and 1965 to obtain an internationally recognized legal neutrality for Kam- puchea, but without success. It was this point that he hedged his bets by moving leftward, making common cause with the communist pow- ers in Southeast Asia. Not too surprisingly, as Sihanouk's relations with the DRV improved, those with the U.S. and the RVN worsened.

Relations with the United States deteriorated as American arms deliveries to Thailand, Laos, and the RVN steadily increased. Even a 1961–62 American decision to provide increased military aid to Kampuchea failed to placate him and in 1963 he ordered termination of all American aid—which since 1955 totaled US$405.7 million. He publicly charged that the United States actively supported Khmer Serai operations against his government from across Thai and South Vietnamese borders, and accused the U.S. Central Intelligence Agency and the RVN of financing Khmer Serai radio broadcasts which attacked him personally. Anti-American sentiment quickly rose to match Sihanouk's rhetoric and in March 1964 the U.S. embassy in Phnom Penh was sacked by mobs. In early 1965 indications of infringement of Kampuchean airspace by American and RVN aircraft in pursuit of the Vietcong led Sihanouk to break diplomatic relations with the United States.

Lon Nol As Premier In 1966, at the very nadir of Kampuchean-U.S. relations, the domestic political solidarity which Sihanouk enjoyed began to fragment. In that year the prince, smarting under charges of one-man rule, for the first time allowed Sangkum candidates to oppose one another in National Assembly elections. Over 400, ranging from one extreme of the political spectrum to the other, competed for 82 seats. The voters elected a right-wing majority which in turn chose General Lon Nol as premier—another first-time process permitted by Sihanouk. Although Sihanouk remained as chief of state (the title he had assumed on the death of his father, the king, in 1960), the election returns clearly revealed a significant reaction against the prince's rhetoric, poor governmental performance and statist economics. More importantly, they showed an adverse reaction to Sihanouk's love-affair with the Vietnamese communists. Sihanouk responded to the election results by attempting, through the medium of the Sangkum, to construct a shadow government of his personal followers and certain leftist leaders as a counterweight to the rightist government.

The Lon Nol government's program—denationalization of the economy, encouragement of foreign investment and overtures to the West—embittered the leftist deputies in the National Assembly who tried to undermine him. Their tactics encouraged the Khmer Rouge, which was augmented by the Vietcong, to commence an armed uprising in Battambang and Kompong Cham provinces in April 1967. Although the revolt was quickly suppressed it appeared to frighten Sihanouk. He was unable to control his shadow government—some of his leftist friends having become extremists as evidenced by the revolt they allegedly led. Nor was he able to halt the Lon Nol government's decided shift to the right. Sihanouk, therefore, changed tactics and made amends with Lon Nol. He blamed three young leftist leaders in the National Assembly—Khieu Samphan, Hu Nim and Hou Yuon—

for instigating the rebellion, announcing they would have to face a military tribunal at which General Lon Nol would "confront" them. The three fled to eastern insurgent-controlled areas. By mid-1968 new Khmer Rouge attacks had extended the insurgency to other provinces, forcing Sihanouk to acknowledge finally that its success was linked to Vietcong military assistance.

Search for Security   With Kampuchean territorial integrity in jeopardy from the Khmer Rouge and the Vietcong. Sihanouk became amenable to American overtures to repair relationships. Jacqueline Kennedy's visit to Phnom Penh in November 1967 had been followed by a trip to Kampuchea in January by American ambassador to India, Chester Bowles. Bowles assured the government that the United States, in cases of "hot pursuit" of Vietnamese forces, would do everything possible to avoid acts of aggression against the Kampuchean state.

Although Sihanouk welcomed President Johnson's March 31, 1968 announcement of a complete bombing halt of the DRV, he said later the same year: "If the U.S. were to leave Asia completely, it would be the end of my [sic] independence."[6] When President Nixon began unacknowledged American aerial bombardment of DRV bases in Kampuchea in the spring of 1969 Sihanouk did not object. Moreover, Nixon's assurance of Kampuchea's "sovereignty, neutrality and territorial integrity" in April impelled the Lon Nol government to restore diplomatic relations with the U.S. in June, and Kampuchea rejoined such western supported institutions as the International Monetary Fund, the Asian Development Bank and the International Bank for Reconstruction and Development. These measures, however, alarmed Sihanouk, who was driven by an overwhelming compulsion to avoid any semblance of compromising the political neutrality which he espoused so fervently. He feared that such moves, coupled with Lon Nol's anti-socialist economic program and his effort to force the withdrawal of the Vietcong from Kampuchea, might stimulate to drastic counter-measures both the DRV and the PRC—the latter in the most radical period of its Cultural Revolution.

Thus Sihanouk decided to appeal directly to the Chinese and to the Soviets to call off their Vietnamese allies. In August 1969 he requested Lon Nol, at that point not occupying the premiership but nevertheless the leading politician, to form a "Salvation Government"; he also reportedly asked Lon Nol not to make any military decisions before he visited the PRC and the USSR to present his case.[7] Sihanouk departed for Paris, Moscow and Peking in January 1970.

In his absence Lon Nol and Deputy Premier Sirik Matek apparently decided that the military action they perceived as necessary to dislodge the Vietcong from Kampuchean territory and to crush the Khmer

Rouge, could not be mounted unless Sihanouk himself was removed. Their first move was to allow the steadily rising sentiment in Kampuchea against the Vietnamese to go unrestrained. On March 11 thousands of demonstrators sacked the DRV and the communist Provisional Revolutionary Government of South Vietnam embassies and indiscriminately attacked residences and businesses of Vietnamese living in the capital. On March 18–19, meeting in joint session, the National Assembly and the Council of the Kingdom granted Lon Nol full emergency powers and deposed Sihanouk as head of state and forbade his return. Lon Nol thereupon requested the U.N. Security Council to verify the presence of Vietnamese communist troops on Kampuchean soil and announced the government's intention to seek arms from any country which would help it defend its political neutrality and territorial integrity.

On October 9, 1970 Kampuchea was proclaimed "a united and indivisible Khmer Republic"; the 1,168 year old monarchy came to an end. Chen Hang was designated chief of state pending election of a president. Rather than branding either rightist or leftist dissidents as traitors the government appealed for domestic unity. Political prisoners were released and in May the Khmer Serai leader Thanh announced his support of the new government and became a senior advisor to Lon Nol.

Sihanouk's National Front   Prince Sihanouk learned of his deposition in Moscow and flew on to Peking where on March 20 he announced that the 1947 constitution precluded the National Assembly from replacing the chief of state. By implication he had been granted life tenure. At first he proposed a national referendum to settle the issue, but on March 23 declared instead that he would dissolve the Lon Nol government, organize a national army of liberation and form the National United Front of Kampuchea (Front Uni National de Kampuchea or FUNK). On May 5 the formation of FUNK and a statement of its political program were announced in Peking. The declaration listed Prince Sihanouk as head of state and chairman of the Front which would be comprised of all Khmer—including the Khmer Rouge—within and outside the country. Its political program included opposition to "United States imperialist schemes and aggression,"[8] development of a profiteering-free nationalized economy, emphasis on the traditions of Angkor civilization and pursuit of a politically neutral foreign policy.

At the same time Sihanouk announced the formation of the Royal Government of the National Union of Kampuchea (Gouvernement Royal d'Union Nationale de Kampuchea or GRUNK). Penn Nouth (an old friend) was named prime minister and Khieu Samphan (a former enemy) was designated deputy prime minister and minister of defense.

All thirteen members of FUNK's Political Bureau also held positions in the GRUNK Cabinet. The FUNK-GRUNK strategy was to operate both from Peking, where Sihanouk and the cabinet ministers were "temporarily" located, and from inside Kampuchea through the Khmer Rouge. The in-country operations were placed under the control of Khieu Samphan, Hu Nim and Hou Yuon, the leftist deputies of the National Assembly who had defected to the Khmer Rouge in 1967.

The National Front immediately attracted adherents within Kampuchea, ranging from simply pro-Kampuchean through pro-Sihanouk to communist elements. These diverse groups were difficult to unite, thus enabling the Khmer Rouge, who were already united and more disciplined, to dominate the Front. Bitter memories of Sihanok's earlier persecution of the leftist deputies were incentives for them to reverse the tables.

Khieu Samphan also became commander in chief of FUNK's military arm, the Kampuchean People's National Liberation Armed Forces. In an extremely important development, infusion of DRV and Vietcong forces into the Liberation Army dramatically increased. The organization's strength grew from 3,000 Khmer Rouge guerrillas in 1970 when Sihanouk was deposed, to a force of about 85,000 by mid-1971, some 70 percent comprising DRV and Vietcong soldiers; the remainder were Khmer Rouge guerrillas, Sihanouk's personal followers, opportunists, bandits and peasants forced into military service. By mid-1972, while the indigenous forces were still mainly in the western provinces, DRV-Vietcong elements were occupying roughly the eastern half of the country. Sihanouk's Liberation Army was on the road to victory, but Sihanouk in Peking had lost control.

The PRC and the Provisional Revolutionary Government of South Vietnam headed a list of 25 countries which by mid-1972 had extended diplomatic recognition to GRUNK. The Soviet Union stalled about recognizing Sihanouk's government-in-exile, a cause of growing dissatisfaction to Sihanouk but a reflection of the fundamental Sino-Soviet quarrel which, after 1975, completely dominated and determined the course of Kampuchean politics.

KHMER REPUBLIC

Tensions and cross political objectives quickly became evident in the new Khmer Republic. In 1969 the Americans had begun aerial bombardment of DRV bases in Kampuchea which were used as springboards for attacks against the RVN. The bombing was followed in April 1970 by a large ground "incursion" of U.S. and RVN forces into the southeast to destroy communist border sanctuaries. The action, undertaken with the acquiescence of Lon Nol, plus Nol's request to the United States for resumption of military assistance, assured extension of the war in Vietnam to Kampuchea.[9]

Military Problems When Sihanouk was deposed in March 1970 Kampuchean government forces comprised about 35,000 men. As the war in Vietnam increasingly involved Kampuchea, government recruitment efforts and the response to its appeals for foreign assistance, especially from the RVN, raised military strength by 1972 to 200,000 plus some 145,000 paramilitary personnel.

Initially high morale; air support from Thailand, the RVN and the U.S.; and volunteer battalions from the RVN, produced military successes. However, in the succeeding years the nation suffered heavy destruction. Angkor and its priceless monuments were ravaged in 1971 and the city fell to the leftists who ignored appeals for its internationalization and neutralization. During the period 1970–1973 the U.S. Strategic Air Command reportedly carried out 2,875 raids over Kampuchea, dropping 240,000 tons of bombs, over 50 percent more than were dropped over Japan during World War II.[10] But lack of training in counter-guerrilla tactics, and traditional Khmer-Vietnamese animosity, impeded the government's efforts. Defeats began to outnumber victories and DRV troops and the Khmer Rouge guerrillas continued their advance. After withdrawal of the last American toops from Vietnam in 1973, the cessation, ordered by the U.S. Congress, of American air bombing after August 1973, the Khmer Republic's capacity to resist steadily declined. RVN help shrank because South Vietnam had been weakened by its war for survival. Thailand, seeing the writing on the wall, became less enthusiastic about support and began to mend its international political fences in expectation of communist victories throughout Indochina. By 1974 the DRV-Vietcong-Khmer Rouge forces controlled 80 percent of the country and 5,500,000 of its 7,400,000 people.[11] Sapper attacks against Phnom Penh, the capital, were common after 1972.

The Khmer Republic had little chance of survival. The fact that it was a pawn among powerful external political forces—the PRC, USSR, United States and the DRV—practically assured its demise and internal factors guaranteed it. War casualties, loss of territory, tides of refugees, inflation, and physical destruction caused by aerial bombardment and ground combat destroyed what remained of the Khmer Republic's economy. Industrial output fell by 50 percent after 1970. In the agricultural sector, production of rubber, one of two main export crops, was practically abandoned as the war progressed. Exports of rice, the other main agricultural product, ceased entirely.

Initial enthusiastic support for the Lon Nol government began to diminish in 1971. Cabinet crises became common. On October 18, 1971 Lon Nol, by decree, took the lawmaking power from the National

Assembly. In March 1972 he proclaimed himself the republic's first president, as well as its prime minister, and dissolved the commission which had been authorized by the National Assembly to draft a new constitution. A Lon Nol-appointed successor body produced a new draft which was approved overwhelmingly in a national referendum in April and went into effect in May. The 1972 constitution provided for a strong president, elected for a five year term, with authority to appoint a prime minister and cabinet solely responsible to him. The bicameral parliament, comprised of the National Assembly and the Senate, was accorded legislative powers. Lon Nol won reelection as president with 55 percent of the votes cast in the election of June 4, 1972. He thus won popular endorsement of his regime for the first time, but only 30 percent of those eligible voted.

The new president's troubles multiplied in 1973. During that year several attempts were made on his life when defecting Kampuchean air force pilots bombed the presidential palace while flying en route to "liberated" regions of the country. He closed newspapers and magazines, forbade public meetings and arrested numerous members of the royal family. The communist advance on, and encirclement of, Phnom Penh repeatedly cut the city's supply routes. A new state of emergency was proclaimed in March and the National Assembly was suspended after conferring complete authority to run the country on the president and a four-man High Political Council. Rice and petroleum shortages grew worse.

Fall of the Khmer Republic   In July, seeing no alternative, Lon Nol adopted a course of action envisioned as early as 1971, namely an offer to negotiate for peace with the "Cambodians on the other side," but specifying that Sihanouk would not be an acceptable negotiator. When the offer was rejected, Lon Nol modified it in December, stating he was ready to meet Sihanouk at a conference table with no preconditions except the departure from Kampuchea of DRV troops. But the offer went unheeded because time was on Sihanouk's side. In April 1974, when American military and economic support amounting to US$1.5 million daily was the sole factor preventing collapse of the government, Sihanouk said he would never negotiate with Lon Nol.

Student riots in June, resulting in the murder of the education minister, climaxed weeks of demonstrations by teachers, students, workers and government employees. On July 9 Lon Nol made an unconditional offer to begin "dialogue," a move supported by the British and American governments. Sihanouk denounced the proposal "as a piece of hypocritical and cynical propaganda inspired by Mr. Lon Nol's American backers."[12] During the remainder of 1974 the offer of unconditional peace talks was renewed and rejected several more times as the victorious DRV-Vietcong-Khmer Rouge armies tightened the noose around Phnom Penh.

In January 1975 communists blockaded the Mekong River, preventing food and ammunition from reaching the capital by convoy from the RVN. Thus with all water and land supply routes cut, Phnom Penh depended exclusively on C-130 transport aircraft—mostly from Thailand—for vital supplies during the last months before its fall. In late March the Soviet Union acknowledged GRUNK as the sole legal government of Kampuchea, ending USSR diplomatic recognition of Lon Nol which had irritated Sihanouk and the Khmer Rouge.

The actual collapse of the Khmer Republic began April 1 when Lon Nol flew to political exile in Indonesia and from there to the United States. His departure, he said, was intended to open a way for settlement of the country's conflict through peaceful negotiations between the government and the opposition. General Sankham Khoy was president until April 5 when he was evacuated to Bangkok by U.S. helicopter. On April 17 government forces in the capital surrendered to the Khmer Rouge who responded: "We enter Phnom Penh as conquerors and we have not come here to speak about peace with the traitors of the Phnom Penh clique."[13]

During the period 1970–1975 the U.S. provided the Khmer Republic with US$1.18 billion in military materiel and training and US$503 million in general economic assistance.

DEMOCRATIC KAMPUCHEA: 1975–1978

Seldom in the course of nation-state history has so dismal a record been compiled as in Kampuchea beginning in 1975. The events were a direct reflection of: 1) the Sino-Soviet quarrel and the competition between the two powers for influence in Southeast Asia, 2) the centuries-old conflict between Thailand and Vietnam over control of Kampuchea, and 3) the effect of extremist political ideology on human beings and social institutions. Some of the consequences included utter disregard of human rights, genocide, physical and moral disintegration and the intensification of the Sino-Soviet rivalry.

Between April and August 1975 no central governmental structure appeared, although a GRUNK National Congress confirmed Sihanouk and Penn Nouth, both in Peking, as head of state and prime minister respectively. Instead Deputy Prime Minister Khieu Samphan, who derived his power from his position as commander-in-chief of the Khmer Rouge forces, acted apparently for the dreaded secret directorate, the Angha Loeu (Higher Organization). The conquerors immediately set out to mobilize the masses, after first beheading the leaders of the government who had remained behind. Within days they ordered evacuation of all cities and towns, sending the entire population to the countryside to till the land; resisters and questioners were executed immediately. The wholesale disequilibrium that resulted ensured that privation, disease and death quickly became widespread.

In the beginning the rulers turned inward politically, espousing a nonaligned foreign policy which repudiated DRV, Soviet and even Chinese influence in the country's affairs. Any rapproachement with the United States was impossible after the Khmer Rouge forces on May 12 seized the U.S. merchant ship *Mayaguez* and its crew of 39 about eight miles off Koh Tang Island in the Gulf of Siam. The ship was retaken by U.S. marines with an American loss of life of 41. The Kampuchean government called the American recapture of the vessel a "savage, ferocious, insane and flagrant act of aggression."[14]

Government Prince Sihanouk returned to Phnom Penh September 9, 1975 to head Kampuchea's first communist government and embarked the same month on an international tour as an ambassador of goodwill. He returned at the end of December and "ratified" a constitution, drafted and adopted in his absence. Pointedly the new document, which went into effect January 3, 1976, did not include the position of "head of state" which Sihanouk had enjoyed for 15 years, even during his time of exile.

The constitution of Democratic Kampuchea specified that the means of production belonged to the state and the people. A People's Assembly of 250 deputies (200 peasants, 50 workers), to be elected for five-year terms, was empowered to draft legislation. Pending election of the People's Assembly FUNK, which had convened after the capture of Phnom Penh, was transformed into the Legislative Assembly. This body designated Sihanouk to be chairman of the State Presidium for five years. Khieu Samphan and Ieng Sary were named vice presidents and Premier Penn Nouth was selected to head the cabinet.

Deputies to the new People's Assembly were chosen in general elections March 20. Inexplicably, the election results, which were signed by Deputy Premier Khieu Samphan, did not include among the names of the elected deputies Sihanouk, Penn Nouth or Ieng Sary, although all three had "garnered 100 percent victory."[15] Suddenly, on April 5, Radio Phnom Penh announced Sihanouk's "resignation" and his replacement by Khieu Samphan as Chairman of the State Presidium. On April 7 the entire cabinet resigned to enable the newly-elected People's Assembly to choose a new premier, a new cabinet and a special committee of 50 members "who will be the real leaders of the country."[16] The little known Pol Pot soon emerged as prime minister. Quite clearly Khieu Samphan, the French-educated economist who was an avowed admirer of Mao Tse-tung, was in a position to carry out his radical economic ideas. King-Prince Norodom Sihanouk, now a private citizen, was granted a quarterly allowance of US$2,000 and was assured that a statue depicting him as an anti-imperalist fighter would be erected.

Genocide Joseph Stalin reportedly once said, "one death is a tragedy; a million deaths are a statistic." Stalin's aphorism almost proved true as one of the most grisly sagas of modern history unfolded in Kampuchea in 1975–76 with surprisingly mild initial world reaction. In April 1976 *Data Asia* noted that "the forced expulsion from Phnom Penh in April 1975 had reportedly caused the deaths of 600,000—an estimated 20 percent of the capital's former population."[17] John Barron and Anthony Paul, authors of *Murder of a Gentle Land,* concluded that "at the very minimum, more than 1,200,000 men, women and children died in Cambodia between April 17, 1975 and January 1, 1977, as a consequence of actions of Angha Loeu (the revolutionary Higher Organization)," from disease, starvation, massacres, execution and during escape attempts.[18] In April 1980 the United States government stated that "of some 7 million Khmer in 1975 when Pol Pot came to power, up to 2 million had died from war, brutality and hunger."[19] (The population in 1984 was estimated by the Population Reference Bureau at 6.1 million).

Triad: Khieu Samphan, Pol Pot, Ieng Sary Government and politics in Kampuchea were dominated from mid-1975 to the end of 1978 by two men of similar backgrounds, Khieu Samphan and Pol Pot, assisted by their henchman Ieng Sary.

Khieu Samphan, born in 1931 to a judge and a half Chinese mother, went to Paris on a government scholarship in 1954 where he became a communist. He received a doctorate in economics in 1959, thence returning to Kampuchea to found a newspaper devoted to the communist movement. In the early 1960s Sihanouk literally rescued the shy Samphan from a life of harassment at the hands of the royalist police, permitting him to be a candidate for the National Assembly and a member of the prince's political front. Sihanouk's act assured Samphan of election and the prince designated him minister of commerce. However after the 1967 rebellion in Battambang and Kompong Cham provinces, Sihanouk identified Samphan as a ringleader and he defected to the Khmer Rouge, then in the jungle. In 1970 Sihanouk, himself in exile after his deposition, reembraced Samphan and the heretofore introverted ideologue emerged as deputy prime minister and minister of defense in GRUNK. As noted, Samphan later replaced Sihanouk as chief of state (Chairman of the State Presidium) in the Khmer government.

Pol Pot, apparently an alias for Saloth Sar, was born in 1924 or 1928, and also studied in France where he too became a Marxist. He returned to Kampuchea in 1953 to become a journalist and high school teacher, and secretary general of the tiny Communist Party of Kampuchea (Parti Communiste du Kampuchea—PCK) which was secretly formed in 1960 in an effort to counter Vietnamese-communist domination of the loose groups known collectively as the Khmer Rouge. Pol Pot was unknown to the outside world until he became premier in 1976, and the existence of the PCK was not officially acknowledged until 1977 when it was divulged that the Angha Loeu and the PCK were one and the same.

Ieng Sary, the shrewd and resolute diplomat of the ruling triad, had also been a teacher. He and his beautiful wife, Ieng Thirith, specialized in cultivating foreign diplomats, especially Chinese and Soviet, and devoted many years to recruiting students and intellectuals to the communist movement. Ieng Sary became deputy prime minister and foreign minister in April 1976.

Policies The new regime pursued two overriding objectives: to cement relationships with the PRC and, conversely, to curtail Vietnamese influence; and to transform the state into an agrarian society with small industry scattered in the countryside.

Kampuchea's pro-Chinese posture evoked immediate response from Mao Tse-tung, Chairman of the Communist Party in China, who promised shortly before his death that the PRC would fight "shoulder to shoulder" to support Kampuchea's "revolutionary cause."[20] China became the new regime's main window to the outside world; even travel into or out of the country was via Peking. Nevertheless Sary managed during the regime's first year to initiate diplomatic relations with all of the ASEAN states save Indonesia, a fact which was to stand the government in good stead subsequently.

In the field of economic planning the government sought to achieve agricultural self sufficiency through water projects—similar to the irrigation systems of the ancient Khmer empire—which would permit three rice harvests per year. Therefore the entire population was mobilized to dig irrigation canals or to cultivate rice. Every other aspect of social and economic life was subordinated to these activities. The money economy was completely extinguished. Cities and towns were virtually abandoned. Markets, telephones, telegraph facilities, shops, private land and paid labor disappeared. In a setting reminiscent of William Golding's *Lord of the Flies* armed teenagers supervised the dawn to dusk work of the people. The extreme measures prompted the *Japan Times* to charge that "Cambodia is creating the most radically communist society in the world" and that "the human cost of this transformation is staggering."[21]

In September 1976 Pol Pot suddenly resigned "temporarily" for "health reasons" amid rumors that the real reason was his criticism of development programs as being inadequate. Nuon Chea replaced him for several months as prime minister. A coup attempt against the government was discovered in the planning stage in February and the mass execution of government officials and military units allegedly involved followed, wrath being directed this time at early Khmer Rouge leaders thought to have become untrustworthy.

Pol Pot now reemerged as prime minister, stronger than ever. His absence from the political scene from late 1976 to mid-1977 was apparently related to a behind the scenes struggle for control of the PCK. The struggle allegedly pitted Pol Pot's pro-Chinese leadership against the old Khmer Rouge—comprising the PCK bureaucracy in the countryside—that was planning a new revolution to organize a government along Soviet lines. Henceforth the pro-Chinese elements would be the "genuine" communist party.

Reaction against the Khieu Samphan-Pol Pot-Ieng Sary triumvirate was inevitable. It came from at least three sources: 1) ardent Khmer nationalists opposed to communism, such as the old Khmer Serai and the right wing Khmer National Liberation Movement, 2) Khmer Rouge defectors who wished to retain the basic objectives of the revolutionary movement but rejected its extreme policies, and 3) the Vietnamese, Kampuchea's ancient rivals, who refused to accept Chinese ascendency over the country.

Coup attempts against the government emanating from one or another of these sources had begun in 1975 and became more frequent in the next several years. Moreover, by 1977 the regime found itself involved in border wars with both Thailand and Vietnam, precipitated mainly by the enormous refugee exodus from Kampuchea into those countries. Some 400 border incidents with Thailand—to which 35,000 Kampucheans had fled after April 1976—occurred in 1977 alone. The quarrel with Vietnam, where 330,000 Kampucheans and ethnic Vietnamese living in Kampuchea had sought refuge after 1975, became the more serious problem. Vietnam, searching for support within Kampuchea against the regime, found it in 1977 when for the first time young field-grade Khmer Rouge officers led an unsuccessful revolt to protest the regime's harsh methods. Their defeat and frustration made other officers and some provincial chiefs easy targets for Vietnamese blandishments. A major uprising in three eastern provinces near the Vietnam border took place in May 1978. It was led by Heng Samrin, the Khmer Rouge's chief military-political leader in Kompong Cham province. When it failed, Samrin escaped to Vietnam. The stage was thus set for the December 1978 invasion.

The Vietnamese decision to move against the government of Kampuchea stemmed basically from: 1) the history of Vietnamese-Kampuchean relations, 2) Vietnam's perception of the threat from China, and 3) Vietnam's role in the Sino-Soviet contest for influence in Southeast

Asia, reflected a month previously by the 25-year treaty of friendship and cooperation with the Soviet Union. The treaty, which contained a defense clause, in effect bound Vietnam in a partnership with the USSR. At the same time the treaty was Vietnam's response to China's proposal in October of a PRC-Khmer Rouge military alliance against Vietnamese aggression.

On Christmas Day 1978 Vietnam launched a several pronged attack against the cities of Kratie and Kompong Cham, the Mekong provinces northeast of Phnom Penh, and Takeo south of the capital. In each case they trapped the Pol Pot armies, smashed them with heavy artillery and air bombardment, destroyed command headquarters, and fanned out in "blooming lotus" fashion. The five Vietnamese divisions converged on the capital, pushing before them the forces of the Khmer Rouge defector Heng Samrim. Phnom Penh was surrounded and captured on January 7. When it fell the Vietnamese gave full credit to the "army" of the Kampuchean National United Front for National Salvation whose Central Committee was headed by Samrin. The Central Committee made public in Phnom Penh an eight-point policy statement for the "Liberated areas." On January 11 the Kampuchean People's Revolutionary Council proclaimed the founding of the People's Republic of Kampuchea. Pol Pot escaped to the jungle, Ieng Sary to Thailand and Prince Sihanouk, who had been under virtual house arrest in Phnom Penh since 1976, was permitted to fly to Peking several days before the fall of the city. From Peking he denounced the Heng Samrin regime and threw in his lot with the previous government. In February 1979 Vietnam and the People's Republic of Kampuchea signed a 25-year treaty of friendship and cooperation which permitted unlimited garrisoning of Vietnamese troops in Kampuchea.

PEOPLE'S REPUBLIC OF KAMPUCHEA

Problems immediately beset the new regime. The People's Revolutionary Council, formed shortly before the capture of Phnom Penh, appeared unable to form a government. Sihanouk claimed from Peking that the Council had even offered to place him at the head of the new republic. The Vietnamese, who until then had repeatedly denied both their involvement and presence, obliged the new regime by taking over most of the administrative duties in the capital. This act confused the people, fanned inherent Kampuchean distrust of Vietnam, and encouraged resistance from the approximately 30,000 scattered Pol Pot forces in the jungle who had become guerrilla fighters. China's enmity increased and the ASEAN states expressed explicit disapproval. World opprobrium over the events was widespread.

In an endeavor to build national support, the Revolutionary Council announced an extensive program to undo the restrictions and radical measures of the Pol Pot regime. A money economy was reintroduced along with an eight-hour paid work day. Elections were promised for an assembly which would write a constitution to create "genuine socialism." Meanwhile "self management" committees were elected to insure order and security, and to restore agricultural productivity by means of production teams.

Vietnamese domination of Kampuchea meanwhile continued, eclipsing the fledgling government's presence and making a mockery of its plans. The Vietnamese plundered the country taking, according to one correspondent, "rice, tires, machinery from factories, cloth, furniture, spare parts for vehicles, anything of value."[22] By 1980 some 100,000 Vietnamese troops were stationed in the south. Their primary mission was to rout the remaining Khmer Rouge guerrillas who had been able, with Thai and Chinese help, to establish a "government" in the Cardamon mountains. From this mountain hideaway Khieu Samphan had announced in December 1979, formation and leadership of the Patriotic and Democratic Front of the Great National Union of Kampuchea. Within the new front Pol Pot remained commander of the military forces and chairman of the PCK.

A second reason for the continued Vietnamese military presence in Kampuchea was anticipation of Chinese retaliation for the humiliating defeat of its client-government; Hanoi feared an invasion of Kampuchea as a follow-on to the Chinese invasion of Vietnam in February–March 1979. Giving credence to this concern, Samphan flew to Peking in March 1980 where his "government" received fresh endorsements and promises of material support.

A third reason for the large Vietnamese troop presence concerned Thailand. Hundreds of thousands of Kampucheans—ranging from simple peasants, to Son Sann's anti-communist National Liberation Front which claimed 30,000 followers among the refugees in border camps, to soldiers of the solidly communist Khmer Rouge—had fled toward or into Thailand in 1979, pursued by major Vietnamese forces. One result was engagement of Thai and Vietnamese military units in cross-border fighting, each blaming the other for border intrusions.

On the other hand, the Thai as well as the Chinese were known to be supplying the Khmer Rouge guerrillas, and the United States was backing the Thai under provisions of the 1954 defense agreement that had created SEATO. When a 2,000-man Vietnamese unit briefly invaded Thailand on June 23, 1980, the United States strongly condemned the action and speeded up delivery of, and promised further, military aid. The ASEAN states joined in condemnation of the Vietnamese intrusion on their fellow member's territory. Of greater consequence to Thailand, more than 75,000 additional Kampucheans fled across the border, intensifying relief and resettlement problems and further destablizing the frontier.

Politics of Starvation Disruption of planting in May and June 1979, as a result of the military actions in the country and the uprooting of further thousands of people, combined with unfavorable climatic conditions to produce famine. The Vietnamese exploited the condition. The remark that "Lon Nol bombed us, Pol Pot killed us and the Vietnamese are starving us," summarized the Kampuchean nation's plight. Quite literally the Vietnamese had begun to use "food denial" as a "principal weapon" against the retreating Khmer Rouge and as a means of compelling cooperation among the general population.[23]

As the famine reached crisis proportions another wave of refugees began crossing into Thailand and thousands starved to death before an international relief effort could get underway. In October the International Red Cross and the UN Children's Fund (UNICEF) began a coordinated relief program in the Thai-Kampuchean border area; the World Food Program, OXFAM of the United Kingdom, the World Council of Churches and the Christian Conference of Asia subsequently participated. Approximately 600,000–1,000,000 persons were given food and medical assistance by July 1980, including 400,000–800,00 people within Kampuchea. The latter received aid through the "oxcart and bicycle brigade," i.e., Kampucheans who traveled each week to border distribution points and then redistributed the food and medicine in the interior. Such devices were necessary because Heng Samrin and Vietnamese authorities, convinced that relief would be used to keep Khmer Rouge resistance alive, insisted on controlling distribution with Kampuchea. Subsequently restrictions were lifted and throughout the 1980s the UN Border Operation coordinated food distribution to refugees in makeshift camps whose shifting populations averaged some 250,000 souls.

International Political Response The international relief program of 1979–80 (food and medical assistance; provision of first asylum for refugees provided by Malaysia, Thailand, Indonesia, the Philippines and Hongkong; and permanent resettlement provided mainly by the United States, France, Canada, Australia and Germany) was a catalyst which stimulated further international response to the Kampuchean tragedy. UN Secretary General Kurt Waldheim had convened an international conference in Geneva in July 1979 to draw world attention to the plight of the refugees and of the beleaguered countries of first asylum. A second international conference on Kampuchean relief, convened in May 1980, was initiated by the ASEAN states and the member states of the UN Economic and Social Council.

The flood of refugees forced upon the ASEAN states—which had their own problems of feeding, uplifting and integrating large rural populations—coupled with the blatant use of force by Vietnam to achieve suzerainty over Kampuchea, provoked ASEAN to take the lead in rejecting the Vietnamese-installed Heng Samrin regime on the grounds that it was not the free choice of the Kampuchean people. Since 1979 ASEAN has consistently prevailed in the UN General Assembly in preventing the Heng Samrin government (supported strongly by the Soviet bloc) from assuming Kampuchea's seat in that body.

Early in 1980 ASEAN joined the European community in proposing withdrawal of all foreign troops from Kampuchea, a proposal immediately rejected by Phnom Penh. An ASEAN formula for a UN-supervised demilitarized zone also came to nought. In October the ASEAN states secured General Assembly approval of an international conference which would negotiate the withdrawal of foreign troops from Kampuchea within a specified time frame, to be verified by the UN and to be followed by UN-supervised elections. Both Heng Samrin and the Vietnamese turned down the conference initiative as interference in Kampuchea's internal affairs. In January 1981 the foreign ministers of the three communist states of Indochina proposed instead a withdrawal of some Vietnamese troops and a regional summit conference with the ASEAN states to resolve their differences. This was rejected in March by ASEAN which continued to insist on a full international meeting. Philippine Foreign Minister Carlos P. Romulo, speaking for the group, added that ASEAN would refuse to recognize the validity of any election in Kampuchea while Vietnamese troops remained.

The non-communist Southeast Asian nations, including most actively Burma, had also worked assiduously to prevent the Heng Samrin government from being seated at the 92-nation association of non-aligned states meeting in February 1981 in New Delhi. The Kampuchean seat was left vacant and the meeting unamimously adopted a declaration calling for the withdrawal of foreign troops from that nation. Meanwhile the United States intensified its political and diplomatic pressures. In June in Peking Secretary of State Haig announced that the United States had lifted its restrictions on arms sales to China and that the two countries were following parallel courses in opposing Vietnam's occupation of Kampuchea.

Economic and Political Turnaround Despite the horrors of the Khmer Rouge period, the harsh military occupation by the Vietnamese, and the political and economic isolation imposed upon the government by most of the international community, Kampuchea miraculously began an economic recovery in 1981. Its resurgence was directly traceable to three factors: 1) the international food and medical relief operation which succeeded in reducing the death rate and the degree of malnutrition—even though a substantial amount of the aid was "requisitioned" by the Vietnamese occupiers, 2) the delay of the Heng Samrin regime in organizing a centrally planned economy—although it remained committed to some form of socialism, and 3) the combination of the traditionally industrious Kampuchean farmers, good weather and a fertile countryside.

By mid-1981 Phnom Penh no longer resembled the ghostly city of 20,000 to which it had been reduced by the Khmer Rouge policy of emptying the cities and returning the country to an agrarian economy. Instead the capital had again become a bustling center of 400,000, with small shops and restaurants abounding. The government permitted unrestricted private trading in farm produce and handicrafts, and even in consumer goods which were smuggled in from Thailand and southern Vietnam. Small entrepreneurs had begun to make boats, bicycles and farm tools. The rapid recovery occurred in an environment where the government had not yet begun to collect taxes, and provided free, if sporadic, water and electricity.[24]

The economic policies, whether deliberate or simply the consequence of inattention, were matched by relatively liberal political policies which seemed to be a response to international pressures.

In early 1981 the government had embarked upon intense political activity that included local elections, elections to a National Assembly and the organization of a new party structure. The new 117-member National Assembly, chosen in June, elected its own leaders and adopted a new constitution. The People's Revolutionary Party, which was designated as the "leading force" of the republic, took the place of the PCK. It was headed by Pen Sovan as secretary general. He was also chosen head (premier) of the Council of Ministers of the new government which in turn replaced the Revolutionary Council. The highest body, the seven member Council of State, was led by Heng Samrin who thereby became president of the republic.

Coalition Government of Democratic Kampuchea At the time of the government changes, the political and military opposition made moves of their own. The Chinese-backed Kampuchean Communist Party of the Khmer Rouge announced that it had formally dissolved, apparently in an effort to make itself more acceptable to the non-communist elements in opposition. However the armed guerrillas of the Khmer Rouge, militarily supplied by the PRC, had reached an estimated level of 20,000–30,000. They were augmented by two other resistance groups: the approximately 9,000-man force of the Khmer People's National Liberation Front of former rightist Kampuchean premier Son Sann, and the 1,000-man, largely peasant, force of Prince Sihanouk's National Army (ANS).[25] (By 1983 the Son Sann group had some 11,000 men under arms and the Sihanouk faction had increased to 5,000 armed soldiers; Khmer Rouge forces remained at approximately 30,000.[26])

In September Khieu Samphan, prime minister of the Khmer Rouge "government" encamped along the Thai-Kampuchean border, proposed a coalition government and offered the post of prime minister to Son Sann and the presidency to Sihanouk. The offer came at a Singapore meeting among the three which was convened at the urging of China as an expression of unity among the anti-Vietnamese factions. During the meeting Sihanouk obliquely expressed his discomfort over lending his prestige to a performance forced upon him and Son Sann by Chinese pressure.[27] Five months later, following a meeting with Samphan in Peking, Sihanouk reluctantly accepted the tripartite proposal commenting: "the Khmer Rouge have killed my children and my grandchildren. [But] the problem is to unite to fight the Vietnamese."[28]

In June 1982 Sihanouk, Samphan and Sann, meeting in Kuala Lumpur, proclaimed the formation of the Coalition Government of Democratic Kampuchea ((CGDK)—although collectively they held only a tiny portion of the western sector of the country. Sihanouk assumed the presidency on the grounds that he would be best able to attract both the loyalties of the Kampucheans and world support. Samphan became vice president and minister of foreign affairs while Son Sann accepted the premiership. The declaration contained an escape clause for the Khmer Rouge to the effect that if the coalition should reach an impasse the legal government of Kampuchea would revert to them.[29]

Sihanouk immediately undertook a tour of the ASEAN capitals to gain political and diplomatic support for the CGDK. It quickly became apparent, however, that while non-communist countries were willing to provide political support and humanitarian assistance, they would not, except for Singapore, admit to being willing to supply arms. Thus the PRC remained its principal military supplier.

The UN General Assembly annually through 1989 accepted the credentials of the CGDK as Kampuchea's legitimate government (124 aye, 17 nay and 12 abstentions in 1989). But in Indochina conflict over Kampuchea dominated politics in the region during the 1980s. The CGDK factions quickly reverted to their individual roles as surrogates of competing external influences. Sihanouk, maximizing his role as the father figure of his country, rallied broad international support including, from 1982, official "non lethal aid (some analysts believe "lethal" as well) from the U.S. for his and Son Sann's non-communist factions. The PRC continued to supply military assistance to the stronger Khmer Rouge communist resistance faction which now identified itself as Democratic Kampuchea (DK). Sihanouk's and Son Sann's forces were frequently at odds with the Khmer Rouge and the term "Coalition Government" became meaningless.

The character of the protracted struggle began to change significantly, beginning in 1986, with promulgation of the USSR's openness *(glasnost)* policy. As Sino-Soviet relations began to improve, the Soviets' Vietnamese client became less intractable, as did the PRC's Khmer Rouge client. By 1988 Sihanouk had begun talks with both the Khmer Rouge (minus its notorious Pol Pot element), and the Heng Samrin (president)—Hun Sen (premier) government in Phnom Penh. The ASEAN states, specifically Indonesia, Thailand, the Philippines and Singapore, began to ignore their professed trade embargo against Vietnam, and mounted efforts in February 1989 to find a solution to the Kampuchean issue. In April Vietnam announced it would remove its troops from Kampuchea by September, giving no indication that its previous demand for a prior political settlement was any longer a factor.

The July–August 1989 Paris peace conference on Kampuchea, orchestrated by the ASEAN states to bring together the four contenders for power, was attended by all interested parties, including the U.S., the USSR and the PRC, but did not succeed in achieving an accord. Nevertheless Vietnam continued with its promised troop withdrawal, claiming to have withdrawn its last forces from Kampuchea on September 26. The Khmer Rouge responded by launching attacks along the border and against several cities, apparently making serious inroads. In mid-January 1990 France called for a meeting of the five permanent members of the UN Security Council to discuss the situation.

WHITHER KAMPUCHEA?

When closely examined, 1986–89 developments in Indochina reveal complex national agendas. These suggest that the road to conflict resolution in Southeast Asia will be long and difficult despite Sino-Soviet rapprochement and Vietnam's 1989 troop withdrawal from Kampuchea. Political realities dictate such a conclusion.

The Vietnamese are unlikely to sacrifice their traditional influence in Kampuchea despite their military withdrawal. Vietnam dominated parts of Kampuchea for long periods until the advent of 19th century French colonialism. And their persona, as Asian authority Lucius Pye has remarked, is characterized by arrogance, a sense of superiority and obsession with achievement of "status."[30] Its political elite has repeatedly demonstrated that it will not tolerate threats to Vietnam's preeminence in Indochina.

Nor will the Chinese forfeit the influence in Indochina they have enjoyed for centuries. Chinese diplomacy negotiated Vietnam's military withdrawal and has sought to assure a role for the Khmer Rouge in a Kampuchean political settlement. In 1989 the PRC responded to two years of Soviet supplication by inviting USSR President Mikhail S. Gorbachev to a Peking summit where the Soviet leader acquiesced to both demands. The communist leadership in Peking apparently perceives the PRC's role in contemporary Southeast Asia as similar to that played by the emperors of the Middle Kingdom, before whom the barbarian world was expected to prostrate itself.

If, as suggested here, conflict resolution in Indochina is a more complex matter than overt declarations and acts of the nation-players suggest, what are the likely longer term political outcomes? The fact is that war-ravaged Kampuchea is not a sovereign state, but rather a collection of diverse ethnic groups, historically united mainly by allegiance to traditional monarchs who capitulated to western colonialism to ward off the predations of neighboring China, Vietnam, Thailand and Burma. Nor could concepts of governmental responsibility and constitutional procedures flourish in the wake of post-World War II independence because the region immediately became a zone for battle by proxy among external interests.

Little evidence is at hand to suggest that fundamentals have changed. Sihanouk has outrageously exploited all the players—non-communist and communist, internal and external—exploiting the near reverence he has enjoyed as past monarch within a culture which embraced god-kings during the golden centuries of the Angkor empire. But Sihanouk's rhetoric and his lack of a coherent political philosophy wore thin at the July–August 1989 Paris peace conference on Kampuchea. He was unable to bring together the opposing factions—the Phnom Penh and the Khmer Rouge communists, and his own non-communist forces—each of which are politically significant. All will likely continue to play major roles in Kampuchea, as will Kampuchea's powerful neighbors among the ASEAN states, the People's Republic of China, and the Soviet Union.

FOOTNOTES

1. Roger M. Smith, *Cambodia's Foreign Policy* (Ithaca, N.Y.: Cornell University Press, 1965), p. 13–14.

2. Robert Heine-Geldern, "Conceptions of State and Kingship in Southeast Asia" reprinted in John T. McAlister (ed.), *Southeast Asia: The Politics of National Integration* (N.Y.: Random House, 1973), p. 82.

3. Martin F. Herz, *A Short History of Cambodia: From the Days of Angkor to the Present* (N.Y.: Praeger, 1958), p. 75.

4. David J. Steinberg, *Cambodia, Its People, Its Society, Its Culture* (New Haven: Human Relations Area Files Press, 1959), p. 16.

5. Herz, *op. cit.,* p. 111.

6. Peter A. Poole, *Cambodia's Quest for Survival* (N.Y.: American-Asian Educational Exchange, Inc., 1969), p. 43.

7. Sheldon W. Simon, *War and Politics in Cambodia: A Communications Analysis* (Durham, N.C.: Duke University Press, 1974), p. 24.

8. *Area Handbook for the Khmer Republic (Cambodia)* (Washington: U.S. Government Printing Office, 1973), p. 191.

9. In December 1970 the U.S. Congress forbade use of American combat forces or advisers in Kampuchea, a reaction to the earlier "incursion."

10. Steven Warshaw, *Southeast Asia Emerges* (San Francisco: Canfield Press, 1975), p. 175.

11. *Ibid.*

12. *Data for Decision* (Manila: Press Foundation of Asia), 1974, p. 2078.

13. *Ibid.,* 1975, p. 2838.

14. *Ibid.,* p. 2911

15. *Data Asia* (Manila: Press Foundation of Asia), 1976, p. 3676.

16. *Ibid.*

17. *Ibid.*

18. John Barron and Anthony Paul, *Murder of a Gentle Land* (N.Y.: Reader's Digest Press, 1976), p. 206.

19. "Khmer Relief," *GIST* (Washington, D.C.: Department of State), April 1980.

20. *Data Asia, op. cit.,* p. 3740.

21. *Japan Times,* April 17, 1976.

22. Elizabeth Becker, "Vietnam Rewrites History of Cambodia," *Los Angeles Times,* October 24, 1979, p. 3.

23. Roger Kershaw, "Multipolarity in Cambodia's Crisis of Survival," *Southeast Asian Affairs* (Singapore: Institute of Southeast Asian Studies), 1980, p. 184.

24. "Conditions Better in Cambodia, But Dissent Evident," *Pomona Progress—Bulletin,* April 28, 1981 and Barry Wain, "Heng Samrin Regime Brings Cambodia Near Normalcy, But Problems Remain," *Wall Street Journal,* December 22, 1981.

25. Michael Parks, "Ousted Cambodian Regime Dissolves Its Communist Party," *Los Angeles Times,* December 8, 1981.

26. Bob Secter, "New Arms, Tactics Spark Cambodian Rightist Forces," *Los Angeles Times,* January 20, 1983.

27. Henry Kamm, "Three Cambodian Ex-Leaders Sign Pact on Anti-Hanoi Front," *New York Times,* September 5, 1981.

28. Jonathan Sharp, "Chinese Sweeten Sihanouk's Deal with Khmer Rouge by Giving Arms," *Asia Record* (Palo Alto, Calif.: Asia-Pacific Affairs Associates), March 1982.

29. *Asia Record, op. cit.,* July 1982, p. 6.

30. Lucian Pye, *Asian Power and Politics: The Cultural Dimensions of Authority* (Cambridge, M.A.: Belknap Press of Harvard University Press, 1985).

Laos

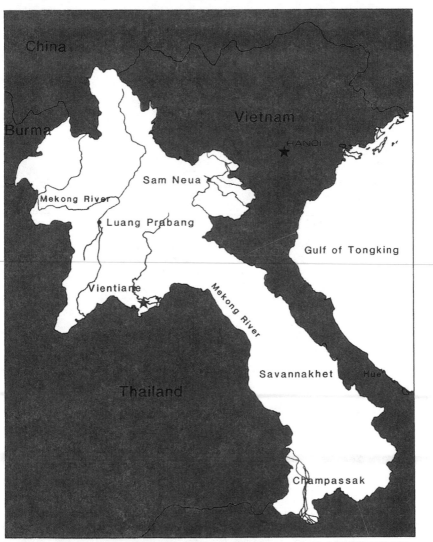

CHAPTER 4

LAOS

Laos is the only landlocked state in Southeast Asia. It is bordered on the north by China, on the west by Burma and Thailand, on the south by Kampuchea and on the east by Vietnam. The Mekong River, which rises in the Himalayas, forms much of its western boundary, and the Annam Cordillera its eastern border.

Most of Laos is mountainous, drained by short rivers flowing into the Mekong, and covered by monsoon rain forest and savannah. Its climate is the most extreme in Southeast Asia and the country suffers drought from December through February when the headwaters of the Mekong are frozen.

The Lao are a Tai people, related to the Thai of Thailand and the Shan of Burma, who penetrated the present state of Laos over the course of centuries from the Yunnan and Szechwan provinces of southern China. Moving down the valley of the Mekong they settled in what was then a border state of the Khmer empire. It was populated by a probably Negrito people, less developed than the Lao, called Kha, the Laotian word for slave. With the conquest of Yunnan by the Mongols in 1253 the Lao fled south in increasing numbers and found themselves in the position peaceably to assume leadership in the Kha areas.

The Lao brought with them Chinese arts of war, the techniques of wet rice cultivation and rice terracing, but no written language; they learned to write from the Khmer.

EARLY KINGDOMS

The first historic king was Fa Ngoum (1353–1373) who considered himself the 23rd successor of the legendary progenitor of the Lao—Khoum Lo. Fa Ngoum had been exiled (or perhaps held hostage) in the court of Angkor where he married a Khmer princess, accepted Theravada Buddhism and was sent back to the Lao center of Muong Swa with the blessing of the Khmer emperor. He brought with him the

Pra Bang (Golden Buddha) which became the most revered national religious image—even though the populace by and large remained animist. Fa Ngoum conquered all of present-day Laos and much of northern and eastern Thailand, and formed the first Lao state—Lan Xang, Land of a Million Elephants.

His excessive military demands brought about his deposition twenty years later and he was succeeded by his son who took the dynastic name of Sam Sene Tai (Lord of Three Hundred Thousand Tai) in consequence of a census taken in 1376 which showed the land was occupied by 300,000 Tai males and 400,000 non-Tai. Women and children were not counted. Sam Sene Tai consolidated the kingdom and organized the administration, setting a pattern of government that persisted for three centuries. Lan Xang became an absolute monarchy, administered by princes of the blood who held office at the pleasure of the king. A *maha uparat*, or second king, became chief adviser and could in theory be anyone of talent, but in fact was usually chosen from the family of the incumbent. This may have been a faint reflection of the Chinese bureaucratic system, but was more likely a Malay tradition as the same custom pertained in Thailand and Malaysia.

The kingdom apparently prospered throughout the 15th century and was able to beat back the Vietnamese of Annam after they briefly captured the capital, Muong Swa. In the 16th century Lan Xang became embroiled in a struggle for control of the Thai state of Chieng Mai, a dispute that preoccupied Laos, Burma and Ayutthia for the next century.

The Laotian king Potisarath, who had based his dynasty on trade and royal marriages, intervened in the case of the Chieng Mai succession by placing his own son, Settathirath, on the throne. Upon his father's death Settathirath returned to Muong Swa, carrying with him the Pra Keo, Emerald Buddha, religious and political symbol of Chieng Mai whose possession signified sovereignty over the area. In retaliation Burma twice invaded Lan Xang seeking to seize the Pra Keo and Settathirath was forced to move his capital to Vientiane where, around 1563, he built the Wat Keo to enshrine the Emerald Buddha. At the same time he renamed Muong Swa, Luang Prabang in honor of the Pra Bang, Golden Buddha, enshrined there.

Settathirath later disappeared on an expedition against the Kha and Burma succeeded in conquering Lan Xang, holding it for 20 years. When Ayutthia attacked the Burmese and took control of Chieng Mai, Laos was able to regain its independence (1591).

The golden age of Laos was the 17th century when its boundaries exceeded those of the present-day nation and included parts of southern Yunnan, Annam, Kampuchea and northeastern Thailand. Soulinga Vongsa ruled from 1637 to 1694 and during this period the first

Europeans appeared briefly, unsuccessfully seeking trade and diplomatic ties. They found a nation secure and strong and described Vientiane as a beautiful city with a splendid court. Soulinga Vongsa settled a boundary dispute with Annam on ethnic grounds which gave Lan Xang all the land on which resided people who lived in "houses on piles with verandas," and Annam the areas where the people lived in houses "without verandas," an ethnic-cultural distinction still valid between the Malay and the Chinese.[1] Soulinga Vongsa precipitated the dissolution of his country, however, by executing his only son for adultery, leaving the question of succession open on his death. As a result the country was divided into three centers, which obtained until the present, Vientiane, Luang Prabang and Champassak.

Upon Soulinga Vongsa's death his nephew Sai Ong Hue returned from Annam and seized Vientiane with the help of the Annamese and accepted a tributary relationship to Annam. A grandson, Kisarath, took the old capital of Muong Swa, now Luang Prabang, and another prince gained control over Champassak (Bassac, the old capital of Chenla), in the far south. The country remained divided, the three states quarreling among themselves. At the same time all three were forced to fight for their existence against the Annamese on the east, Chinese bandits on the north, Burmese on the west and the Thai of Ayutthia, now called Siam, on the south.

In 1778 Vientiane was conquered by Ayutthia and to regain its independence had to pay tribute to that nation as well as to Annam to whom it was already in vassalage. Fifty years later it was savagely sacked by the Thai who carried off 10,000 of its inhabitants as well as the Pra Keo image. The Thai subsequently used Vientiane as a path of attack on Annam, and when forced to retreat took with them large numbers of Laotians, on the theory that depopulation of an area assured the conqueror that no army could rise against it or assist its enemies for at least another generation. By the middle of the 19th century the population of Vientiane was barely a fourth of what it had been at the beginning of the century.

Champassak had also been captured in 1778 by the Thai and remained under their suzerainty throughout most of the next few decades. Luang Prabang was devastated during the 18th and 19th centuries by wars with Vientiane, Thailand and Burma, and by raids by Meo tribes and Chinese bandits. When the French appeared on the scene in the 19th century all three states of a divided Laos were under Thai suzerainty. Only Xieng Khouang, a tributary state to Vientiane, had survived as an independent unit.

FRENCH COLONIAL PERIOD

French influence rose rapidly on mainland Southeast Asia after 1850. Annexation of Cochinchina was completed by 1864 and Annam and

Tongking in central and northern Vietnam were transformed into protectorates between the years 1882 and 1884, thus solidifying French control of Vietnam. Kampuchea had become a French protectorate in 1863 at the expense of Thailand, which did not abandon its residual claim to that territory until 1867. In the meantime, displeased by the loss of Kampuchea and perceiving the rise of French power in northern Vietnam as a direct threat to its own security, Thailand launched a military expedition against northern Laos, ostensibly to suppress Chinese bandits, but actually to make it a Thai province and buffer zone.

France thereupon informed Thailand that it had inherited Vietnam's claims to Xieng Khouang and Luang Prabang, and proposed a Thai-French boundary commission to determine the Luang Prabang-Tongking border. Although the boundary matter was left unsettled, France emerged from the negotiations with Thai permission to open a vice consulate in Luang Prabang. The move seemed to confirm French recognition of Thai sovereignty over that portion of Laos. However, the vice consul appointed, Auguste Pavie, was an official experienced in Southeast Asia, who from the beginning used his office to promote French interests in the area.

Pavie's opportunity occurred in 1887 when Thai troops, who were supposed to protect the kingdom, withdrew at the onset of the rainy season and Luang Prabang was sacked by a powerful dissident chief. Pavie, who personally saved the old king's life by spiriting him down river, persuaded him to opt for a French protectorate rather than Thai suzerainty which had proved ineffective. Thus began actual French colonial rule in Laos.

Pavie's success in Luang Prabang impelled the French to move strongly into the Mekong valley and in March 1893 Pavie, by then the French minister in Bangkok, claimed for France—in the name of Vietnam—all territory east of the Mekong River from Kam Mon southward. The Thai rejected the French claim in May and appealed to the British for support but the British declined to intervene. The French followed up their claim by sending a naval force to Bangkok and, under pressure, Thailand signed a treaty October 3, 1893 giving up all pretensions to the east bank of the Mekong River, north and south.

Modern Laos took further shape when an Anglo-French declaration of January 15, 1896 made the Mekong River the boundary between British Burma and French Laos. In 1896–97 French agreement was reached with China to fix the northern border. In 1904 and 1905 Thailand specifically ceded to France west bank portions of Luang Prabang and Bassac. The upper portions of the former Lan Xang kingdom west of the Mekong remained in Thai hands.

Government and Administration In 1899 Vientiane became the seat of a resident general and the administrative capital of French Laos, which comprised the states of Luang Prabang, Xieng Khouang, Champassak and Vientiane and was termed Laos for the first time. French protection secured the country against threats from Thailand, Vietnam and Burma, but internal tribal conflicts, especially those involving the Kha, Meo and Tai (as distinct from Thai) frequently required French military intervention.

The resident exercised only indirect rule over the royal capital of Luang Prabang where the king retained his title and royal prerogatives. In the remaining area, which was divided into eight provinces, French rule was direct but lighthanded. The resident's major roles were collecting taxes, setting fiscal policy, providing educational facilities, organizing and administering a judicial system and suppressing slavery. In other matters the French administrators adopted a live-and-let-live approach and maintained existing local governmental institutions. The councils of village headmen elected one of themselves to represent their villages before a French-appointed district officer.

Unlike the hostile and suspicious Confucian mandarins in Annam, the Laotian Buddhist elite accepted the French open-mindedly. French quickly became the language used even at village level, and teachers from France created a keen interest in French education among the tiny Laotian elite. The French reciprocated, many of them developing strong emotional bonds to the Lao people.

The last king to ascend the throne before World War II was Sisavang Vong, who was crowned instead of his elder brother on recommendation of the French senior resident.

WARTIME POLITICS

Germany invaded and defeated France in June 1940. In Asia Germany's ally Japan, which had been engaged in military operations in China since 1931 and had almost reached the border of Indochina in its southward drive, had already signed a compact with an expansionist, militarist Thailand. After the German victory Japan demanded and obtained from the German-sponsored Vichy French government the right to station troops in Indochina, including Laos, and to use airfields there; in return the French civil service and armed forces were left in place.

In January 1941 Thailand demanded from the French the return of the Laotian provinces on the west bank of the Mekong. The Thai army occupied the provinces and, with Japanese diplomatic support, obtained a settlement which returned to Thailand Bassac Province in the south, and Sayaboury Province on the west bank of the Mekong opposite Luang Prabang in the north. King Sisavang Vong was compensated for these territorial losses, which included some of Laos' best teak forest, when the Vichy government agreed to incorporation within the Kingdom of Luang Prabang the territories of Vientiane, Xieng Khouang and Nam Tha. In Hanoi in August 1941 Marshal Henri Petain, head of the Vichy French regime, and the king signed a treaty that defined the terms of the French protectorate over the expanded Kingdom of Luang Prabang. The *maha uparat*, Prince Phetsarath, became wartime prime minister in addition to his viceregal duties.

After the liberation of France from the Germans in 1944, contacts developed between the Free French mission in Kunming, China, and Vichy French administrators and commanders in Indochina. The apprehensive Japanese on March 9, 1945 suddenly disarmed and imprisoned French military forces and interned French civilians throughout Indochina. They declared the end of the French colonial regime and ordered Emperor Bao Dai in Vietnam, Prince Sihanouk in Kampuchea, and Sisavang Vong in Laos to declare their independence from France. Instead, Crown Prince Savang Vatthana, in the name of his father, proclaimed the loyalty of the royal court and the people of Luang Prabang to France and, on March 16, decreed a mass uprising against the Japanese. The angry Japanese occupied Luang Prabang April 5 and removed the crown prince to Saigon. King Sisavang Vong on April 8 was forced to declare the termination of the French protectorate and the independence of the kingdom within the Japanese Co-Prosperity Sphere, the new political-economic order the Japanese sought to achieve in Southeast Asia.

The removal to Saigon of the crown prince gave a relatively free hand to Prince Phetsarath, the viceroy and prime minister. He was the eldest of three remarkable brothers and the founder-to-be of the Lao Issara (Independent Laos) movement. Phetsarath was anti-French, but he also feared the revival of an aggressive Vietnam—traditional enemy of the Laotians—which he perceived to be taking place with growth of the communist Vietminh. Phetsarath therefore cooperated with the Japanese who in turn merely appointed advisers to his administration. He was thus largely free to lay plans for genuine independence when the time came.

Lao Issara Government In August 1945, within days of Japan's surrender, Phetsarath in Vientiane, without informing the king in Luang Prabang, reaffirmed the April 8 proclamation of independence from France which the Japanese had forced on the king. Phetsarath declared Laos to be a single, independent monarchy under King Sisavang Vong, and proclaimed the union of the Kingdom of Luang Prabang and the territory of Champassak. He then formed a committee of Lao Issara, consisting of his family, others of the elite and a few

Vietnamese who held official positions in Laos, to resist any attempt to return Laos to colonial status.

But Phetsarath encountered immediate difficulties. Prince Boun Oum of Champassak, the foremost political leader in the south, objected to Phetsarath's temerity in claiming leadership throughout Laos and invited French troops to enter his territory; the king welcomed the French mission which parachuted into Luang Prabang September 14. Three days later the king informed Phetsarath that he regarded the protectorate as still in effect, and on October 10 announced that Phetsarath's titles of viceroy and prime minister had been withdrawn. The king's rebuff coincided with the return to Luang Prabang of French agents who gave every indication that France intended to resume the protectorate.

Phetsarath's independence group in Vientiane countered on October 12. It proclaimed a provisional constitution for a united Laos and formed a Provisional National Assembly which nominated a government and chose Phaya Khammao, former governor of Vientiane, as prime minister. Phetsarath's brother, Prince Souvanna Phouma, was named minister of public works, and his half-brother, Prince Souphanouvong, who was liaison between the Lao Issara and the Vietminh, was appointed minister of defense and commander in chief of the Lao Issara armed forces. Just as they had facilitated Ho Chi Minh's cause by flying him into Vietnam, the Americans facilitated Souphanouvong's by arranging a military flight for him to Hanoi. There he had received Ho Chi Minh's enthusiastic endorsement to form a Lao national government, with a promise of all possible assistance from the Vietminh, and Ho had given him 100 of the Vietminh's reserve of 240 rifles. Despite the king's rebuff, Phetsarath invited Sisavang Vong to head the new constitutional monarchy because the Lao Issara realized that the king's French advisers would be more amenable to a monarchy than to a republic. The king declined, pronouncing the provisional government illegal and against the popular will. Simultaneously, he summoned Phetsarath to Luang Prabang.

Phetsarath refused to obey. Instead, on October 20 his National Assembly voted to depose the monarch on the grounds that, isolated as he was in Luang Prabang and under the influence of the French, the king was no longer a free agent. However, a Lao Issara delegation was dispatched to Luang Prabang in early November to convince the king of the strength of the constitutional movement, to recount for him the place reserved for the monarch in the constitution and to suggest to him that his own legitimacy and that of the movement would be reinforced by his participation. Under pressure and with great reluctance, Sisavang Vong finally agreed to put himself under the authority of the provisional government. The Lao Issara then requested him to take the throne of a united constitutional monarchy of Laos. His coronation in Luang Prabang on April 23, 1946 was accompanied by a traditional and elaborate ceremony.

POLITICAL INDICATORS

1. Laos had come to nationhood late in history and was from the beginning an amalgam of tribes and peoples on the outskirts of earlier empires.
2. Landlocked, Laos occupied the western slopes of the Annamite mountains, whose eastern slopes were held by its usually more powerful and warlike neighbor, Vietnam; and the eastern bank of the Mekong River, whose western flood plain was held by its equally powerful and warlike neighbor, Thailand.
3. Prior to French occupation the country had been split into three geographical units. These were perpetuated by the French and were to become centers of conflict in the long post-World War II fight for political control.
4. The unifying and legitimizing force was the monarchy which was to continue as a political value until full communist accession to power.

THREE PATHS TO INDEPENDENCE: 1947–1960

The Lao Issara government was shortlived because two days after the pomp and circumstance of its inauguration French forces occupied Vientiane. On March 21, 1946 at the town of Thakhek in central Laos, the French were confronted by the combined Lao Issara forces under command of Prince Souphanouvong and Vietminh irregulars and agents. In the mortar and machine gun battle which ensued the Laotians and the Vietnamese were routed and Souphanouvong was badly wounded, although he escaped. French forces entered Vientiane with only minor further skirmishes on April 25 and the Lao Issara government, including Phetsarath and Souvanna Phouma, fled en masse to Thailand to continue a government in exile and to conduct cross-river operations against the French. On May 13 the French reoccupied Luang Prabang and King Sisavang Vong speedily changed his position and reaffirmed the link with France.

A joint Franco-Laotian commission was formed to draft a provisional agreement regarding the future relationship between France and Laos and to recommend the form of the Laotian government. In August the two states signed a *modus vivendi* which recognized the unified, autonomous entity of Laos under the sovereignty of Luang Prabang, and provided for a constituent assembly to write a constitution. Crown Prince Savang Vattana headed the interim provisional government; elections to the constituent assembly were held at the end of the year under difficult security conditions occasioned by guerrilla activity. Simultaneously France successfully pressured Thailand to return the provinces it had acquired in 1941. The constitution promulgated by the king May 11, 1947 formally transformed Laos into a constitutional monarchy within the French Union.

After the flight of the Lao Issara government from Vientiane, Phetsarath became the de facto leader of the independence movement. His government-in-exile in Bangkok considered the *modus vivendi*—and thus the governmental arrangements fashioned from it—totally unacceptable. Phetsarath's intransigence was counterproductive. He refused to have any contact with the French, a self-defeating posture given the reality of French physical control of Laos. Prince Souvanna Phouma, who had become deputy prime minister, held different views; he and the independence movement's chief publicist, Katay Don Sasorith, were prepared to trust the French. Meanwhile, until the opportune moment arrived, Souvanna Phouma was content to work for the Thai Electric Company in Bangkok and plan ambitiously the economic development of Laos.

Souphanouvong took a third view. His meeting with Ho Chi Minh in 1945, his armed struggle against the French with Vietminh support at Thakhek, and his fascination with the Vietminh's brilliant tactician, Vo Nguyen Giap, convinced Souphanouvong that only armed rebellion in alliance with the Vietminh could achieve real independence for Laos. This view was rejected by many Lao Issara leaders because of their traditional fear of Vietnamese hegemony—whether cloaked in communist ideology or otherwise. By 1948 the rift between Souphanouvong and the more moderate leaders led to a break in their relations.

Souphanouvong also recognized that the economic and political expectations of the hill peoples were not being addressed, either by the French or by the Lao elite who were devising the country's institutions. He therefore made repeated trips into the hills to gain support of the tribes. His followers, principally along the Thai border, became skillful as guerrilla fighters and expert at ambushing French convoys. Common cause with the Vietminh enabled the prince and his chief of staff, Phoumi Nosavan, who later became a right-wing leader, to raise mixed Lao-Vietminh armed units. The guerrillas even created primitive small arms workshops, fashioning crude rifles from automotive scrap metal.

The French, meanwhile, had become more attentive to Lao national aspirations, principally because they were involved in a full-scale war in Vietnam and could ill afford a backyard conflict in Laos. A Franco-Laotian convention of July 1949 gave Laos greater autonomy in foreign

affairs to enable it to qualify for United Nations membership, and a
Laotian territorial army was established under French command.
These appurtenances of sovereignty had the desired effect. The Lao
Issara leaders in Bangkok decided to disband the government-in-exile
and the French obligingly flew 25 of them back to Vientiane in
November 1949. Within a year the United States, the United Kingdom
and a number of other western nations, as well as Thailand, extended
diplomatic recognition to Laos. Only Prince Phetsarath, the proud and
bitter ex-viceroy and the initial leader of the Lao independence movement, remained in Bangkok; he eventually returned to Laos in 1957,
his title of vice-king finally restored, where he died in 1959.

After 1950 France became even more preoccupied by the military
threat in Vietnam and began to withdraw troops from Laos to meet
that threat. Assisted by United States funds and material provided
under an aid agreement of September 9, 1951, the French built up a
Royal Lao Army to replace French troops. Souvanna Phouma, newly
returned from exile, became prime minister in November but could
not persuade his half-brother Souphanouvong that, by joining together,
they could free the country from French domination.

Under increasing pressure to achieve complete independence, Sou-
vanna Phouma in August 1953 formally approached the French and in
October a treaty was signed, the first article of which states: "The
French Republic recognizes and declares that the Kingdom of Laos is
a fully independent and sovereign state and a member of the French
Union."[2]

Pathet Lao   Prince Souphanouvong had been removed from his
position as commander of the Lao Issara forces by his colleagues in
the government-in-exile in May 1949 because the political paths of the
moderate independence leaders and of the "Red Prince" had parted.
The prince exploited his personal prestige, his military reputation and
the assurance of Vietminh support he had received in Hanoi to establish that same year a separate political front variously called the
Progressive People's Organization or the Lao Free Front. In 1950, with
Vietminh encouragement, a "congress" of this organization met in the
Laotian jungle to organize a national resistance government with
Souphanouvong as prime minister. In a 12-point political manifesto
bearing "the notation 'Pathet Lao,' literally 'Land of the Lao,' referring to the areas Laos claimed to have 'liberated' from French rule,"[3]
the group presented itself as the free government of all Laos and the
successor to the Lao Issara. Pathet Lao became the name by which
the organization was popularly known.

The Pathet Lao was an inconsequential force until April 1953 when
Vietnamese communist troops crossed into northern Laos in large
numbers and forced French and Royal Lao army units out of areas in

the northern provinces of Phong Saly and Sam Neua. There the Pathet Lao set up an "administration" within striking distance of Luang Prabang.

In 1954 the Geneva Conference mandated the withdrawal of the Vietnamese "volunteers" from Laos and the confinement of Pathet Lao forces and administration to Phong Saly and Sam Neua pending a "political settlement," including national elections, to determine party strength in the new national government. However the Vietnamese forces did not withdraw, and the Pathet Lao refused to cooperate with the International Commission for Supervision and Control set up to supervise execution of the conference mandate, or allow restoration of central government authority in the two provinces. In effect, the Geneva Conference produced a de facto division of Laos rather than a settlement.

Nevertheless, following the Geneva Conference and after five years of alienation the two princes engaged in a brotherly reunion and hopes were expressed by Katay Don Sasorith, who had succeeded Souvanna Phouma as prime minister in Vientiane in October 1954, that a united nationalism might prevail. "I believe Souphanouvong is a nationalist," he said, and that "it is possible to cooperate with these people if we can get them away from the Vietminh."[4] However, negotiations between the government and the Pathet Lao over the regrouping of forces, a ceasefire or any other positive step failed; the one exception was in the north where the elections mandated at Geneva were held in December 1955. When Souvanna Phouma became prime minister anew in March 1956 he announced again that reconciliation with the Pathet Lao was his most urgent task. Simultaneously, a new political manifesto of the Pathet Lao stressed the desirability of a united front, with the implication that it might include the Royal Government.

FIRST COALITION GOVERNMENT

The Pathet Lao announced a new organization in 1956, the Neo Lao Hak Sat, or United Lao Patriotic Front (NLHS), as a framework for possible coalition. Simultaneously, however, a true communist party was formed within the Front, the Phak Khon Ngan (Worker's Party), later known as the People's Revolutionary Party, which carried on operational work at village level under the umbrella of the NLHS. The term Pathet Lao came to be synonymous with the military arm of the NLHS.

The organization of the Front, with presumed accommodation for varying political sentiments, brought the Royalists and the NLHS to negotiations. As Souvanna Phouma hoped, the latter agreed to defuse factionalism in return for representation in a coalition government.

Accordingly NLHS leaders Souphanouvong and Phoumi Vongvichit became ministers in the coalition government, the NLHS was accorded official political party status, Sam Neua and Phong Saly provinces were turned over to the authority of the Royal Government, and in November 1957 supplementary elections to the National Assembly were scheduled. Finally, a portion of the Pathet Lao military forces were integrated into the national army and the remainder were to be demobilized. In the elections held May 4, 1958 leftists won 13 out of the 20 supplemental seats. Souphanouvong received more votes than any candidate in the country and when the new members of the National Assembly convened he was chosen to head the assembly.

The Americans, who had been supporting non-communist elements in Laos since 1951, were disappointed over the election outcome and over the rampant inflation arising from misuse of the U.S. military and economic assistance program which had begun in 1953; by 1958 the United States was providing almost 100 percent of the entire Laotian budget. The United States suspended its aid programs in June and the National Assembly withdrew its confidence in Souvanna Phouma on the issue of monetary reform; he resigned in July.

Phoui Sananikone Government: 1958–1960   Phoui Sananikone, who succeeded the prince in August 1958 as prime minister, had a very different idea about political neutrality; it did not, in his view, preclude anti-communist action at home. Thus Phoui's cabinet excluded the NLHS ministers and included four representatives—not even assembly members—of the new rightist group, the Committee for the Defense of the National Interest (CDNI).

Phoui ended many of the abuses in the U.S. aid program, attempted monetary reform, made overtures to non-communist governments in Southeast Asia and let it be known that he considered the Pathet Lao to be Vietnamese agents whose provincial centers he would clear out. His hard line created apprehension among the north Vietnamese communists that their north-south communications and supply routes through Laos to southern Vietnam, known collectively as the Ho Chi Minh Trail, would be jeopardized. In late December 1958 they moved several companies of regular troops into Laos in Savannakhet province just west of the demarcation line between north and south Vietnam. In response Phoui secured special governing power from the National Assembly, added three army officers to his cabinet and stated that his government did not consider itself bound by the terms of the Geneva Conference as long as a political settlement had not been reached in Vietnam.

The government's apparent repudiation of coalition politics in 1959 was encouraged by the hard line CDNI element in the cabinet, especially Colonel Phoumi Nosavan, the erstwhile aide to Souphanouvong who had become a firebrand rightist. When the government in May insisted upon immediate integration of two battalions of Pathet Lao troops into the Royal Army, as had been agreed earlier, one of the battalions defected. The government retaliated by placing Souphanou-vong and other NLHS leaders under house arrest in expectation that the move would have a dampening effect on Pathet Lao terrorist tactics. Instead Pathet Lao guerrilla activity increased, it was rumored with the assistance of troops of the Democratic Republic of Vietnam (DRV) operating on Laotian soil. Sporadic fighting, greatly exaggerated by the western press, took place from June to October. On July 29 the government announced that new elements, entirely equipped and supported by the DRV, were assisting Pathet Lao forces. Using this claim as a basis, the government requested and received from the United States 100 additional technicians for an emergency technical and weapons training program. A United Nations investigation of the military situation requested by Prime Minister Phoui could not, how-ever, substantiate the presence of DRV troops and UN Secretary General Dag Hammarskjold advised the government to pursue a more neutral policy. Prime Minister Phoui, embarrassed, blamed Phoumi Nosavan and the other CDNI ministers for misrepresenting minor Pathet Lao military activity as major clashes between DRV forces and the Royal Laotian army. Meanwhile in October Sisavang Vong died after a 54-year reign, and was succeeded by Crown Prince Savang Vatthana.

The CDNI group, headed by Phoumi Nosavan and four other gener-als, demanded intensification of pressure against the Pathet Lao and postponement of elections for the National Assembly. They forced Phoui on December 30 to submit his resignation, which the new king, who also advocated a hard line toward the Pathet Lao, quickly ac-cepted. Fearing emergence of a military dictatorship the ambassadors of the United States, France, the United Kingdom and Australia persuaded the king to appoint a civilian interim government responsi-ble to himself and to hold the elections as scheduled.

Since the April 24, 1960 elections produced landslide victories for pro-government factions, both the NLHS and some western analysts concluded that they were rigged. Tiao Somsanith emerged as prime minister in the new government. Phoumi Nosavan became minister of defense and leader of the new Social Democrat Party that had been formed from a CDNI nucleus and was the real wielder of power. The government promised a firm anti-Pathet Lao policy. Anticipating that the new government might bring them to public trial, Souphanouvong and 15 other Pathet Lao leaders who had been in detention at a police camp near Vietiane escaped, with the aid of their guards, to the safety of the jungle and the Pathet Lao forces.

The Kong Le Coup and Its Aftermath   On the night of August 8, 1960 the 24-year-old commander of the 2nd Parachute Battalion, Captain Kong Le, seized Vientiane's radio station, airfield, power plant and arsenal. He announced the next morning in his simple and direct manner that he had done so to end the rising civil war, to resist foreign pressures, to secure removal of foreign troops from Laos and to suppress those who were "making their harvest on the backs of the people."[5] Kong Le proposed reestablishment of a neutral government under Souvanna Phouma who had been elected chairman of the National Assembly following the April 1960 elections.

On word of the takeover the assembly immediately split into factions. Under Phoumi Nosavan's leadership some cabinet ministers and 21 assembly deputies flew to the town of Savannakhet where they denounced the coup. The remaining 34 assembly deputies in Vientiane deposed the Tiao Somsanith cabinet and asked the king to call on Souvanna Phouma to form a new neutral government. The latter accepted, a new government was formed and Kong Le and his paratroopers handed over the prime minister's office to Souvanna Phouma on August 17.

Phoumi in Savannakhet, however, refused to accept defeat. With the support of most of the country's military commanders he proclaimed martial law which, he claimed, suspended all normal government activity including investiture by the king of the new Souvanna Phouma government. Souvanna Phouma flew to Savannakhet and convinced Phoumi that both factions of the assembly should meet in Luang Prabang—neutral ground—to resolve the impasse. "This is our last chance," he said. "If we cannot come to an agreement civil war will certainly follow."[6] Phoumi agreed and the reunited assembly met in Luang Prabang. On August 31 Phoumi and Souvanna Phouma announced complete accord. Phoumi entered the cabinet as deputy prime minister but, significantly, not defense minister.

Nevertheless, Phoumi, several ministers and the assembly deputies who were his followers, were reluctant to return to Vientiane where Kong Le and his 600 paratroopers had announced that they would not accept Phoumi in the new administration in any capacity. Instead they returned to Savannakhet where they, and the commanders of three of the five military regions, began to organize a revolutionary group to oppose the new government. Boun Oum of Champassak, the venerated southern leader, was chosen to head the resistance movement.

The Pathet Lao retaliated by stepping up pressure against the Royalist-held town of Sam Neua, where 150 defenders surrendered. Souvanna Phouma blamed the Phoumi resistance movement for inciting the attack. After a final unsuccessful attempt at reconciliation, Souvanna Phouma dropped Phoumi from the cabinet. The Pathet Lao's strategy of divide and conquer was achieving success.

Foreign Intervention   Although formal United States policy, as that of France and the United Kingdom, was to support the government of Souvanna Phouma, evidence suggests the United States perceived its real interest to lie with Phoumi, and supported his drive to retake Vientiane and regain control of the government. As Arthur Dommen, a close student of Laos, notes:

> From mid-September, Savannakhet was the scene of an increased number of landings and takeoffs by unmarked C-46 and C-47 transports, manned by American crews. These planes belonged to Air America, Inc., a civilian charter company with U.S. Air Force operational support and under contract to the U.S. government. The aircraft, giving the Phoumist forces a badly needed logistical supply system, ferried military supplies from Bangkok to Savannakhet, the headquarters of the Revolutionary Committee, and shuttled between Savannakhet and outlying garrisons loyal to General Phoumi.[7]

In October the Pathet Lao, having secured a strong base area in northern Laos with Vietnamese support, proposed negotiations with Souvanna Phouma and the Royal Government. The prince accepted the initiative, disturbing the Americans who then modified their policy to "compromise between all-out support for General Phoumi and all-out toleration of Souvanna Phouma's predilection for co-existence with the Pathet Lao."[8] United States Ambassador Winthrop G. Brown was personally sympathetic to Souvanna Phouma and suggested that the United States would renew grant aid in cash if the prince would permit American military deliveries to General Phoumi for use against the Pathet Lao. Souvanna Phouma agreed, but the problem with this "gentlemen's agreement" was that provision of U.S. military aid to Phoumi implied that he enjoyed official American support. As U.S. war materiel for Phoumi's forces began to arrive in large quantities, the psychological effect was to encourage regular Laotian units to defect to Phoumi. In November the Luang Prabang garrison mutinied against the Vientiane regime and joined Phoumi, as did a government militia force sent out to quell the mutiny. The king, in Luang Prabang, was thus cut off from Souvanna Phouma's government in Vientiane.

General Phoumi prepared for an assault on Vientiane while Souvanna Phouma was engaged in fruitless negotiations with Pathet Lao units who, aided by "stiffener" elements of DRV troops, consolidated their hold over the entire tier of Laotian districts along the Vietnamese border. Souvanna Phouma appealed to his brother Souphanouvong

who agreed to a coalition among representatives of Souvanna Phouma's Vientiane government, the Pathet Lao and General Phoumi, but
the latter turned down the proposal.

As Phoumi's forces approached the city the government began to
dissolve. Many deputies departed the city on December 7 to join
Phoumi's ally, Colonel Kouprasith Abhay, military commander of the
Vientiane region who was encamped nearby. Souvanna Phouma fled
to Kampuchea, and Quinim Pholsena, an influential pro-communist
senior government minister, escaped to Hanoi to enlist aid from the
Soviets and the Vietnamese. On December 11 the 38 deputies in
Savannakhet who were Phoumi supporters voted to depose Souvanna
Phouma. They were supported by the king who issued ordinances
dismissing him, giving powers provisionally to the Savannakhet group,
and nominating a provisional government headed by Prince Boun
Oum.

In Hanoi Quinim Pholsena secured an immediate response from the
Soviets who apparently had already decided, in exchange for a formal
alliance between Kong Le's troops and the Pathet Lao, to airlift arms
and supplies into Laos to provide resistance against Phoumi's U.S.-
supplied forces. By December 12 heavy 105mm howitzers and mortars
were arriving in Vientiane. The Soviet decision and the formal Kong
Le-Pathet Lao alliance changed the nature of the struggle in Laos.
Although Phoumi's forces captured Vientiane in the December 13–16
battle that cost 600 lives and 1,000 injuries, Kong Le and his troops
were able to make an orderly withdrawal to the Plain of Jars (midway
between and slightly east of Luang Prabang and Vientiane) with their
jeeps, trucks and armored cars intact. Airlifted Soviet supplies of food,
gasoline and arms permitted Kong Le's men to continue operation as
an effective fighting force, and Soviet military aid enabled Souphanouvong to transform his guerrilla Pathet Lao into effective combat
troops.

Superpower intervention in the Laotian civil war deepened. The
Soviets castigated the United States for backing Phoumi, assuring
Souvanna Phouma that they regarded him as the legal prime minister.
The United States, for its part, charged that responsibility for the civil
war lay squarely with the Soviet government and announced a program
of military assistance to the Revolutionary Committee—headed by
Phoumi and Boun-Oum—that had been designated as the provisional
authority by the king. From the Soviet point of view, their outright
and massive military assistance which had begun to transform the
Plain of Jars into a vast armed camp, was necessary to maintain their
position in the area and, most importantly, to retain the allegiance of
the Vietnamese communists in the emerging Sino-Soviet quarrel.
United States officials, meanwhile, appeared to have come to the

conclusion that the capitulation of Laos to north Vietnamese pressures would have serious consequences of U.S. policy throughout Southeast Asia.

It was the protagonists themselves who initiated a solution in 1961. On February 19 the king denounced all foreign interference and declared Laotian neutrality. Responding to the king's message, Souvanna Phouma returned from Kampuchea to make contact with Quinim Pholsena's skeletal government in northern Laos. Next the prince confounded the diplomatic world by managing to have a cordial meeting with General Phoumi in Vientiane. Souvanna Phouma and Phoumi issued a communique March 10 calling for an international conference on Laos.

While the Vietnamese communists, the Chinese, the Americans and the Soviets all gave lip service to the idea of an international conference, the Kong Le-Pathet Lao forces, with close DRV support and operating from the Plain of Jars, began to inflict serious defeats on Phoumi's troops. By mid-March they had cut the Royal Road between Luang Prabang and Vientiane, and by the end of March controlled six provinces. The Americans were suddenly face to face with the probability that Laos would fall to communist forces. President Kennedy ordered formation of a land, air and sea task force and notified Moscow and Peking that the U.S. would intervene to prevent a communist takeover. He advised the world on March 23 that the U.S. supported the U.K. initiative for a joint British-Soviet appeal for a ceasefire, followed by an international conference.

The conflicting forces in Laos then proceeded to negotiate a curious kind of unstructured ceasefire on their own in early April. Their agreement did not identify troop locations nor terrain under their control. It did not prohibit troop movements nor make any reference to airlift of supplies from abroad. The entire scenario was without precedent. The Pathet Lao—the military arm of the NLHS, whose political program supported Souvanna Phouma but whose leaders held no offices in his government—had no legal justification for participation in the ceasefire which was between two rival "governments." Another anomaly was that Soviet aid officially was helping the Royal Lao army led by Kong Le, not the Pathet Lao, and the Royal Government of Souvanna Phouma, rather than the NLHS headed by Souphanouvong.

Geneva Conference A conference of 14 foreign ministers was convened at Geneva on May 16 and the International Control Commission (ICC), created by the 1954 Geneva Conference but long dormant, was reactivated. Convening of the Geneva Conference in the spring of 1961 was a fortuitous development. Had the conference not materialized the United States almost certainly would have undertaken military intervention in Laos with unpredictable international consequences. The

conference met for 13 months before agreement was reached to provide a neutral status for Laos through accommodation among contending internal political factions and through international guarantees to
be monitored by the ICC. During the long period of negotiation
Souvanna Phouma and his shadow government in the small town of
Khang Khay near the Plain of Jars concluded a series of agreements
with the DRV—for economic and cultural cooperation, exchange of
specialists of various sorts and commercial relations—all of which
facilitated uncontrolled and unsupervised access by the Vietnamese to
Laos and to the Kong Le-Pathet Lao forces. One result was a rise in
the number of DRV military personnel on Laotian soil to approximately 5,000 by mid-1961. By early 1962, as the conference in Geneva
dragged on, DRV troop strength in Laos increased further and by May
combined Vietnamese-Pathet Lao forces defeated Phoumi's forces so
severely that Kennedy announced he had ordered U.S. ground and air
units to Udorn, Thailand, at the invitation of the Thai government, in
the event that communist forces, in the wake of their violation of the
ceasefire, crossed the Thai border.

United States objectives at the time of the conference were twofold:
to persuade Thailand to accept neutralization of Laos in return for
U.S. guarantees of Thai security; and to persuade the Phoumist forces
in Vientiane headed by Boun Oum, the neutralist forces of Souvanna
Phouma in Khang Khay, and the NLHS faction of Souphanouvong, to
form a coalition government as a foundation for political neutralism.
But the Phoumists, claiming to be the only legal representatives of
Laos, refused to participate in the conference if the NLHS and
neutralist representatives were also present. Because of this attitude
Laos was not formally represented at the conference for a long period
and actual negotiation among the three Laotian factions about formation of a coalition government took place elsewhere.

Prince Sihanouk of Kampuchea had persuaded the three principal
elements to meet in Zurich in June 1961, but little was accomplished.
Prince Boun Oum and his mentor, General Phoumi, proved the most
recalcitrant of the three, repeatedly declining to meet with Souvanna
Phouma and Souphanouvong until after the United States began to
withhold the monthly cash payment which was essential for the survival of the Vientiane government. The three princes finally held a
series of meetings on the Plain of Jars in early June 1962 and agreed on
the division of portfolios in a coalition government. The eventual
Provisional Government of National Union was headed by Souvanna
Phouma, as prime minister and minister of defense; Souphanouvong
as deputy prime minister and planning minister; and Phoumi as a
second deputy prime minister and finance minister, since it was he
who had been handling the American aid. The remaining portfolios

were apportioned by the mutual agreement of the three factions. Either deputy prime minister could veto a decision in cabinet sessions. The "troika" took office June 24 to begin work to reunify the country.

Emergence of the coalition government permitted Laos to be represented at last by a single delegation at the conference. On July 9 the government made a formal statement of neutrality to the conferees who incorporated it into the "Declaration to Respect the Neutrality of Laos." The Declaration and a Protocol spelling out the duties of the reactivated ICC were signed by the foreign ministers on July 23.

SECOND COALITION GOVERNMENT

Reunification posed many economic and political problems. The two sets of currencies in circulation—the American dollar-backed *kip* issued in Vientiane and the unsupported *kip* issued by Souvanna Phouma—had to be reconciled. Aid agreements had been made by Souvanna Phouma at Khang Khay with the Soviet Union, the DRV and the People's Republic of China (PRC); Boun Oum in Vientiane had made an agreement with the United States. All four agreements were continued. Road construction by the Chinese between Yunnan and northern Laos was disclosed in 1962, as was the construction by the DRV of four separate roads through the Annamite mountains between Vietnam and Laos. Agreements concerning these projects had been concluded by Souvanna Phouma and all were honored by the coalition government, even though the main purpose of the roads was to facilitate movement into Laos by the DRV and the PRC.

According to the mandate of the conference all foreign troops were to be removed from Laos. "American forces, already reduced, were meticulously counted out of the country by the International Control Commission—666 Americans and 403 Filipino technicians."[9] DRV withdrawal totaled only 40 military personnel[10] of the estimated 10,000 in Laos at the time of the creasefire.[11]

The DRV troops were primarily occupying the mountain passes to protect continued use of eastern Laos by the DRV as a corridor for reinforcing the insurgent movement in southern Vietnam—a violation of the 1954 Geneva Conference mandate. The United States, meanwhile, was increasing its commitment to defeat the communists in southern Vietnam. Thus the continued presence of DRV troops in Laos virtually guaranteed continuing U.S. involvement in Laotian affairs and U.S. determination to assure the survival of the new coalition government.

The task of unifying the military forces of the three political factions, as anticipated by the Geneva settlement, proved impossible to accomplish because of the continued intervention of external forces. Before the Geneva settlement was signed all three factions were being assisted from the outside. The "neutral" forces of Kong Le and Souvanna Phouma were supplied by a Soviet airlift. The Pathet Lao or pro-communist forces of Souphanouvong were supplied both by the Soviet Union and by the DRV. Phoumi's forces were supplied by the U.S. economic aid mission.

Since the U.S. mission operated under an agreement with the Royal Government, continued flights by Air America after the Geneva settlement were perfectly legal. However, the Pathet Lao faction in the government complained about Air America, accused the U.S. of obstructing the settlement and charged that the Phoumists had broken the ceasefire.

At this point the Soviets suddenly discontinued their airlift to Kong Le, apparently to appease Hanoi and the Pathet Lao, whose relations with Kong Le's forces on the Plain of Jars were steadily deteriorating. The Soviet action thus reduced the Kong Le forces to utter dependence upon the Pathet Lao and Hanoi for supplies and ammunition for their Russian-made weapons. When the latter deliberately withheld supplies, the position of the Kong Le neutralists—now become centrists—became endangered. Souvanna Phouma appealed for help in providing Kong Le with vitally needed materiel. The Soviets promised an airlift via Hanoi but Hanoi stalled. The United States immediately arranged to supply Kong Le through Air America.

In early 1963 tensions between Kong Le and the Pathet Lao intensified. An intimate of Kong Le was assassinated on February 12, outraging the Kong Le forces; the pro-communist foreign minister of the coalition government, Quinim Pholsena, was assassinated April 1, an act which enraged the Pathet Lao. Full scale fighting between the two military elements broke out.

In Vientiane the coalition government began to fall apart as a result of the fighting. By mid-April NLHS ministers began to disperse to Pathet Lao headquarters at Khang Khay where Souphanouvong had already gone. Prime Minister Souvanna Phouma appealed to the USSR and the UK, which had co-chaired the conference in Geneva, asking them to intervene to end the ceasefire violations. Acting on his request, and despite obstructionist tactics by the Polish representative on the Commission, the ICC sent a team to the Plain of Jars to investigate. As fighting continued the United States announced it was resuming arms and ammunition shipments to Kong Le—for the first time since 1960—at the request of the Royal Government (presumably requested by a Phoumist minister since Souvanna Phouma remained silent). By June Souvanna Phouma was openly condemning the Pathet Lao for its dependence on foreign arms.

Civil War: 1964–1973 Pathet Lao agents began appearing in southern Laos in significant numbers in April and May 1963 and by mid-year 11 Vietnamese battalions of 450 men each were on the Laotian side of the border as part of the DRV force. By 1964 the NLHS was administering nine of Laos' 16 provinces. In April 1964 two Phoumist generals attempted to carry out a coup in Vientiane. They held Souvanna Phouma under house arrest until western diplomats, led by U.S. Ambassador Leonard Unger, reaffirmed western support for Souvanna Phouma, causing the coup to fail. In May U.S. reconnaissance flights over the Plain of Jars resulted in two planes being shot down by the Pathet Lao. The U.S. retaliated with bombardment of Pathet Lao installations by fighter-bombers based in the Republic of Vietnam (RVN). In June the U.S., the UK, Thailand, the RVN and Canada accused the DRV of flagrant violations of the Geneva agreements.

Although NLHS participation in the coalition government ended in a practical sense in 1963, Souvanna Phouma kept open four cabinet posts for the NLHS in the event of their return to the government. Curiously, in the meantime, the NLHS was allowed to maintain a "legation" headquarters in Vientiane. Defying the odds, Souvanna Phouma's regime survived with the support of the Americans and the toleration of the Soviet Union. A new bid to overthrow the government by forces loyal to Phoumi failed in February 1965 and Phoumi, who had become increasingly unpopular for his corrupt financial practices, fled to Thailand. In 1964 heavy Pathlet Lao attacks had driven Kong Le's forces from the Plain of Jars, upsetting him to the point of mental breakdown and his own troops forced him into exile in early 1966.

Withal, the persistent Souvanna Phouma continued to try to maintain the tripartite structure by retaining Souphanouvong as one deputy prime minister and a representative of the right-wing Phoumi group as the other. National Assembly elections were held in July 1965, although the NLHS refused to participate or allow the elections to take place in areas under its control. Nevertheless, Souvanna Phouma continued to allocate cabinet posts among the three factions.

By 1967 the NLHS sulked at its headquarters—now moved to Sam Neua town—lacking vigorous leadership and entirely dependent upon Hanoi for funds and guidance. It again refused to participate in National Assembly elections, called because the king dissolved the assembly after it rejected the government's budget. A majority of the new assembly's 59 members supported Souvanna Phouma, who renewed his condemnation of DRV intervention in Laos but managed to remain on friendly terms with both Moscow and Peking. In 1968, after cessation of U.S. bombing of the DRV and announcement of peace talks in Paris, Souphanouvong and Souvanna Phouma agreed upon integration of the Lao People's Liberation Army—the name given the

Pathet Lao after 1965—with the Royal Army. But integration failed
when Souvanna Phouma refused to request the halt of U.S. bombing
raids in Laos "as long as an estimated forty to fifty thousand Vietminh
troops occupied Laotian territory."[12]

U.S. Bombing   During the long years of civil war in Vietnam the
DRV had developed an intricate system of infiltration routes from
northern Vietnam through southern Laos, thus avoiding the heavily
armed and guarded demilitarized zone. Over half a million DRV troops
had used these paths which became known as the Ho Chi Minh Trail.
In 1965 the U.S. had begun bombing the trail—with the acquiescence
of Souvanna Phouma—to support both Laos and its own operations in
behalf of the Republic of Vietnam (RVN) against the DRV. In late
January 1970 the DRV suddenly sent 13,000 troop reinforcements and
heavy equipment into the Plain of Jars where the Royal Army was
heavily engaged against the People's Liberation Army. U.S. Ambassador G. McMurtrie Godley, fearing a large offensive, requested
Washington to order B-52 bomber strikes against DRV troop concen-
trations in northern Laos. On February 13, after the feared offensive
had begun, Souvanna Phouma made the first of several requests for
such strikes which were finally authorized by Washington for February
17–18, the first by B-52 strategic bombers in Laos other than along the
Ho Chi Minh Trail. The strikes triggered widespread protest in the
United States from the press and Congress, and the administration was
forced to reveal publicly that both the U.S. and the DRV had been
violating the 1962 Geneva accords throughout the presidencies of
Kennedy, Johnson and Nixon.

In 1971 U.S. air operations in Laos conducted by the air force and
navy averaged 340 sorties a day, down from 350 per day in 1970 and
400 per day during most of 1969. B-52 sorties, begun in February 1970,
continued through 1971. These operations were being carried out
against the 39,000-man Lao People's Liberation Army and the 100,000
DRV troops that were estimated to be in Laos after the war in Vietnam
had wound down.[13]

On the ground military ebb and flow became predictable. Each dry
season the People's Liberation Army would commence an offensive
which would gain territory before the beginning of the monsoon in late
May. Fighting would cease in the mud of the rainy season. Government
and Meo and Yeo tribal forces, trained by the Americans, would
counterattack in August at the end of the rains, since superior American transport services made it possible to cope with the rain-damaged
road system as the weather cleared. The counterattacks would lose
momentum before the end of the year and the annual cycle would be
repeated. By 1972 the net seasonal gain had begun to favor the People's
Liberation Army, partly because government forces depended more

heavily on American bombing than on their own fighting skills and initiative. The territory of Laos under Vientiane's control had dwindled to about 25 percent and, except for the irregular revenue from opium traffic along the Burma border, the economy continued to be totally dependent upon United States largesse. In early 1973, with little authority remaining to him, even along the Mekong River, Souvanna Phouma offered to accept 50 percent NLHS participation in the government.

THIRD COALITION GOVERNMENT

On January 30, 1973 the Royal Government proposed a ceasefire to be accompanied by withdrawal of all foreign troops in 90 days, and formation of a new provisional coalition government within 60 days. After almost a month of negotiations, a ceasefire and the Agreement on Restoring Peace and Achieving National Concord was signed on February 21 by Souvanna Phouma for the government and by Souphanouvang for the NLHS. A follow-up protocol providing for machinery to implement the agreement was added in September. Both sides were allocated equal representation within the new provisional government. Both the administrative capital of Vientiane and the royal capital of Luang Prabang were declared neutral areas and negotiating teams from both sides formed a Joint Political Committee whose task was to draw up a constitution and to supervise the transitional period.

The country's third coalition government in 17 years came into operation on April 5, 1974 when King Savang Vatthana in Luang Prabang presided over the investiture of the new government which comprised two principal organs. The National Political Consultative Council (NPCC), headed by Souphanouvong and composed of 16 leftist representatives, 16 rightists and 10 neutralists, was designated as the chief policymaking body. The Cabinet, led by Prime Minister Souvanna Phouma and comprising 10 leftists, 10 rightists and 4 neutralists, was designated to head the administrative branch of government and was answerable to the NPCC.

On April 23 the cabinet approved a 20-point program for national reconciliation which addressed the budget, the timing of withdrawal of foreign troops, foreign policy, repatriation of refugees and the soaring cost of living. On April 24 the 42-member NPCC began its first session under the chairmanship of Souphanouvang; it pledged to respect the throne and to carry out the peace agreement to the benefit of all the Laotian people. On May 22 the cabinet decided not to reconvene the 60-member National Assembly elected in 1972, even though the 1947 constitution under which the government was operating provided that the National Assembly must meet every year from May 11 for five months. The decision was a victory for the NLHS which had not participated in the 1972 elections.

The foreign troop pull-out period expired June 4. The last U.S. military advisers and paramilitary agents of the U.S. Central Intelligence Agency (CIA) departed Vientiane June 3, leaving in Laos only 31 military personnel in the defense attaché's office and 19 marine guards; 9,000 Thai mercenaries who had been employed by the CIA also departed. Some 9,000 to 12,000 Chinese troops who had been building roads in northern Laos reportedly began to withdraw. Only the DRV troops did not comply.[14]

Another opportunity for the NLHS to gain an advantage occurred when Souvanna Phouma, following a heart attack on July 12, departed for France to recuperate, designating NLHS Deputy Premier Phoumi Vongvichit to act in his place, rather than rightist Deputy Premier Leuam Insisiengami. The latter reacted by forming a provisional rightist politburo to consolidate his power; it comprised other rightist ministers who had been in the preceding administration and their advisers. Souvanna Phouma was unable to regain his former role or influence after he returned in November.

Sporadic violence had occurred almost from the inception of the new coalition government. Within a month local military commanders of the Royal Army and the People's Liberation Army were jockeying for better positions. Neither the military forces nor the territories held by each were integrated. In August the People's Liberation forces fired upon a government Joint Peace Committee helicopter.

The economy deteriorated rapidly. By November 1974 prices in Vientiane were 100 percent higher than the previous year. Strikes and social unrest became endemic. In private sector enterprises strikers demanded a general wage increase which the government viewed as inflationary. In the public sector—police, army, telephone, post and electricity services—the outcry was for removal of top officials accused of "abuse of power, incompetence and corruption."[15] Rightists claimed that foreign agitators were behind every demonstration that challenged them, and they blamed the NLHS. The NLHS in response asserted that the People's Liberation Army and the joint police force were needed to provide security and moral support for the strikers. Clashes intensified between the politico-military forces associated with prime Minister Souvanna Phouma (whether termed "rightists," "royalists," "neutralists" or "Vientiane faction") and those of the NLHS. In mid-1974 General Vang Pao, a Meo leader of Vientiane forces on the Plain of Jars, warned that the People's Liberation Army was preparing to isolate Vientiane.

General fighting had broken out in April between Vientiane forces and the People's Liberation Army—backed by DRV troops—in northern, central and southern Laos. It was described by the defense minister as "flagrant violations" of the ceasefire agreement. He asserted that 15,000 DRV troops were confronting the Vientiane forces throughout Laos and that an additional 35,000 Vietnamese were encamped on the Ho Chi Minh Trail.[16] The fighting escalated from company-size engagements in which mortars and rockets were utilized, to battalion-size encounters in which tanks, long range artillery and 122mm rockets were employed.

In March 1975 the king's 12-man Privy Council refused to dissolve the predominantly rightist National Assembly as ordered by the coalition government. The Privy Council was unwilling to endorse dissolution in the absence of firm arrangements for new elections within 90 days. The following month, assured that new elections would be held within the prescribed time, the king dissolved the assembly. In May five right-wing ministers who had been closely identified with U.S. policies resigned under mounting pressures from student groups and left-wing labor organizations. Students stoned the American embassy, hauled down the American flag and demanded U.S. withdrawal from Laos. Simultaneously rightist generals with whom the United States had worked were dismissed.

By the latter part of April, following the capture of Saigon by the communists, the collapse of the Republic of Vietnam, and the victory of the communist Khmer Rouge in Kampuchea, Souvanna Phouma had moved toward the left. He approved deployment of the People's Liberation forces throughout Laos, including principal cities which were once controlled by rightists, and decreed an orderly surrender to the NLHS.

NLHS Takeover   A province by province takeover by the People's Liberation forces followed. Vientiane Province was officially taken on August 26, 1975. The Popular Revolutionary Power (PRP)—the committee formed to manage the government—proclaimed a 10-point program "to serve the real interests of the people and rapidly normalize the situation in the capital." The program sought to "respect the position of King Sri Savang Vatthana, of Premier Souvanna Phouma and of NLHS leader Souphanouvong, the head of the National Political Council."[17]

General elections for a new National Assembly were postponed until 1976 and administrative committees were set up at all levels of government. Within a month Souvanna Phouma and other neutralist office holders were stripped of real power and rightist leaders who had fled to Thailand were condemned to death in absentia. Some 1,500 Soviet technicians replaced the U.S. economic and military aid mission that once numbered 1,000 and was closed June 26, American aid having ended as ordered by the U.S. Congress. In September over 3,000 military officers were shipped to the interior for reeducation and the remainder of the 60,000-man Royal Army was dispersed into labor teams. Virtually every person in the country was obliged to undergo ideological indoctrination through compulsory attendance at reeducation seminars.

LAO PEOPLE'S DEMOCRATIC REPUBLIC

The 700-year old monarchy and the 20-month coalition government were dissolved and the Lao People's Democratic Republic was proclaimed December 3, 1975 following a two-day All-Laos People's Congress in Vientiane. King Savang Vatthana abdicated, saying he was renouncing the throne "to help the country advance favorably." Prime Minister Souvanna Phouma resigned, stating that "the existence of the Provisional Government of National Union is no longer compatible with the situation."[18] A Supreme People's Council was created to be the policy making body of the government with Souphanouvang serving as President of the Council. The cabinet was retained as the chief administrative organ. Kaysone Phomvihane, a hard line, pro-communist, became prime minister. Souphanouvong became chairman and Phomvihane general secretary of the Lao People's Revolutionary Party, the controlling political force within the NLHS. The new People's Republic pointedly renounced political neutrality in favor of an active policy of friendship with communist countries, but it simultaneously called upon the United States to contribute to healing the country's war wounds. The new regime also announced it did not consider itself to be bound by the 1962 Geneva accords.

Almost immediately the People's Republic was beset by problems which impelled it to harsh actions and extreme positions. A substantial resistance movement, centered in the Meo area of northern Laos and in the southern province of Champassak, stronghold of the right-wing Champassak family, undertook a campaign of ambush and sabotage. The anti-communist Revolutionary People's Front for National Liberation and the Committee for Reconquest of the Nation, Religion and Throne combined forces to sabotage the regime's communication lines and military convoys to and from Vietnam.

The communist authorities retaliated. Dusk to dawn curfews were imposed in cities and massive manhunts were undertaken to find saboteurs. By June 1977 some 37,600 persons who had taken part in "reorientation" seminars were reportedly detained in camps indefinitely;[19] In April 1980 Amnesty International reported that between 10,000 and 40,000 persons in Laos had been imprisoned without trial for over five years, and over 100,000 persons had been transplanted to resettlement programs on the Plain of Jars.[20]

"Medicine from the Sky" Special efforts were made to eliminate recalcitrant hill peoples, many of whom had been identified with the United States. In January 1979 the *Hongkong Standard* reported that 1,200 Meo tribesmen were killed by gas when Vietnamese and Laotian planes fired rockets at villagers who had been blockaded inside a communist troop cordon.[21] Other reports of communist use of lethal chemical agents soon appeared: "Laotian tribespeople call it 'medicine from the sky.' Falling as yellow or red or white rain, it causes convulsions, nausea, bleeding from the nose and mouth, and death."[22]

In August 1980 the U.S. Department of State made public a collection of more than 100 reports it received alleging use of Soviet-supplied chemical weapons in Laos, Kampuchea (and Afghanistan), and in a major speech September 12, 1981 U.S. Secretary of State Haig officially stated that the U.S. had "physical evidence" that poisonous chemicals had been used in Indochina. The Department of State reiterated the claim in November, implying that the chemicals came from the Soviet Union.[23] Finally, in a special report to Congress of March 22, 1982, Haig said:

> The U.S. Government has concluded from all the evidence that selected Lao and Vietnamese forces, under direct Soviet supervision, have employed lethal trichothecane toxins and other combinations of chemical agents against H'Mong resisting government control and their villages since at least 1976. Trichothecane toxins have been positively identified, but medical symptoms indicate that irritants, incapacitants, and nerve agents have also been employed. Thousands have been killed or severely injured. Thousands also have been driven from their homeland by use of these agents.[24]

It should be noted, however, the UN corroboration has not been forthcoming.

Sino-Soviet Competition for Influence Sharp Sino-Soviet competition for control of the new communist regime was quickly evident. In March 1976 Prime Minister Phomvihane and a large People's Revolutionary Party delegation were feted in Peking by Premier Hua Kuo-feng and Chairman Mao Tse-tung in one of the latter's last appearances before his death; the Laotian prime minister had just returned from Moscow where he had attended the Soviet Communist Party Congress. Immediately after the Peking visit several Chinese experts arrived in Vientiane to discuss renewal of work on a highway near the Chinese border. But in September Phomvihane was back in Moscow—the second time in five months—to receive from Soviet Communist Party General Secretary Leonid I. Brezhnev a pledge of Soviet "friendship, solidarity and cooperation."[25] Throughout 1977 both the Soviet Union and the Soviet-oriented regime in Vietnam forged close links with Laos. A Laotian economic agreement with the USSR in July was followed the same month by three new accords with Vietnam: a 25-year treaty of friendship and cooperation, a treaty defining the frontier between the two countries, and an agreement on loans and assistance. By 1978 Laos had signed economic accords with all of the Eastern European COMECON countries.

When the regime in 1978 began a program, on the Vietnamese model, of forcing the departure from Laos of ethnic Chinese, it was severely criticized by the PRC. In July Phomvihane declared, in an obvious reference to the PRC, that Laos would stand fast with Vietnam against imperialist aggression. In March 1979 Laos expelled the Chinese technicians in the country and accused the PRC of imperialist designs on Laotian territory. Hostility between Laos and the PRC reached a new height in April 1979 when the Vientiane government requested that the United Nations end "armed threats" by China whose troops allegedly occupied Laotian territory in the north. In a note to UN Secretary General Kurt Waldheim, the government declared that China had continued to mass troops on the border "to help exiled Laotian reactionaries disturb peace and harmony among different ethnic groups."[26] The April note also confirmed for the first time the presence of about 50,000 Vietnamese troops in Laos, stressing that the troops had been requested under the 1977 treaty of friendship and cooperation. On May 9 the Laotian Revolutionary Party newspaper, *Sieng Pasason*, said that the "presence of Vietnamese troops in Laos guaranteed the country's independence, sovereignty and territorial integrity as well as peace, stability and order in Southeast Asia."[27]

Despite the active Soviet-Vietnamese presence in Laos—or perhaps because of the intelligence possibilities it affords—the United States continued to maintain diplomatic relations with that nation, but after 1977 the Laotian government limited the U.S. Embassy staff in Vientiane to 12. The United States operated no economic, cultural or military programs in Laos and American law prohibited U.S. Government assistance to Laos except for humanitarian purposes. The latter was provided from time to time, mostly in the form of rice contributions.

Socialization and Radicalization   Galloping inflation in 1976, combined with failure of the rice crop, led the new regime to nationalize most of the business enterprises of the Indians, Chinese and Vietnamese in Vientiane and to exercise government control over agriculture, although much of the land was allowed to remain in private hands. The slender industrial economy of the country was reorganized into joint state/private enterprises under state control. French-owned tin mining property was nationalized, creating friction with France that led to a break in diplomatic relations between the two nations in 1978.

Some 150,000 persons had fled to Thailand to escape forced integration into the new government's political and social framework in the several years following the communist takeover. Nevertheless in-country resistance drove the government to ever more severe measures. In March 1977 former King Savang Vatthana, Crown Prince Si Savangvong and two other royal family members were suddenly arrested for resistance activities and condemned to death by a special court, but he died, apparently of natural causes, in 1989.

By mid-1978 Vientiane's population had shrunk from 150,000 to 100,000. While forced transfer of persons to upcountry reeducation centers had lessened, compulsory service with rural agricultural cooperatives increasingly produced claims on the population. Adding to the difficulties of transforming Laos into a productive socialist state were the vagaries of weather which seriously diminished agricultural output. The population was forced to subsist on a meager rice ration and a gruel made from wheat which had been donated by the international community; the Laotians were unfamiliar with wheat and did not like it.

In mid-1979 the government suddenly called a halt to the creation of new cooperatives and in December Premier Phomvihane announced the ruling party's "Seventh Resolution," ending forced cooperativization, permitting return to traditional farming methods, encouraging private incentive and easing controls on trade between the Laotian provinces and Thailand.[28] The change of policy occurred because the economy was in shambles, a fact openly admitted by the government. Only half of the 80 saw mills that had operated in 1974 were functioning—in a country where wood is the largest export product and where timber processing accounts for some three-fourths of all industry. At least 250,000 Laotians—about 10 percent of the population—had left the country since the communist takeover, mostly because of economic hardship; the exodus continued during 1980 at the rate of 1,000 per month.[29]

The years since then have been marked by a lessening of economic problems, mainly a consequence of assistance from external sources. In 1981 Moscow and Vientiane entered into a long-term economic aid agreement; the Asian Development Bank lent Laos US$41.1 million to fund socio-economic projects, including a low interest loan for electrification and support for the Nam Ngum hydropower project; and the small UN development program continued. Stepped up agricultural collectivization was announced for 1984 in the wake of a 1983 drought that caused a temporary food shortage.

By mid-1981 Laos and Thailand began seriously to discuss keeping open the Mekong River border, (previously often closed in the wake of cross-river shooting incidents) which is vital to landlocked Laos as an import-export route, and in 1982, the Laotian government indicated it would shed its "hermit state" image, allowing tourists into the country under closely controlled circumstances to earn much needed foreign exchange.

Politics   Factions soon surfaced within the Laotian leadership, apparently along nationalist/internationalist lines. Premier Phomvihane and Deputy Premier Nouhak Phoumsavan led the "international wing," distinguished by its close ties with Vietnam and the Soviet Union. The "nationalist" group included Souphanouvong, Phoumi Vongvichit, Khamouan Boupha and the 60 percent of Laotian officials who served in former non-communist governments. The latter, relatively unfamiliar with Soviet administrative procedures, reportedly had displeased the approximately 2,000 Russian advisers in the country who were "very relentless in setting conditions about the use of their aid."[30]

Nevertheless, unlike the internal conflict which characterized Kampuchea throughout the 1980s, politics in Laos were surprisingly stable. Kaysone Phoumvihane retained his twofold position as premier and general secretary of the LPRP throughout the decade. He gradually modified his tough Pathet Lao stance and led the party toward moderation. In 1989 he stressed Laos' "new way of thinking," defined as cooperation with any country, regardless of ideology.[31] Old guard member and acting President Phoumi Vongvichit, maintaining his nationalism-first posture, lent support to Kaysone's "creative model" of socialism which was reflected in the Second Five Year Plan (1986–90) set forth at the Fourth Party Congress in 1986.[32] The new course in economic policy sought elimination of state-subsidized bureaucratic management and devolution of authority in tandem with similar policy adoption in Vietnam.

In 1988, at the first elections since the party's accession to power in 1975, district and provincial committees were chosen. The Supreme People's Council was expanded from 45 to 79 representatives and authorized to: 1) write a constitution and "necessary laws," 2) elect the chairman of the Council, 3) propose changes in the structure of government, and oversee government activity. In March 1989 an estimated 1.8 million citizens voted to choose the 79 members of the new National Assembly which, in turn, was charged with ratifying the new constitution.[33]

A non-communist resistance movement, the United Lao National Liberation Front (ULNLF), headed by exiled General Phoumi Nosovan, emerged in the early 1980s but achieved little progress. Phoumi died in 1986 and the ULNLF apparently resorted to terrorism. It was blamed for a bomb blast at the Soviet Cultural Center in 1987 which coincided with the visit of Soviet Foreign Minister Shevardnadze. Exiled General Vang Pao's hill tribe guerrillas, who opposed the communist government, centered their activities in the Hmong villages of northern Vientiane province.

Foreign Affairs   Lao relationships within the international community began to improve in the late 1980s. The Thai-Laotian armed border conflict of 1987 ended with a truce in 1988 and significant economic cooperation between the two states ensued. China and Laos agreed in 1988 to exchange ambassadors after a 10 year interim, and trade negotiations began. Also, during 1987–88 and after 35 years of military presence, Vietnam withdrew half its estimated 40,000 troops. Relations with the United States improved. The U.S. continued humanitarian aid, deleted the country from the list of nations ineligible for official bilateral assistance, and the two states agreed to cooperate concerning American MIAs (missing in action) and narcotics control. However, the U.S. imposed new assistance restrictions in March 1989, charging that Lao opium production continued to expand. A proposed "Lao-Pacific Airline," a venture between Laos and Brunei, was announced in January 1989. The project was expected to involve participation of foreign investors from 16 countries.[34]

WHITHER LAOS?

Laos is economically dependent upon its neighbors. It is landlocked and thus depends upon the aquiescence of Thailand for supply and/or transhipment of 90 percent of its required imports. Its population comprises some 68 diverse ethnic groups, a condition which guarantees difficulty in achieving national integration. Laos is also a captive of the political agendas of its neighbors. Their agendas, in turn, are conditioned by the policy objectives of China and, since 1945, the Soviet Union. Withdrawal of Vietnamese troops from Laos, resumption of diplomatic relations with China, reduced ideological fervor and trends toward a market-oriented socialism all coincide with political and economic change beyond the borders of Laos. Its future will take whatever form the larger players decide.

FOOTNOTES

1. Frank M. LeBar and Adrienne Suddard, eds., *Area Handbook for Laos* (New Haven, Conn.: Human Relations Area Files Press, 1972), p. 13.

2. Quoted by Arthur J. Dommen, *Conflict in Laos* (N.Y.: Praeger, 1965), p. 38.

3. Dommen, *op. cit.*, p. 70.

4. *Ibid.*, p. 83.

5. Hugh Toye, *Laos: Buffer State or Battleground* (London: Oxford University Press, 1968), p. 141.

6. Quoted by Toye, *op. cit.*, p. 147.

7. Dommen, *op. cit.*, p. 154.

8. *Ibid.*, p. 160.

9. Toye, *op. cit.*, p. 187.

10. Henry A. Kissinger, *White House Years* (Boston: Little Brown and Co., 1979), p. 450.

11. Dommen, *op. cit.*, p. 240.

12. John F. Cady, *The History of Post-War Southeast Asia* (Athens, Ohio: Ohio University Press, 1974), p. 414.

13. LeBar, *op. cit.*, p. 282.

14. *Data for Decision* (Manila: Press Foundation of Asia), 1974, p. 1960.

15. *Data Asia* (Manila: Press Foundation of Asia), 1975, p. 2375.

16. *Ibid.*, p. 2821.

17. *Ibid.*, p. 3282.

18. *Ibid.*, p. 3409.

19. *Ibid.*, 1977, p. 4709.

20. *Ibid.*, 1980, p. 6982.

21. *Ibid.*, 1979, p. 5989.

22. Jim Leach, "Medicine from the Sky," *Foreign Service Journal*, January 1981, p. 16.

23. Text of speech reproduced in the *New York Times,* September 14, 1981; see also U.S. Department of State *Current Policy No. 342,* November 10, 1981.

24. U.S. Department of State, *Special Report No. 98,* "Chemical Warfare in Southeast Asia and Afghanistan," Report to the Congress from Secretary of State Alexander M. Haig, Jr., March 22, 1982.

25. *Data Asia, op. cit.,* 1976, p. 4033.

26. *Ibid.*, 1979, p. 6229.

27. *Ibid.*

28. John Burgess, "Laos Regime Slows Collectivization," *Los Angeles Times,* December 19, 1980.

29. *Data Asia, op. cit.,* 1980, p. 7429.

30. *Asia Record* (Palo Alto, Calif.: Asia-Pacific Affairs Associates), December 1982, p. 26.

31. "Enticing Investors," *Far Eastern Economic Review,* April 13, 1989, p. 32.

32. Geoffrey C. Gunn, "Laos in 1987," *Southeast Asian Affairs 1988,* p. 139.

33. *Asia Yearbook 1989,* p. 158; see also *Indochina Chronology (Berkeley Institute of East Asian Studies),* January–March 1989, p. 12.

34. *Indochina Chronology, op. cit.,* p. 11.

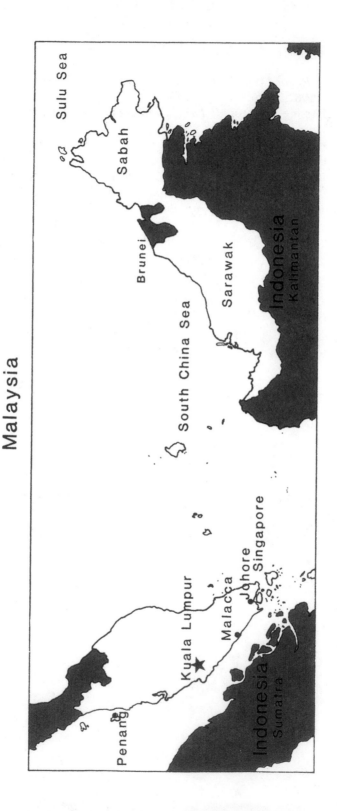

CHAPTER 5
MALAYSIA

Malayasia is a nation of two parts, Peninsular Malaysia (consisting of the 11 states of Johore, Kedah, Kelantan, Malacca, Negri Sembilan, Pahang, Penang, Perlis, Perak, Selangor and Trengganu) which occupies roughly the southern third of the Malay peninsula; and East Malaysia (Sabah and Sarawak) on the northwestern coast of the island of Borneo. The two sections are separated by 400 miles of South China Sea.

Peninsular Malaysia is bounded on the north by Thailand and on the west by the Strait of Malacca which separates that nation from the Indonesian island of Sumatra; the strait has long been a major sea route between India and China. On the south Malaysia is separated from Singapore by the Johore Strait which is only one-half mile at its narrowest and spanned by a causeway. On the east Peninsular Malaysia is separated by the South China Sea from the East Malaysian states of Sarawak and Sabah. The latter share the island of Borneo with the tiny coastal nation of Brunei and the large Indonesian state of Kalimantan. To the north of Borneo lies the Philippine archipelago.

The Malay peninsula consists of steep forest-covered mountains and narrow coastal plains with few bays or harbors. East Malaysia also has a mountainous interior, with an often swampy coastal plain drained by numerous rivers. Both regions were originally settled by the Proto-Malay, but in Peninsular Malaya the Deutero-Malay pushed the Proto-Malay into the jungles and mountains, as the latter had earlier displaced the aboriginal Negritos. The Deutero-Malay are those known today as Malays and are the main population stock of Peninsular Malaya; the Proto-Malay are the largest racial group in Borneo.

In this discussion the term Malaya will be used when it applies to the peninsula alone, Malaysia when referring to both areas or when it refers to the modern state.

PRE-BRITISH MALAYSIA

Throughout the centuries the peoples of Malaysia were influenced by Indian trade and missionary activity, and by contact with the Indianized states of Southeast Asia. Around 200 A.D. Funan, the first great Southeast Asian empire, extended its control over the northern part of Malaya from its capital in the Mekong River delta of Indochina. Funan was supplanted in 627 by Chenla, but the center of political influence over the peninsula soon shifted from the Mekong delta to Sumatra where the Srivijaya kingdom ruled from Palembang.

By the end of the 8th century the Indianized Mahayana-Buddhist kingdom of Srivijaya controlled both the Malay peninsula and the west coast of Borneo, commanding the waters on both sides of the peninsula. By so doing it was able to curtail piracy, traditionally a hazard to shipping in these seas and straits, and trade among China, India and the west flourished. As Srivijaya declined during the course of the 13th century its influence on the peninsula was replaced by that of the Theravada Buddhist kingdom of Thailand, centered at Sukhothai and later Ayutthia; and in Borneo by the Hindu state of Majapahit of Java. However, throughout this period Malaysia was at the edge of empire and the peninsula in particular remained rural and isolated from the mainstream of Southeast Asian life.

Kingdom of Malacca The first kingdom centered on the Malay peninsula was the Kingdom of Malacca, founded by a rebel Sumatran prince whose name—or title—was Parameswara. He established himself and his followers in Malacca, a fishing village with a small harbor on the narrow middle portion of the Strait of Malacca, and gained control of the strait and the trade that passed through it. He went on to conquer the interior of the peninsula which at the time owed nominal vassalage to Thailand or to Sumatra.

From its beginning Malacca comprised a mélange of peoples: the indigenous Malays; Javanese mercenaries and shipwrights; Sumatran rulers and immigrants; Chinese merchants; and Indian, Arab and Persian traders. Islam and Islamic institutions early began to replace Hinduism and Buddhism in the kingdom as merchant-converts from south India and Gujerat (west India) spread their new faith. Since they were traders and not missionaries, and Islam had come to them in diluted form through Persian and Turkish conquerors of India, the faith they introduced into Malaya lived tolerantly with older Hindu, Buddhist and animist customs, and was quickly accepted by the ruling class. By 1450 Islam had become broadly accepted, and Arabic numerals, alphabet and script adopted.

Since Malacca controlled the main sea route between India and China it soon became a major world entrepot. The city had a population of 40,000 by the middle of the 15th century, with separate quarters for members of the various foreign trade communities. Except for the ruling elite, the indigenous Malay were not integrated into the city's life, but remained farmers and fishermen. Malacca was, as were later Malayan entrepots, a foreign enclave in a rural Malay society.

Symbols and traditions which still pertain to Malayan royalty were developed at that time and spread to other courts on the peninsula. The king, who adopted the Muslim title of sultan, formally possessed absolute power and owned all land. The actual ruler for most of the century, however, was not the sultan but his chief adviser, the *bendahara*. The greatest of these was Tun Perak who ruled for kings and princelings from 1456 to 1498.

During the 15th century the Sultanate of Brunei on Borneo was also in the ascendency. The present dynasty came into power at the same time Parameswara was consolidating his power in Malacca. Brunei extended its sway over all of present day Sabah and Sarawak and by the time the Europeans appeared on the scene it controlled much of Borneo, the Sulu archipelago and neighboring islands. Trade with Malacca was extensive and after Malacca fell to the Portuguese Brunei became a haven for many of that kingdom's refugees.

Portuguese Malacca   Portuguese navigators were the first Europeans to find a route to the East by sailing around Africa. Their assault on Malacca was part of a concerted plan to gain access to the spice trade of the East Indies, and to deny it to the Arab traders who had long controlled the traffic. Profit seeking was accompanied by missionary zeal. In Portuguese eyes eastern expansion was a continuation of the Crusades and of the centuries-old Christian attempt to drive the Moors from Europe and to throw off the economic shackles imposed on Christian Europe by Muslim control of the Mediterranean.

The capture of Malacca by the Portuguese in 1511 caused the rapid decline of the Kingdom of Malacca. Sultan Mahmud fled to the south and eventually established his court on the small island of Bintan, south of Singapore. He remained as nominal ruler of the rest of the peninsula but the countryside was rural and poor; Malacca, which controlled the strait, was the only center of trade and wealth.

Mahmud repeatedly tried to retake Malacca, but the Portuguese fortified the city so well that it withstood all assaults for the next hundred years. The Portuguese, however, counterattacked and destroyed Bintan in 1526. The sons of Mahmud eventually established small fiefdoms on the peninsula—in Perak in the northeast and in Johore in the south—and the Sultanate of Johore became the Malay successor state to the Kingdom of Malacca.

The Portuguese never tried to conquer the peninsula. Their tactics worldwide were to control the sea and a few key ports. In this respect they were similar to the Malay kingdoms which they succeeded and with which they were in competition—all were sea empires, trading or raiding from and between isolated commercial centers. The influence of the Portuguese on the Malays of the peninsula outside Malacca was minimal and never friendly. With the Kingdom of Brunei, however, Portugal maintained cordial relations and the two signed a commercial treaty in 1526 which permitted Portugal to build a factory on Borneo. Brunei as well as Portugal prospered. Portugal maintained its seaport fortresses and control of the sea lanes for a century, but possessed neither the manpower nor the resources to maintain its far-flung conquests in the face of the Dutch challenge of the 17th century.

Dutch Malacca   The Dutch, with the assistance of Johore, besieged Malacca in 1640–41, taking the city after a six month siege and great loss of life on both sides due to disease. The Dutch took Malacca, not because they desired it as an entrepot (they had developed a new route further south—around Africa and through the Sunda Strait—which gave quicker access from Europe to the spice islands, China and Japan) but to prevent others from so using it. They therefore purposely neglected the city and made little effort to control other parts of the peninsula, except for a partially successful attempt to monoplize the tin trade of Perak.

Dutch disinterest permitted the Sultanate of Johore to grow in strength. The capital was returned to the mainland and much of the peninsula and parts of Sumatra were recaptured. Like other Malay empires, however, the sultanate was a lightly held feudal kingdom; chieftains paid tribute and had military responsibilities to the center but were absolute rulers in their own territories. At the end of the 17th century the sultan made a decision that influenced Malay peninsular politics for the next hundred years: he hired Bugis—Malays from Celebes Island, east of Borneo—to staff his army. The Bugis soon achieved primary influence at court. They legitimized their position in 1722 by creating and holding the office of under-king (*yang di pertuan muda*) whose occupant became the actual ruler, and they used but neglected the Johore sultanate in order to conquer the rest of the peninsula.

By the time the British made a serious appearance on the Malayan scene in the 19th century the states of Kedah (which included Perlis) in the northwest, and Kelantan and Trengganu in the northeast, were nominally under the suzerainty of Thailand; Selangor had a Bugis dynasty, and Perak was independent but under pressure alternately from Kedah and Selangor. The mini-states in the interior behind Malacca were forming themselves into what would become the state of Negri Sembilan, and Pahang on the east coast was nominally vassal to Johore; Malacca remained Dutch.

POLITICAL INDICATORS

1. Throughout history the foreigner—Sumatran, Javanese, Indian, Arab, Chinese, Bugis, Portuguese and Dutch—controlled the commerce and trade of Malacca, which in turn controlled the Strait of Malacca and thus the peninsula's contact with the outside world. The indigenous Malays, with the exception of the ruling class, continued as farmers and fishermen, living in small villages along the coasts and inland rivers, little touched by urban life.
2. The ruling elite remained Malay—whether indigenous Malay, Javanese, Sumatran or Bugis—except in Malacca.
3. In Malaysia political and cultural maturation occurred later than in most of the other states of Southeast Asia and much of the peninsula was not effectively brought into the mainstream of Southeast Asian life until the European period.
4. Brunei, which included today's Sabah and Sarawak, developed a more sophisticated Malay commercial life than did the peninsula, and was in contact with, but politically separate from, the peninsula. It was not conquered, or controlled for any period of time, by other Asian or European powers prior to the 19th century.
5. Islam came early and easily to Malaysia because court and urban life were late in developing and there was no strong Hindu or Buddhist culture in place. The Islam introduced was a modified Indianized form that tolerated rather than excluded earlier religious and secular customs.
6. The powerful political offices of *bendahara* and *yang di pertuan muda,* which developed early, enabled their occupants to rule while the sultans reigned, a tradition that prepared the sultans for their roles in the British residency system.
7. Inter-area contacts, Malay and foreign, were by sea rather than by land, and empires were sea-empires.
8. The Malay-ruled states of present day Malaysia had evolved on the peninsula by the time of the arrival of the British.

BRITISH STRAITS SETTLEMENTS

British interest in the peninsula was motivated by need for a naval base on the eastern side of the Bay of Bengal to protect British India and Britain's extremely valuable India/China trade. Of lesser concern was the procurement of Malayan tin for the Far Eastern markets.

Penang   On behalf of the English East India Company (which had been formed in 1600) Francis Light in 1780 negotiated with the sultan of Kedah for rights to Penang, an island at the northeastern entrance to the Malacca Strait. In a treaty signed in 1791 the company agreed to pay US$6,000 a year for the use of the island, but disavowed Light's promise to help Kedah against attackers—establishing a precedent which was followed by Britain for the next century. In 1800 the company bought a piece of land on the mainland opposite and named it Province Wellesley in honor of the then governor general of India, i.e., the governor of the English East India Company and ipso facto the ruler of British India. The two territories were incorporated as Penang and became in 1805 the fourth presidency of India, taking its place with Bombay, Calcutta and Madras as the major adminstrative units of the East India Company. This organizational arrangement was indicative of British hopes to develop the area. Penang, however, failed to become either an economic or military asset. The Strait of Malacca had slipped to secondary importance; when it regained primacy after the opening of the Suez Canal and the elimination of the long voyage around Africa, Singapore, at the southern end of the strait, became the major British naval and commercial base.

Malacca Wars in Europe at the end of the 18th century brought Malacca temporarily under British control. The French Revolutionary Army's occupation of the Netherlands caused the Dutch to assign their East Indies possessions to British protective custody. On this authority Britain occupied Malacca and, to prevent it being a threat to Penang in the future, began systematically to dismantle its great fortress. Malacca was returned to Holland in 1818 but Dutch repossession was brief.

Singapore In 1819 Sir Stamford Raffles signed a treaty, on behalf of the East India Company, with two Malay leaders, the territorial chieftain and a pretender to the throne of Johore whom Raffles recognized as sultan on his own authority, even though the British government had acknowledged his brother. The treaty gave possession of Singapore Island to the company in return for annual cash payments to the two signators. The Dutch protested Raffles' action. While the British and the Dutch debated the issue, with the British government inclined to demand Raffles' withdrawal, Singapore boomed. By 1824 when the two governments signed the Treaty of London, Singapore's trade was already more than twice that of Penang and eight to ten times that of Malacca.

Institutionalization of the Straits Settlements The Treaty of London was a milestone in Malasian history, institutionalizing what became the British Straits Settlements and laying the framework for British Malaya. In the treaty the British and Dutch agreed that all territories to the south and west of a line drawn down the Strait of Malacca would be Dutch; all territories to the north and east would be British. The Dutch thereby recognized Singapore as British and exchanged Malacca for a British possession on Sumatra. The effects of the treaty were several. The three territories to become the Straits Settlements—Penang, Malacca and Singapore—were now firmly in British hands; Britain's trade route to China was secure; the peninsula was removed from the European power struggle; and Sumatra, which had long played a role on the peninsula, was now within the Dutch sphere of influence and constrained from involving itself in Malaya. Lastly, the sultan of Johore, whose capital was (again) on a southern island in the Dutch zone, was cut off from his mainland domains which were within the British sphere of influence; these territories soon fell under the control of other members of the sultan's family. Also in 1824 the East India Company signed a second treaty with the territorial chieftain and the sultan-pretender which ceded the island of Singapore permanently to the British.

In 1826 an act of parliament placed the three Straits Settlements under the English East India Company and in 1829 they were downgraded from a presidency to a residency under the Calcutta Presidency. Three years later the administrative headquarters were removed from Penang to Singapore, but the residency was still governed from India.

One result of the administrative relationship with India was that the British, like the Portuguese and Dutch before them, restricted themselves to the three port towns, displaying little desire to become involved in the interior. They considered the ports of value strictly as collection, distribution and provisioning stations in the India-China trade; there was no peninsula trade. Moreover, since the Straits Settlements was an economic drain on the British Indian government—with only Singapore meeting its own administrative costs—any additional territorial acquisition was seen by the government of India as a further financial burden. British policy during the next forty years therefore remained a policy of non-interference and non-involvement in peninsular affairs; with two minor exceptions Malay-Malaya remained free of foreign intervention until 1867.

During this period Singapore prospered and its population increased from 5,000 in 1820 to more than 80,000 by 1860; a preponderance of the new inhabitants were Chinese. The city developed into a banking and insurance center, as adjunct to its position as a world entrepot. After 1842, however, Hong Kong and Canton on the China coast began to displace Singapore as a distribution center, which became more and more a coaling and provisioning way-stop. Its decline was halted by the opening in 1869 of the Suez Canal, an action that resulted in a restructuring of trade routes. The Strait of Malacca once more became the primary artery to the Far East.

Chinese in Malaya   Until the middle of the 19th century peninsular Malaya remained a rural, feudal Malay society. Malays, either indigenous or from Sumatra and Celebes, formed the main racial stock. Society was hierarchical, comprising aristocratic landowners, and peasant agriculturists who were bound to the land by custom, preference or debt-slavery. The picture changed dramatically when tin became a major item in international commerce and the tin mines of Malaya proved of immense value. The landowners, who did not themselves engage in industry except to tax it, encouraged Straits Settlements Chinese and Europeans to operate the mines and to import vast numbers of Chinese laborers to work them. The workers, who came primarily from southern China to escape the consequences of overpopulation and political repression, were indentured for a year to repay their passage money. Without families they lived in large, unassimilated communities, organized and manipulated by the notorious secret societies which accompanied them from China. These societies sought to exploit their members as well as to protect them. They fought among themselves for control of the mines, enforced their own laws, ignoring or rejecting local laws, and became a danger to the peace of the countryside. Since the societies were also entrenched in the towns, the riots they incited at the mines resulted in riots in the Straits Settlements. To prevent lawlessness in the Settlements the British ultimately were forced to take action on the peninsula itself.

BRITISH MALAYA

Tin mining not only led to the introduction of the disruptive secret societies and of the ethnic Chinese who would later pose a serious political problem, it also led to a breakdown in the old feudal relationships among the territorial chiefs and the sultans. The chiefs who owned mines had greater wealth and power than the sultans whom they nominally served. Resultant dissensions led to civil war in Selangor, a succession dispute in Perak and a quarrel in the small but important tin mining state of Sungei Ujong. The Straits merchants—British and Chinese—stood to lose much if these disorders were allowed to continue and they pressured the British government to act. Britain in turn was apprehensive about possible French or German expansion onto the peninsula. The new governor in Singapore, Sir Andrew Clarke, largely on his own authority, decisively intervened. The result was to establish the British government as the mediator in disputes between, and within, heretofore independent states, and to develop the British residency system (1874) in Malaya. Under this system the sultans were required to accept British residents at their courts whose advice they were supposed to seek in all matters other than religion and custom. The last thing the British wanted, however, was outright annexation of Malay territory. Experience in India and

Burma in the 19th century had demonstrated the problems of direct rule.

By 1889 British residents, responsible to the governor general in Singapore, had been provided under treaty arrangement to the states of Perak, Pahang, Selangor and Negri Sembilan—the last comprising the numerous small chieftainates in the central interior, including Sungei Ujong. In all the states the residents insisted the tax on tin be used for infrastructure and general welfare, instead of to enrich chieftains and sultans as previously. Thus the former absolute rulers became, in essence, salaried officials. State councils were established to discuss policy. Composed of the sultan, his major chiefs, one or two Chinese and the resident, they were used by the resident as a forum to win adherents to the policies he advocated. These policies, too, further undermined the position of the sultan.

The residency system worked well to insure peace and order and a degree of modernization, but the system was flawed: residents were becoming independent, bypassing the rulers and the state councils in their desire to achieve goals, and states were developing differing laws and land and tax policies. Both the residents and the Straits government recognized the need for the states to form common policies and to cooperate, especially in developing transportation and communication systems.

Federated Malay States   In 1895 Johore accepted a British protectorate arrangement and in the same year the Federation of the States of Perak, Negri Sembilan, Pahang and Selangor was proclaimed. Kuala Lumpur, the new and modern capital of Selangor, became the federal capital. This was the first time since the Kingdom of Malacca in the 15th century that the central states of Malaya had achieved such a measure of unity. At the Rulers' Conference held two years later the sultans of the four states met for the first time.

The Rulers' Conference of 1897 set the pattern for the development of modern Malaysia. The conference agreed to the appointment of a resident general who would reside at Kuala Lumpur and who would coordinate policy and supervise the various residents. The purpose of the conference was to increase the power of the rulers vis-a-vis the residents, but the result was that the rulers became almost powerless because the conference had failed to distinguish between the powers of the states and those of the federal government. This permitted the central power in Kuala Lumpur to increase to the point that the federation became a de facto union. Moreover as state governments expanded and became more complex, the number of federal departments to oversee the activities increased; the power to coordinate became the power to initiate and direct. In addition, since the emphasis on economic growth required a mindset and an expertise that the indigenous Malay administrators lacked, the unified civil service, agreed to at the conference, increasingly became a British civil service.

By 1909 when a Federal Council was established—which included the governor of the Straits Settlements as council president, the resident general, the four residents and the four sultans—the sultans had essentially exchanged roles with the residents: they were now the advisors rather than the advised. Nevertheless the authority structure was not entirely undesired by the sultans who reflected a history of delegated authority, and whose offices and incomes were assured while their ceremonial perquisites were actually enhanced. As the Federal Council assumed increasing legislative authority, the real governing power continued to lie with the governor in Singapore and the resident general in Kuala Lumpur.

Unfederated States   Throughout the 19th century the British endeavored to maintain good relations with Thailand in order to limit French influence in Southeast Asia, and in the latter decades, to prevent the establishment of French, German or possible American bases on the east coast of the Malay peninsula or on its offshore islands. In consequence Britain had acknowledged Thai suzerainty over the northern Malay states of Perlis, Kedah, Trengganu and Kelantan, despite Malay resistance.

By the beginning of the 20th century the European pattern of alliances was changing as was the British role on the peninsula. In 1902 and 1905 Thailand was forced to acknowledge British interests in the northern tier states and to appoint British advisers—in the employ of the Thai government—to their courts to supervise foreign affairs. In 1909, under terms of the Anglo-Siamese treaty of that year, Thailand relinquished all claims to suzerainty and recognized a British protectorate over the area.

Noting the centralization of authority within the federation, the sultans of the four northern states declined to join it, although they accepted British residents at their courts. Johore in 1914 accepted a British adviser but maintained the relationship spelled out in the 1895 protectorship agreement.

Thus at the beginning of World War I the contemporary boundaries of Peninsular Malaysia had been established and Britain had extended its control, directly or indirectly, over the whole peninsula. The five unfederated states were under British protection and indirect rule on an individual basis. They had little in common among themselves but their relationship with the British. They remained more Malay, less westernized, dependent on their own sources of revenue, and with more Malays and fewer British in their administrative services than the Federated States. In the Federated Malay States British power was exercised, presumably indirectly, but actually directly, through the resident general in Kuala Lumpur who was subject to the high commissioner, the governor in Singapore. British rule over the Straits Settlements, carried out by a governor and the resident commissioners in each settlement, was direct and absolute. Persons born in the Settlements were British subjects and citizens.

BRITISH BORNEO

Conditions in Brunei began to decline in the mid-17th century when trade routes shifted and the Dutch instituted a monopoly of trade in the Indonesian archipelago. The process was accelerated in the 19th. The capital city of Brunei shrank from 40,000 inhabitants in 1730 to little more than a very large village by the 1840s. The sultan of the Sulu archipelago to the north occupied Sabah, and the province of Sarawak in the south was in rebellion. At this point James Brooke, an Englishman of substance who had been in the army of the English East India Company, inadvertently became involved in Brunein affairs.

Visiting Sarawak at the request of Singapore merchants, Brooke was offered the governorship of the province by the local raja (chieftain) in return for his aid in putting down the revolt. He was confirmed in this office by the sultan in 1842. He first undertook to control piracy, which was rampant, and incorporated (with the sultan's grudging approval) the pirate bases he seized into this fiefdom. In 1863 he returned to England, bestowing Sarawak, which by this time included most of southern Brunei, on his nephew, Charles Brooke. The following year the British government recognized Sarawak as an independent entity under the rule of the Brookes, but vassal to Brunei.

Sabah came into British hands in a similarly unplanned fashion, although the British government had held the Sabahan island of Labuan as a crown colony since 1847. In 1865 an American adventurer secured title to the mainland of Sabah from the sultan of Brunei in return for annual payments. The title changed hands several times, eventually coming into the possession of Dent Brothers, a British company in Hong Kong, that concluded further agreements with the sultan of Brunei to whom the territory belonged by law, and the sultan of Sulu who held it in fact. Dent Brothers in 1881 obtained a Royal Charter from the British government creating the British North Borneo Company and giving it administrative control over Sabah, with provisions that the company would make facilities available to the British navy, would not interfere with the religion or customs of the area, and would not transfer the territory without British government permission.

Seven years later (1888) the British government declared a protectorate over North Borneo (as Sabah was now called), Sarawak, and what was left of the Kingdom of Brunei. The governor of the Straits Settlements became High Commissioner of the Borneo States. Agreements were reached in the next few years with Spain, which recognized British rights to North Borneo in return for British recognition of Spanish claims to the Sulu archipelago; and with Holland, defining the boundaries of North Borneo and Dutch Borneo.

MALAYSIA BETWEEN THE WARS

Economy   Rubber had begun to compete with tin as the major income earner on the peninsula at the turn of the century and by 1920 Malayan rubber accounted for 53 percent of the world total. It was heavily planted in the Federated States and Johore by small landholders, as well as on plantations where it was worked by Tamil laborers imported in large numbers from south India. By 1921 Indians constituted 14 percent of the population of the peninsula, but were transient, with about two-thirds as many leaving annually as entering.

Rubber and tin prices dipped in the post World War I slump, and both dropped disastrously during the worldwide depression of the 1930s. The weakness of the Malayan economy was evident: it relied upon two raw materials, the demand for which, and therefore the price, was determined elsewhere. It also became evident that both the rubber and tin industries were uneconomically structured: they were labor-intensive, administratively top-heavy and in need of modernization.

Sabah and Sarawak were more diversified, with rubber, timber, pepper and copra the major money earners, and were under- rather than over-populated. Thus they were not faced with the unemployment problems that led to the restrictive immigration ordinances of 1928 and 1930 in the Straits Settlements and Federated States which were aimed at Chinese and Indian labor. However, by 1937 Sabah found it necessary to restrict Chinese immigration, which had increased in the intervening years in the wake of revolution and war in China.

Peninsular Politics   Declining prices for their products in the 1920s made the sultans of the Federated States increasingly aware that they had traded political power for economic prosperity, and now the latter was disappearing. Moreover, the unfederated states, whose economies had been less developed and therefore less dependent upon world trade, were growing stronger. At the same time the British government recognized that the eventual goals for Malaya should be decentralization of administration and union between the federated and unfederated states.

In 1924 and 1925 the government attempted to address these issues, but opposition from the British and Chinese business communities succeeded in limiting the decentralization of revenue control and in retaining legislative power in the Federal Council in Kuala Lumpur which enacted the laws for all four states. Again in the early 1930s the high commissioner for the federation, Sir Cecil Clementi, called for a decentralization of all departments except those such as customs, immigration and railways, and for the further subordination of the chief secretary to the residents who were to have powers similar to those of the advisers in the unfederated states. Clementi's attempts to decentralize the federated and move toward union with the unfederated states were opposed by the Chinese community, Singapore and the unfederated states. The Chinese and Singapore feared a policy of Malayization; the unfederated states feared a loss of independence.

The Chinese were justified in their assumption. The high commissioner's effort to reorganize the governmental structure was precipitated by the fact that in 1931, for the first time, ethnic minorities in British Malaya outnumbered Malays. The Chinese, by far the largest minority, had become a settled community and were demanding the rights of residence and citizenship. The British Colonial Office viewed decentralization as the only means to prevent the Malay from being overwhelmed. Actual steps taken at this time were more limited than their proposer hoped, but the state councils were strengthened.

The several educational systems in Malaya contributed to the political problems besetting the country. Because the Chinese had earlier been considered transient, they had been left to provide their own social and educational institutions. The result was their schools reinforced Chinese ethnicity, language and customs. In the 1920s and 1930s they also began to propagate anti-imperialist doctrines current in China—including virulent anti-British Chinese nationalism, and the pro-communist ideas of the left wing of the Kuomintang (KMT), the revolutionary party in power.

Concurrently the British had encouraged the Malay to maintain their own religious-language schools. Education of the preponderantly rural Malay in the traditional manner, failed to prepare them for leadership positions in a modernizing society. Only the few English-language schools located in cities attempted to do so. In consequence, Malayan society was divided racially and linguistically, and between the rural and urban and the traditional and modern.

Nationalism Nationalism in Malaya—in sharp contrast to other emerging Southeast Asian nations—was delayed for two major reasons. First, the British had brought together a splintered multi-racial society and had done so with a minimum of governmental coercion, leaving the sultans as physical Malay symbols of common language, religion and custom. Second, the British brought productivity and

prosperity to the region, especially with the expansion of the rubber
industry in the 20th century.

The Chinese in Malaya were the first to develop political awareness,
a spin-off in the 1920s from the revolution raging in China. The Malaya-
based branch of the Chinese KMT, heavily influenced by the pro-
communist wing of the party, advocated communism and anti-coloni-
alism in Malaya rather than Malayan nationalism. In 1930, after the
KMT in China broke with the communists, the Comintern (Communist
International) organized the Malay Communist Party (MCP). Comprised primarily of ethnic Chinese, the party immediately sought
control of youth and labor organizations. It was initially successful,
but lost ground when it instigated a series of strikes and many of its
leaders were jailed. Following 1937, when the communists and the
KMT in China united to fight Japan, the MCP played an active anti-
Japanese role in Malaya. Party membership however, remained primarily Chinese.

Malay nationalism was also foreign inspired and foreign oriented,
and was neither revolutionary nor national. Originally an outgrowth of
the Islamic Reform Movement in the Middle East, it sought to
strengthen and modernize Islam; its leaders were primarily Arabs. A
Pan-Malay nationalism, led by Indonesian intellectuals, promoted union with Indonesia. Neither movement was widespread.

Sabah and Sarawak   Sabah was preoccupied during the inter-war
years with extending governmental authority into the interior and
developing legal and administrative systems akin to those of the
peninsula. Sarawak, under the third Brooke raja (1917–1946) began to
modernize, depersonalize and decentralize administration. A modern
judicial system was developed and legal codes were adopted. Although
the decline of rubber prices was offset by new oil revenues, income
was insufficient for undertaking major social services or public works.
In 1941, on the 100th anniversary of the Brooke dynasty, the raja
presented the state with a new constitution. It was negated by the
Japanese invasion in December the same year.

POLITICAL INDICATORS: BRITISH MALAYSIA

1. British policy in Malaysia, except in the Straits Settlements, was to
   maintain the sultans in power and to rule indirectly through the
   British adviser-residents attached to their courts. In actual fact the
   residents in the Federated States became the rulers and the sultans
   the advisers, and the federation became a union with control
   centered in Kuala Lumpur.
2. The importation of Chinese and Indian labor was originally welcomed by the Malay since it did not compete within the Malay

economic structure but produced new wealth for the states from the tin mines and rubber plantations. However political problems arose when the total minority population exceeded that of the Malay and when the Chinese became permanent residents and sought resident and citizenship rights.

3. British educational policies forced the Chinese community to develop its own schools and encouraged rural Malayan schools to continue in traditional patterns. The system seriously impeded assimilation of the two communities and limited the spread of modern ideas and attitudes among the Malay, simultaneously encouraging Chinese ethnocentrism and making the Chinese more vulnerable to political proselytizing by China.

4. Governmental authority was fragmented among the Straits Settlements, the Federated Malay States and the individual unfederated Malay states; actual authority and power were exercised primarily by the British in Singapore and Kuala Lumpur. Little political or economic coordination developed between Peninsular Malaya and Sabah and Sarawak.

5. A true Malaysian nationalism failed to materialize.

WAR AND THE BRITISH RETURN

When Germany in May 1940 occupied France and Holland and defeated Britain on the continent, the metropolitan powers became unable to contain the Japanese advance into Southeast Asia. Japanese forces landed on the coast of Kelantan in northeast Malaya in December 1941 and moved down the peninsula. Sarawak, which was invaded the same month, offered no resistance because the leadership was out of the country. Sabah fell in January. Singapore fell in February. The Malaysian campaign was over.

Before Singapore fell the British arranged for "stay behind" groups which were to organize resistance, maintain communication with British forces in India and prepare to assist in retaking Malaya whenever that might be. The most effective group was the Malayan People's Anti-Japanese Army (MPAJA). It was spearheaded by Chinese communists (mainland agents and partisan guerrillas) who had the most to fear from the Japanese, as Chinese and as communists. They were joined in 1943 by British officers from India from whom they kept secret their plans to establish a People's Republic of Malaya at the war's conclusion. In Borneo, also, the active resistance was primarily Chinese.

The Japanese perpetrated numerous atrocities, particularly in Singapore, and attempted with some success to foment conflict between Malays and Chinese. However they lost the support of the Malay leaders when they turned over the four northern states to Thailand in October 1943. Japan's surrender in August 1945 was sudden and there was no effective authority ready to take over. The MPAJA attempted to seize control in some areas, but it, too, was unready. Little damage or loss of life occurred in the last days, but the occupiers had allowed the economy to deteriorate and the mines and rubber industry had been severely damaged.

Upon their return in September the British established an interim military government and proposed the creation of a Malayan union. The union would have reversed the prewar trend toward decentralization. All political entities except Singapore were to be combined into a highly centralized state, the sultans would lose nearly all their authority, and citizenship was to be granted equally to Malay, Chinese and Indian. The intent was to make all of Malaya a British colony under British law. Singapore was to be excluded because of its strategic importance and because its large Chinese population was perceived as adding immeasurably to the political problems of the union.

In reaction to these proposals an "instant" Malay nationalism emerged. Led by the prime minister of Johore, Datuk Onn bin Jaafar, the United Malay National Organization (UMNO) came into being, the first indigneous Malay nationalist party. Resentment was so great that a new plan was presented in February 1948 providing for federation rather than centralization. Special rights were reserved for the Malays and citizenship requirements were tightened. The goal spelled out in the Federation Agreement was "ultimate self-government." Although the agreement called for a federation, in effect it created still another union; each state retained its own ruler and bicameral parliamentary legislature, with specific rights, but control remained in Kuala Lumpur.

The Emergency In June 1948 an insurgency broke out, pitting Chinese communist terrorists against the Malays and the bulk of the Chinese community. For several years the survival of the federation was in doubt. The insurgents employed the now classical Maoist terrorist tactics of village harassment and encirclement, in combination with assassination and extortion.

The MPAJA had disbanded after the war without turning in its caches of arms and had joined the reorganized Malayan Communist Party. The MCP quickly took over the trade unions and began a series of strikes to prevent economic recovery. Main targets were rubber estates and tin mines. The British declared a State of Emergency in June after a coordinated series of 67 assassinations. The small British defense force and the understaffed police were augumented by a 24,000 Malay defense force, and later by Chinese who organized to protect the mines.

Squatters and others living in isolated areas (some 500,000) were removed to New Villages where they could be protected. This move also had the desired effect of cutting communist supply lines since many isolated villages had been terrorized into becoming communist support groups. An unexpected dividend of the New Village Movement was that it forced the government to pay attention to rural Malaya which had been largely ignored. Roads and modern facilities—such as a water supply and electricity—provided for the New Villages, were demanded by the old *kampongs* (villages) which had remained loyal.

The communists were decisively defeated after General Sir Gerald Templer became high commissioner in 1952. With the help of Commonwealth troops he took the offensive and forced the communists to retreat further and further into the jungles. As an area was declared safe, emergency regulations were relaxed. Templer's recognition of the value of actively engaging the populace in the political process is considered the decisive factor in his success; he effectively equated communism with the destruction of Malayan nationalism rather than simply with anti-imperialism.

During the campaign for the first important postwar election (December 1951) UMNO and the Malayan Chinese Association (MCA)—made up of moderate Chinese who accepted Malaya as their homeland—worked together. In 1953 Tunku (Prince) Abdul Rahman of Kedah succeeded in bringing these two parties and the Malayan Indian Congress (MIC), representing a similar moderate Indian group, into the Alliance. The Alliance was an umbrella multi-communal party seeking to achieve responsibile self government.

The general elections of 1955 gave the Alliance a sweeping victory—51 of the 52 elective seats in the federal legislature. Rahman became chief minister and within two years the Alliance persuaded the British to transfer sovereignty to the federation.

Although the emergency officially continued until 1960, the communist danger was no longer as threatening. The main problems faced by the newly independent government—which continue to plague Malaysia to the present—were the economic imbalance among the three major ethnic groups, but particularly between the Chinese and the Malay; and the need to assimilate the Indians and the Chinese into the Malayan community and create a national unity and a national identity.

FEDERATION OF MALAYSIA

Political Organization   The Federation of Malaya was proclaimed August 31, 1957; it became the Federation of Malaysia on September 16, 1963 when it incorporated the Bornean states of Sabah and Sarawak, and for two years Singapore. The 1957 constitution, amended to allow for these political changes, was retained.

The constitutional arrangements are unique. Malaya/Malaysia is a federation of 13 states headed by a constitutional monarch (*yang di pertuan agong*), chosen for a five year term by, and from among, the sultans of the nine states which are headed by such hereditary rulers. The other four states—Malacca, Penang, Sabah and Sarawak—are headed by governors who have no vote in the matter. The king, who ceases to be head of his own state while he is head of nation, acts on the advice of the federal cabinet, as do the sultans and governors on the advice of their state cabinets.

Malaysia is a parliamentary democracy with a written constitution and a bicameral legislature. The House of Representatives, in 1990 consisting of 177 members, is popularly elected. The Senate is composed of 32 members appointed by the king and 26 others elected by the assemblies of the individual states (two each). The prime minister is head of the majority party in the lower house and responsible to it.

Although Malaysia is a federation of 13 states, its constitution *enumerates the powers of the states*; all other powers are vested in the central government. This is a reversal of prewar arrangements and of the U.S. constitutional system under which the states delegated powers to the central government. Nevertheless some states are given broad powers such as the power to make independent economic arrangements with foreign governments.[1] The judicial system of the federation is unitary. There are no state courts, although religious courts are under state jurisdiction; federal courts enforce both state and federal law. Islam is the official religion of the federation but freedom of religion is guaranteed in the constitution. However in recent years states have passed more and more restrictive religious requirements.

The federal constitution expressly provides favored treatment for Malays and, since 1963, for natives of Sarawak and Sabah which include large numbers of aborigines and Proto-Malay. The electoral districts are weighted in favor of the rural areas which are largely Malay, and there are special citizenship requirements and restrictions for non-Malays. This form of "affirmative action," is expressly designed to keep Malaysia Malayan and to give the Malays an opportunity to reverse the economic imbalance they suffer in relationship to the Chinese and, in lesser degree, to the Indians.

The Conference of Rulers, a carryover from the Federated Malay States, is expressly recognized by the constitution. It consists of the nine hereditary sultans and the (now) four governors. The conference meets with the king and the prime minister three or four times a year to discuss and decide "policies of national importance," to appoint senior civil servants and all higher court judges and, with the governors abstaining, elect a king.

Problems of Union   By 1960 the mutual apprehension of the federation and Singaporean governments concerning the strength of the communists in Singapore had caused the two to enter into discussions of union. Each considered that the communist threat could better be contained by a united effort. Since Malaya had long feared the inclusion of Singapore's million Chinese in the Malay state, the British proposed that the three Bornean states, which had a total Malay majority, be simultaneously incorporated into the federation. Inclusion in the federation of the British colony of Singapore and the British Bornean states would also secure for all four independence from foreign rule and would relieve Britain of further colonial responsibilities in Southeast Asia.

At the end of World War II the three Bornean states were in dire economic straits. Sabah and Sarawak, lacking the financial resources to rehabilitate themselves, applied for British crown colony status; Brunei had oil revenues. Although as crown colonies Sabah and Sarawak differed from the protectorate of Brunei in their political-legal relationship with Britain, the three states developed a unified court system and discussed closer administrative and political associations. Brunei, ironically in view of later events, evinced a stronger interest in relations with Peninsular Malaya than with its neighbors, perhaps because its neighbors occupied lands which had once been Brunei's and now wanted to share in her oil revenues which meanwhile had become considerable.

In 1962 a British commission canvassed opinion in Sabah and Sarawak and reported a large majority of the population favored union with Malaya; in Brunei the sultan was known to favor it. However, in Brunei the first general elections, held in August–September 1962, produced a sweep by the leftist National Brunei People's Party headed by A. M. Azahari. Backed by the Philippines and Indonesia, both of whom now made claims to territory in British Borneo, Azahari led a revolt in Brunei which had the broader aim of preventing all three states from joining Malaya.

British troops called in by the sultan put down the revolt, but in January 1963 President Sukarno of Indonesia announced a policy of "confrontation" toward Malaya. In April Indonesian troops attacked across the borders in Borneo but were repulsed. Elections in Sabah and Sarawak confirmed the desire of those states for union, but Malaya sought to mollify Indonesia and the Philippines by suggesting a United Nations team be sent to Borneo to sample public opinion. Despite the UN report that the people of the area favored federation, Indonesia stepped up its policy of confrontation.

The Federation of Malaya nevertheless became the Federation of Malaysia on schedule. The Sultan of Brunei elected not to join the new nation and on the same date Indonesia and the Philippines broke off diplomatic relations with the state.

Indonesian attacks occurred both in Borneo and Peninsular Malaysia and infiltrators succeeded in increasing racial tensions in Singapore where serious riots broke out in mid-1964. Although Indonesian aggression was easily repelled, racial tensions between the Malays and the Chinese increased. The Malay states were nervous about the influence of Singapore in the federation, and the Alliance Party was disturbed by what it considered meddling by the People's Action Party (the party in power in Singapore) in elections in the Malay states during 1964. In August 1965 Singapore was pressured to leave the federation.

Malaysia's problems with Indonesia were resolved when Indonesia suffered an attempted communist coup in September 1965 and was forced to concern itself with near civil war and political change. On August 11, 1966 an official end to the unofficial war was concluded and in June the following year the Philippines and Malaysia restored diplomatic relations without, however, the Philippines giving up claim to Sabah.

Relationships between the less politically and economically developed states of Sabah and Sarawak (now known as East Malaysia) and the central government were difficult at times, although economic development of East Malaysia was spurred by membership in the federation. When Singapore withdrew from Malaysia in 1965 Sabah and Sarawak talked of revising their relationship with the federation as well. The central government responded by promptly removing the chief ministers of both states.

During this period the federation, which had remained under the protective military umbrella of the Commonwealth, adopted a third world position in foreign affairs. It declined to join the western-oriented Southeast Asia Treaty Organization (SEATO), although during the Vietnam War it recognized the western-backed regimes in south Vietnam and Kampuchea. In 1963 Malaysia joined with Indonesia and the Philippines to form "Maphilindo," a regional social and economic association. It had aligned itself in 1961 with the Philippines and Thailand in a similar tenuous economic and cultural relationship, the Association of Southeast Asia, which was expanded in 1967 to include Indonesia and Singapore as the Association of Southeast Asian Nations (ASEAN).

Racial Problems   Racial problems, always just beneath the surface, erupted in serious riots in Kuala Lumpur in May 1969 in the aftermath of general elections which had polarized racial feelings. The urban Chinese resented the fact that the Malay enjoyed superior legal status and thus greater access to political power, while the rural Malay were distressed because they did not share the economic prosperity of the country—as Malays or as farmers. A second State of Emergency was called as rioting between the rightist Pan Malaysian Islamic Party (PMIP) and the leftist Chinese Democratic Action Party (DAP) reached a level of violence that required army assistance to the police. An Emergency (Essential Powers) Ordinance was proclaimed. Parliament was suspended and for the next two years the country was governed by the National Operations Council. Deputy Prime Minister Abdul Razak was appointed chief executive by Prime Minister Abdul Rahman.

A National Consultative Council was called to examine the issues that led to the riots and to suggest measures to prevent unrest in the future. The basic approach, strengthened by constitutional amendments, was to prohibit any questioning of the provisions of the constitution that enumerate "right, status, position, privilege, sovereignty or prerogative established or protected by the constitution."[2] By decreeing a national consensus, and requiring political parties and politicians to accept the ideal as the real, the government sought to gain time to bring the Malay into the economic mainstream and thus defuse dissatisfaction.

When Abdul Rahman retired in 1970, Abdul Razak succeeded him as prime minister. In 1971 the National Operations Council was downgraded to National Security Council and Parliament was called back into session. Recognizing the need to extend the range of economic benefits, the federation organized government corporations and other quasi-public bodies to carry out the New Economic Policy whose avowed goal was to generate greater economic prosperity in the Malay community. The Chinese acquiesced.

Economy The New Economic Policy, with goals to be achieved by 1990, placed emphasis on *bumiputra* (son of the soil) participation in the economic growth of the country. Use of the term *bumiputra* underscores government intent to benefit the Malay agrarian poor. Efforts are devoted to developing rural communities, opening up new lands for settlement, upgrading the quality of and standards for rubber (since many small farmers are rubber growers) and encouraging palm oil production as an alternative to rubber to diversify Malaysia's agricultural base and to bring a quicker return to the smallholder.

Malaysia is the world's largest producer and exporter of rubber, tin and palm oil, and by 1982, after only a decade of production, had become a leading exporter of electronic products, in part because of its favorable wage scale. Petroleum has been found in increasing amounts in the waters off the east and west coasts of Peninsular Malaysia as well as off Sabah and Sarawak, and with Eurodollar loan assistance the nation has embarked on a venture in Sarawak to liquify offshore natural gas. Should worldwide demand for petroleum and petroleum products increase, petroleum and natural gas may become Malaysia's prime foreign income earner.

Although it is an agricultural exporter, Malaysia is not self sufficient in rice, importing as much as 35 percent of its needs; Thailand is its major supplier. Acknowledging this dependence, Malaysia entered a long-term oil pact with Thailand in January 1980; however its main customers remain Japan and the United States.

Petroleum production has served as a catalyst to reinforce Malaysia's ties with Islamic producer states in the Middle East. In 1975 the Arab-Malaysian Development Finance Corporation was formed to "manage and invest capital from the Arab Gulf States in a wide range of Malaysian developments and enterprises."[3] In the same year Saudi Arabia lent Malaysia over US$78 million for medical, technical and land development projects, and in 1979 Libya provided funds for a headquarters for the Malaysian Muslim Welfare Organization.

Malaysia has encouraged foreign industrial investment, with certain restrictions. The government requires that Malays hold a specific minimum number of shares in any new company, although it is often difficult to find Malays with capital sufficient to finance joint ventures; in the tin industry, for example, 30 percent *bumiputra* capital is required. Targets imply that Malays must comprise 66 percent of the industrial workers in jobs created between 1976 and 1990, and 54 percent of those in service areas, to better match their percentage of the total population.[4] In the corporate sector the target is 30 percent *bumiputra* ownership by 1990, 40 percent other Malaysian and 30 percent foreign.[5] Projects located in the several free trade, or export processing, zones may be entirely foreign owned as long as they are export oriented and do not exploit depletable resources. Indicative of the need for Malay affirmative action, six years after the introduction of the New Economic Policy, Malaysians of Indian descent (11 percent of the population) were still earning 60 percent more than Malays, and Chinese Malaysians (36 percent) were earning 108 percent more. The Chinese in 1983 held 75 percent of all the sales jobs and half of all industrial production positions; nearly half of the *bumiputras* (53 percent of the population) held low-paying agricultural jobs.[6]

Despite such restrictions, the gross national product (GNP) from 1976 to 1980 grew at a rate of over 8 percent annually; the worldwide recession of the early 1980s caused it to drop 4 percent. Negative factors included the decline in tin exports following collapse in 1985 of the International Tin Agreement, and depressed commodity prices (rubber, palm oil, timber, petroleum). The economy rapidly regained momentum in 1987, however, with a growth rate of 5.2 percent. The upward trend continued the following year with a gain of almost 8 percent due to the recovery of the commodities market and a booming manufacturing sector, the consequence of high external demand for rubber products and electric and electronic devices. By 1989 Malaysia had become the world's third largest exporter of semiconductors, after Japan and the United States.[7]

Internal Politics Since the nation's inception the unifying force in both national and state politics has been the National Front (Barisan Nasional), successor to the Alliance Party, which compromises the three moderate ethnic parties: UMNO (Malay), MCA (Chinese), and MIC (Indian), plus eight small parties. Each of the major parties maintains a state counterpart, closely tied to the national party, as does the National Front itself. The parallel party structures have helped minimize conflict between the states and the national government through intra-party political communication. Moreover, since passage of the constitutional amendments which forbid questioning basic racial policy, much party business and inter-communal bargaining is conducted within the National Front; public party discussion of communal issues is minimal. In consequence, the National Front's dominant political position enabled four strong prime ministers—Abdul Rahman; Abdul Razak; Hussein Onn who became prime minister in January 1976 on the death of Abdul Razak; and Mahathir Mohamad who took office in July 1981—to control the political process.

The Front has been challenged, however, by the extremist parties, the Chinese-leftist DAP and the Malay-rightist PMIP, now known as the PI. In July 1978 the National Front swept the general elections, with UMNO strengthening its position vis-a-vis the PI, but the moderate Chinese MCA fared less well against the DAP, primarily because the MCA was unsuccessful in gaining government permission to establish a new private Chinese university. Although it rejected the ten-year-old plea for a charter, the government agreed in July 1979 to increase the number of non-Malays admitted to instructions of higher education, thus easing the concerns of the Chinese community and strengthening the MCA. In the 1982 elections, called early by Mahathir, the National Front cut into the DAP constituency. It won 132 of 154 parliamentary seats (88.9 percent) and controlled all 11 state assemblies in Peninsular Malaysia. In the succeeding federal elections of 1986 the Front won 147 of 177 seats in the expanded parliament, a 3 percent decline from 1982.

Despite the success of UMNO against the PI, closer ties with Islamic countries have encouraged an increased sense of the racial-religious identity of the Malay—all of whom are by constitutional definition, Muslim—and a growing Islamic fundamentalism which has begun to have political repercussions. Johore in February 1979 began to enforce strict Muslim laws concerning sexual behavior, drinking and Friday prayers; other states are following suit. The Malayan Moslem Youth Movement, which is urban based, but has ties to the rural-based PI, is another purveyor of fundamentalism.

Security In the aftermath of the war in Vietnam, domestic security problems increased. Student demonstrations in late 1974 caused the government to suspend the Student Union and arrest a number of leaders who were accused of "using democracy to destroy democracy." Urban violence increased throughout 1975, apparently, according to Prime Minister Razak, the result of communist successes in Vietnam and Kampuchea.[8] American weapons left behind were reportedly being transported into Malaysia via Thailand. As a result, new police regulations and security laws were promulgated which established a presumption of guilt, removed the need for warrants, eliminated jury trials and mandated the maximum penalty for certain crimes. The Emergency Ordinance of 1975 became enshrined in law as the Emergency Act of 1979. Razak also proclaimed compulsory guard duty for all males aged 18 to 55, making each neighborhood responsible for its own security against both criminals and urban terrorists—a plan similar to that used during the 1950s Emergency. These restrictions, plus the Internal Security Act of 1969 to counter subversion, have remained in effect.

In the countryside communist guerrillas were again active, destroying tractors, bulldozers and earth moving equipment in Perak and Pahang in an effort to forestall the completion of development projects, and attacking police and security personnel. The Malayan Communist Party, once 90 percent Chinese, gained support from the Malay rural poor, and Malay membership by 1980 amounted to about 55 percent, although leadership was confined to the ethnic Chinese.

Guerrilla operations, limited primarily to the Malay-Thai border, persisted. In November 1975 the Malaysian anti-guerrilla force deployed along the border was expanded by 50 percent—to 60,000 men. In 1979 the two countries agreed to permit the other's security forces to penetrate its borders in "hot pursuit" to a distance to 20 miles and the Malaysian armed forces budget was increased. As Vietnamese activities in Southeast Asia expanded, Prime Minister Hussein Onn announced at the opening of the UMNO General Assembly in July 1980 that Malaysia would further increase defense installations, troops and armament and urged the entire nation to assume responsibility for the defense of the country.

In April 1981, just before Mahathir became prime minister, the government passed the Societies (Amendment) Act. The Societies Act of 1966 had defined "political society" so broadly it included almost any grouping. The 1981 amendment gave the government wide powers of authority over such societies, forcing them to amend their rules and subjecting their aims to government scrutiny. Although strong opposition was expressed to the terms of the amendment, the Mahathir government has been unwilling to make any major concessions. The Printing Presses and Publications Act, passed March 28, 1984, represented a further step towards government control. It imposed virtual censorship on "undesirable publications" and established Malaysia's Bernama News Agency as the sole distributor of foreign news.

Mahathir   Prime Minister Mahathir Mohamad, who assumed office on July 16, 1981 upon Hussein's resignation for reasons of health, represents a break from the past and is the first of Malaysia's "second generation nationalists" to achieve the office. In contrast to the first three premiers, Mahathir was educated in Singapore rather than at a prestigious British university, and is a product of the middle class rather than of the traditional elite. He speaks and acts with a bluntness uncharacteristic of the Malay; his father was Indian. It was he who in 1979 as deputy premier stated that Malaysia would "shoot on sight" the Vietnamese boat people if they persisted in trying to land on Malaysian shores.

Mahathir's assertive stance and his extreme nationalism appealed to the Malay electorate, enabling him to defeat repeated challenges to his leadership throughout the 1980s. When opponents within UMNO tried to oust him from its presidency at party elections in 1987, Mahathir narrowly defeated Tunku Razaleigh Hamzah, his former cabinet colleague now rival. Mahathir's chauvinism, cloaked in a populist appeal to Malay hearts and minds, led him to authoritarian practices. Relying heavily upon antisubversion provisions of Malaysian internal security legislation which allows detention without trial, he used the police to quash public dissent. Newspaper licenses were revoked and 106 prominent persons were detained, including most of the leaders of DAP, the main opposition party, as well as some politicians of the PI.

Mahathir's tactics aroused serious concern within UMNO. *Bapa Malaysia* ("Father of Malaysia") Tunku Abdul Rahman, the nation's first prime minister; Azlan Shah, the Sultan of Perak, a respected jurist and king (1989); and High Court Justice Datuk Harun Hashim joined other judges in calling for adherence to the constitution and a review of its provisions. Mahathir responded that such proposals would cause "tensions" among the people. Justice Harun, pursuing the issue through the judiciary, ruled on February 4, 1988 that UMNO was an unlawful organization because it was not legally registered under terms of the Societies Act. Thereupon Mahathir's intraparty opponents again tried to unseat him and to resuscitate the party under the sobriquet UMNO Malaysia.

Mahathir again met the challenge successfully. He managed to derail registration of UMNO Malaysia, which proved to be its death knell, and to register instead UMNO Baru (New UMNO). Mounting "Loyalty to the People" rallies, he secured enough pledges from parliamentary and local party leaders to assure his continued control of the House of Representatives. Finally, and transparently, Mahathir took aim at the courts. He publicly blamed the judiciary for allegedly usurping parliament's law-making role and engineered the resignation and subsequent successful prosecution in 1988 of Lord President of the Federal Court Tun Mohammed Salleh. The supremacy of UMNO Baru over Malaysian politics, personified by Mahathir, continued.

Foreign Relations   Malaysia's foreign relations since 1971 have been multifaceted and sometimes contradictory. For example, as a member of the Commonwealth of Nations, Malaysia is active in Commonwealth affairs and is a member of the Five Power Defense Arrangement with Singapore, Britain, Australia and New Zealand (ANZUK). The latter three promised to provide aid if Malaysia or Singapore were faced with an "armed attack externally organized or supported or the threat of such attack." In February 1981 Britain announced that it would continue to support the five power arrangement although its role would be reduced.

Malaysia nevertheless supported the ASEAN proposal that foreign bases be removed from the area and that Southeast Asia become a "zone of peace, freedom and neutrality." The state is also an enthusiastic member of the group of nonaligned nations that seeks reform of the international economic system.

Malaysia clearly aspires to a leadership role in Southeast Asia and in the decade of the Mahathir government has acted accordingly. In recent years the regime has questioned the utility of ASEAN's dialogues and criticized ASEAN's meager progress toward more substantive intraregional economic cooperation. Attuned to world rather than regional trade, Malaysia's robust export economy is the envy of its ASEAN partners. Reversing the "Buy British Last" and "Look East" policies of the early 1980s, the nation has found profit and prestige in courting its fellow members of the Commonwealth, especially the United Kingdom.

Kuala Lumpur's opposition, in tandem with its ASEAN neighbors, to Vietnam's 1979 military occupation of Kampuchea, began to change in the mid-1980s. In 1985 Malaysia initiated the notion of indirect or "proximity" talks among competing Vietnamese and Kampuchean interests, the first step toward many ensuing regional discussions on the Kampuchean issue. With Indonesia, Malaysia sees the value of Vietnam as a buffer against China.

Indicative of Malaysia's assertive perception of its regional role, the nation has continued to upgrade its air and naval strength. Malaysia's land forces, no longer preoccupied by internal security problems as communist subversion has abated, are seeking a region-wide role. Malaysia immediately accepted Yassir Arafat's 1988 proclamation of an independent Palestine state, thus buttressing its popularity among the very large Muslim populations of Southeast Asia.

The nation's growing military-political power is a signal to other Southeast Asian states that Malaysia intends to use its power to influence the policies of its ASEAN partners, particularly the Philippines because of its unrenounced claim to Sabah, and Indonesia because of its continuing record of territorial expansion.

Malaysia's relations with the Philippines had been troubled by the revived Philippine claim to Sabah in 1968, with subsequent suspension of diplomatic relations and clandestine Malaysian assistance to the Muslim rebels in the southern Philippines. In 1975 such aid, arriving primarily from Sabah, was drastically curtailed when the political leadership in that state was changed. Sabah was also a haven for Philippine Muslim refugees whose status was in contention between Malaysia and the Philippines. In 1977 Malaysia agreed to allow the 90,000 refugees in Sabah to remain, on condition that they assimilate and become permanent residents. In August that year Malaysia, the Philippines and Indonesia signed a border agreement designed to halt smuggling, piracy and drug traffic across their mutual borders; Malaysia agreed to stop smuggling from her shores into the southern Philippines in return for the Philippine offer to renounce its claim to Sabah. However, the Sabah claim has never been resolved.

In April 1980 the nation unilaterally declared a 200 mile "economic zone" in the seas around the peninsula and off Sabah and Sarawak, which gives it exclusive rights to the exploration, conservation and management of the waters, but does not affect freedom of navigation and overflight rights of other nations nor encroach into the territorial waters or islands claimed by other states. Malaysia expressed willingness to negotiate the latter. This set off counteractions by Thailand, the Philippines, Indonesia, Singapore and Vietnam. In December 1981 Malaysia and Indonesia drafted a treaty which spelled out their mutual rights over territorial seas and airspace. Malaysia recognized Indonesia's "archipelagic" principles (rights to waters and air space around the entire archipelago rather than around each individual island) as defined by Indonesian laws, and Indonesia recognized Malaysia's rights and interests over its territorial seas and archipelagic waters and its right to free and unhindered air and sea passage between Peninsular and Bornean Malaysia.

Increasingly Malaysia has strengthened its ties with Islamic nations. In 1969 it called for an Islamic Summit and a Malaysian became the first secretary general of the Islamic Secretariat created at the ensuing conference. The state has taken a strong position against Israeli expansion and has supported the Palestine Liberation Organization and its goals, formally recognizing the latter in August 1981.

When the United States began withdrawing troops from Vietnam in the early 1970s, Malaysia—and other nations of Southeast Asia that had supported western-backed regimes—sought to mend relations with the communist states. In May 1974 Malaysia became the first ASEAN state to recognize the People's Republic of China. The PRC agreed at that time that it would not try to influence the Chinese communities of Southeast Asia, and in particular of Malaysia; in return Malaysia broke relations with the Republic of China on Taiwan. Nevertheless the PRC continued to support the internal communist parties and continued to permit the outlawed MCP to broadcast the Voice of the Malayan Revolution from Yunnan. The two nations drew closer, however, when Soviet-backed Vietnamese troops overthrew the pro-Chinese government of Kampuchea in 1979.

The relationship between Malaysia and Vietnam has shifted significantly since the end of the Vietnam war. Malaysia attempted to achieve an accommodation with Vietnam in 1976 and the two nations exchanged ambassadors. In January 1978 they signed a most favored nation agreement and issued a joint communique recognizing the new political atmosphere in Southeast Asia as conducive to peace in the region. Although Vietnamese refugees were becoming a serious problem, Malaysia began a short-lived program to help rehabilitate the Vietnamese rubber industry. Aid was discontinued after Vietnam invaded Kampuchea in December.

Along with the other ASEAN nations, Malaysia took a lead in condemning Vietnamese military and political domination of Kampuchea, although strongly disapproving of the preceding Pol Pot regime there. Since 1979 it has consistently voted in the United Nations against UN recognition of the Vietnamese-installed Heng Samrin regime as the legitimate government.

Nevertheless, in the mid-1980s in tandem with its ASEAN neighbors, Malaysia began to modify its opposition to Vietnam's occupation of Kampuchea. In 1985 it initiated the idea of indirect or "proximity" talks among Vietnamese and Kampuchean interests, a first step toward ensuing regional discussions. Quite simply, Malaysia saw Vietnam as a buffer against China.

Refugees   Together with the invasion of Kampuchea by the government of Vietnam, the massive refugee problem arising from the actions of the communist governments of Vietnam, Kampuchea and Laos, has been the most destablizing factor in Southeast Asia since the end of the Vietnam War.

Refugees began fleeing South Vietnam following the communist takeover in April 1975, but the flow only reached Malaysia in meaningful numbers in 1977. A year later refugees were pouring in at the rate of 3,000 a month, 40 to 50 percent of them ethnic Chinese. They were arriving on Malaysia's east coast, its poorest region, and they increased the proportion of Chinese to Malays in a country already divided along racial lines. By October 1978 the refugees numbered 30,000 and Malaysia requested the United States and European countries to increase the number of persons they would accept for permanent settlement. When, during the first two weeks in November, 9,000 "boat people" arrived, Malaysia began to turn them away and some died when their ships foundered. By December the total was 52,000 and Malaysian patrol ships were towing refugee boats back to sea.

The situation continued to worsen, reaching a crisis point on June 15, 1979 when Malaysia announced that it would push the 70,000 refugees in camps back into the sea, and shoot on sight any others entering Malaysian waters. It had reached an agreement with Thailand and Indonesia, the government added: the three nations would drive away all refugees trying to land on their shores and their navies would "mount joint patrols in certain parts of the South China Sea soon to curb the refugee influx."[9] To deflect criticism, Malaysia accused the West of hiding behind its immigration laws while pointing the finger of "human rights" at Southeast Asian countries which could no longer bear the burden of the enormous influx; the cost to Malaysia alone, by that time, was US$22,400,000.

The following week Prime Minister Hussein Onn assured the UN secretary general that his forces would not actually shoot on sight, but urged the international organization to move quickly to resettle the refugees elsewhere. Malaysia's firm, if harsh, stand prompted western nation action.

The 1979 Geneva Conference produced agreement that Southeast Asian nations would provide first asylum for boat people, with the understanding that the refugees would ultimately be resettled permanently in third countries. Until 1987 the exit rate from Vietnam roughly matched resettlement availability. At that time the United States and other western nations introduced resettlement screening criteria based upon "well founded fear of persecution." The requirement coincided almost precisely with a sudden and massive increase in the number of arriving boat people. The relative equilibrium collapsed and large numbers of refugees filled the camps in Thailand and Malaysia.

Thailand reacted by redirecting its refugees to Malaysia, whose case load increased from 9,120 in December 1987 to 13,334 by August 1988. The Kuala Lumpur government responded by announcing it would close its Pulau Bidong refugee camp and by calling for a new conference on refugees. The ensuing 1989 Geneva Conference on Refugees attended by the affected nations accomplished little more than refining resettlement procedures already in place.

WHITHER MALAYSIA?

Malaysia enters the final decade of the century as one of the most successful new political entities of the post-World War II era. It has achieved enviable rates of economic growth despite a serious recession in 1985. The federal government in Kuala Lumpur enforces a national unity policy, and the nation enjoys a position of influence in Southeast Asia as well as within the broader international community. But Malaysia's initiatives have been costly.

The Mahathir government has *imposed* its version of appropriate social integration upon three ethnically, linguistically and religiously disparate communities—Chinese, Indian and Malay—with mixed results. The Fourth Economic Plan, for the decade of the 1980s, drew to a close far short of its goal of achieving *bumiputra* commercial and industrial sectors holding at least 30 percent of Malaysian companies' equity. In fact, economic success came at least partly at the expense of *bumiputras* following liberalization of policy toward foreign and locally owned ventures in 1986. If their interests are further sacrificed in the new ten-year plan the *bumiputras,* the largest component of the population and heretofore largely dependent upon government largesse, could well disrupt UMNO unity anew. If, on the other hand, policy favors *bumiputras* the economically powerful Chinese may be further alienated.

Malaysia also faces the threat of rising authoritarianism. During the decade of the 1980s the government frequently violated constitutional rights of individuals by its exceedingly broad perception of internal security requirements. Prime Minister Mahathir also deliberately impaired the autonomy of Malaysia's judiciary, a valued legacy of British constitutionalism, in what appeared to be a campaign to achieve executive dominance over all governmental institutions.

FOOTNOTES

1. See Sabah and Indonesian agreement to sell and market timber in Japan. *Data Asia* (Manila: Press Foundation of Asia), 1979, p. 6268.

2. Gordon P. Means in *Politics and Modernization of South and Southeast Asia,* Robert N. Kearney, ed. (N.Y.: John Wiley and Sons, 1975), p. 188–194.

3. *Data for Decision* (Manila: Press Foundation of Asia), 1975, p. 3185.

4. *Data Asia* (Manila: Press Foundation of Asia), 1978, p. 5531.

5. *Malaysian Digest* (Kuala Lumpur: External Information Division of the Ministry of Foreign Affairs), February 28, 1982, p. 2.

6. Eduardo Lachica, "Malaysian Growth Strategy Praised by U.S. Think Tank," *Asian Wall Street Journal Weekly,* July 18, 1983.

7. *Asia Yearbook 1989,* p. 171; *Far Eastern Economic Review,* August 25, 1988, p. 72.

8. *Data for Decision, op. cit.,* p. 3090.

9. *Data Asia, op. cit.,* 1979, p. 6300.

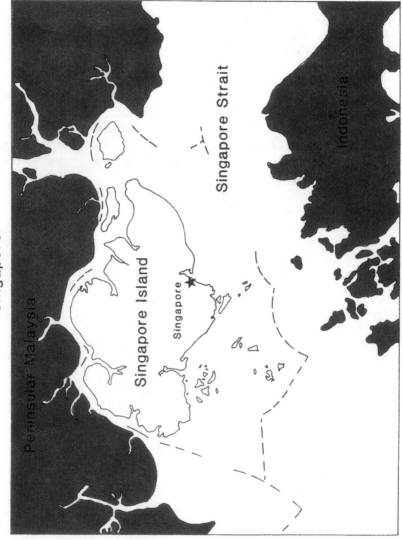

CHAPTER 6
SINGAPORE

The Republic of Singapore consists of Singapore Island—an area extending approximately 26 miles east to west and 14 miles north to south—and 55 offshore islets. On the north it is separated from the Malay Peninsula by the narrow Johore Strait, which at one point is only half a mile wide and spanned by a road and rail causeway. The Strait of Malacca separates Singapore on the west from the Indonesian island of Sumatra, and on the south the Singapore Strait forms a passage between the Strait of Malacca and the South China Sea to give the city-state its commanding geographic position.

Singapore Island was originally swamp and jungle, but was blest with a fine, natural deepwater harbor. Its early inhabitants were Malay, but 75 percent of its 2.6 million population by 1990 were Chinese who migrated there during the last 150 years.

From the 11th to the early 19th century Singapore, then more commonly known as Tumasek, was a minor Malay entrepot. The island gained significance when Sir Thomas Stamford Raffles, an officer in the English East India Company, recognized its geographic importance in the struggle between the British and the Dutch to control the trade between Europe and the Far East.

ENGLISH EAST INDIA COMPANY

Singapore typifies in historic times the island kingdoms and empires of the South China Sea and the Malay Peninsula which were based on trade and control of the sea lanes. The center of each kingdom was an entrepot where cargoes were traded or stores obtained, and the kingdom controlled the seas around it. An empire controlled the sea lanes between entrepots. At no time did these sea powers settle or hold sway over the interior—lands behind their trading centers. Singapore was to fit this mold.

When Raffles landed at Singapore on January 28, 1819 he found 120 Malay and 30 Chinese living in a community which was little more than a pirate lair. It was under the suzerainty of the Sultan of Johore, whose headquarters at the time was on the small southern island of Riau. Raffles signed a treaty, of uncertain validity, with the sultan's brother on February 6, 1819, which permitted the company to establish factories on Singapore or on any islets within ten miles of the coast; on June 7, 1823 a second agreement gave the company formal authority. By the Treaty of London March 17, 1824 both Singapore and the Malay peninsula were ceded to the British by the Dutch, who claimed the Sultan of Johore as their vassal. Singapore was incorporated into the Penang Residency in 1826, along with the Malay port cities of Penang and Malacca, as the Straits Settlements and administered from India by the East India Company as a free port. In 1851 the Penang Residency, with Singapore as its seat of government, came under the direct control of the governor general of India, and in 1867 administration of the Straits Settlements was transferred to the Colonial Office in London.

Singapore was a successful commercial venture from the beginning. Within three years of its founding 1,575 ships from Europe, India and China were visiting the port annually, and the trading community consisted of Arabs, Armenians, Eurasians, Indians, Chinese, Bugis and an assortment of Europeans. Although Malays were the original settlers, the Chinese population grew rapidly, exceeding 32,000 by 1845. They came as merchants and planters of gambier and pepper, and developed into bankers and moneylenders. They controlled the opium trade in the colony, an item of some importance since government revenues depended heavily upon opium duties, and imported indentured labor from south China to do the heavy work in the port and harbor.

Since the company expected the various ethnic groups to monitor themselves, the development of social and political infrastructure was neglected. Chinese secret societies *(huis),* based on dialect groupings, arrived in Singapore and Malaya with the coolie labor and grew rapidly. The societies, manipulated by leading Chinese merchants, ruled their members in mafia fashion, alternating protection with extortion and terror. During the mid-19th century *huis* were a threat to the city's very survival, controlling as they did the majority of Singapore's population. Simultaneously Singapore's Chinese merchant-entrepreneurs were deeply involved in tin mining on the peninsula. Blood feuds among the *huis* for control of the mines led the Straits government, in 1874, to intervene in the internal affairs of the Malay states because warfare at the mines was spilling over into the Settlements.

CROWN COLONY

In 1867 Singapore became a colony under the British crown and as such flourished both administratively and economically for the next half century. It became one of the most important ports in the world, as well as a major trader and processor of Malayan tin and rubber, products essential to the industrializing West.

Government   When the Straits Settlements, with Singapore as its major component and administrative headquarters, was transferred to the crown, it possessed few characteristics of self government. Sir Harry St. George Ord, the first colonial governor, formed an Executive Council consisting of senior colony officials in 1867. It was to meet in private to advise the governor; the latter, however, was not obliged to accept its advice. A Legislative Council was also created which met in public and included the members of the Executive Council, the chief justice and four non-officials appointed by the governor. By 1924 the Legislative Council comprised an equal number of officials and non-officials. Its first Asian member, a leading Chinese businessman known as Whampoa (from his place of origin), was appointed in 1869. The governor possessed a tie vote in Legislative Council decisions; at the same time he initiated most legislation but was required to take into account the advice of the council, particularly in fiscal matters.

The Municipal Commission, established in the 1860s, was the first elective governmental body in the colony. However elections were abolished by the Municipal Ordinance of 1913 since neither the European nor the Chinese merchants desired an elected officialdom. The power to nominate commissioners and draw up the budget was given to the governor.

The Straits government was supposed to have representatives from Penang and Malacca, but as a rule representatives from those areas had little input. Rather Singapore, as the premier colony, played a greater and greater role in Straits affairs and its influence began to be felt on the peninsula as well.

In 1874 a residency system was set up under the governor in Singapore to advise the sultans of four peninsular states, and in 1895 the four sultanates were joined to form the Federated Malay States. The office of Resident General was established at Kuala Lumpur (Selangor) to coordinate the work of the residents. Although the Federated States were not part of the Straits Settlements, the resident general was subordinate to the governor who represented the crown as High Commissioner to the Federation and was in addition the senior British government administrative official of Malaya.

Social Strains   While Britain provided the administration and public works necessary for the smooth running of a major port, the social infrastructure it provided was minimal. This was left to the individual ethnic communities. It was not until 1902 when the Education Code was passed, that the government even undertook to provide English language primary schools.

Nevertheless, under the crown the government undertook to curb the licence that existed during company days within the Chinese community. The Chinese Immigrants Ordinance and the Crimping Ordinance were passed in 1877. These required licensing coolie agents and reduced the worst abuses of the indentured labor trade. The Societies Ordinance, adopted in 1890, broke up the secret societies, reducing them to manageable gangs, and created the Chinese Advisory Board to provide an official link between that community and the government.

China technically forbade emigration until about 1870, and the law was not formally changed until 1893. This had not deterred hundreds of thousands of Chinese from seeking to better themselves as laborers or traders throughout Southeast Asia. Although most hoped to return home—since few women migrated—their loyalty to their homeland, as well as to their adopted land, was minimal. When China changed its policy to permit emigration, it also took action to recapture the loyalties of the *nanyang* (south seas) Chinese, using Singapore as a base of operations. Conflict within the Chinese community between loyalty to the government of Singapore and to that of China became apparent after 1909 when the Chinese government proclaimed *jus sanguinis* (the law of blood) as the basis of nationality, thereby insisting that all persons of Chinese blood were citizens of China—regardless of their place of birth or residence—and owed first loyalty to the mother-land. The strains increased as revolutionary ideas gained in China and the revolutionaries used Singapore as a safe haven and a source of financial support. Nationalism, which included anti-imperalism and anti-British sentiments, began to be taught in Chinese schools and churches. By and large the few English-educated Chinese remained loyal to British Singapore; the Chinese-educated majority were torn by the philosophies in contest in their homeland. Nationalism in Singapore thus equated with Chinese nationalism. The Malay population exhibited little nationalist sentiment.

Malays represented about 13 percent of the population of Singapore by the beginning of the 20th century, their proportion declining as that of the Chinese rose. Their number included peoples from Sumatra, Java and the Celebes as well as from the peninsula. Like the Chinese, they had been encouraged to maintain their own ethnic schools. Since Malay schools were Islamic religious institutions, the education Malay students received did not prepare them for a modern commercial society. Instead, the religious schools reinforced Malay language and ethnicity and kept the community intact but relatively isolated. Most Malays in Singapore held menial jobs.

Economy   When the Straits Settlements were transferred to the Colonial Office in 1867 Singapore was one of the more profitable ports in the British empire, yet its trade increased eightfold in the next four decades. The increase was the result of: 1) opening of the Suez Canal and the return of trade to the Strait of Malacca from the Sunda Strait to the south, 2) increased trade with Thailand under the modernizing King Chulalongkorn, 3) colonization by France of Indochina and the resultant increase in trade and shipping, and 4) liberalization of Dutch trade policies in Indonesia. Singapore was the natural entrepot and coaling station for trade within the area, and for the far more important trade between Europe and the Far East. Moreover, by World War I commercial rubber plantings on the peninsula and in Indonesia were reaching major proportions and most of the crop was exported through the colony, rubber vying with tin as Singapore's most important export. Oil, which was being pumped in Indonesia and Brunei by British Shell Corporation, was also being transshipped from Singapore and the city became the oil supply center for the entire Far East.

The colony supported Britain in World War I with both money and troops, and the postwar years differed little from the prewar in terms of government structure and authority. The economy fluctuated with world economic conditions. In the "boom years" of the 1920s, when rubber and tin were in great demand by the industrial west, Singapore's economy flourished. Worldwide depression, coupled with earlier over-planting of rubber, created great hardship in Singapore in 1930–32. Not only were unskilled laborers without work, but the major trading companies that depended upon international trade suffered, and European planters were without jobs.

In 1933, however, Singapore succeeded in balancing its budget and in 1934 worked out a rubber agreement which stabilized the rubber market and remained in effect until World War II. At the same time Britain began to develop the naval coaling station at Singapore into a major base. By 1938 Singapore had the only drydock outside England that could service the world's largest ships and the following year the new naval facilities opened, although the British lacked a fleet to station there. The defenses of the port and city were strengthened but only to withstand an attack from the sea.

POLITICAL INDICATORS

1. The basic socio-political change that took place during the century and a quarter of British control was that the British replaced the Malays as rulers and the Chinese replaced them as merchants.
2. During this period Singapore had become the center for trade between Europe and Asia as well as for trade within Southeast Asia; it had also become a major commercial and banking center.
3. Little or no self government and little demand for it was evident.

4. The city was overwhelmingly Chinese, yet its politics and economics were closely interwoven with affairs on the Malay peninsula. As the seat of government of the Straits Settlements, Singapore was the residence of the governor who was also the High Commissioner to the Federated (and unfederated) princely Malay states. Singapore provided the naval defense of the area and was economically integrated with the peninsula as chief shipper and processor of Malayan rubber and tin.
5. Nationalism was primarily Chinese nationalism and was manipulated by both the government and the revolutionary forces of mainland China, creating divisions and divided loyalties among the Chinese community in Singapore, and dissipating the loyalty of the Chinese to the Singapore government.

1941–1965

On December 7, 1941 the Japanese, in their march through Southeast Asia, bombed Singapore and landed troops in the northeastern sector of the Malay peninsula. From the beginning the Japanese commanded the air; after sinking the British warships *Prince of Wales* and *Repulse* which had been sent to strengthen Singapore's defenses, they commanded the sea as well. The army then quickly moved down the peninsula to take Singapore, which was not prepared to defend itself from land attack. Its water supply from Johore was cut, and on February 15, 1942 the city fell. The occupation was harsh, and as elsewhere in Southeast Asia, food was scarce, imports were nonexistent and the Chinese community bore the brunt of the repression.

The war ended abruptly on August 10, 1945 after the U.S. dropped atomic bombs on Hiroshima and Nagasaki, and the British returned in September. They had been engrossed with military operations and were ill prepared for postwar civil administration. Because of its strategic location Singapore became headquarters of British military government in Southeast Asia. Under the command of Lord Louis Mountbatten, British forces were responsible for administering French and Dutch colonies in the area, as well as British, pending the return of the metropolitan powers.

The communists, who had organized the Malayan Peoples Anti-Japanese Army (MPAJA) in the early days of the war, had played the leading anti-Japanese role in both Singapore and Malaya, and in the immediate postwar years were looked upon as heroes. Although the MPAJA was disbanded, the group retained its arms and combined with the newly legalized Malay Communist Party (MCP). During the early postwar years the MCP could count some 70,000 supporters in Singapore, primarily Chinese, and it quickly gained control of the labor union movement.

Government and Politics   After the war Singapore remained a crown colony, although the other Straits Settlements, Penang and Malacca, became part of the new nation of Malaya. Singapore was specifically excluded from the merger on the grounds of its strategic importance to Britain, and because its large Chinese population would impose an unbearable burden of assimilation on Malaya.

The prewar Legislative Council was expanded, although still partially appointed, and all British subjects over 21 were given the franchise. The first general election in Singapore's history was held in 1948. David Marshall, head of the Labor Front, became the first prime minister of the emerging state after the legislative election of 1955. Talks with London on achieving full independence were undertaken in 1956, but because of the strength and actions of the communists in both Singapore and Malaya (where they had launched an insurrection in 1948), the British refused to relinquish control of internal security. Marshall resigned and Lim Yew Hock of the same party became prime minister.

Under Lim's leadership a new constitution came into effect in 1958 and Singapore achieved limited self-government on June 3, 1959. Foreign affairs and defense remained in the hands of the British and security was to be supervised by three Britons, three Singaporeans and one Malayan—since Malaya had almost as much interest in Singapore's internal security as Singapore itself.

At the first election to choose a City Council in 1957 the People's Action Party (PAP) won 13 out of the 30 seats, by far the most taken by any party. The election showed the trend of the country—away from the British-educated middle class with its values of moderation, toward a left-oriented socialism and a more intense nationalism. PAP had been formed three years earlier and stood for socialism and a single Malayan nationality based on the principle of *jus soli*, i.e., all persons born in Singapore, whether Malay or Chinese, were to be considered Singaporeans. However, to win enough support, PAP had to court the communists and other left-wing elements, who were for the most part ethnically Chinese. The communists in turn hoped to use PAP as a front to achieve political control. The student riots of May and June 1955 were thought to have been PAP fomented and the riots and strikes of 1956, which required 10,000 police and army personnel to quell, were suspected of being instigated by the communist elements within the party.

Nevertheless in the elections of 1959, with 90 percent voter turnout (voting was compulsory), PAP won 43 of the 51 seats in the Legislative Assembly (changed from Legislative Council in 1955). Lee Kuan Yew became prime minister, a position he has held uninterruptedly through 1989. Lee insisted on the release of communist detainees before taking office—but later found it necessary to jail them himself—and he abolished the City Council as an unnecessary level of government for the small island state. Singapore thus began an era of self government marked by political freedom, a unitary governmental structure and a dominant political party.

The political struggle for the next few years was between elements within PAP—the socialist-nationalists, represented by Lee and the PAP hierarchy, and the communists, whose strength lay in the labor unions and the general membership of the party—for control of both party and government.

To achieve party control the PAP hierarchy in July 1961 maneuvered the withdrawal from the legislature of the 13 pro-communist members of PAP who, with their large following, immediately formed the Barisan Socialis (Socialist Front). The same year, in an attempt to break communist control of labor, the PAP leadership dissolved the Singapore Trade Union Congress which had been formed by PAP but which was now controlled by the new pro-communist Front; it established in its place the National Trades Union Congress.

Union with Malaysia   The outcome of the struggle between PAP and the Barisan Socialis for control of Singapore was enough in doubt to be of concern to the Federation of Malaya, which had just defeated communist insurrection and guerrilla terrorism on the peninsula and could not afford a communist success on its southern border. Union with Singapore seemed a feasible solution; if Singapore was not strong enough to control internal communism Kuala Lumpur could add the weight of its military and security arrangements to tip the scale. In Singapore union had always been the goal of all political parties because it seemed unlikely that a Chinese city-state could survive in a Muslim-Malay society of nations.

The two governments achieved agreement on the specifics of union in May 1962. British power in foreign affairs was to be assumed by the central government at Kuala Lumpur; Singapore would have 15 seats in the 59 seat federal legislature, and the city would retain intact its own parliamentary system for local matters. In the September referendum Singaporeans voted for merger. The British Bornean Malay states of Sabah and Sarawak agreed to join in the federation at the same time in order to assuage Malay concern about Singapore's Chinese identity. The Federation of Malaya therefore became the Federation of Malaysia on September 16, 1963.

Problems arose from the beginning. Aggressively expansionist Indonesia objected to the inclusion of the Bornean states in Malaysia—making claims to them itself—and immediately declared a "state of confrontation'' against the new federation. Incursions by Indonesian troops or guerrillas were easily turned back, but Indonesian *agents provocateurs* were suspected of infiltrating Singapore and inflaming tensions between the Malays and Chinese. Serious racial riots occurred in mid-1964 on the birth-anniversary celebration of the Prophet Mohammad, when hundreds were injured and 22 killed, and rioting occurred again in September the same year.

The Barisan Socialis lost the elections held almost immediately after the merger, polling 33 percent of the vote to PAP's 47 percent. The party thereupon called for a general strike in an attempt to overthrow the government; the government forestalled the action by arresting the Front's leaders and withdrawing the registrations of seven unions.

Perhaps seeking to strengthen its internal position vis-a-vis the Front by becoming a nation-wide party, PAP entered nine candidates in the peninsular elections of April, 1964. It succeeded, however, only in alarming the Malay power structure which wanted neither Chinese nor socialist domination of peninsular politics. Moreover the Alliance Party, which was formed by a coalition of the moderate Malay, Indian and Chinese parties on the peninsula, looked with disfavor on the divisiveness of a competing majority-Chinese party. Even Lee's aggressive personality caused resentment among the Malays. Problems reached crisis proportions in 1965 when Lee suggested that the Alliance no longer represented a recognizable constituency and called for a Malaysian-Malaysia to replace the Malay-Malaysia which guaranteed special rights to Malays.

In consequence on August 9, 1965, after a series of talks between Lee and Malaysian Prime Minister Abdul Rahman, Singapore was forced to withdraw from the federation and became fully independent.

REPUBLIC OF SINGAPORE

The Singapore legislature met after the withdrawal/expulsion and amended the constitution—basically the 1958 constitution as amended in 1963 to permit federation—to meet Singapore's changed status. The unicameral Legislative Assembly became a 65-member Parliament. The prime minister continued to head a cabinet responsible to the legisature, and Yusef bin Ishak became president and titular head of state after Singapore declared itself a republic on December 22, 1965.

Singapore retained the Emergency Powers section of the Malaysian federal constitution to enable it to deal with subversion, and agreed to cooperate with Malaysia in defense, foreign policy and on economic issues. Malay remained the official language, but English continued to be the de facto medium of business and government. However, despite its agreement to cooperate, Singapore, partly out of necessity, immediately set out to develop a competitive economic policy. As a first step it proposed reestablishing trade with Indonesia which, prior to "confrontation," had been its major trading partner. Malaysia responded by threatening to restrict commercial relationships with Singapore which therefore withdrew from the joint defense council that the two states had agreed upon.

The prospects for a viable independent Singapore appeared bleak, particularly after Britain in 1968 announced it would withdraw its military forces within the following three years. Singapore survived because, first, the government immediately undertook aggressive economic programs to industrialize, woo foreign investment, and modernize the skills of its society. Second, the People's Republic of China was preoccupied by its "cultural revolution" and neglected the MCP. Third, the Chinese community had developed a sense of permanence and loyalty to the state. In 1968 PAP sought and received a new mandate from the people by calling for general elections. Because the Barisan boycotted the elections PAP won every seat, as it did again in 1972.

Security Britain's announced determination to give up its bases in Singapore by 1971 prompted enactment of legislation making all 18-year old males subject to military service. Israeli advisers were brought in to train the armed forces, much to the irritation of the Muslim-Malay world. Government determination plus Israeli know-how produced a small but well-trained army. Even more importantly, military service was exploited to help create a sense of national identity.

The British in fact extended their military presence beyond 1971 because of the uncertainties arising from mounting communist successes in Indochina, and a Five-Power Commonwealth Defense Council came into effect November 1, 1971 which included Britain, Australia, New Zealand, Malaysia and Singapore. A small Australian, New Zealand and British presence (ANZUK) was established in both Singapore and Malaysia. Nevertheless, final withdrawal of the British began in 1975 and was completed by March 31, 1976. Singapore and Malaysia were thereafter basically responsible for their own defense, but all five nations agreed to respond if either Malaysia or Singapore faced an external attack.

The early 1970s saw renewed Chinese communist activity in Singapore. In May 1971 Lee closed two newspapers and jailed four executives from another—*Nanyang Siang Pau,* the city's largest—for "alleged race baiting and the use of secret foreign funding."[1] In January 1973 he arrested the chairman and managing director of *Nanyang* and released two of the editors jailed earlier. The following year the government proposed a law making it more difficult for the media to receive foreign funding. The bill passed in August after the government assured Parliament that it had no intention of taking over the press or of inhibiting its legitimate commercial transactions.

In June 1974 the government also arrested 30 suspected communists and saboteurs—the largest number since February 1963—declaring that the communists had abandoned their political association with the Barisan Socialis and were preparing for armed struggle. At the same time the Singapore Muslim Action Front protested against government treatment of Muslims and the presence of Israeli advisers although, according to the government, the last Israelis had ended their duties the preceding month.

Economy Singapore is a commercial city as it always has been, and its concerns have traditionally been economic rather than political. PAP came to power as a left-wing socialist party, but experience in office quickly brought out a strong streak of economic pragmatism within the leadership that significantly modified its socialist economics, particularly after the Barisan element was banished.

The government had early addressed the pressing problem of housing, both to relieve the terrible conditions brought on by poverty and overcrowding, and to stimulate the economy. Under the Housing Development Board tremendous strides were taken in building multi-storied apartment buildings in housing estates, i.e., complexes which included the essentials of community living—shops, schools and eventually entertainment facilities. Slum dwellers were moved into these units. The slums they evacuated were razed and rebuilt with like apartments to which the original dwellers could return if they desired. By 1966 Singapore was constructing annually 10 new dwellings for every 1,000 persons.

The equally severe problem of unemployment was addressed by the Economic Development Board (EDB) which began to develop industrial estates, the largest and most notable of which is Jurong, built on the site of a former coastal swamp. The Jurong Industrial Estate, which was designed to increase port facilities and build an infrastructure to attract new and foreign industries, was well underway before merger with Malaysia. After separation the success of this project was essential. The government sought to enlist the cooperation of labor and capital but did not hesitate to use authoritarian measures to assure that its programs were carried out. Employment and industrial relations acts were passed in 1968 restricting union disputes and eventually outlawing strikes.

Deciding that Singapore needed to develop exports in order to acquire foreign capital, and technologically advanced industries to force labor to acquire modern technical skills, PAP leadership pushed the Economic Incentives Act through Parliament in 1967 to provide financial inducement to modern export industries. The Development

Bank was organized to provide financing for industrial projects; the International Trading Company, which was jointly owned by the government and the Development Bank, was established to promote and expedite international trade; and the EDB was reorganized to manage industrial estates, provide technical and financial assistance and join foreign companies in joint ventures.

Benefiting from the new shipbuilding and repair center at Jurong, new free industrial zones, and government encouragement of international trade, Singapore by 1970 had become the busiest port in the Commonwealth, exceeding London. Its free market monetary policies, combined with absence of restrictions on foreign banking, had also enabled it to become the headquarters of the Asian dollar market and a major financial center. Multinational oil companies had selected the city for administrative and service headquarters while they prospected for oil in waters throughout Southeast Asia. Singapore itself had developed oil refining facilities and ranked as the third largest refining center in the world, surpassed only by Rotterdam and Houston. Singapore's GNP grew at an annual average rate of 14 percent, but slackened in the mid-1970s in the wake of the rise in oil prices and world inflation.

Social Problems   Singapore recognized earlier than most developing nations the problems caused by unchecked population growth in a finite economic situation. The rate of growth was checked in the 1950s, and in the 1960s the government set zero growth as its goal; by 1981 the rate was 1.2 percent, and the population 2.4 million. The Singapore Family Planning and Population Board has been extraordinarily successful for three reasons: 1) Singapore is an urban area with a basically literate population which can be readily reached by various media— TV, radio, press and posters, 2) the government supported the program with punitive measures, denying housing and schooling advantages to families with more than the specified number of children, and 3) the government made birth control measures readily available. One effect of the one or two-child family is that women have entered the labor market in ever increasing numbers, the percentage doubling in less than two decades. This is a significant plus since Singapore suffers a chronic labor shortage. Ironically, in 1984 the government backtracked and urged educated women to have more children by offering them tax breaks.

In its first nine years in power PAP allocated one-third of its budget to education, with an emphasis on technical, scientific and physical education, the first two to improve the economic skills of the nation, the latter to improve the health of the community. A second language was required and facility in English was quickly perceived as the road to advancement. Fully one-fourth of the citizenry speak English, although Tamil, Malay and Mandarin are also official languages. In 1971 English became the language of the military.

The government invested vast sums in infrastructure and public housing (40 percent of the people lived in public housing by the end of 1975), education, and in providing jobs, but Singapore did not become a welfare state. The elderly and the handicapped were left to the care of family and charitable institutions. Singapore instead was dedicated to economic achievement, hard work and self-reliance. This attitude was not wholly admired by outsiders and by the mid-1970s the government itself sought to alter the materialistic mindset of the nation.

Foreign Affairs   After separation from Malaysia Singapore was too small to defend itself except in limited fashion and being an entrepot it needed to maintain ties with as many states as possible. Thus a continuing military relationship with Britain and other Commonwealth countries did not dissuade the state from establishing cordial relations with Eastern Europe nor from embracing the political posture of the third world. It joined both the nonaligned bloc and the Association of Southeast Asian Nations (ASEAN)

Singapore's relations with its ASEAN neighbors have not always been good however. Malaysia resented Singapore's aggressiveness and its Israeli advisers, and Indonesia accused Singapore of wanting to take over Japan's earlier role in the area. Singapore's insensitivity to its neighbors' concerns was exemplified by its execution of two Indonesian saboteurs in spite of Indonesian President Suharto's plea for leniency. The action produced anti-Singapore riots in Jakarta and a further effort on the part of Indonesia to develop its own trade patterns and reduce its dependence on Singapore as a transshipment center.

As Singapore surmounted immediate post-separation problems and felt secure in its ability to survive despite Britain's planned troop withdrawal, it began to mend its political fences. In 1970 Singapore passed tax incentives for nationals to invest in Malaysia and in 1972 Lee visited Kuala Lumpur for the first time since separation; the Malaysian prime minister returned the compliment in November 1973. Despite the still bitter feelings between the two countries, the leaders recognized the need to unite in the face of common threats, i.e., renewed fighting in Vietnam and increased communist activity in Malaysia. In 1973 Lee also visited Jakarta, for the first time in 13 years, and Suharto reciprocated in 1974. The visit of Suharto resulted in the signing of an economic treaty and the ratification of an agreement delineating the sea boundaries between the two states. The agreement drew a line through the Strait of Singapore—basically following the course taken by supertankers—but did not posit the boundaries at the entrances of the strait nor of the continental shelf.

POST-VIETNAM WAR

The defeat and total elimination of the Republic of Vietnam by communist Vietnamese forces created a shock wave throughout Southeast Asia. Singapore was perhaps in the most favorable position to weather the immediate postwar period. "The best thing we can say about the American intervention in Southeast Asia," one government official said in May 1975, "is that it bought us 10 years time. . . . We here have not wasted the precious time—but I am very much afraid that some of our neighbors have."[2]

Security Throughout the region communist guerrilla operations increased and communist political action intensified. The MCP doubled the number of broadcasts in English, Tamil, Malay and Chinese dialects on its "Voice of Malayan Revolution" from its station in southern China. During the first six months of 1976 a communist network—apparently run from Hong Kong and Sydney, Australia—was uncovered and 50 members were arrested. To deal with the increase in communist subversion the Singapore government doubled its police force by the end of 1976 to 12,000, one per every 170 residents.

In May, after allegations by the Dutch Labor party that Singapore was violating human rights and civil liberties by not releasing those being detained for communist activities, PAP withdrew from the Socialist International, the organization of socialist parties to which the ruling parties of both Singapore and Holland belonged. In submitting the party's letter of resignation, PAP representative C.V. Devan Nair charged that the Malay Communist Party "was an illegal organization both in Malaysia and Singapore against whose elected governments it has been waging armed revolution for many years," that since the communist takeover in Vietnam "there had been a significant increase in armed guerrilla activities and clandestine organizational work," and that those detained had been arrested "following the detection of an underground net of CPM [MCP] agents and the discovery of large caches of arms and explosives."[3] The Socialist International did not accept Nair's explanations, objecting perhaps as much to PAP's pragmatic capitalism as to its authoritarianism, and concurred in Singapore's withdrawal.

Further arrests occurred during 1976 in connection with reported communist infiltration of Singapore Polytechnic College. Most of those arrested were students who were warned, as were their parents, of the dangers of associating with subversives. Those who renounced communism were released. Lim Hock Siew, founding member of PAP, and Said Zahari, former newspaper editor, both of whom had been detained for 15 years without trial, were released but restricted to two offshore islets because they refused to foreswear communism.

As communism was contained, a new threat arose—the worldwide phenomenon of Muslim extremism. In January 1982, 10 Muslims, including four opposition politicians, all members of the clandestine Singapore's People's Liberation Organization, were arrested for plotting to overthrow the government "by creating communal unrest, arson and by planting bombs in shipping centers."[4] They were also charged with soliciting help from foreign powers and individuals. Five of them pleaded guilty and were given jail terms of three years.

Politics In July 1976 the government announced that Parliament would be increased to 69 members, and a new coalition—comprising mainly Malay organizations—emerged to oppose PAP in the December election. Not unexpectedly PAP won all seats as it did again in the February 1979 by-elections. The by-elections, however, produced two surprises. The secretary general of the Workers' Party, against whom Lee had just won a slander suit, won an unexpected 38 percent of the vote for the seat for which he was standing. The other unusual event was that some of the candidates chosen by PAP to run were highly experienced bureaucrats rather than party members, and Lee announced in advance the cabinet positions they would hold if elected. This move reflected Lee's "recruitment and promotion drive" to bring bright young technocrats and bureaucrats into top positions of government and train them as a "successor generation." Lee appointed Lim Chee Onn as secretary general of the National Trades Union Congress, a technocrat instead of a union leader, and informed union members that their job was to find the most qualified persons to lead them, not necessarily those who had seniority or had worked within the union.

Goh Keng Swee, who had long been the government's major trouble shooter and had alternated between being minister of finance and minister of defense, depending upon which department was most in need of his talents, was made minister of education, indicating that education was the government's current concern. As minister of defense Goh had pointed out that soldiers from lower backgrounds could speak neither English nor Mandarin, although the schools had been supposed to teach English as the second language and Mandarin as the Chinese "dialect" for the past 10 years. As minister of education, Goh pragmatically began to "stream" children to eliminate slow learners from the bilingual program; he also insisted that Mandarin be used in teaching Chinese.

In December 1980 PAP again made a clean sweep of all—now 75—parliamentary seats, the fourth such success since 1968. Lee campaigned on the slogan, "help me test a new team"; 18 of the PAP candidates were less than 43 years old. The seven opposition parties which fielded 43 candidates campaigned on the proposition that one party rule was not true democracy.

PAP's monopoly was finally broken in December 1981 when J.B. Jeyaretnam, a member of the Workers' Party, won the seat vacated by Devan Nair who had just been unanimously chosen president of the nation (October 23) following the death in May of Benjamin Sheares. Jeyaretnam, of Indian ancestry, won in a 78 percent Chinese district, even though he could not speak Chinese and had to use an interpreter when campaigning. His success was due in part to the fact that Nair had chosen a rich Chinese as his replacement candidate in this heavily working class district, but evidence suggests that the vote was primarily against rising prices and the harsh attitude of the government toward labor. Although frequently the subject of scathing government comment, Jeyaretnam's presence forced the "traditionally closed and hierarchical government . . . to disclose a great deal of information about its policies—the sort of information that is readily available in most democracies but which has normally been withheld in the island republic."[5]

Lee's PAP achieved renewal of its mandate in the 1984 elections, winning 77 of the now 79 parliamentary seats. His traditional opponent, Jeyaretnam, was reelected; the Democratic Party's Chiam See Tong won the remaining seat.

In the wake of his election victory Lee began to criticize the one-man-one-vote system, a prelude to his campaign to change electoral politics. His plan was to mix parliamentary and presidential systems by creating multi-person constituencies and a popularly elected president. A constitutional amendment of the same year allowed the opposition three non-constituency seats even if fewer than that number are elected. The amendment was designed to defuse criticism that Singapore is a one party state.

The 1988 elections were again swept by PAP. Only Chiam See Tong of the opposition was reelected. The government had rid itself of the troublesome Jeyaretnam by successfully prosecuting him for false declaration of Workers' Party funds.

By 1988 Lee mainly achieved his goals. First, Singapore had modified the electoral system by creating 13 three-member "super" districts, or team constituencies, while retaining the remaining 40 single-member districts. At least one candidate in each super district must represent a minority community, and in eight of the super districts one candidate is required to be a Malay. The device is supposed to ensure multi-racial and multi-religious political participation.

Second, direct election of the president was mandated. The popularly elected president, to be chosen when Prime Minister Lee retires, will have veto authority over certain expenditures, and civil service and judicial appointments. The president may not initiate policy or make executive decisions.

Economy   Singapore is an economic creature. It was founded by merchants and continues to be a center of trade. By 1980 it was the third largest port in the world, next to Rotterdam and Yokohama.

Singapore nevertheless has been engaged in a massive effort to expand its economic base by creating and encouraging industrial developmnent, particularly since its separation from Malaysia in 1965. So successful has it become that surveys made in 1977 and 1978 by Business International Corporation (an American research firm) rated Singapore as the best investment country in the world. The criteria on which the surveys were based were primarily political and economic stability and freedom of movement of capital. On a scale of 100 Singapore ranked 15 points higher in 1978 than either the U.S. or Canada.[6] However, the "second industrial revolution" launched by Singapore that year caused some foreign entrepreneurs to pause before investing in new industries. The new policy was intended to eliminate cheap "guest labor" and thus force employers to increase productivity by mechanization, and to develop middle-technology industries. The means to these ends were government-dictated higher wages. The cost to employers the first year alone was about 20 percent of the median pay. To increase the pool of skilled labor the government established a Skills Development Fund and persuaded the French in November 1980 to establish the Singapore-French Institute of Technology in Jurong. This, France's biggest investment in the transfer of technology, was a major vote of confidence in the future of Singapore.

The higher wage scale, however, did not produce instant mechanization nor upgraded labor, and the government found it necessary to maintain an open door policy to foreign skilled and unskilled labor in order to complete on schedule Singapore's largest industrial investment, a US$1 billion petrochemical complex. Ironically, when the major facilities were completed in 1982, the worldwide petrochemical glut impeded their startup.

By 1981 the wage policy was being perceived negatively by employers. Wage costs had risen more than 60 percent and were beginning to force some foreign as well as local firms out of business. A new 10-year plan to raise Singapore to the rank of an industrialized nation was announced in March and one-half of the 1981–82 budget was earmarked for development. The "main pillars" of growth were to be manufacturing, trade, tourism, transport and communications. The wage policy was seen as a hindrance to this plan since it was pricing Singapore out of the international labor market. As a result the government decided to discontinue the higher wage policy, try to eliminate job-switching, and give employers greater determination on use of manpower by allowing them to demand longer hours without overtime, particularly in the key shipbuilding and repair industries. In

November Parliament, without debate, passed a trade disputes amendment to the Labor Code that brought "such union activities as go-slow
and work-to-rule under the government's stringent rules governing
labor strikes."[7]

In another move to improve its economic position the government
proposed to dismantle all import tariffs except those on a few traditional revenue items such as tobacco, liquor and petroleum products.
It also plans to reduce personal income taxes periodically. At the same
time it seeks to persuade all ASEAN nations to lower their own tariffs
progressively, an action that would basically benefit Singapore since it
is the most industrialized state in the association.

Singapore opened a Gold Exchange in 1978 to widen the scope and
diversity of the country's financial markets and to enhance its position
as the fourth largest banking center in the world. To improve business
communications the state began to build two new satellite receiving
stations and inaugurated two legs of the intra-ASEAN underwater
cable linking it with the Philippines and Indonesia. In the new Jurong
Town Corporation master plan for the 1980s the government emphasized decentralization of industry onto offshore islets; both polluting
industries and petrochemical plants are presently being sited there.
The worldwide recession of 1981–83 slowed Singapore's economic
growth and prompted the government to increase infrastructure projects, e.g., roads and Changi International Airport expansion.

Singapore recovered rapidly from the oil crisis of the late 1970s.
Workers in commerce enjoyed an average growth in earnings of 12
percent a year between 1979 and 1985, while manufacturing grew to
earn more than 50 percent of the republic's foreign exchange. The city
state also recovered quickly from the worldwide recession of the mid
1980s. Broad based growth in electronics, electrical goods, machinery,
fabricated metal products and the chemical and printing industries
resulted in a gross domestic product increase of over 9 percent in 1988.
More than 3,000 multinational corporations from the U.S., Japan and
Europe operate in Singapore's cosmopolitan environment.

Foreign Affairs   A Chinese state in a Malay sea, Singapore has been
wary of too close a relationship with the PRC. The March 1975 visit to
Peking by Foreign Minister Sinnathamby Rajaratnam was the first
official visit by a Singaporean official; in July 1981 the two countries
established formal commercial relations. However, when PRC Vice
Premier Teng Hsiao-ping made a grand swing through Southeast Asia
in November 1978, Lee warned him not to meddle in Singapore's
affairs, reminding him that Singapore's Chinese are Singaporeans. Lee
reiterated that neither Singapore nor ASEAN wished to become involved in the PRC-USSR/Vietnam power struggle in Indochina, point-

ing out that the five states were concerned instead with building an economically strong and politically secure Southeast Asia.

Fiercely aware of its national sovereignty, Singapore has not hesitated to take contrarian positions. Despite its highly vocal opposition to Vietnam's military occupation of Kampuchea, and the nation's commitment to the formal ASEAN policy of economically isolating Vietnam for its sins, Singapore is "first on the list of Hanoi's clients" and second among non-communist states in supplying imports to Vietnam.[8] Conversely the nation provides covert aid to the Kampuchean factions that resist the Vietnamese-supported government.

A similar anomaly is evident in Singapore's posture toward the People's Republic of China and the Republic of China (ROC) on Taiwan. Singapore has not formally recognized the ROC, although Prime Minister Lee Kuan Yew has visited Taiwan informally at least 20 times, and in 1989 he invited ROC President Lee Teng-hui to Singapore. Coincident with the Taiwan leader's visit it was announced that Singapore intended to extend full diplomatic recognition to the PRC!

Relations with its immediate neighbors during the post-Vietnam War years were generally good. In 1975 Singapore entered into a shipping agreement with Indonesia, "based on equality and mutual benefit," and in 1978 agreed to help that country develop Batam Island, just 13 miles south of Singapore, as a tax free, bonded industrial estate—in competition with its own industrial developments. Fearing a loss of port fees and a negative impact on its refining industry, however, Singapore did not support Malaysia and Indonesia when they first proposed limiting the tonnage of ships passing through the Strait of Malacca after a Japanese supertanker had run aground there. Following a second such accident which resulted in an oil spill in the Singapore Strait, Singapore agreed to the February 24, 1977 Safety of Navigation in the Straits of Malacca and Singapore Accord by which the three nations unilaterally established an under-the-keel clearance minimum of 3.5 meters (11.5 feet). Despite this action Singapore continues to consider the straits as international waterways. In 1980 Singapore again followed its two neighbors by extending territorial limits to 12 miles from shore and its economic zone to 200 miles, agreeing to settle any boundary dispute—sure to arise in these narrow waterways—through negotiations.

Together with its Malaysian partner, Singapore nevertheless continues to subscribe to the Five Power Defense Arrangement of 1971. The nation seeks regional respect, but as in Malaysia the political elite is uncertain as to the future role of ASEAN. In 1989 Prime Minister Lee announced that Singapore's trade dependency upon the ASEAN countries had fallen from 50 to 20 percent.

WHITHER SINGAPORE?

Singapore has achieved enviable rank among the four economic "smaller dragons" of East Asia. It enjoys a per capita income exceeding that of the Republic of Korea or Taiwan. Its foreign reserves are greater, per capita, than those of Taiwan, and its proportion of gross domestic product earned through trade is higher than that of Hong Kong. Indonesia and Malaysia depend significantly upon Singapore for port and financial services. Seemingly the republic's future economic importance in Southeast Asia is constrained only by its small physical size and a population of only 2.6 million which is barely replacing itself.

During its post independence decades Singapore essentially escaped the communal strife suffered by Malaysia. Malay and Indian minorities (24 percent of the population) joined the Chinese majority to pursue with spectacular success economic interests essential to the survival of the city state. Ethnicity and ideology were of secondary importance. Despite the hitherto socialist philosophy of PAP, market forces—within a political framework predicated upon individual rights, the rule of law and democracy—have predominated.

In 1989 the government appeared to be changing course. Policy makers called for Singaporeans to evolve a "national ideology." The concept was challenged immediately by the Malay and Indian minorities who perceived its tenor as abandonment of the multi-ethnic approach epitomized by the term "Singaporean." The predominantly Chinese political leadership was apparently influenced by recent studies of western scholars who have concluded that the economic miracles of Japan, the Republic of Korea and Taiwan are in part the result of "communitarian" rather than "individualistic" values.[9]

These nations are usually categorized by scholars as Confucian states, products of an ethical system which has influenced more people than any other, and is in a broad sense embraced by the two-thirds Chinese majority of Singapore. The ethic subjugates the individual to the family, and traditionally has conferred authority to govern on the worthy.

Since 1988 both Prime Minister Lee and his chosen successor, Goh Chok Tong, have demonstrated a decided bias in favor of Confucian principles. Lee has publicly referred to them as underlying the successes of other post-Confucian states of East Asia.

Singapore policy makers, along with their counterparts in other Asian nations who are smitten with ardent nationalism, seem to want modernization and increased ethnic awareness while simultaneously resisting western materialism and individualism. But such views could lead to unacceptable levels of authoritarianism, as restrictions on a free press and the arbitrary detention of individuals during the 1980s confirm.

FOOTNOTES

1. *Data for Decision* (Manila: Press Foundation of Asia), 1972, p. 278.

2. Quoted by William Tuohy, "Indochina Outcome Leaves Rest of Region Confused," *Los Angeles Times,* May 25, 1975.

3. *Data Asia* (Manila: Press Foundation of Asia), 1976, p. 3813.

4. *Ibid.,* 1982, p. 8627.

5. *Asia Yearbook* (Hong Kong: Far Eastern Economic Review Ltd.), 1983, p. 240.

6. *Data Asia, op. cit.,* 1978, p. 5709.

7. *Ibid.,* 1981, p. 8446.

8. *Foreign Broadcast Information Service, EA,* June 8, 1988, p. 51.

9. See George C. Lodge, and Ezra F. Vogel, *Ideology and National Competitiveness: An Analysis of Nine Far Eastern Countries* (Boston: Harvard University Business School Press), 1987.

Brunei

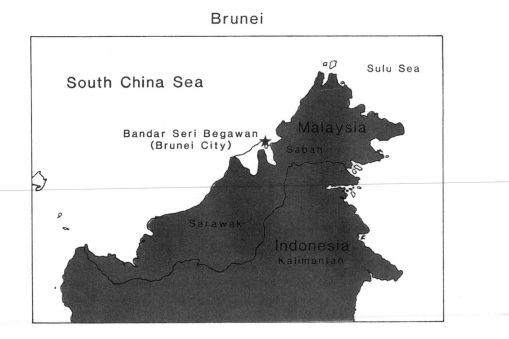

South China Sea

Sulu Sea

Bandar Seri Begawan
(Brunei City)

Malaysia

Sabah

Sarawak

Indonesia
Kalimantan

CHAPTER 7
BRUNEI

The state of Negara Brunei Darussalam is located on the northwest coast of the island of Borneo (which is a European corruption of the word "Brunei"). Divided into two unequal parts by the Limbang River, the tiny state of 2,226 square miles is surrounded on three sides by the Malaysian state of Sarawak, and on the fourth by the South China Sea. Brunei has a tropical climate, with heavy rainfall, a hilly and swampy jungle terrain, and a coastline of 100 miles. The capital, Banda Seri Begawan, previously known as Brunei or Brunei Town, is the only city. For most of historic times the sultanate of Brunei included the contemporary Malaysian states of Sarawak and Sabah, i.e., most of western and northern Borneo.

The indigenous population is a mixture of 15 percent Negrito and Proto-Malay, and 60 percent Deutero-Malay, with an admixture of Arab blood. Chinese merchants and entrepreneurs who immigrated in recent years make up the remaining 25 percent.

EARLY CENTURIES

Chinese annals first mention the region in the 6th century A.D. when it was known in them as Po Ni, with a trading center at Kota Batu, near the site of the present capital. Po Ni supplied China with camphor and birds' nest for soup, and sent tribute missions to the imperial court. The present dynasty came into power on Borneo in 1405, coincident with the establishment of the Kingdom of Malacca on the Malay peninsula. Trade between these states grew and Brunei exchanged wax, sago, rice and gold with Malacca, for cloth from India. During the 15th century Brunei at various times paid tribute to Malacca, China, and Java and developed an adminstrative structure and court ceremony derived from all three. It meanwhile expanded its territories to include all of Sarawak and Sabah.

When Malacca fell to the Portugese in 1511 many Malaccans of the merchant—and some of the ruling—class established themselves in

Brunei. Their influence was felt in two ways: the economy prospered and Islam, the faith of the Malaccan Malays, became the religion of the Brunein upper class. Trade increased, partly because many of the Malaccan merchants had brought with them their capital as well as their expertise, and partly because the Portugese found Brunei a useful ally. Alone among the Malay states, Brunei was treated as a friend. It was a convenient waystation between Malacca and Macao, the Portugese entrepot in southern China, and Malacca and the Moluccas, the spice islands whose products they sought. It was also a market for Chinese currency, the accepted exchange in that part of the world.

Brunei experienced its greatest territorial expansion and prosperity during the 16th century. Sultan Bolkeiah, (exact dates unknown) extended his sway over most of Borneo, the Sulu archipelago and much of the southern Philippines—including perhaps the Visayan Islands—and raided as far north as Manila. Pigafetta, an Italian who accompanied Magellan on his 1521 world encircling voyage, remarked upon the highly civilized court he observed in Brunei, the number of Chinese merchants in residence and the amount of silk brocade, and gold and silver tableware, in use.

As the century waned, however, the state was wracked by internal strife. Outlying territories fell away and European powers moved in. Spain laid claim to the southern Philippines and the Sulu archipelago as a result of Magellan's explorations, and in 1577 the Spanish attacked and captured Brunei Town. They also launched two later successful expeditions against the sultanate (1588 and 1645) but could not maintain control because they, in turn, were forced out of their base in the southern Philippines by the Dutch who had replaced the Portugese in the islands of Southeast Asia. Brunei's relations with the Dutch were cordial despite loss to them of vassal states in eastern Borneo and of traditional trade routes in the Moluccas. However, as its legitimate trade was circumscribed by the Dutch in the spice islands and, to a much lesser extent, by the Spanish in the Philippines, Brunei turned to the age-old island enterprise of piracy.

Political authority and economic conditions continued to deteriorate throughout the 18th and 19th centuries, as the sultan lost control over his chieftains, and the area became feared as a pirate base and slave mart. The state dwindled in size to include only Brunei proper, Sarawak and portions of Sabah. Brunei Town, which in 1730 still had a population of 40,000, with thousands of Chinese raising pepper in the countryside, by 1842 was little more than a large village.

BRITISH INTERESTS

The English East India Company initially expressed interest in Brunei in the late 18th century because of its strategic position athwart the trade routes to China and Japan. The sultanate was subsequently perceived as too far east for use as a entrepot or naval base, and the company turned to developing ports along the west coast of the Malay peninsula instead. During the 19th century Brunei became a serious threat to international trade, attacking shipping, not only along the coastal sea lanes but in the straits of Singapore and Malacca as well.

Encroachment   The company found an ally in its struggle against these predations in James Brooke, a young Englishman formerly with the company's army in India. At the request of Singapore merchants in 1841 he helped the ruler quell a rebellion in Sarawak, a vassal state of Brunei, and in recompense was made governor of the territory. With the aid at crucial times of British naval vessels, Brooke destroyed pirate centers and in 1846 foiled a pro-piracy coup at the capital, in return for which the sultan ceded him full sovereignty of Sarawak; he remained nevertheless a vassal. In his role as Raja of Sarawak Brooke continued to move against pirate havens to the north, extending his own control over the cleared area at the expense of Brunei. Each territorial gain was explained on the grounds that the sultan could not control the pirates still infesting his domains.

Brooke retired to England in 1863, transfering his suzerainty over Sarawak to his nephew, Charles Brooke. The following year Britain recognized Sarawak as an independent state by appointing a consul to the capital, yet it reminded Charles in 1877 that he was still the sultan's vassal.

The policy of the sultan of Brunei during the 19th century was to make the best of a bad situation. Unable to control his territorial chieftains or protect settled people from the predations of the piratical elements of society, he was willing to allow the Brookes to increase their dominions. Always in need of money, he was also willing to "sell" or "lease" other lands. Thus in 1846 he ceded Labuan Island to the British as a commercial and naval base in return for an annual payment, and promised not to dispose of further portions of his territory without British government permission. Against such a back-drop he encountered the American adventurer, Charles Lee Moses, in 1865.

Moses, the American consul to Brunei in the days when a consul was paid no salary but was expected to support himself from consular fees and by his own business acumen, persuaded the sultan to give him 28,000 square miles of northern Brunei—roughly the modern state of Sabah—in return for an annual payment of US$9,500 that he never made. Moses sold his title to the territory, which eventually was acquired by Dent Brothers, a British trading firm. Dent Brothers was given full sovereignty over Sabah by the sultan, in return for a yearly payment of US$10,000 to the sultan and US$3,000 to his chief adviser.

Recognizing that the Sultan of Sulu also had claims to the area, the company the following year signed a treaty with Sulu agreeing to pay that ruler US$5,000 annually. The monetary settlements may be indicative of the strength of the two sultan's claims.

In 1881 Dent Brothers was reorganized as the British North Borneo Company under British royal charter to manage Sabah, with the understanding that the company would make facilities available to the British navy if sought, would not interfere with the religion or the customs of the natives, and would not "transfer away" any part of the territory without British government permission.

Protectorate   During the next decade Britain undertook to legalize the status quo of the area. A treaty with Spain in 1885 acknowledged Spanish rights to the Sulu archipelago in return for Spanish recognition of British rights to Sabah (now called North Borneo); the boundaries between British and Dutch Borneo were agreed to in 1891. In 1888 Britain had declared Sabah, Sarawak, and what was left of the Sultanate of Brunei, as British protectorates, for the most part stabilizing their boundaries, although both Sarawak and Sabah continued to expand their territories at the expense of Brunei.

Disregarding its status as a British protectorate, Charles Brooke in 1890 sought to absorb all of Brunei by seizing the Limbang River Valley, thus splitting the already tiny kingdom in two. He thought, erroneously, that the parts would fall into his hands. The sultan for many years refused to acknowledge this annexation of his land and refused the proffered compensation. Relations between Sarawak and Brunei were normalized only after the British assigned a resident to the court of Brunei in 1906. Sabah, on the other hand, rounded out its borders by land grants from Brunein nobility in 1898.

The British protectorate over all three states gave Britain control of their foreign affairs, guaranteed them protection from external forces, and in Brunei provided extraterritorial rights for British citizens. The governor of the Straits Settlements in Singapore was designated high commissioner to each. It is probably fair to say that with the proclamation of the British protectorate the sultan of Brunei's legal suzerainty over Sabah and Sarawak ceased.

Brunei: 1906–1945   In 1906 Britain assigned a resident to the court of Brunei. James Brooke had proposed this move more than a half century previously, and if Brooke's suggestion had been followed when made, the state of Brunei would in all likelihood still encompass Sabah and most of Sarawak.

Under the residency system the relationship of the British government to Brunei was similar to its relationship to the members of the unfederated Malay sultanates. The resident was appointed from the (British) Malayan Civil Service and British officers were eventually brought in to head various government departments. As in Malaya, the residency system assured a reasonable concern for law, order and economic and social development without attempting to force change.

The years between 1906 and 1941, therefore, were years of slow but steady progress. Roads were built, trade improved and the people were encouraged to settle down and become farmers and fisherman. Schooling remained traditional: Islam was the religion of the land and education followed primarily Islamic modes. Discovery of oil in the 1920s and the output from the Seria field beginning in 1929 made a considerable difference in the finances available to the state and to the importance of Brunei in international affairs. The oil fields, developed by the British firm, Burnei Shell Petroleum, became of major importance to the Commonwealth. They also attracted the attention of Japan.

The Japanese attacked and occupied the oil fields of Seria on December 16, 1941. Six days later they seized Brunei Town. In the immediate prewar years the British had stockpiled food for fear that the war in Europe would interfere with shipping. Brunei thus weathered the first year of occupation fairly well, even though trade came to a standstill. However, by the war's end the population faced starvation. Medicines were unavailable and malaria was rampant; roads were neglected and overgrown, and people had sought refuge in the jungles. During 1944 Brunei suffered daily air raids as the Allies fought their way through the islands of the Pacific, and the capital was almost completely destroyed. Immediately before the British retook Brunei on June 10, 1945 the Japanese killed all political prisoners and bombed the oil fields.[1]

Postwar Borneo All three of the Bornean states were badly damaged during the Japanese occupation and Sabah and Sarawak were financially unable to rehabilitate themselves and sought crown colony status to become eligible for British aid. Brunei, more fortunate, looked to potential oil revenues. Initially, all three were subject to British military government.

When administration was returned to civilian authority in 1946 the three states were more unified than they had been in prewar years and they continued to build upon this new base. The British resident at Brunei became responsible to the governor at Sarawak instead of to the high commissioner in Singapore. The three accepted a unified court system and discussed further administrative and political ties. But Brunei evinced more interest in a relationship with Malaya than with the neighbors who occupied her former territories and now seemed interested in sharing her oil wealth as well. However, there was much interstate trade and labor moved back and forth freely, primarily from Sarawak to the oil fields in Brunei.

During the next few years the possibility of federation with Malaya was discussed. In April 1962 a British commission canvassed opinion in Sarawak and Sabah and found sentiment heavily in favor of union; in Brunei the decision was up to the sultan who was known to favor it. Fate deemed otherwise.

Brunei's first constitution was promulgated by the sultan in 1959, at which time its administration was separated from that of Sarawak. Elections for a partially-elective Legislative Council were held in August-September 1962 and the left-leaning National Brunei People's Party won all the contested seats. The leader of this party was A.M. Azahari, of Arab parentage, from Sabah, and Indonesian trained. Unopposed, the party had presented itself as all things to all segments of society: denouncing feudalism, the British and Malaya; supporting the Chinese businessmen, yet advocating socialism and Islam; and calling for the retaking of Sabah and Sarawak as Brunei *irredenta*.

Shortly after his electoral sweep, and backed by both Indonesia and the Philippines which were advancing claims of their own to the states of British Borneo, Azahari led a revolt to prevent the three British protectorates from joining the projected Federation of Malaysia. The sultan called in British forces who soon suppressed the insurrection. Partly as a result of the revolt—but perhaps more importantly because of the sultan's developing concern over taxation of Brunei's oil revenues by the proposed federation, his position in the hierarchy of Malaysian sultans, and his loss of personal power as the result of required internal changes—Brunei, which had been the closest to peninsular Malaya of the three states of Borneo, declined to become part of the federation.

In preparation for joining Malaysia the sultan had already dismissed his British department heads and hired Malayans. After he decided against federation he dropped the Malayans and rehired British civil servants, a situation that still obtained upon independence.

INDEPENDENCE

Political Affairs In 1964, at British urging, Sultan Ali Saifuddin introduced internal constitutional reforms to achieve limited ministerial government. Under the constitution of 1959, as amended in 1964, Britain remained responsible for Brunei's defense and foreign affairs. Legislative authority was vested in the Legislative Council—a majority of whose members were appointed by the sultan—which also acted in an advisory capacity. A judicial system—independent of Sarawak and Sabah—was established, with a High Court, a Court of Appeals and magistrates courts. New elections to the Legislative Council were held in 1965.

Saifuddin, unwilling to accept the further changes urged on him by his British advisers, abdicated on October 4, 1967 in favor of his 21-year old son, Hassanal Bolkiah who was crowned sultan on August 1, 1968, the 29th of his dynastic line. Only Saiffudin's death in 1986 ended constant quarreling between father and son over each other's prerogatives.

Bolkiah as the head of state presided over a Council of Ministers, comprising the British high commissioner (akin to the resident of former years), six officers ex-officio and four assistant ministers drawn from the Legislative Council. He dissolved the existing Legislative Council in 1970, replacing it with a new council of 22 members appointed solely by him. He was advised by a Privy Council on constitutional matters, a Religious Council, and a Council of Succession, but for the most part he ruled by decree on the basis of emergency powers in effect since the insurrection.

In 1971 Brunei and Britain signed an agreement recognizing Brunei's full independence in internal affairs, although Brunei continued to rely on the high commissioner for advice, and on British adminsitrators in major government departments (especially finance); Britain retained responsibility for defense and foreign affairs. Under pressure from the United Nations decolonization committee, its neighboring states of Malaysia and Indonesia, and Britain's labor government which was eager to be rid of its last colonial responsibility in the East, Brunei in 1979 agreed to accept full independence on January 1, 1984. It did so reluctantly, perceiving no advantage in severing its ties to Britain and cognizant that its larger and more powerful neighbors, Malaysia and Indonesia, were possibly more interested in its oil than in its self determination.

In 1984 the sultan further consolidated the power of the monarchy by suspending the State Legislative Council which he had established in 1970. He appointed technocrats to development-oriented ministries, but kept key ministries in the hands of the royal family. Following his announcement (1984) that political parties, with the exception of Azahari's Brunei People's Party, were *not* banned, an "opposition" Brunei National Democratic Party (BNDP) emerged, as did a vague pro-government splinter group which called itself the National Alliance Party. In 1988 the two leaders of the BNDP were arrested and the party "deregistered."

Since independence the sultan has retained the 1,000-man Gurka battalion, which had been deployed to protect the sultan and the oilfields, by continuing to pay Britain one million pounds annually for its services. Meanwhile the tiny oil-rich nation has dramatically expanded its arsenal, raising a third local army battalion, and allocating as much as one-third of the annual budget for defense; education, public works, medical care and the police, in that order account for

the other major expenditures. By the mid-1980s this mini-nation possessed heat-seeking ground-to-air missiles, French surface-to-surface
missiles, an armored reconnaissance squadron, modern British scor-
pion tanks, an air wing of American and German helicopters, a flotilla
of fast patrol boats, and a highly sophisticated tactical communication
system.

Brunei's primary security concern is Indonesia, which supported
the Azahari rebellion and facilitated incursions by Indonesian-trained
forces into Brunei during its 1963–65 period of "confrontation" with
Malaysia. At the time Indonesia claimed all three states of British
Borneo as part of "greater Indonesia" and sought to incorporate them
into the rest of Borneo which it had acquired from the Dutch.

Economy   Brunei is, on a per capita basis, the wealthiest state in
Southeast Asia and the fourth richest nation in the world. Income from
oil and gas has accounted for nearly 90 percent of state revenue in
recent years, and revenues frequently exceed expenditures. Brunei has
no income tax, and education and medical care are free. The state
offers everyone a pension plan and subsidizes government employees,
including members of the armed forces and employees of Brunei Shell.

Brunei's wealth is, in singular fashion, a product of its relationship
with Brunei Shell Petroleum. Shell struck oil in commercial quantities
in 1929. The government subsequently became an equal partner, a fact
which inevitably causes Brunei to be referred to as the "Shellfare
State." Also in partnership with the Japanese firm of Mitsubishi, Shell
operates the largest liquid natural gas plant in the world, whose output
of 5.5 million tons is purchased by Japan and ferried by a fleet of seven
tankers that ply regularly between the two countries. Until 1980 Shell
was the state's largest employer after the government; the construction
boom of the early part of the decade relegated the company to third
place. The state hopes to develop its vast reserves of high grade silica.
The only other natural resource being exploited is timber and experts
predict the coastal jungles will be depleted within a few years unless
more selective cutting or reforestation takes place.

Five-Year plans to diversify and to develop a modern infrastructure
were adopted in 1974, 1979, and 1986. Each plan emphasized the need
to accelerate development in agriculture and industry, the former
because close to 90 percent of Brunei's foodstuffs are imported; earlier
attempts to plant rice on a large scale failed. Industrial expansion has
been chronically slowed by interdepartmental red tape, labor shortages
and the reluctance of Chinese entrepreneurs to post the high bond
required of them. Nevertheless two earth satellite stations have been
constructed to establish direct communication links with the world, a
floating dry dock services oil support vessels, and Brunei has been the

training locale for British Airways and Singapore Airlines pilots at one of the world's most modern and uncrowded airports.

In November 1986 the government disclosed large scale misuse of funds by the National Bank of Brunei, 75 percent of whose shares were held by a Singapore financer. Charging fraud, the authorities closed the bank. A new, locally owned International Bank of Brunei was formed. It is expected that the Bank will enable Brunei to play a larger financial role in the region, eventually becoming the merchant banker for ASEAN.

The Chinese have long been of major importance in the economic life of the nation, dominating 60 percent of the economy—commerce, services, manufacturing and construction. Agriculture and fishing (2 percent) and government employment (38 percent) are the monopoly of the Malay.

Foreign Affairs Upon independence Brunei immediately joined ASEAN, a move in part to insure that its powerful neighbors would abandon further designs on the state. Brunei has strengthened its political and economic ties with Indonesia, including offering that nation an interest free loan of US$100 million in 1987, and expressing a desire to invest in Indonesia's ailing cement and aluminum industries. In response to his interest the sultan is believed to have "obtained an unwritten Indonesian guarantee for the security of his state."[2] Brunei is also an investor in Malaysia, possibly for similar reasons.

Brunei maintains a special relationship with Singapore. Its currency is linked to the Singapore dollar on a par basis, the major weekly is owned by the *Singapore Times,* and Singapore's armed forces continue to use the British-developed training facilities in the Temburang jungle. In 1988 Brunei chaired ASEAN and hosted its 1989 Foreign Minister's Meeting.

A member of the Organization of the Islamic Conference, Brunei takes a strong position in support of the Palestinians and is highly critical of Israel, but the government is wary of Islamic fundamentalism and refuses to permit such influence within its educational system. Also a member of the Commonwealth of Nations, Brunei's relations with Britain are warm: in 1985 the government transferred large monetary sums to London to prop up British currency, and in 1989 was "edging closer" to membership in the Five-Power Defense Agreement among Great Britain, New Zealand, Australia and the ASEAN states of Singapore and Malaysia.[3]

WHITHER BRUNEI?

Despite its economic stength, Brunei face potentially serious social problems. Islam, the state religion practiced by 60 percent of the population, and the sultan are the cohesive forces within a society otherwise fragmented by tribal loyalties. As in other Muslim states, Brunei has a large Chinese minority, some 60,000 among a total population of approximately 226,000. Legal restrictions severely limit citizenship for the Chinese, and non-citizens are legally discriminated against: they cannot own land and foreign companies are required to post large bonds to compete for government contracts. Additionally, as non-citizens, Chinese hold only an identification certificate and thus are technically stateless—an untenable situation over the longer run.

The sultan's absolutism also suggests future problems within the Malay community itself. The increasingly better educated Malay already demonstrate some restlessness over lack of accountable government and meaningful political participation. Finally, border disputes between Brunei and the Malaysian states of Sabah and Sarawak are potential irritants. Nor is Indonesia's record of "confrontation" regarding Brunei, Sabah and Sarawak, plus its past expansion into East Timor and West Irian easily forgotten.

FOOTNOTES

1. State of Brunei, *Annual Report* (Brunei: Government Printer), 1956, p. 184–185.

2. *Southeast Asian Affairs* (Singapore: Institute of Southeast Asian Studies), 1988, p. 69.

3. *Asia Yearbook* (Hong Kong: Far Eastern Economic Review, Ltd.), 1989, p. 90.

Burma

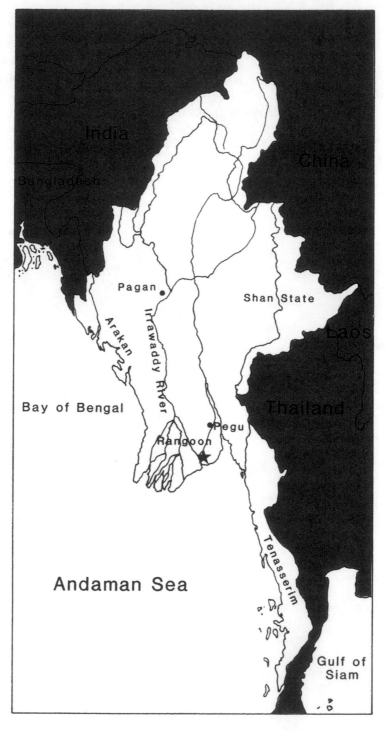

CHAPTER 8

BURMA

(MYANMAR)

Burma is bounded on the east by Thailand and Laos, on the north by China and on the west by India and Bangladesh; on the south it is washed by the Bay of Bengal and the Andaman Sea. The land mass includes four geographic regions, and Burmese history, inevitably, is influenced by this factor.

The Arakan mountains on the west, whose foothills descend to the Bay of Bengal, form the region of Arakan. On the east is the mountainous Shan plateau, a continuation of the Yunnan plateau of southern China and part of the Indo-Malayan mountain system which continues into Thailand and Laos. Between the Shan plateau and the Arakan foothills lies the central plain, the heartland of Burma. It is drained by two major rivers, the great Irrawaddy, with its tributary the Chindwin, and the lesser Sittang, which empty into the Andaman Sea and the Gulf of Martaban respectively, both part of the broad waters of the Bay of Bengal. Attached like a tail to its southeastern extremity is 500 miles of narrow coastline, forming the northern and western part of the Malay peninsula, bounded on the east by Thailand and on the west by the Bay of Bengal. This Tenasserim coast, like the coast of Arakan, is backed by mountains and possesses little arable land. But its ports and mountain passes made possible the historic portage of goods between the Bay of Bengal on the west and the Gulf of Siam on the East. Burma's mountain ranges and rivers, like those of all other states of mainland Southeast Asia, run north and south. The climate is tropical and monsoonal.

The antecedents of the modern Burmese were tribes who pushed south into Burma from the Tibetan and Yunnan plateaus of southwest China. They were preceded by the Mon, and followed by the ethnic Tai who constitute most of today's tribal groups, e.g., the Shan and Karen. Although the movement of peoples was from the borderlands of China, the cultural influences came from India, through the moun-

tain passes of Manipur and Assam into Upper Burma (roughly the
north-central plain) and by sea across the Bay of Bengal from south
and eastern India into Lower Burma (the delta of the Irrawaddy and
the Tenasserim peninsula).

EARLY DYNASTIES

The first people to develop a known civilization in Burma were the
Pyu from Tibet who had established a state in the Irrawaddy delta by
at least the 6th century A.D. and possibly as early as the 1st century
B.C. The ruins of their capital city of Srikshetra (Prome) show strong
Indian commercial and cultural ties, with evidences of both Hindu and
Buddhist religious practices.

In the south the Mon, a tribe akin to the Khmer of Kampuchea, had
migrated into the Irrawaddy delta from Thailand, probably before the
advent of the Pyu. In the 8th century they defeated the Pyu and ruled
Lower Burma for the next three hundred years. Also heavily influenced
by India, the Mon gave Burma its present form of writing which is
derived from the south Indian Pallava script, a centuries old civilization
based on trade and rice cultivation, and Theravada Buddhism which
was to be a unifying force in Burma until the present.

The Burmans, who have given their name to the country and today
make up 71 percent of the population, came from the hills to the east
of Tibet. The term Burman is applied to this ethnic group, Burmese to
the people of the country as a whole. In the 11th century the Burmans
established a kingdom at Pagan, in Upper Burma, where the Chindwin
joins the Irrawaddy. The heydey of Burman power and culture began
with King Aniruddha who ruled from 1044 to 1077, and reached its
zenith under his successors. Moving out of the plain, Aniruddha
conquered Arakan on the west and the Mon kingdom in the south, and
carried back to Pagan the Mon court, its artists, craftsmen, scholars
and Theravada priests. He replaced the practice of Mahayana with the
Theravada form of Buddhism of the Mon. He subjugated the Shan in
northeast Burma, and built a line of forts along the Shan plateau to
protect his kingdom.

Burman culture reached its apex under a successor, Narapatisithu
(1173–1210), when scholars in Pagan were producing Buddhist com-
mentaries which were recognized as authoritative throughout the Theravada world. The wealth of the kingdom was lavished upon temple
building, as some five thousand pagodas still testify today.

The kingdom of Pagan was overthrown by the Mongol empire of
China. When Chinese occupation ended (1301) the princes of the Shan
plateau—who had accepted the Burman language and Buddhist culture
and had led in resisting the Mongols—gained control of the fragmented

states. Ava, on the upper reaches of the Irrawaddy at the base of the Shan plateau, became the capital. The next two and a half centuries were ones of constant warfare, but as is often the case in times of political strife, it was a golden age of Burmese literature and depicted an era of chivalry and romance.

In the meantime Arakan and the Mon kingdom, whose capital was Pegu in Lower Burma, prospered as Muslim Indian and Arab traders brought both commerce and their religion to Southeast Asia. The king of Arakan took the Muslim title, Ali Khan, and the state became rich through trade with Malacca and Bengal (India). The Mon kingdom, which had been in a constant state of war with the Shan, was strengthened politically as well as commercially when Shin Saw Bu (1453–1472) became queen regnant. (She is the only woman to have ruled Burma, although the status of women has always been high and women frequently played a prominent role in official, cultural and commercial life.) Under her successor, Dhammazedi (1472–1492), who epitomized the ideal Buddhist ruler (wise, learned and a benevolent administrator), Mon civilization reached its apogee. Trade increased, continuing to do so after the appearance of the Portuguese in the Bay of Bengal in 1511. When the Portuguese were permitted to open a trading station in Mon territory in 1519, unbeknownst, the day of the Indian and Arab Muslim merchant was setting and that of the Christian European trader and church was dawning.

The Burmans, who had gained strength as the Shan at Ava declined, were eager to share in the new-found commercial wealth of the Mon and the Arakanese, but were landlocked. In 1531 Tabinshwehti (Toungoo Dynasty) became strong enough to break out of the plain, defeat the Mon, and make Pegu his own capital (1539). He was killed during a Mon rebellion, but his brother-in-law, Bayinnaung, reconquered Pegu and resubdued the Shan, incorporating all of the present day Shan state into his kingdom. In a sweep across the northern plateau he seized the states of Chieng Mai in northern Thailand, and Luang Prabang and Vientiane in Laos, and conquered the great Thai kingdom of Ayutthia. For a time Burma was the most powerful state in Southeast Asia. During his son's reign, however, the Thai successfully revolted and thousands of Mon sought refuge from his rule in Thailand. Burma was again broken into fragments.

In the first half of the 17th century Anaukhpetlun reunited the country, restoring Pegu as its capital. He retook Chieng Mai and was planning a new invasion of the Thai heartland when he was killed. He was succeeded by his brother Thalun, who abandoned Burman expansionist policies and moved his capital from Pegu to the old Shan capital of Ava, turning his back on trade and contacts with the nations of the Indian Ocean and the increasingly aggressive intruders from the West.

During the next century a long line of weak kings reigned and the country was at the mercy of Indians from Manipur who raided the northwest, and bandit followers of the last Ming emperor of China who ravaged the country from the northeast. In 1752 the revived Mon, with the help of the French who were interested in a concession in Mon territory, threw off Burman rule and captured Ava.

A Burman resistance leader who titled himself Alaungpaya, "the great Lord who shall become a Buddha," soon rose to retaliate. He defeated the Mon at Ava and reestablished control over Upper Burma. In 1755 he stuck at the Mon in the south. He made the small port of Dagon his headquarters and—looking well into the future—renamed it Rangoon, "the end of opposition." After reestablishing control over all of Burma previously under the Toungoo dynasty, he occupied Manipur and prepared to besiege Ayutthia but died before he could succeed. His son, Hsinbyushin returned to attack Thailand in 1767 and permanently destroyed Ayutthia after a long siege, leveling the walls and putting the city to the torch. Thousands of Thai were taken prisoner, particularly craftsmen, artists, musicians, dancers and scholars. The result of this infusion of Thai talent was a reflowering of Burmese literature and the arts. The remainder of Hsinbyushin's reign was devoted to defending his northern borders against the Chinese who, though not interested in the conquest of Southeast Asia, pursued a policy of attempting to prevent any state from becoming preeminent in the area. In this instance they were unsuccessful, and in the midst of a fourth indecisive invasion (1769–70) agreed to a treaty of peace and withdrew behind their borders.

The arrogant behavior of the Burmans after their successes against Ayutthia and China provoked a revolt by both the Mon and the people of Chieng Mai. The Mon rebellion was quickly suppressed and thousands of Mon again fled to Thailand to swell the ranks of the Thai who had established a new capital south of Ayutthia. The people of Chieng Mai declared themselves an integral part of Thailand. Bodawpaya, who succeeded his half-brother after executing all who stood between him and the throne, again put down a Mon rebellion with great severity. In 1784 he invaded Arakan, partly to prevent it from being used by the British who now controlled India, and partly at the request of the Arakanese chieftains who sought an end to the chaos in that country.

Arakan Since 1430 the Kingdom of Arakan had survived as an independent principality, in part because of its geographic isolation, in part because the Burmese kings had turned their attention toward greater centers of power and commerce in the south and east, and in part because it maintained a strong navy. It grew rich and became a factor in the European exploitation of East Asia, both the Portuguese and Dutch establishing footholds at ports on its coast. But its wealth and power were eventually dissipated and it never recovered from a defeat handed it by India in 1666.

When the Burmans invaded Arakan in 1784 they were at first welcomed. However, mistreatment of the populace and seizure of the great statue of the Buddha—a treasure and national symbol—caused half the population to flee across the border into northeastern India. This displaced population became a catalyst for the first Anglo-Burmese War.

POLITICAL INDICATORS

A number of patterns emerge from scrutiny of Burmese history in the 1,300 years prior to the country's close contact with Britain, patterns that can be expected to recur and can help explain political actions or attitudes today.

1. Burma was divided into four major groupings, more or less mutually antagonistic, each with its own geographic power center. The Arakanese, isolated and restricted to the western seacoast by mountain ranges, were outside the main arena of conflict and thus maintained their independence much of the time, although frequently paying tribute to the central power. The Shan, related to the Tai of China and Thailand, with their power center in the interior, were reinforced by direct contact with the Tai hinterland, but isolated from other foreign and civilizing influences. The Mon in the delta and on the Tenasserim coast, with strong Indian and later European contacts, were closest to the mainstream of South and Southeast Asian cultures. And lastly the Burmans, confined to the central plain by the other three major ethnic groups, sought constantly to push out of the plain and exercise control over the others.
2. The major dynasties were Burman, but the Burmans tended to look politically inland, toward the Shan states of Burma and Thailand, rather than outward to contacts beyond the sea.
3. Political power splintered after brief periods of centralization.
4. Theravada Buddhism was the state religion and the cement that held the various ethnic groups together.
5. Warfare or repression resulted in massive movements of peoples, in part because the terrain permitted escape and often offered sustenance, and in part because there were ethnic "cousins" across the border to accept them. This applied to the Mon who frequently sought refuge in southern Thailand, the Shan who could cross into northern Thailand and the Arakanese who on occasion fled into northeastern India.

GRADUAL BRITISH ANNEXATION

The geo-political interests of the English East India Company—de facto ruler of eastern India—collided with those of Burma along the borders of Assam and Manipur, mountainous states which were Indianized but at times paid tribute to Burma. British economic and political expansion was motivated primarily by the desire to secure India from other European powers (French and Dutch) by controlling the Bay of Bengal, and to inhibit French expansion into Southeast Asia. Burma, like other countries of Southeast Asia, was caught up in the European power struggle.

In 1795 the British sent Captain Michael Symes to the court of Bodawpaya in Ava to: 1) persuade the Burmese king to close his ports to the French, 2) conclude a commercial treaty, and 3) settle the problem of the Arakanese refugees in India. No formal agreement was reached but an understanding of sorts was achieved. The second Symes mission in 1802 was accompanied by a regiment of soldiers to impress the king with British might. At this time the king agreed to allow a British commercial agent to take up residence in Rangoon and gave up his demand that the British return the Arakanese refugees in India. The British on their part agreed to assign a regiment to guard the Indian border to prevent further use of the border area as a rebel base.

The political situation among the border states deteriorated, however, and in 1822 Burmese forces occupied both Assam and Manipur and demanded that British Indian authorities return Arakanese and Assamese political refugees. To enforce these demands the Burmese commander made plans to march on Calcutta, at that time the capital of British India.

The British responded by sending a naval expedition against Rangoon, thereby drawing the Burmese back from Bengal, relieving tensions on the border and forcing the conflict to Burmese soil. The war between the British and the Burmese in Lower Burma dragged on until 1826, complicated by a rebellion by the Mon and Karen (a southeastern hill people). Burma was forced to accept the Treaty of Yandabo under whose terms Burma agreed to: 1) pay a large indemnity, 2) evacuate Assam and Manipur, 3) cede Arakan and Tenasserim to British India, and 4) forego further attacks on Thailand where Britain had interests. The British thereupon withdrew their troops from Rangoon.

The return of the Burmans to Rangoon was accompanied by a brutal repression of the Mon and Karen, creating another flood of refugees, this time into Thailand. In consequence of the war, this harsh treatment, and earlier excessive manpower demands by Bodawpaya for his vast building schemes, Lower Burma was depopulated and its agriculture and commerce were destroyed; the final Mon rebellion of 1838 was equally severely quelled.

In Upper Burma demoralization arising from the treaty conditions, misrule, and actual lapses into insanity by the next three kings—as well as the "slaughter of the kin," i.e., murder of all royal relatives thought capable of succeeding—resulted in the deterioration of the monarchy and the state.

By contrast, British rule in Arakan and Tenasserim succeeded in improving the economic condition of these areas, at the expense, however, of introducing Indian and Chinese labor into the country and sowing the seeds for the major socio-economic problems of the next 100 years. Rice acreage increased 50 percent in Tenasserim by 1852, as did the population. In Arakan production rose 400 to 500 percent and produced a profit for the English East India Company.

The Second Anglo-Burmese War (1852) arose over a minor point of honor between Burman authorities and British shipowners. Positions hardened and the British seized Lower Burma. The outgrowth of this one-sided war was the unilateral annexation of Lower Burma, formally announced in Calcutta in December 1852. Almost as galling to the court as the loss of territory was Britain's refusal to deal with Burma as an equal and sovereign state; London insisted on conducting treaty negotiations and diplomatic relationships with Burma through Calcutta. To add insult to injury, Thailand, which had collaborated with the British in both wars against Burma, was accorded equality.

When Mindon Min (1852–1878), who had seized the throne in an effort to stop the war, was unable to regain Lower Burma, he turned his back on Ava and Amarapura, the capitals associated with the defeats of the First and Second Anglo-Burmese Wars, and built a new capital at Mandalay on the upper reaches of the Irrawaddy. Like his contemporary, King Mongkut of Thailand, but less successfully, he turned his energies to modernizing his country. He invited European specialists to help improve the economy; he tried to control bribery and the misappropriation of monies by establishing salaries and stipends for administrative officers; and he attempted to establish a just system of land taxation. His economic measures, however, suffered from the demands he himself placed upon the economy in building his new capital.

Recognizing that not only the morale but the morals of the country were deteriorating as Buddhism lost its government patronage in Lower Burma, and its vitality as a mainstay of the social order throughout the country, Mindon purified the *sangha* (priesthood) by introducing public examinations in religious learning. He encouraged a revival of interest in the scriptures among the laity, and most importantly, he organized the Fifth Buddhist Synod; the last had occurred around the 1st century A.D. Mindon invited monks from all over the world, Mahayana as well as Theravada. The recognition he gained from Buddhist countries for this act was psychological compensation for the lack of recognition by the British.

In 1862 the three parts of Burma held by the British—Arakan, Tenasserim, and Lower Burma—were amalgamated into one province under the Government of India. The move formally perpetuated a major irritant in British-Burmese relations—Britain's insistence on treating Burma as part of India and Burmese needs as identical to India's. In 1875 Mindon was forced to cede to the British the Karen states adjacent to Lower Burma, which had been part of Burma since the Kingom of Pagan.

THIRD ANGLO-BURMESE WAR AND ITS CONSEQUENCES

Britain's policy toward Burma during the latter half of the 19th century was determined primarily by her continuing concern over French expansion in Indochina and her own interests in China. Britain viewed Burma—incorrectly as it turned out—as a potentially rich trade route to southern China, and forced the Burmese in 1867 to allow British steamers passage up the Irrawaddy to Bhamo where the caravan road to Yunnan began.

Mindon in turn sought to outflank Britain by establishing trade and diplomatic relations with France, Italy and the United States, but these moves came to little. The British resented the Burmese actions, as well as the presence of French and Italian traders and adventurers at the Burmese court, but were constrained from taking over Upper Burma by events in other parts of their empire which claimed their attention and resources.

By 1885 the international situation had changed and a conservative government had come to power in London. The French had recently signed a commercial treaty with Burma and posted a consul to Mandalay; more importantly, they had effected a consolidation of power in Vietnam and parts of Laos. At this point the Burmese made the mistake of levying an exorbitant fine on a British trading company for the alleged illegal export of teak logs. This gave the British pretext for delivering an ultimatum demanding that the government of Burma allow the government of India to handle its foreign relations. Thibaw, who had succeeded to the throne, refused and the British forces moved against Mandalay, taking it two weeks later. On January 1, 1886 the British government announced the annexation of the Kingdom of Burma.

Thibaw was exiled to India where he died in 1916. For lack of a suitable successor (the only viable candidate for the throne was a protégé of the French) the British decided to rule Burma directly, rather than through traditional channels of leadership. The decision to eliminate the court was to prove costly, both to the Burmese and to the British. The country was left without any symbol of indigenous authority, and Buddhism without official support. Direct British rule, moreover, resulted in British administrative law replacing customary law, and in the introduction of British immigration policies that allowed unrestricted immigration of Indian labor, with detrimental consequences that persisted until recent years.

Economy Annexation brought to Upper Burma the export-oriented, money economy that the British had already introduced into Lower Burma. Since Lower Burma was governed as part of India, the British had developed the Irrawaddy delta as a rice bowl for India's rapidly growing population. British firms controlled the wholesale trade and had created a cartel among themselves, dictating the price of rice on both the local and international markets. Chinese (primarily from Malaya) and Indian merchants controlled the retail trade; they were also moneylenders, lending farmers money for seed and other needs between harvests, as well as capital to open up new lands as population pressure and the demand for rice increased. These practices were introduced into Upper Burma with similar economic consequences for the Burmese. The failure of many of the peasants to meet their debt payments, and their frequent inability to establish title to their lands under British law, led farmers to lose their lands to the foreign moneylenders. Landlessness led to rural unemployment, which was intensified when Indian migrant labor was introduced into the country to work at lower wages. At the very time the Burmese peasant was losing his land and his livelihood, the value of rice exports was rising from 160 million rupees in 1899–90 to 390 million in 1913–14. By 1942 Burma was exporting two-fifths of the world's supply of rice. The profits, however, were largely remitted out of the country: to England by the great trading companies, and to India and China by the retail merchants. The pattern also characterized the trade in forest products, minerals, and after 1900, oil.

Although the British administration created an agricultural infrastructure—roads, railways, steamship systems, wharves, river bunds—it was unable to accumulate a surplus for social infrastructure. Nor did it recognize that lack of land and resultant unemployment were the root causes of the social disintegration that was expressing itself in rural and urban violence.

Politics By 1890 resistance in both Upper and Lower Burma had been suppressed; the Shan were pacified and the law minimally adjusted to their local customs; borders with Thailand and Laos were established; and titular independence of the Karenni State had been recognized in appreciation of Karen assistance during the years of pacification. (Karen support had been based in part upon anti-Buddhist as well as anti-Burman grounds, since British missionaries had opened schools and proselytized among the animist and relatively primitive Karen tribes.) The British also discriminated in favor of the Karen and other tribal minorities by accepting them in the army, thus intensifying ethnic separateness. Such policies of "divide and rule" were to give Karen, Shan and Chin (on the Indian border) a heightened sense of tribal identification which would lead to the ethnic uprisings against Burmese authority that began after World War II and have yet to be effectively quelled.

The British introduced an administrative system into Burma based on the villages. They eliminated the upper echelons of traditional hierarchy and attempted to coopt the village headmen who were placed under the direct supervision of British district officers. One major problem was that resistance to the British had come from this same class of village elders in the early days of pacification and many of them had been killed or displaced.

In 1897 Burma was granted limited legislative autonomy under a lieutenant governor and an advisory and appointive Legislative Council. Originally including only two Burmese members, the council was expanded to include thirteen by 1920. The lieutenant governor was appointed by the Governor General of India, who in turn served under the Secretary of State for India in the Colonial Office in London. Each of these three officials could veto council actions. The Burmese bitterly resented this authority structure and their subordination to the government of India.

Buddhism as an institution and as a moral influence declined with direct British rule. While not forbidden, it was deprecated by Europeans and European-educated Burmese, and was denied the financial support and prestige it had enjoyed throughout the preceding centuries. Demoralization set in, discipline within the *sangha* declined to new lows, and the order lost its power to enforce social and moral standards. Buddhist schools forfeited government financial support unless they followed the prescribed government curriculum, and were, for the most part, except in rural areas, superseded by government or missionary institutions. Superstitious priests, lacking the discipline of the court-supported *sangha,* roamed the countryside, and became an incipient force for riot and revolution.

20TH-CENTURY NATIONALISM AND COLONIAL POLICY

Burmese reaction to the increasing inability of the government to solve the ills of society was to revive Buddhism. In 1906 the Young

Men's Buddhist Association (YMBA) was formed, based on the organization established earlier in Sri Lanka and modeled on the Young Men's Christian Association. The YMBA professed an interest only in revitalizing Buddhism and encouraging the moral uplift and religious life of the people. As a first step it opened a number of schools around the country and requested and obtained grants—from a reluctant government—equal to those given to Christian institutions. Two other major cultural associations were established in the pre-World War I years: The General Council of Buddhist Associations which became a recognized spokesman for the educated Burmese laity, and the Burma Research Society, made up of intellectuals, both European and Burmese.

These bodies sought to revitalize national religious and cultural pride, and began to attract more active nationalists, in particular a number of young barristers who returned from the freedom of British universities as highly trained professionals and were not beholden to the government for civil service jobs. In 1917 and 1918 the YMBA played a role in an unsuccessful effort to obtain for Burma the same concessions toward self government that the British were prepared to give India. The YMBA eventually joined with other more outrightly nationalist organizations to form in 1920 the General Council of Burmese Associations.

Rangoon College had been established in 1880, and became the University of Rangoon on December 20, 1920. Since Indian universities had quickly become hotbeds of nationalism, the government sought to prevent a similar situation in Burma by vesting university control in a council appointed by the government, and in a Senate restricted to faculty members of senior grade, none of whom were Burmese. The students of the newly proclaimed university immediately walked out on a strike which quickly spread to the lower schools. Nationalist leaders organized the Council of National Education, and national, i.e., non-government, schools were opened around the country; all YMBA schools became national schools. The government was eventually forced to placate the nationalists by appointing a committee, including their leaders, to amend the University Act. The strike was a clear-cut victory for the students and the nationalists, and had a powerful effect on public opinion. It also set a precedent of student involvement in politics.

Constitutions   The 1917–1918 British plans for progressive self government for India did not include Burma in its proposals. The explanatory statement that Burma was not as ready as India to govern itself inflamed Burmese sensitivities. The Burmese Constitution of 1922, promulgated in 1923, further angered the nationalists and three provisions that were particularly galling were to have long-term adverse effects on Burmese politics. First, Burma remained under the government of India which retained control of foreign affairs, defense, communications, transportation, taxation, monetary policy and law. Second, the legislature was to be partially appointed and partially elected, with 58 members to be elected from general constituencies, 21 by specified minorities and 24 appointed by the governor; the result was a fragmentation of society and a personal scramble for power. And third, the British kept the three major hill peoples (Chin, Karen, and Kachin—meaning barbarian) under direct rule, insisting they were not ready to participate in self government. This drove further the wedge between the minorities and the majority of the Burmese, and insured that future national integration would be difficult.

The new constitution specified that self government would extend to district councils which were to be elected indirectly by tax-paying villagers. The deteriorating economy however reduced the number of villagers able or willing to pay taxes in order to participate in the marginal political process. Instead, as the effects of a worldwide depression intensified, resentment of the ordinary Burmese toward the Indian and Chinese shopkeepers, moneylenders and cultivator-competitors flared and riots broke out in Rangoon—against the Indians in 1930 and the Chinese in 1931—followed later by riots against the Indians in the countryside. At the same time anti-British sentiment came to a head in the Saya San rebellion. Saya San, an ex-monk who declared that an earthquake that almost leveled Pegu foretold the fall of the British, rallied the villagers of Lower Burma, proclaiming himself king and reviving traditional forms of court symbolism. His followers, armed with little more than swords and magic amulets, but goaded by a sense of desperation, revolted; the movement spread. It was suppressed in 1933, but only after 10,000 rebels had been killed and 9,000 captured, including Saya San who, with 128 others, was tried and hanged.

The Simon Commission, sent from London in 1931 to study the effects of the Constitution of 1922, proposed that Britain grant Burma greater self-rule under a new constitution and separate the government of Burma from that of India. The British commercial class, which had always had a stong voice in the government of Burma, agreed. Paradoxically, Burmese nationalists, unhappy because the terms of the proposed constitution were not spelled out, and suspicious because the British community approved of separation, adopted an anti-separation stance and won a referendum on the issue. However, dissension within the nationalist camp vitiated its efforts and the constitution was drafted in London with little Burmese input and promulgated by the British in 1937.

The new constitution provided for a parliamentary form of government with a bicameral legislature. The House of Representatives was to be elected by voters comprising all males over 21, and all females over 21 who could pass a simple literacy test. Half the Senate was to be elected by the House and the other half appointed by the governor who continued to be responsible for defense, monetary policy and foreign affairs. Despite the referendum the constitution separated Burma from India, but denied the Burmese immediate control over immigration and tariffs, both issues of vital concern vis-a-vis India. The governor retained the right of veto and the administration of the hills areas.

Student Strikes: 1936–1938   The Rangoon University Student Union, built in the late 1920s with private funds, was, in British tradition, the center of free student discussion. It early became the center of the student nationalist movement. Students had become alienated from traditional society as a consequence of their Europeanized education, and many were also frustrated by their inability to obtain diplomas (40 percent annually failed) or to obtain suitable employment. They were therefore a volatile, homogeneous body with few ties to the status quo and with at least a smattering of knowledge of western liberal and socialist thought. They were also in Rangoon and accessible to Rangoon politicians—to use or be used.

The Dobama Asiayone, or Thakin Party (*thakin,* meaning master, was used as a sly dig at their British rulers), initially consisted of two university student organizations which united in 1935 and won control of the student union. It successfully recruited high school students as members but was unsuccessful in organizing workers and villagers. The Thakins precipitated a strike in Feburary 1936 which quickly spread to the high schools, forcing educational institutions throughout the country to close for some months.

Strike demands called for further changes in the University Act. Among the changes granted by the government was broadening the University Council by including a majority of members from outside the university or civil service; this opened the council to politicization which led in turn to a deterioration of educational standards in the post World War II era. The Thakin Party success in 1936 led to Thakin strikes in 1938 which effected a change in prime ministers.

SELF GOVERNMENT

The period between the implementation of the constitution in 1937 and the beginning of Japanese occupation in 1942 gave Burmese prime ministers less than five years to address Burma's basic economic and political problems. Moreover, although the political elements that held power tended to act constructively and responsibly, the opposition factions were irresponsbile and destructive. An anti-Muslim riot, for example, was apparently instigated and inflamed by the political opponents of Ba Maw, the first prime minister.

Ba Maw was British trained, a leader of the European-educated Burmese, a leftist, an Anglophobe, a member of the General Council of Buddhist Associations and an opportunist. Nevertheless in office he attempted to govern responsibly. The Tenancy Act and the Land Purchase Bill he advanced undertook to remedy problems of land dispossession and to make cultivator credit less difficult to obtain, but neither bill was implemented during the short time he held office. He was defeated in Feburary 1939 by U Pu, who instituted a study on the problems of village administration. Bribery and corruption were found to be so widespread throughout the lower and middle administrative systems that success of any administrative reform seemed highly unlikely.

Upon outbreak of war in Europe in 1939 Ba Maw joined the Thakins in forming the Freedom Bloc. The organization took an ultra-nationalist stance, demanding a pledge of independence in return for the support of Britain in the war, and attacked Pu for his ultimate support of Britain without such. The defection from the government of U Saw—who became the next prime minister—caused the collapse of the Pu cabinet.

Saw used emergency powers to suppress internal dissension. He arrested Ba Maw and other Freedom Bloc spokesmen for supporting Japanese activities in China and Southeast Asia, although his own newspapers prior to his assumption of office had taken the same position. Some members of the Thakin Party, who were later to be known as the Thirty Comrades, avoided arrest by slipping out of the country to Taiwan, then part of the Japanese empire, where they received military training and returned in 1942 as Japanese collaborators. They were destined to become the nationalist leaders of postwar Burma.

POLITICAL INDICATORS: PATTERNS AND EFFECTS OF BRITISH COLONIALISM

British colonialism brought Burma into the modern world, albeit piecemeal and half-heartedly. The political, economic and social patterns then established have affected, or are affecting, Burmese society in the post World War II era of independence.

1. British treaties and colonial rule ended Burma's warfare with her neighbors and established national boundaries which have remained stable.

2. British use of the technique of divide and rule—employing hill tribes and minorities in the army and police, and governing the hill states directly rather than through the government of Burma—led to internal destabilization, frequent insurgencies and a continuing demand in the post World War II period by these minorities for some form of autonomy.
3. The concept of a bicameral parliamentary system and its attendant strong legalistic traditions influenced the behavior of postwar politicians until 1962, and the expectations of the educated elite into the 1970s.
4. The student nationalist movement of the 1930s led to formation of the Thakin Party from whose ranks has come the principal political leadership. It also set a pattern for disruptive student strikes that continued to bedevil the Burmese government.
5. By modernizing public administration, communications, transportation and health services, the British administration not only introduced standards, but spurred development of a Europeanized elite to address these attributes of a modern state. At the same time modernization created social unrest and political instability.
6. The Europeanized educational system compounded social disintegration by alienating youth from traditional society without providing soci-economic philosophic alternatives or suitable employment.
7. The new money economy, emphasizing export markets, undermined the traditional non-money, rural, economic patterns and led to indebtedness, drastic turnover of land ownership and economic and social unrest in the countryside, a precursor to general political unrest.
8. Governing Burma as a province of India resulted in unlimited Indian immigration with disastrous economic consequences and the creation of serious postwar political problems.

WORLD WAR II AND ITS AFTERMATH

Japan's interest in Burma centered on the Burma Road that was being used by Britain to supply arms to China; ironically it was the same route to Yunnan that had sparked the British desire to control Upper Burma in 1885.

In 1942 Japan quickly consolidated its power in Thailand and invaded Burma through the Tenasserim mountain passes. The Thirty Comrades returned with the invaders and organized the Burmese Independence Army, made up primarily of politicized monks and youth groups. These volunteers were of no military importance and were quickly disillusioned when the Japanese not only failed to declare Burma's independence as promised, but treated Burma as a conquered territory—although there had been little actual Burmese resistance to the Japanese military takeover.

As the British retreated to India they employed a "scorched earth policy," destroying Burma's transportation system, mines and oil wells; as the Japanese advanced they bombed the Burmese cities.

After the capture of Upper Burma the Japanese disbanded the Burmese Independence Army and set up the Burma Defense Army. Thakin Aung San was made commander, but was under the control of his Japanese advisers. On August 1, 1943 Burma was declared "independent" and given a new constitution. Ba Maw became "head of state," but he allowed himself to be used by the Japanese to the extent that he was unacceptable to the Burmese after liberation. Aung San, on the other hand, secretly contacted the British and organized the Anti-Fascist League, later retitled the Anti-Fascist People's Freedom League (AFPFL), incorporating all nationalist elements, including the communists.

During 1943–45 Burma found itself a front line, as the Japanese made plans to invade India through Manipur, and the British counter-attacked, slowly returning to the central plain. Initially the British were welcomed as liberators by a population that had suffered grievously from Japanese cruelty and arrogance as well as from a disastrous Japanese economic policy which had cut off both imports and exports. However, their errors in judgment during the immediate post-liberation period transformed Burmese public opinion. Rather than asking for self government within the Commonwealth, the Burmese were soon demanding complete independence. In an attempt to quiet political unrest, Sir Hubert Rance—appointed governor of Burma in September 1946—chose Aung San as deputy chairman of his new cabinet, giving him the portfolios of defense and foreign affairs, and allowing him to appoint five other AFPFL members to the nine-man body.

In December 1946 Aung San led a Burmese delegation to London to discuss the future relationship between the countries. The two parties signed an agreement in January 1947 whereby the British agreed to conduct immediate elections for a constituent assembly to determine the future status of Burma; to hold a joint meeting of Burmese and British representatives with the hill tribes to discuss their political relationship with the government of Burma; and to recognize Aung San's cabinet as the interim government.

In the elections for the Constituent Assembly in April the AFPFL won 200 of the 210 seats, and the hill tribes opted for union with Burma. At the height of these successes, Aung San, and six cabinet members who were meeting with him at the time, were murdered at the instigation of former prime minister U Saw. Saw, returning with a vengeance to the prewar pattern of opposition irresponsibility, apparently resented Aung San's success and hoped to place the blame for the murders on the British in order to create a political situation that would allow him to regain power. His plan failed and he was tried and executed.

As a result of the mass assassination of Burma's major postwar leaders, U Nu, a Thakin who had been foreign minister under the Japanese-sponsored government of Ba Maw and was currently president of the Constituent Assembly, was asked by Rance to form a new cabinet. He accepted reluctantly, preferring, at that point in his life, religion and writing to politics. Therefore it was Nu who on October 17, 1947 signed the formal treaty of independence. On January 4, 1948—at 4:20 a.m., the time chosen by astrologers—Burma entered the postwar world as an independent nation.

INDEPENDENCE: 1947–1962

The Union of Burma was established under a constitution originally drawn up by Aung San with a western-style bicameral parliamentary system of government based on full adult suffrage, but on a basis of ethnic representation. States with limited self government were designed for the Shan, hill Karen and Kachin, and a special division was created for the Chin in the northwest. The upper house, or Chamber of Nationalities, represented specific constituencies. The Burmans were given two-fifths representation, and the remaining peoples were represented according to their percentage of the population. Executive authority was vested in a prime minister who was elected by and responsible to the lower house, the Chamber of Deputies. The president, a figurehead, was to be chosen by the two houses and the position rotated among representatives of the major ethnic communities. Because of chaotic conditions in the postwar years the first election did not take place until 1952. The result was an overwhelming victory for the AFPFL.

Insurrection In 1948 the communists dropped out of the AFPFL and engaged in open rebellion against the government. They were divided into two groups, the White Flag Maoists led by Thakin Than Tun until his assassination in 1968, and the Red Flag Trotskyites, led by Thakin Soe until his arrest in 1970 and his execution in 1973.

The most serious uprising, however, that of the Karen of the Irrawaddy delta, began in January, 1949. These lowland Karen had supported the British during the war and often found themselves in conflict with the Burma Defense Army, remnants of which roamed the countryside in post-war years as little better than bandits. To protect themselves the Karen had formed the Karen National Defense Organization (KNDO). They feared also that in independent Burma they would be politically submerged by the Burmans among whom they lived; their concerns were increased because, in a Buddhist society, some 15 percent of them were Christian. By spring the KNDO held much of rural Burma and had joined with the communists to set up a joint government in Mandalay. General Ne Win, one of the Thirty Comrades, slowly but successfully defeated the rebels and reestablished government rule. Amnesty was offered in 1950 and was accepted by many, and in 1951 the Karen were promised a separate self governing state within the Union of Burma. The rebellion might have been completely quelled had not external factors intervened.

In 1950 Chinese nationalist (Kuomintang, KMT) forces, fleeing the victorious communists in China, crossed the border from Yunnan and established themselves in the north. Although the KNDO and the nationalist Chinese did not unite, the KNDO began to obtain military supplies from the latter. The situation was exacerbated during 1952–53 by the airlift from Taiwan of men and supplies to the KMT. U.S. air force planes and U.S. army materiel were involved, evoking Burmese resentment against the United States. Not only did the government fear increased infiltration of arms to Burmese insurgents, but it worried about possible communist Chinese military reprisals across the 1,200 miles of shared frontier. Although under UN and U.S. pressure many of the refugees were evacuated, an unknown number stayed on to engage in raising opium poppies in the "Golden Triangle," the remote mountainous region where Burma, Thailand and Laos meet. They created national and international problems which have yet to be resolved.

Minority problems existed on the western border as well, where a small number of Arakanese Muslims sought to join the new Islamic nation of East Pakistan (now Bangladesh). Although they finally surrendered in 1961, agitation for a separate Arakan state within the Union led to political unrest in 1962. A separate state was finally granted the Arakanese in 1974.

Economy   With the gradual return of law, order and government control to central Burma the state turned its attention to the economy which had been devastated by World War II and had suffered further during the years of civil insurrection. So-called land "nationalization" had already begun. The government forbade holdings of over 50 acres. It distributed the excess lands to tenants in approximately 10-acre plots, reimbursing the original landholders. Redistributed land could not be transferred or resold except under special conditions. In effect the reform expanded the number of private owners of land, rather than nationalizing land ownership. In 1952 the eight-year Pyidawthar (Happy Land) Plan, to create "a country of peace and prosperity," was announced. It posited creation of a socialist welfare state, as well as raising the gross national product (GNP) one-third above pre-World War II levels.

There was little debate in postwar Burma about socialism. The concept was accepted by most politicians as an outgrowth of their prewar resentment of British, Indian and Chinese capitalists. In addition, capital accumulation was unknown in pre-colonial Burma. The problems faced by the government vis-a-vis socialism were, therefore, of implementation rather than acceptance, and mainly arose from lack of funds, management expertise and technology, and faulty governmental administration. Compounding the situation was Burma's rejection of foreign aid.

Burma declined United States technical and economic assistance in the spring of 1953 because of U.S. involvement with KMT refugee forces, and took a position against accepting foreign loans from any major power to avoid entanglement in superpower conflicts. Colombo Plan aid—supplied primarily by members of the Commonwealth—was welcomed, but it was confined mainly to technical help. Private banks, with the exception of one Indian bank, would not take a chance on the stagnant Burmese economy. External aid was, therefore, mostly confined to Japanese war reparations which began in 1954 and amounted to US$200 million by 1977. To add to the bleak economic picture the world price of rice, on which Burma depended for foreign exchange to finance the Pyidawthar Plan, fell drastically in the mid and late 1950s. Low prices, combined with the government's failure to find markets for the surplus produced, led ultimately to lower production and to the erosion of the financial basis of the government development plan.

Politics During his first period in office Nu achieved a coup by convening the Sixth Buddhist Synod in Rangoon (May 1954–May 1956) to honor the 2,500th anniversary of the Buddha's death. The costs of hosting the massive, lengthy conference were great, but the prestige, as well as the religious merit acquired, were considered greater. Buddhists from 30 countries attended the synod and Burma's image in the Buddhist world, and among non-western nations generally, was greatly enhanced.

In 1955 Burma played a second major role on the world scene as an organizer, with Indonesia, Sri Lanka, India and Pakistan, of the Bandung Conference. It was convened by Asian nations to: 1) protest the West's lack of consultation with them on Asian matters, 2) evaluate their own relationships with China, 3) air their opposition to colonialism, and 4) express their concerns over the split between China and the U.S. The conference was a first step in establishing the influence of newly independent nations outside, and in opposition to, the western and communist blocs. Their power as a "neutralist" or "nonaligned" force grew increasingly until by the late 1970s the nonaligned nations dominated the United Nations General Assembly and the specialized UN agencies. Recognition of Burma's importance in the nonaligned bloc was underscored by the election of U Thant as Secretary General of the United Nations Secretariat in 1961, and his reelection to a second five-year term in 1966.

U Nu and the AFPFL were overwhelmingly reelected in the parliamentary elections of 1956, but within 18 months the AFPFL political alliance began to fall apart. The socialists withdrew, provoked ostensibly by the AFPFL's non-adherence to socialist principles, but the split more nearly resembled a return to the personality politics of prewar years. The emergency conditions of war and insurrection which had held the politicians together had passed; the jealousies and opposition that had existed within the League resurfaced. Nu responded by resigning "temporarily" in October and General Ne Win was requested to form a caretaker government for six months as provided for by the constitution. His interim government was extended another year through adoption of a constitutional amendment.

Ne Win: Interregnum, 1958–1960 Ne Win, a socialist, nationalist and authoritarian, moved firmly to take over the decaying political situation brought about, in large part, by the indecision and reluctance of U Nu to act. He arrested political opponents, including students and workers, reduced crime, and improved public services by installing army officers in the middle levels of administration. He appointed a cabinet of senior judges, academics, bureaucrats and businessmen who represented no political faction and were therefore responsible only to him. He cancelled the contract of the private American economic planning advisory team (Nathan Associates) which had helped develop the Pyidawthur Plan, and dismissed Russian consultants. The country increasingly turned inward. He also took a strong pro-Burman stance vis-a-vis the national minorities, abrogating the hereditary rights of the Shan princes and rejecting the tentative proposals advanced by Nu to give the Mon a separate state in Tenasserim. At the same time he attempted to secure Burma's northern flank by concluding a Treaty of Peace and Mutual Non-Aggression with China in 1960, after resolving a long-standing border dispute.

The army—made up primarily of rural Burman youth, and strongly nationalistic—became increasingly involved in the political process. "Solidarity associations," organized to do volunteer work such as firefighting and providing the army with intelligence, were structured in a paramilitary fashion and were forerunners of the political councils of a later period.

U Nu's Return Ne Win returned the country to civilian government on schedule. Local elections were held in December 1959 and a general election in February 1960. Nu and the Clean Wing of the AFPFL—

later to be called the Union Party—were reelected overwhelmingly. However the Union Party again represented a disparate political assemblage—from reactionary Buddhist priests to ethnic minorities seeking greater self government. Trouble began when Nu tried to carry out a campaign promise to make Buddhism the state religion in spite of constitutional provisions for a secular state.

During this period of "second wind democracy," rice production rose to its postwar peak, generating funds to permit importation of needed consumer goods. But Nu was unable to profit from the improved economic situation and was unable to deal effectively with the political fragmentation.

On March 2, 1962 General Ne Win returned with the army, carried out a successful *coup d'état,* arrested 52 high level officials—including U Nu, the Shan princes who had gathered with him to discuss the relationship of the Shan state to the Union, and the Chief Justice—and declared that he had intervened to save the country from self destruction.

MILITARY RULE

This time Ne Win abolished the constitution and all legislative, judicial and executive bodies, including the National Assembly and the Supreme Court, retaining only the civil service. He set up a Revolutionary Council, made up primarily of senior army officers, which conferred on him, as chairman, all legislative, judicial and executive power.

He selected a Council of Ministers to administer the laws which he promulgated, and replaced the Supreme Court with a High Court headed by ordinary citizens—with former judges acting as advisers. In March 1964 he banned all political parties except the Burmese Socialist Program Party (BSPP) which had been set up by the Revolutionary Council in July 1962 to assist it in organizing the masses. The Revolutionary Council manifesto of April 30, 1962, termed *The Burmese Way to Socialism,* was utopian and vaguely humanitarian. It envisaged governmental control of production through cooperatives in a new anti-capitalist system which was to be defended by the armed forces. The new order rapidly drifted toward communist-style regimentation but was forced to come to terms with Buddhism which was too deeply ingrained in Burmese consciousness to be overthrown or ignored.

This time the only two groups that gave Ne Win their full support were the army, with its communist-oriented leadership and young officers eager for renewed power, and the Marxist National Unity Front (NUF). Even though democracy had worked poorly under U Nu, political activists—including educators, students, the press and minorities—refused to support a military dictatorship. As a result the government leaned more and more on its communist backers and became more and more dictatorial.

Student unrest surfaced first. A student protest in June 1962 led Ne Win to order the army to fire on the demonstrators, a large number of whom were killed. A second demonstration provoked the army into demolishing the student union, symbol and meeting place of student agitators since the 1930s. At the same time the university was ordered closed for a month. When new demonstrations erupted in 1963 the university was shut down for a year. It reopened in 1964 with a socialist curriculum that deemphasized social science and stressed technology; student political activities were forbidden, and students seeking to study abroad were sent to Eastern Europe. Educational standards however continued to deteriorate and entrance requirements were further lowered.

Economy In line with the thinking of Ba Nyein, leader of the NUF who advocated the Chinese brand of communism, capitalism was to be eliminated from all elements of society, and agriculture was to be given precedence over industry. Between 1963 and 1965 over 1,000 private firms were nationalized and Indian and Chinese businessmen were expelled or decided to leave, taking with them what little the government would permit. The state thus gained control over industry and commerce, but lost the entrepreneurs, merchants, technicians and managers necessary to maintain and expand the economic order.

Although the new government placed special emphasis on agriculture, food production, which in 1959–60 had almost reached prewar level, declined. Food supplies henceforth barely kept pace with the increase in population and in 1973, for the first time in modern history, Burma had no rice to export. The decrease in rice exports also reduced the availability of foreign exchange for infrastructure improvements and industrial development. Rice production fell because of the inefficient and lax government credit system, government monopoly of the rice trade, and the low price scale. Cultivators used loans for purposes other than those for which the loans were made, planted inefficiently, and grew only enough to serve their own needs, or sold their surplus on the black market or to insurgents who paid one third more than the state stores.

Since half of Burma's land is forest, timber—and in particular teak—has traditionally been second only to rice as an export product. Government monopoly in this field failed to produce notable gains; by 1974 teak export had returned to only two-thirds of its 1940 level. Mining and oil production also remained below prewar levels, partly as a result of British destruction of mines and wells in the early days of World War II, and partly as a result of nationalization, lack of equipment, capital, management and technological expertise, and government refusal to accept foreign aid. The figures for per capita income were no more encouraging—US$80 in 1974, the lowest in Southeast asia.

Foreign Affairs In foreign affairs Ne Win continued U Nu's policy of neutralism and isolation. His main concern was his country's relationship with the People's Republic of China (PRC) which Burma had recognized in 1949, the first non-communist country to do so. Ne Win visited Peking four times between 1962 and 1967. Relations between the two states noticeably cooled, however, after demonstrations in 1967 by Burmese-Chinese in favor of the "cultural revolution" then unfolding in China, which resulted in severe anti-Chinese riots. The demonstrations had apparently been instigated by the Chinese embassy. Pro-Chinese and Chinese-supported rebels in the north and southeast continued to be a problem, and China's own turbulence was reflected in those areas. By 1971 relationships improved, ambassadors were exchanged and the 1961 aid agreement was revived.

Burma's relationships with its neighbors to the west were marred by the fact that between 1962 and 1967 some 177,000 Indians and Pakistanis had fled or been expelled from Burma in the course of Ne Win's policies of nationalization which forced non-nationals out of the economy. Burma's relations with India improved however in the early 1970s and Burma was quick to recognize Bangladesh when it declared its independence from Pakistan in 1971.

Other meaningful international contacts continued to be confined primarily to the United Nations, its specialized agencies and, until 1979, to the nonaligned nations whose political neutralism had become institutionalized.

SOCIALIST REPUBLIC

Politics Ne Win resigned from the army in 1972 to give Burma the appearance of civilian government. On January 4, 1974, acting on the basis of a 1973 national referendum, he legitimized his government by putting into effect a newly approved constitution. Burma was declared a Socialist Republic with one political party, the BSPP. The Revolutionary Council was disbanded and the State Council replaced it as the primary policy-making body, with the chairman of the Council to be the president of Burma. Not surprisingly Ne Win was so selected.

The new legislature, the People's Assembly (Pyithu Hluttaw), was elected for four years from a BSPP slate; its chairman was also prime minister. The State Council comprised 29 members, 14 of whom represented the seven newly designated minority states—Arakan, Chin, Kachin, Karen (Kathule), Kayah, Mon and Shan. People's councils of BSPP-approved candidates were chosen at division, township and village levels.

The BSPP, established in the constitution as the single official party, maintained a nationwide system of party cells and committees to assure party purity in all government activities. Although the constitution had been approved by a ten-to-one margin in the national referendum of 1973, by mid-1974 strikes rocked the country. Neither aspirations for more effective participation in the political processes nor material demands were being met. In December students of Rangoon University used the symbolic opportunity provided by the death of U Thant—former secretary general of the United Nations and a widely admired humanitarian in the democratic tradition—to riot against the government. Ne Win responded by declaring martial law, which was not lifted until September 1976, almost two years later. In 1974, also, opposition to the BSPP became a crime.

After general elections in 1978 the new People's Assembly elected Ne Win to another four-year term as Council chairman and thus president. Of his associates, General San Yu was reelected secretary of the Council and Maung Maung Kha chairman of the People's Assembly, and thus prime minister. Ne Win formally resigned in 1981 and, following new general elections, the Assembly elected San Yu to the Council of State which chose him chairman and president of the Socialist Republic. General elections in October 1985 ushered in a newly expanded Hluttaw of 489 members, chosen from a single slate of party-nominated or approved candidates.

San Yu followed in Ne Win's political footsteps, taking his cues from the latter who remained chairman of the BSPP, and the power behind the government. Ne Win was reelected party chairman at the regular quadrennial congress of the BSPP in August 1985, as were joint party general secretaries Aye Ko and Sein Lwin, both retired generals. San Yu became party vice-chairman. The "big four," plus Prime Minister Maung Maung Kha, a retired colonel, dominated the party's 17-man Central Committee. The committee's report to the congress asserted that "socialist democracy" was now flourishing among the people and applauded the "success" of elections to the People's Assembly although the elections had not yet taken place![1]

Worldwide recession in 1985 seriously affected raw material and foodgrain exports of the marginally successful, centrally planned economy, and eventually led to political crisis. Worsening trade balances, a rising debt service ratio (60–80 percent by 1987) and fuel oil shortages impelled the government suddenly to "demonetize" the currency— render worthless *kyat* banknotes of 75, 35, and 25 denominations—in September 1987, a fateful move. Overnight 60–80 percent of the currency in circulation could not be exchanged for new money.

By March 1988 thousands of rural people had flocked to the cities seeking relief. They were supported by students, already inflamed by anti-government leaflets distributed on campuses. The students marched into central Rangoon where, for the first time, they were joined by thousands of ordinary citizens and riots ensued. Riot police employed to quell them infuriated the students and 283 people were killed.

Through a twist of fate two envoys from Japan, Burma's largest creditor, who were sent to Rangoon in early 1988 to press for economic reforms and more freedom, may have unwittingly helped fuel the March riots. Rather than approaching Ne Win directly—a past-failed tactic—the envoys persuaded the respected and retired Brigadier General Aung Gyi, an advocate of human rights, to write open letters of criticism to Ne Win which were widely circulated.

By May Aung Gyi had emerged as a focal point of opposition to the regime. Ever larger riots took place in June and another 120 people were killed. Anti-government protests had been transformed into demands for overthrow of the regime. In July Ne Win and San Yu resigned, the former suggesting specific economic reforms and a national referendum on demands for multiparty politics. Simultaneously, the current party congress appointed hardliner Sein Lwin as BSPP party chairman and the People's Assembly made him president as well. Aung Gyi and his associates were arrested.

In August ever more massive demonstrations to bring down the government were supported by a nationwide general strike. Sein Lwin responded with unprecedented brutality. The army sprayed automatic rifle fire into unarmed crowds; armored cars machine gunned neighborhoods indiscriminately, killing people inside their homes. "When Sein Lwin eventually stepped down on August 12 estimates of the number of people killed in the August uprising varied from 1,000 to 3,000 in Rangoon alone."[2]

A civilian, Dr. Maung Maung, was appointed BSPP chairman and president of Burma on August 19. Despite his promise of a referendum on the multiparty issue, hundreds of thousands again took to the streets, claiming he was a powerless figurehead. Tens of thousands of BSPP members resigned from the party amidst almost universal demands for democracy. In practical terms, government ceased to exist after troops were withdrawn from Rangoon August 24 and informal citizens committees endeavored to maintain law and order in neighborhoods.

On September 18 a military cabal headed by the chief of staff, General Saw Maung, assumed power and the carnage continued. Another 1,000 persons were killed in violence as a new military-dominated State Law and Order Council banned public gatherings, made mass arrests and summarily executed student activists. On September 20 the Council announced that a new cabinet would rule the country "until general elections can be held."

Anticipating the military takeover, the BSPP had taken measures to ensure its survival. On September 10 the party announced its support for a multiparty system and general elections. The party changed its name September 29, becoming the National Unity Party, and a new Law on Organizations and Associations of September 30 permitted formation of other political parties. In late 1988 the BSPP-controlled government dropped "Socialist Republic" from the official name of the State and in June 1989 the "Union of Burma" became the "Union of Myanmar" and "Rangoon" became "Yangon." Names of towns and provinces were to be written in English according to Burmese pronunciation. The steps help underscore the national unity theme of the renamed BSPP.[3]

Opposition parties quickly emerged. Aung Gyi founded the National League for Democracy (NLD) whose popular secretary, Aung San Suu Kyi, is the daughter of national hero Aung San who was murdered in 1947 as he led the nation to independence. U Nu, the former statesman, led a Democracy Party. Three other parties (People's Democratic Party, Democratic Front for National Reconstruction, and the Unity and Development Party) were organized by Thakins who had been prominent in earlier years. Even the AFPFL of former times was revived. Soon literally hundreds of other groups registered as political parties. By mid-1989 political parties in Burma numbered 234.[4] By then the NLD, claiming membership of over 1 million, had become the main opposition party under the leadership of Aung San Suu Kyi. In June the military government equated the NLD with the still illegal communist party, threatening intervention if the party "remained confrontational."

Minority Politics   Although the 1974 constitution established seven ethnic states, continuous insurrection since then has prevented their political integration within the union. Ne Win offered amnesty to all insurgents in 1974, a move rejected by the hard core Shan, Karen and Mon. Five ethnic groups formed an unsuccessful Federal National Front in 1975, the first rebel attempt at unity. It welcomed all ethnic Burmese resistance groups but showed an aversion to cooperation with the outlawed Burmese Communist party (BCP). Nevertheless BCP guerrillas trained and backed by China, and the Shan United Army soon achieved and retained control of the Shan state adjacent to China's Yunnan province. The Karen National Liberation Army by 1982 controlled much of the countryside in seven provinces along the Thai border. In Late 1988 Shan and Kachin rebel armies, flush with battlefield successes against the Burmese Army, appeared to be distancing themselves from the BCP's northern forces, both physically and ideologically. They formed, with other ethnic groups, a non-communist umbrella resistance organization which they termed the Burma National Democratic Front to oppose the central government.

Foreign Relations   Political neutralism, friendship with its neighbors and peaceful coexistence—within an international political environment where "big powers" get involved in local issues—were Burma's stated foreign policy goals during the early Ne Win years. Nevertheless disputes with neighboring states marked much of the period. The Burmese complained that Thailand has provided arms and safe haven to Burmese rebels; the influx of some 23,000 refugees from Bangladesh during the 1971 India-Pakistan war prompted Rangoon to such harsh deportation measures that the Islamic Council of Europe beseeched the United Nations to stop the Burmese "genocide"; and in 1983 Burma-based Indian insurgents, seeking the independence of Assam and Manipur, were accused of killing an estimated 300 Burmese villagers in a single incident.

Burma's relations with other Southeast Asian states during the post-Vietnam War period were mixed. The Rangoon leadership and the ASEAN partners appeared to be wary of each other. Along with ASEAN, however, the Burmese extended "the hand of friendship" to the new pro-Chinese, Khmer Rouge regime in Kampuchea. Ne Win was the first head of state to visit Phnom Penh in 1977, an act viewed as an indication of Burmese concern over developing Vietnamese dominance in Indochina and inspired by the PRC.

After the overthrow of the Khmer Rouge by the Vietnamese-sponsored regime of Heng Samrin in 1979, the Burmese took the lead in refusing to permit the latter to occupy the seat of the former at the Havana Conference of Non Aligned nations. Burma declared that "no state has the right to interfere, directly or indirectly, in the internal affairs of any other state."[5] When Cuba attempted to influence the conference toward a pro-Soviet, pro-Vietnamese stance, the Burmese withdrew from the body which they had helped establish in 1955. In 1979 Ne Win visited the communist leaders in Laos to discuss security along their 154 mile common border. The two states emphasized "respect for territorial integrity, political independence and non-interference" in one another's affairs, presumably a recognition of growing Vietnamese intervention in the region.[6]

Burma's nonalignment posture was seriously disturbed in October 1983 during South Korea President Chun Doo Hwan's visit to Rangoon, part of an effort to improve diplomatic and economic relations between the two states. North Korean terrorists bombed the site of an official ceremony, killing four Korean cabinet ministers. Chun escaped injury in the assassination attempt, but 21 Koreans and Burmese were killed. Burma subsequently broke relations with North Korea.

Burma has assiduously cultivated China—by 1985 Ne Win had made 12 official visits to Peking—which is viewed as a powerful neighbor, able to assist or withhold aid to the pro-Chinese BCP. Political relations with both the USSR and the western world were proper-to-friendly until the internal violence of 1988 affected them adversely and threw into disarray years of international collaboration to ease Burma's economic problems.

Economic Affairs   The 1974 constitution called for the nationalization of all means of production, permitting retail trade only if it did not undermine the socialist order. The BSPP in turn drew up a 20-year economic timetable (1973–1993) that required reduction within that time of private agricultural production—from 99.8 percent of the national total to 40 percent, with cooperatives accounting for 50 percent and state farms for the other 10 percent. The BSPP plan promised to protect private enterprise from enforced nationalization until March 1994, but it called for the economy to become eventually 48 percent state-owned, with the remaining 52 percent to be divided equally between cooperatives and private ownership.

During the earlier years of military rule, economic progress had been minimal. Neither socialism nor nationalism had solved the problems of a technologically backward economy which was burdened by a relatively high population growth rate and which had rejected international assistance. In 1973, however, the government had begun to demonstrate flexibility within its socialist framework. It invited oil exploration by four western companies—including two from the U.S.—and joined the Asian Development Bank (ADB), receiving its first loan in December that year.

The first year of constitutional dictatorship showed little economic improvement, however. The growth rate was only 2.6 percent compared to the planned 4 and the *kyat* (unit of money) was devalued 30 percent. But 1975 was also the year that the Burmese government began actively to seek outside sources of funding and technical assistance. As a consequence the ADB agreed to supply technical assistance for forest industries, West Germany pledged US$30 million in aid over two years and Japan and Australia agreed to increased loan arrangements. In 1976 it was announced that government trade corporations were to be merged into 11 companies and run like private businesses. The state began to pay compensation for the nationalization of foreign and domestic property, and air travel pacts signed with Singapore and Australia indicated a lessening of isolationism. The government also requested the World Bank's help in acquiring foreign aid.

A Burma Aid Group of the World Bank was organized in 1976 comprising Japan, seven western nations, the ADB, the European Economic Community, the Organization for Economic Cooperation and the UN Development Program. The Group's members agreed to consult one another but to develop their own aid programs for Burma on a bilateral basis. Japan quickly took the lead, its loans and grants to Burma totaling US$1 billion by 1983. By 1985 Japan had developed an advantageous and skillful threefold mix of its annual Burma aid package: 1) highly visible consumer-popular projects (an open air theatre, a stadium, a planetarium); 2) convertible currency credits; and 3) funds for infrastructure (bridges, roads, river and port development, communications facilities). Such assistance was mutually beneficial: in the short run it helped keep Burma afloat financially and created goodwill. More importantly it provided the physical means (access and transport) for Japan to harvest Burma's bountiful natural resources. Other nations adopted Japan's approach, but on a much smaller scale.

Acceptance of international aid had not produced immediate change. In 1977 the World Bank reported that "mismanaged price controls, an overvalued currency, low and misdirected investments, a rampant black market, sluggish employment growth and a stalled transportation system"[7] were still hindering Burma's economic development. The black market still exceeded the legitimate.

Fiscal year 1978–79 began to show the effect of the changes begun earlier. Although not all of the criticisms of the World Bank had been addressed tax reform had been undertaken, an action the World Bank considered a major reason for the observed upswing. The targeted growth rate of 5.9 percent was almost met (5.6) for the first time. Agriculture—which accounted for approximately 27 percent of the gross domestic product, employed 60 percent of the work force and supplied 90 percent of Burmese exports—exceeded its target and registered a 7.9 percent growth.[8] This was accompanied primarily by increasing the extent of cultivated land and by planting 47 percent of the 12 million acres of rice land to high-yielding varieties. The 1978–79 record rice harvest of 10.4 million tons was bettered in 1981 (13 million) and 1982 (14.2 million).[9] Forestry and mining also achieved or exceeded their targets and oil production expanded markedly in 1980, in part due to the completion of a major pipeline; the output of gas rose 600 percent during the decade of the 70s. In fiscal year 1982–83 rice exports—which account for two-thirds of Burma's total exports and therefore a large percent of its foreign earnings—increased 26 percent but other exports remained flat,[10] mainly in consequence of the worldwide recession.

The fragility of the Burmese economy began to show when growth in real terms of gross domestic product slipped from 5.6 percent in

1984–85 to 3.7 percent in 1986–87 and declined the following year to an estimated 2.5 percent.[11] The country's self-styled "socialist production relations" had resulted in the establishment of state-owned enterprises engaged primarily in production of import substitutions. Because these enjoyed a closed market there was little incentive to compete with foreign counterparts.

Imports surged some 21 percent in 1987–88 from the previous fiscal year and export values dropped about 3.6 percent during the same period. Unlike Thailand, Burma had not diversified into export oriented industries. Moreover, when the government in mid-1988 announced a belated move to ease the state monopoly on foreign investment, it retained a monopoly in the sectors most attractive to foreign investors—forest products, mining, precious stones, pearls, oil and gas.

With the August 1988 massacres the western nations, led by the United States, curtailed economic aid. Asian response was ambiguous except in the case of Japan. The latter, acting in concert with the U.S. and West Germany, suspended its Y40 billion (roughly US$357 million) aid program.

WHITHER BURMA?

The four major facts of political and economic life in Burma during the past years have been: 1) authoritarianism, 2) isolationism associated with a strong xenophobia, 3) socialism, and 4) insurgency, including minority and communist rebellions and student riots. In October 1987, almost a year before the summer riots of 1988, the United Nations designated Burma a Least Developed Country. Since then the nation has been reduced to political shambles. But Burma's future may be less grim than the events of of 1988 suggest.

The energies of 40 million persons are being released, albeit violently, after 26 years of rising frustration over political and economic mismanagement. The several hundred political parties emerging from the 1988 summer of violence will not survive individually, but their very numbers, their demands and their persistence indicate that a genuine social revolution is underway. Unlike China's dilemma, namely little experience with democratic concepts and procedures, Burma and its citizens enjoyed accountable government in earlier years. It is quite possible, given the current explosion of popular demand, that responsible governance, including equitable representation of minority groups, will be revived despite the efforts of the military dictatorship to perpetuate itself.

Burma possesses advantages over many developing nations, in fact over many developed and industrialized states: self sufficiency in foodstuffs and vast natural resources. Many analysts consider it has the potential to become the richest state in Southeast Asia.

In the event a viable political system emerges from Burma's current turmoil the international community will likely renew its economic aid commitments. Japan, the largest donor, needs access to Burmese natural resources, and investment in Burma will impel it to come to Burma's assistance.

Turmoil in China in 1989, resulting uncertainty over the political and economic stability of Hong Kong, and a possible settlement of the Kampuchean issue all enhance the attractiveness of investment in Southeast Asia. Burma possesses great potential.

FOOTNOTES

1. *Asia Yearbook* (Hong Kong: Far Eastern Economic Review Ltd.), 1986, p. 119–120.

2. *Ibid.,* 1989, p. 94.

3. See *Foreign Broadcast Information Service,* EAS, October 1988–February 1989.

4. *Ibid.,* June 23, 1989, p. 28.

5. Quoted in *Southeast Asian Affairs* (Singapore: Institute of Southeast Asian Studies), 1980, p. 113.

6. "Editorial." *The Guardian,* (Rangoon), October 25, 1979.

7. *Data Asia* (Manila: Press Foundation of Asia), 1977, p. 5027.

8. *Asian Yearbook, op. cit.,* 1980, p. 149–150.

9. *Asia Record* (Palo Alto, Calif.: Asia-Pacific Affairs Associates), August 1982, p. 5.

10. *Asian Wall Street Journal Weekly,* April 11, 1983, p. 16.

11. *Asia Yearbook, op. cit.,* 1989, p. 6.

Thailand

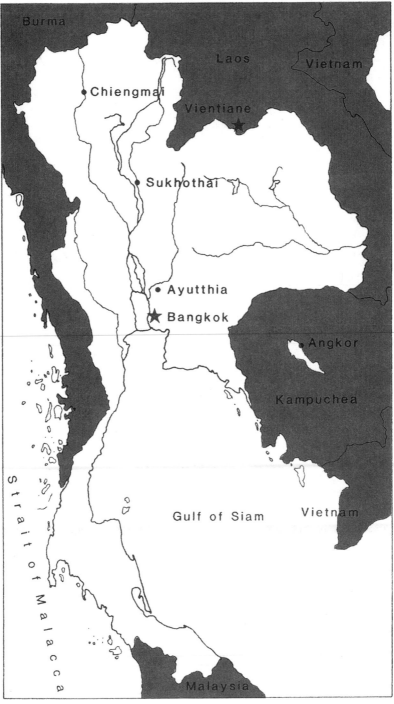

CHAPTER 9
THAILAND

Thailand comprises an area of some 200,000 square miles (about the size of France) in the center of mainland Southeast Asia, with a long narrow corridor stretching two-thirds of the way down the Malay Peninsula. It is bounded on the south by the Gulf of Siam, on the east by Kampuchea and Laos, on the north by Burma and the Andaman Sea (part of the Bay of Bengal) and at its southern extremity on the Malay Peninsula, by Malaysia.

The Menam Chao Phraya (Senior Lord River) drains the central plain which is surrounded by a U-shaped ring of hills and mountains and is the rice basket of the country. Bangkok, the capital, lies on the Chao Phraya 25 miles upstream from the gulf. In the southeast a lowlands extends from the Bangkok delta to the Tonle Sap (Great Lake) area of central Kampuchea. This Thai-Kampuchea corridor is the traditional route which armies of the two countries have used to attack each other's capitals.

EARLY KINGDOMS

Tai is a generic term referring to a parent racial group related to the Chinese who first appeared historically in the 6th century B.C. in western China, and from whom the Shan of Burma, the Laotians and the Thai-Siamese are all descended. By the mid-8th century they had formed the independent kingdom of Nan Chao—with a highly defined political organization—in Yunnan, South China. Over the following years groups of Tai moved slowly southward into Burma, Kampuchea and Laos, settling among the Mon, Khmer and Burmans. By the 12th century they had formed small states in the upper river valleys of present day Thailand. In 1219 (or 1238) a group of Tai attacked and defeated the Khmer commander of the Angkor outpost of Sukhothai in central Thailand. Here they established a center, the forerunner of what was to become an important state in the latter part of the century, a kingdom directly ancestral to modern Thailand. The peoples who settled at Sukhothai were a branch of Tai who called themselves Thai, meaning 'free'; the term Siamese is also applied to this group.

Within a few years of the establishment of the first Thai kingdom at Sukhothai, the southward Tai migration—the last of the massive pre-modern folk movements in Southeast Asia—was accelerated by the Mongol invasion of China and the defeat of Nan Chao. The Mongols did not engage in mass displacement of the conquered population, rather they encouraged development of a series of Tai border states as allies against the existing Southeast Asian powers of Angkor, Pagan and Vietnam.

Such a state arose in northwestern Thailand in 1290–92 when a Thai chieftain, Mengrai, conquered the Mon state of Haripunjaya and in its place founded the Kingdom of Chieng Mai—a state which would be in conflict with the states of Sukhothai, and later Ayutthia, for the next several centuries. The displaced Mon, who were perhaps the earliest people in Southeast Asia to be influenced by Indian culture, contributed much to the civilization of the conquering Thai.

Sukhothai during the reign of Rama Khamheng (1275–1317) has been termed the "cradle of Siamese civilization." Rama Khamheng conquered most of the lower Chao Phraya valley and the northern Malay peninsula, areas which had been Mon territories since before the period of recorded history and, according to some sources, extended his sway to Luang Prabang (Laos), Vientiane (Laos) and Pegu (Burma). Under Rama Khamheng the Thai adopted certain aspects of Mon and Khmer civilizations. Rama reduced the Thai language to writing in 1283, using the Mon alphabet, and adopted Theravada Buddhism (with its ties to Kampuchea and Burma) as the state religion, along with its artistic traditions. At the same time he perpetuated the rituals to ancestral spirits and spirits of earth and sky, thus appeasing followers of the old religious forms. The Thai borrowed other important cultural elements from their neighbors: the Khmer political system; Indian juristic traditions; and the Mongol military organization and threefold division of society into warrior-freemen (Thai), civilian-commoners and serfs.

Ayutthia   In 1349 U Thong, an ambitious prince who controlled much of the area south of Sukhothai, secured the vassalage of that state and established himself in a new capital at Ayutthia. Ayutthia was ideally situated on a defensible island in the lower Chao Phraya River. Surrounded by lush agricultural land and close to the Gulf of Siam, it was militarily within easy reach of the Khmer capital of Angkor.

Thong was crowned in 1350 as Rama Tibodi I (1350–1369) and is regarded as the first king of Thailand. He governed in the feudal tradition which had characterized kingly rule in Sukhothai. He administered the capital and its environs directly; the provinces were held lightly and existed almost as small independent states; the vassal kingdoms acknowledged the sovereignty of Ayutthia and paid tribute to the court.

Boromoraja I (1370–1388) began to centralize Thai administration, adopting the Brahmanic conceptions of absolutism from the Khmer empire, including the idea of the king as *devaraja*. Throughout most of the second half of the 14th and the 15th centuries Ayutthia was the most powerful state in Southeast Asia. During the reign of Boromoraja II (1424–1448) Angkor was captured and Sukhothai was reduced from a vassal state to a mere province, but Ayutthia was unable to subdue its arch enemy Chieng Mai. Boromoraja was succeeded by his son, known in history as King Trailok (1448–1488), who further centralized the state and established functional departments or ministries headed by ranking officers. Civil administration was under the minister of the interior who presided over the Council of Ministers and was in effect the prime minister; the military administration was headed by the minister of war. Trailok promulgated a definitive code of palace law in 1450. Details regarding etiquette suggest the severity and absolutism that had come to characterize Thai kingship: for whispering at a royal audience the penalty was death; for kicking the palace door, the loss of a foot.

Another innovation of Trailok was creation of the office of *maha uparat,* second or vice king; he designated one of his sons as such shortly before his death. This office—which lasted into the 20th century—conferred upon its holder many kingly prerogatives, but not necessarily the succession.

The 16th century heralded a new era in Thailand's political history, with the arrival of the Europeans and their involvement in the affairs of the heartland of Southeast Asia, and the rise of a strong aggressive Burma on the west. In 1564 and again in 1569 the Burmese seized Ayutthia and the Thai struggle to throw off Burmese vassalage continued for the next two decades, culminating in a Thai attack on Burma in 1600. During the same period Ayutthia was engaged in constant conflict on the east with Kampuchea—a continuation of the centuries-long conflict between the two states—and captured its capital in 1594.

The 17th century marked an increase in European contact, with both the Dutch and the English East India companies establishing factories in the capital by 1612. Under Dutch pressure, however, the English were forced to close their factory 10 years later. The Dutch sought to solidify their position in Thailand by helping Prasat Tong seize the throne in 1630, but both Prasat (1630–1656) and his son Narai (1657–1688) feared rising Dutch influence, and Narai invited the English back and welcomed the newly arrived French Missionary Society.

A consequence of opening the door to westerners was that during the next fifteen years a series of European adventurers, both religious and lay—of whom the most notorious was a Greek named Constantine Phaulkon—thoroughly disrupted the court of Thailand. Reaction to European machinations was such that in June 1687 the Thai massacred most of the crew of two English warships, and during Narai's last illness the following year, Pra Petraja, general in charge of the royal elephants, led an anti-foreign conspiracy and gained control of the palace. The coup leaders were joined by thousands of armed Thai, Phaulkon was arrested and executed, and Petraja seized the throne and forced the French to evacuate the country. The feelings against the Europeans—especially Phaulkon—had resulted in "such a powerful upsurge of anti-foreign sentiment that until the days of Mongkut in the middle of the 19th century Siam [Thailand] was to be very chary of granting privileges to Europeans."[1]

Pra Petraja's reign (1688–1703) was marked by a new conflict that would occupy much of mainland Southeast Asia for the next three centuries, the struggle with Vietnam, first for control of Laos, and then under his grandson, Tai Sra (1709–1733), for the control of Kampuchea. During the reign of Boromoraja V (1758–1767), the last king to reign at Ayutthia, the Burmese invaded Thailand twice and Ayutthia fell in 1767. The city was destroyed and was never rebuilt.

CHAKRI DYNASTY: TRADITIONAL PERIOD

While Ayutthia was under seige in 1767 a half-Chinese general, Pya Taksin, escaped with 500 followers. He managed to raise an army on the shores of the Gulf of Siam and was suddenly presented with an opportunity for recovering Thai control of the countryside when the Burmese were attacked on their home front by the Chinese. In October 1767 Taksin sailed up the Chao Phraya from the gulf and captured Thonburi—opposite today's Bangkok—from the Burmese puppet governor, and proceeded to defeat the main Burmese occupation force near Ayutthia. He assumed royal power, Boromoraja V having disappeared, and set up his capital at Thonburi after soothsayers pronounced it a place of good omen. However, the long struggle during his reign to drive out the Burmese, reunite Thailand and extend Thai control over Laos and Kampuchea was accomplished at the expense of his sanity. He was forced to retire to a monastery and the throne was offered to his commander in chief Thong Duang, known by his military title, Chakri. Taksin and his son and brothers were executed to prevent them from becoming a rallying point of later opposition, and Thong assumed the throne, establishing the Chakri dynasty, the line that was still reigning in 1990.

Rama I   Rama I, as Chakri is known (Rama is the title given posthumously to the first five kings of the dynasty by Rama VI and has been used by his dynastic successors), was soon required to defend his country against another long series of Burmese invasions and raids. But Thailand was much stronger and more capably led in 1785 than it had been in 1767. Rama defeated the Burmese and could have revenged himself by an invasion of their homeland but he turned his attention instead to the consolidation of Thailand and to administrative reform. He founded modern Bangkok, built a splendid palace and fortified the city. He secured the allegiance of the provinces by appointing governors absolutely loyal to himself, and established a court system in accordance with ancient legal tradition. Although in theory the power of the king was absolute, in practice it was limited because of loose civil administration. The government provided protection and its revenues came from monopolies, customs dues and taxes. Freemen were obliged to provide labor service for four to six months a year but the obligation could be paid off in money or in commodities. Poor persons therefore often sold themselves into slavery to a patron who would pay off their service obligation to the government. As a result, by the early 19th century approximately one-third of the Thai people were slaves.

Thailand strengthened its position in Kampuchea during the period of the Tay-son rebellion in Vietnam. The Thai removed the Kampuchean boy king, Ang Eng, from the control of the Vietnamese regent and in Bangkok crowned him as monarch in 1794. The next year they sent him back to Kampuchea under the protection of a Thai army. As the price for returning the king, the Thai demanded and received from Kampuchea five provinces, including Battambang and Siemreap, rich border regions.

Thus at the beginning of the 19th century Thailand was more powerful than ever before, extending its influence over the kingdoms of Luang Prabang and Vientiane in the north, Kampuchea in the east and the northern Malay states in the south. Even the continuing wars with Burma finally wound down as the Burmese were increasingly involved with problems on their western border.

Rama II and Rama III   Rama II (1809–1824) ruled Thailand during the period the new Vietnamese empire of Gia Long was gathering strength. When Rama II supported the rebel brother of Kampuchea's King Ang Chan and forced Ang Chan to flee to Saigon, Gia Long with a large force reinstated him. Thus temporarily eclipsed in the matter of succession, Rama II in 1814 occupied more provinces of northern Kampuchea. He also began to exert pressure upon the Malay states in the south, an action which led eventually to problems with the British. Nevertheless he removed some of the impediments of trade with Europeans which had characterized Thai policy since banishment of the French in 1688. However his successor Rama III (1824–1851) reverted to the traditional Thai suspicion of Europeans and actively obstructed their influence—though he signed a treaty in 1826 with Henry Burney of the English East India Company which slowed, but did not stop entirely, Thai encroachments on the Malay peninsula. Rama III increased charges and restrictions upon European traders and at the same time hired more Chinese tax collectors. Chinese control of foreign trade and of the king's commercial operations became so pronounced that Bangkok during his reign appeared to be a Chinese city. Rama III was also the last Thai king to reflect the traditional view that the ruler was a *chakravartin*—universal emperor and embryo buddha, an outgrowth of the concept of *devaraja*.

Since the threat from Burma eased after the British defeat of the Burmese in the first Anglo-Burmese War (1824–1826), Rama III had greater freedom to pursue the Thai policy of territorial expansion in the east. In 1828 Vientiane was sacked and Laos subsequently became a corridor for Thai attacks on Vietnam. Three years later Thai armies occupied most of Kampuchea, before being routed by the Vietnamese. The following decade the Thai again sent armies into Kampuchea— this time at the request of a group of Kampuchean nobles—to thwart Vietnamese attempts to absorb the country. In 1845 the two aggressor nations reached a compromise: Kampuchea was placed under the joint protection of Thailand and Vietnam and Ang Duong was consecrated king of Kampuchea in the names of the sovereigns of both conquering nations; he was therefore vassal to each.

CHAKRI DYNASTY: MODERNIZING PERIOD

Mongkut (Rama IV)   Upon Rama III's death in 1851 Thailand entered a new era. Prince Maha Mongkut, half-brother to Rama III and Rama II's eldest son by a royal mother, became king as Rama IV upon the invitation of the chief princes of the royal family. Mongkut had lived as a monk during his predecessor's reign, eventually becoming chief abbot. His long years of study, first of Pali scriptures and later of western learning, and his wide range of foreign contacts, provided him with a sophistication not hitherto seen in a Thai king. Realizing that his nation's survival depended upon its ability to accommodate to a new world with which Asian traditionalism could not cope, he opened Thailand to the West after almost two centuries of self-imposed isolation. He welcomed nationals of various European states on the assumption that safety for Thailand from dominance by any one western power lay in contact with several.

Mongkut was particularly eager to establish a firm relationship with Britain—which was in the process of carving out its Southeast Asian empire in Burma and Malaya, both Thailand's neighbors—perceiving that the British were less a threat to Thailand than were the French. This was despite the fact that the British prevented Thai expansion on the Malay peninsula in the 1830s and again in 1862. In effect Mongkut was willing to acquiesce to British preeminence throughout Malaya in return for an implicit commitment by the British to preserve Thailand's political integrity.

Mongkut took the first step in permitting western trade and influence when in 1855 he and Sir John Bowring, a particularly perceptive and capable British diplomat, worked out a treaty of friendship and commerce. The agreement not only provided for freedom of trade between the two nations, but restricted the Thai government's authority to levy duties and taxes on British enterprises and granted Britain extraterritorial privileges (i.e., jurisdiction over British subjects within Thailand). Trade immediately increased and other powers quickly requested, and were granted, similar treatment.

Nevertheless it was Britain which benefited most from the dramatic shift in Thai policy. Five British ships had visited Bangkok during 1849; in 1864 the number in port on a single day exceeded 100, most of them in the Hong Kong-Singapore trade. British firms became the dominant foreign enterprises and British experts provided advice to the king on canal and road construction, ship building, reorganization of government services and teaching foreign languages. Many of these advisers subsequently became heads of Thai government departments.

Chulalongkorn (Rama V)   When Mongkut died suddenly of malaria in 1868 he was succeeded by his 16-year-old son, Chulalongkorn, who had been educated by an English governess whom his father had engaged as tutor for the royal children. Since he was a minor, the government operated under a regency for the next five years, and the future king was allowed to travel abroad extensively before he assumed the throne.

When he was crowned in 1873 Chulalongkorn immediately embarked upon what constituted a radical reform of traditional Thai society. He abolished the practice of prostration in the royal presence, forced the children of the aristocracy to follow European educational curricula at the palace schools which he established, sent his own sons to Europe to study and decreed that no one could be born a slave or sell oneself for debt. He ended the forced labor system and developed an efficient conscript army.

Chulalongkorn also undertook major administrative reforms. He transformed the bureaucracy into 12 functional ministries, appointed royal governors for the provinces, embarked upon the long and arduous task of fiscal and tax reform and modernization, and reorganized the administration of justice. Since he was convinced that modernization could only be achieved by a strong leader, he adroitly managed governmental reforms with an eye to increasing the power of the king at the expense of that of the nobility. He enlisted as his supporters younger members of the court who had been exposed to western education. Drawing upon these individuals—known collectively as the Young Siam Party—he formed two new governmental bodies in 1874 as counterbalances to the Senabodi (the council of senior ministers, princes and prelates) which he considered to be obstructionist. The organizations he created were the Privy Council and the Council of State. The former was responsible for bringing issues before the latter, which in turn advised the king regarding legislation.

Although Chulalongkorn developed cordial relations with a number of western royal houses, he continued to face the problem of territorial encroachment by these same powers. The problem had worsened after the French conquest of Vietnam—which began with the seizure of Cochinchina in 1859 and was concluded by the declaration of Tongking as a French protectorate in 1885. During that period France replaced Vietnam as Thailand's competitor for control of Kampuchea, forcing a treaty of protection on that state in 1863. Four years later Mongkut had surrendered his claims to suzerainty over all of Kampuchea in return for French recognition of Thai rights in the Kampuchean provinces of Battambang and Siemreap that Thailand had long held.

In 1885 Chulalongkorn sent a military force to northern Laos because France was threatening Thai suzerainty over that region. Some 22 years of conflict and tension between the Thai and the French ensued, during which Thailand lost some 96,000 square miles on its eastern borders to French aggression. In 1893 French gunboats deliberately shelled Thai forts at the entrance to the Chao Phraya river; their objective was to provoke a war that would provide France with an excuse for seizing the entire central valley. The crisis was resolved when the British persuaded the two sides to negotiate, with the result that Chulalongkorn had to agree to give up all territory east of the Mekong River, to evacuate the provinces of Battambang and Siemreap, and to pay a large indemnity to France.

From 1893 until the Anglo-French entente cordiale of 1904 Thailand continued to be a pawn in the game of French-British rivalry, given moral support by Britain, but constantly forced by France to forfeit territory and claims to maintain its sovereignty. After the Anglo-French rapprochement Thailand had to cede the still disputed Battambang and Siemreap provinces to France (1907), and to abandon claims of suzerainty over the Malay states of Kelantan, Trengganu, Kedah and Perlis in return for the British surrendor of extraterritorial rights in Thailand (1909).

Rama VI   Rama VI, who succeeded his father in 1910, was the first

Thai king to be educated abroad. His reign reflected his diverse interests, some of them contradictory. A dilettante with a flair for the dramatic, Rama VI was uninterested in mundane governmental affairs, yet he initiated significant social reforms. Among other changes, Thai law was recodified to prohibit polygamy, require vaccination and the use of surnames, and establish succession to the throne through male primogeniture. The king encouraged the use of western dress by women, adopted the Gregorian calendar, established the Red Cross Society, founded Chulalongkorn University in honor of his father (1917), and introduced compulsory elementary education (1921).

Rama VI was in many respects the first Thai nationalist in the modern sense. In spite of his gestures toward westernization, he often expressed his love of country in chauvinistic terms. He stressed the revival of Buddhism, in part on the assumption that only a Buddhist could be a good patriot. In his unhappiness over the slow pace of assimilation into Thai culture of the increasingly large Chinese community, he accused the Chinese of placing monetary interests over loyalty to their adopted land.

His most astute move was to support the Allied Powers in World War I. He pointedly disregarded the army's preference for the Central Powers—a preference arising from a lingering resentment over losses of territory to the French and the British—and after the United States entered the war in 1917, sent a small expeditionary force to France. His prescience in coming down on the winning side—a traditional skill of the Thai—paid off handsomely: Thailand gained the approbation of the Allies, millions of dollars worth of German shipping as war booty, and charter member status in the League of Nations.

POLITICAL INDICATORS

1. The Thai appeared late on the political scene in Southeast Asia, but they arrived with a defined political organization, having survived as a kingdom on the edge of the Chinese empire for centuries before moving into central Thailand.
2. They quickly accepted and adapted the superior civilization they found—in particular Theravada Buddhism, writing, art forms and the semi-sacred role of the king—of the Mon and Khmer who became their neighbors and subjects.
3. The Kingdom of Ayutthia succeeded in incorporating the competing Thai states of Sukhothai and Chieng Mai and expanded south into the Malay peninsula, eastward into Kampuchea and Laos, and pressed against Burma on the west. These thrusts against adjacent states were a hallmark of political life for the next six hundred years.

4. The constant conflict between Thailand and Kampuchea changed to a contest between Thailand and Vietnam for control of Kampuchea and, less importantly, of Laos.

5. Although Thai kings showed a marked ability to adapt to changed political and economic conditions in the 19th and early 20th centuries, their attempts to modernize called for centralization of royal power and failed to give the elite a meaningful role in government.

CONSTITUTIONAL GOVERNMENT

The constitutional era in Thailand dates from the reign of Chulalongkorn's youngest son, Prajadhipok, who succeeded to the throne in 1925 upon the death of his brother, Rama VI. Shy and retiring, liberal in outlook, and preferring to share rather than monopolize governmental responsibility, Rama VII began his reign by broadening the powers held by the earlier advisory bodies. He established an advisory Supreme Council made up of five princes, and a Committee of Privy Councillors, representing Thailand's intellectual, commercial and professional communities. One of his most important achievements was the termination of the unequal treaty system with which Thailand had been fettered since the British treaties of 1855–56, and that had provided the legal basis for extraterritorial claims and tax exemptions for almost all foreigners in Thailand.

But new problems arose. Rama VII moved to reduce expenditures in the wake of Rama VI's extravagances and to dismiss his brother's courtiers from sinecure positions. In pursuing these ends the king managed to offend the bureaucracy, the army and the nobility. He also investigated the possibility of granting a constitution to the kingdom— a graphic way of repudiating the traditional absolutist theory of kingship he wished to disavow. But his indecision, his failure to enlist the support of the political elite, his lack of recognition of the depth of social discontent, and the economic depression of 1930 combined to precipitate a more fundamental change.

1932 Coup On June 24, 1932 the political crisis which had been building throughout the reign of two kings erupted. Pridi Phanomyong, a brilliant young lawyer and son of a wealthy Chinese businessman and his Thai wife, led a group of civilian officials and army officers in a successful *coup d'état* which was supported by military units in the Bangkok area. The coup, like most of those which have followed, was bloodless and involved little public participation. Lacking a colonial experience and the popular reaction it engendered, the Thai masses had not demonstrated a desire for political participation nor a sense of nationalism as had other peoples of Southeast Asia. Thai nationalism originated among, and remained limited to, the upper class. It was mainly a tool in the struggle against absolutism by the modernizing elite, a cover to permit them to influence political and social change in accordance with their views and to enable them to achieve power.

Several days after the coup the People's Party, as the leaders termed themselves, announced that a provisional constitution drafted by Pridi was in effect and the kingdom had become a constitutional monarchy. The king accepted his plight readily, declining to attempt to counter the coup by employing police powers or by advancing a reform program of his own, even though the new constitution abolished all kingly prerogatives save the power of pardon. The document also specifically excluded princes from ministerial and army hierarchies.

Pridi and colonels Pibun Songgram and Phaya Phayon, representing young and ambitious army officers, were the key figures in the coup; the first two were to remain major figures in Thai politics for the next thirty years. The three quickly became the most influential members of the Commissariat of the People established under the provisional constitution. The Commissariat, which had the power to make laws and to appoint ministers, was nominally headed by Phaya Manopakorn, a former high court judge who had not participated in the coup but whose conservative credentials provided a counterweight to the radical proclivities of some of the coup leaders. The Commissariat was appointed by a 70-member Senate, which had itself been selected by the coup leadership.

Major social goals were announced: internal peace and order, freedom, equality, economic well being and educational opportunity for all. The specific reforms included a graduated income tax, a merit civil service, lower postal rates and suspension of the land tax. Pridi's ideas were toned down, however, in the permanent constitution promulgated on December 10, 1932. The constitution was a compromise among the party's young radicals, the conservative army elements within the party, and the moderate king. The monarch's authority was substantially restored. He was given the power to appoint half the members of the unicameral National Assembly under a tutelary arrangement, not to exceed ten years, that was deemed necessary to permit gradual transition to a completely elected assembly. Cabinet ministers were to be chosen jointly by the king and the assembly, and the king could dissolve the assembly without cabinet approval and call new elections within three months. The king could also veto legislation, subject to legislative override, and could enact emergency decrees when countersigned by the appropriate functional minister. A State Council, from which princes were excluded, was established. At the king's request the People's Party was dissolved. Phaya Manopakorn became prime minister.

An economic plan put forth by Pridi in 1933 to nationalize land and industrial resources provoked a reaction from Phaya Manopakorn who, with the support of the conservative military group, raised the spector of communism and forced Pridi from the cabinet, persuading him to take a long sojourn in Europe. Phaya Manopakorn then prorogued the assembly, imposed press censorship and promulgated a tough anti-communist law. These acts raised fears among moderate army leaders that he was preparing to restore the absolute monarchy. Disapproving of both Pridi's policies and Phaya Manopakorn's methods, army colonels Phaya Phayon and Pibun Songgram, and navy commander Supa Chalasai resigned their portfolios and carried out a successful *coup d'état* of their own on June 20, 1933. Phaya Phayon took over as prime minister, a new State Council made up of his followers was appointed, and the National Assembly was reconvened. The new government maintained an anti-communist stance, prepared for general elections, and defeated a pro-monarchy rebellion in October 1933 led by the king's cousin. Pibun's actions in successfully defending Bangkok and recapturing the airport from the rebels catapulted him into the political spotlight.

In September 1933 the government had permitted Pridi to return to Bangkok, although he was not allowed to hold high office pending resolution of charges that he was a communist. A commission of investigation cleared him in 1934 and his popularity soared. Pridi, the left-wing civilian champion of the rising middle class, found himself in intense rivalry with Pibun, who had won acclaim for his defense of Bangkok and become the military champion of the same middle class.

The first general elections in Thailand were held in November 1933. Most of the 78 elected assembly deputies were civilians; the appointed half of the assembly was mainly military. The popular and tactful Phaya Phayon continued as prime minister—the only public figure able to maintain a balance between the Pibun and Pridi factions. As the urban middle class rallied around Pridi and the army leaders around Pibun, the significant loser was the monarch. Rightly or not he was suspected of supporting the unsuccessful royalist rebellion and never regained popular confidence. He abdicated from England in March 1935 and urged that a young successor be chosen who would not interfere in political affairs before the government's policies could be carried out. Accordingly the 10-year-old Ananda Mahidol (1935–1948), son of the king's deceased younger brother, was chosen. The new king (Rama VIII) was attending elementary school in Switzerland and a three-member regency carried out his responsibilities until he returned in 1945.

Pridi and Pibun: 1934–1938   Although Phaya Phayon was officially head of government until 1938 when ill health caused his retirement, the most influential cabinet member during most of the period was

Pridi, followed by Pibun. Pridi was successively minister of interior, foreign affairs and finance. Pibun became minister of defense and built the Thai army into a strong political instrument, emphasizing nationalism and the need for a powerful military organization to keep the country from being controlled by outsiders. He asserted the superior efficiency of the military organization over that of the civilian administration. Both leaders opposed interference in politics by the nobility.

During this period government policy increasingly emphasized Thai ethnicity and culture and discriminated against the Chinese in the professions and in business. Citizenship standards were altered, establishing literacy, wealth and military service requirements to discourage Chinese who sought Thai nationality. The political restrictions put into place in 1933 were continued. Newspapers were not permitted because it was claimed the nation was not ripe for political discussion, and the Pibun faction steadily campaigned against "communistic" elements.

The uneasy alliance between civilian and military factions became increasingly strained as more and more civil offices came under the control of the military. The new, more conservative, assembly which was elected in 1937 further tipped the balance towards the military. When the Phaya Phayon cabinet resigned in December 1938 over a budget crisis, Pibun became prime minister and a period of intensified nationalism and chauvinism ensued.

The new government emphasized Thai ethnicity and culture to the extent that true patriotism was equated with being a Buddhist. The kingdom's name became Muang Thai (Land of the Free), or Thailand, rather than Siam which had been its official name since the time of King Mongkut. A pan-Thai movement was initiated that sought restoration of former Thai possessions in Laos, Kampuchea, Burma and Malaya. In 1939–40 the military budget absorbed one-third of the national revenues, and a militant Japanese-style youth organization was established.

WARTIME THAILAND

The fall of France in June 1940 emboldened Pibun—with Japanese encouragement—to assert territorial claims to much of French Indochina. He claimed all of Laos and three provinces of Kampuchea. The same month he signed a treaty of friendship with Japan. In August Japan pressured the Vichy French regime to allow Japanese forces to be stationed throughout Indochina. As a consequence, when the Thai launched an "offensive" in early 1941 along the Laotian-Kampuchean frontiers, Japanese onsite "mediation," and then "arbitration," awarded Thailand the Kampuchean provinces of Battambang and Siemreap and the Laotian territory on the west bank of the Mekong which it had relinquished to France in 1893. With Thailand thus in its debt, Japan's conquest of Southeast Asia was assured, since Thailand was a geographically strategic state.

The day following the Japanese attack on Pearl Harbor (December 7, 1941) which put the American fleet out of action, Japan landed troops in Thailand. Pibun's forces offered token resistance, capitulated and then agreed to declare war on the Allies. The way was thus cleared for a two-pronged attack by Japan on the British in Singapore and in Rangoon, via a base in Thailand.

While Pibun's pro-Japanese policy averted the physical destruction of war, it was not popular. Pridi meanwhile resigned from the cabinet, failed in his effort to form a neutralist government in northern Thailand, and then accepted the relatively non-political job of regent to the young king. He soon initiated a clandestine "free Thai" movement that established contacts with other anti-Japanese Thai groups and with U.S. and British intelligence services. Pibun declared war on the Allies in 1942, but his ambassador to the United States, Seni Pramoj— one of two brothers who became prominent in postwar Thai politics— declined to deliver the declaration. Pridi and Seni between them were effective in promoting pro-Allied policies to such a degree that the United States refrained from declaring war on Thailand and did not consider Thailand as an enemy country in the postwar peace negotiations.

When Japan began to lose the war, beginning in 1943, Pibun's political fortunes waned; Thai leaders realized that the country might well become the physical target of Allied wrath. Moreover the Japanese distrusted Pibun and were threatening to take control of the country themselves. Pridi sought to avert disaster by appealing to the Allies, but the Allies declined to assist Pridi's underground forces unless Pibun was displaced. To achieve their support Pridi secured a no-confidence vote against Pibun who resigned in July 1944 and was succeeded by the civilian Khuang Aphaiwong, a conservative follower of Seni. Pridi however became the dominant political figure of the new government.

In August 1945 Pridi disavowed, via royal proclamation, the 1942 Thai war declaration against the United States and Great Britain, and then ensured good future relations with the United States by requesting Ambassador Seni to return to Bangkok to head the government. France, Britain and the Soviet Union were less easily placated. France required Thailand to return the Indochinese territories so recently annexed. The British demanded Thailand renounce claims to the four northern states of Malaya and pay reparations for war damages involving British investments in Thailand (part of which was to be in the form of rice shipments to British Malaya); and the Soviets insisted that

the Thai repeal their anti-communist laws. These cor
met before the three nations would agree to Thailand
the United Nations.

COUPS AND COUNTER COUPS: 1946–1968

Unlike the postwar history of Indochina—Kampuchea, Laos and
Vietnam—where the political struggle was between anti-communist
and revolutionary-communist nationalists, the postwar political history
of Thailand was a struggle between the military and the civilian elite to
obtain and retain power and yet achieve the semblance of constitutional
democracy. It was fought by coup and counter-coup—usually bloodless. The same prewar actors continued to play center stage.

Upon achievement of the British-Thai agreement of January 1, 1946,
which in essence accepted Thailand into the postwar "free" world,
Seni's government was dissolved. Elections were held to fill the seats
of the elected-half of the National Assembly which returned a large
majority of Pridi's followers. Khuang, with Pridi's blessing, became
prime minister a second time, but resigned in March to found the
conservative, pro-monarchist Democratic Party. Pridi thereupon assumed the premiership and proposed a new constitution which was
approved by the assembly and came into force in May. The main
difference between the 1932 constitution and that of 1946 was that the
latter provided for a bicameral legislature, one in which the lower
house elected the members of the upper house. Thus Pridi was assured
of controlling both chambers. By means of the constitution Pridi in
effect created a packed legislature as the basis of his power to balance
the armed forces which were Pibun's power base.

Pridi's star dimmed, however, when 20-year-old King Ananda Mahidol was found shot to death on June 9, 1946 under circumstances that
aroused a suspicion of murder. Pridi's clumsy and tardy handling of
the incident raised public doubts, not only of his effectiveness, but of
whether or not he was involved in the tragedy. To defuse the situation
Pridi resigned and departed on a world tour. His protégé, retired
Admiral Thamrong Nawasawat, succeeded him. Thamrong built a
following by closing his eyes to an unprecedented level of corruption
within the government. The new king, Bhumibol Adulyadej (Rama
IX), the younger brother of Ananda Mahidol, was 19 years old at the
time of his accession to the throne. He had been born in the United
States and educated in Switzerland, and he returned to Switzerland to
complete his studies, not commencing his royal duties until 1951. A
regent carried out the monarchical role in the interim.

A number of army officers, disgruntled over the near eclipse of
military influence in the civilian government, carried out another

ɔloodless *coup d'état* on November 8, 1947. Pibun emerged as leader of the Coup Group as it was called, and installed Khuang as prime minister for the third time, on the theory that a respected civilian would quiet adverse foreign reaction. Pridi, who had returned from his world tour, fled to Peking. A second but provisional postwar constitution was promulgated, which again provided for a bicameral legislature, with each chamber having 100 members, but membership in the upper house was this time reserved for nominees of the crown.

General elections in January 1948 gave Khuang's Democratic Party a small parliamentary majority in the lower house, while the military party, Tamatipat, fared badly. Khuang's effort to govern with a small majority, but without links to the military, was immediately challenged. Officers of the Coup Group forcibly removed him and urged the regent to request Pibun, by then a field marshal and waiting in the wings, to form a new government.

Pibun Years: 1948–1951 Pibun's return to power in 1948 was on a much less solid basis than that which he had enjoyed during the war years. In 1948 he was forced to compromise and negotiate among army, police and civilian factions. Even so his government was beset by attempted coups. A planned uprising by an anti-Pibun army group was thwarted by the arrest of its leaders in October 1948. In February 1949 supporters of Pridi in the royal marines led an unsuccessful revolt to reinstate a civilian government; it was quelled by forces under the command of General Sarit Thanarat after—for the first time—widespread violence and bloodshed. A broad purge of senior politicians and officials followed.

In June 1951 it was the navy's turn. Naval officers abducted Pibun from a ceremony marking the transfer of United States equipment to Thailand under the military assistance program. He was held for three days. On the third day the Thai air force bombed Thai naval craft, including the one on which Pibun was being held hostage. Pibun managed to swim to safety. The rebellion failed but only after nearly 1,000 civilians and several hundred military personnel had been killed in the worst violence Bangkok had ever witnessed.

From 1948 until the June 1951 rebellion, Pibun's actual public policies differed little from those he favored in the 1930s, although during most of the period he was operating under terms of a constitution whose provisions did not support the philosophy of the Coup Group.

A permanent constitution had been promulgated in March 1949, the third of the postwar period. It did not reflect Coup Group philosophy, but was a liberal document, drafted by experts under former prime minister Khuang's supervision, and designed to limit the power of the military; it retained the bicameral legislature created by the 1946 document. The Group was impelled to accept the new constitution after the marine rebellion in February, but the document did not prevent Pibun from pursuing policies designed to strengthen the military forces, harass the Chinese, enforce a super-patriotism (including efforts to force a Thai Buddhist culture on Malay Moslems in the southern provinces), and vigorously promote anti-communism (during the communist uprisings in Laos, Malaya, Burma and Vietnam and the successful communist takeover of China). The government's tough internal policies were reflected in its international relationships. Thailand refused to recognize the new communist regime in China; instead it supported the United Nations against North Korea in 1950 and became a loyal proponent of United States policy in Southeast Asia. These initiatives endeared the regime to the anti-communist western nations who expressed their appreciation by providing assistance that helped accelerate Thai agricultural and industrial development and contributed to growing Thai prosperity.

During the four year period of attempted coups and revolts, Pibun was obliged, for political survival, to share power gradually with General Phao Siyanon, director general of the police, and General Sarit Thanarat, commander in chief of the Bangkok army. Phao had achieved prominence for his efficient suppression of the Chinese minority and for his skill in combating communist subversion. Sarit had become widely known because he had organized the resistance which quelled the armed rebellion by the marines in February 1949. By mid-1951 the army and the police, in the persons of the two generals, had become the real rulers of Thailand.

Pibun, Phao and Sarit all opposed the civilian bias of the 1949 constitution and on November 29, 1951 suddenly announced on the radio that the 1949 constitution had been abrogated because it was too advanced and that the 1932 constitution had been reinstated. By renouncing the 1949 constitution the military leaders of the "Radio Coup," as it was known, emasculated the power of the legislature, the last significant source of opposition to their control. The official reason given for returning to the 1932 constitution's unicameral assembly—half of whose members were chosen by the government—was the danger of internal communism and the political instability of Southeast Asia. By reviving the anti-monarchical constitution two days before the return to Thailand from Switzerland of King Bhumibol, the coup leaders also sought to minimize the possible assumption of royal power.

The young king at first declined to accept the substitute constitution, raising the threat of non-recognition of the coup by foreign powers. Although Bhumipol was able to exact only a few concessions before conceding, his action signaled that—as the first adult monarch since

1935—he would not remain aloof from politics, a position he has consistently maintained.

Troika The revised constitution was promulgated February 26, 1952. Elections the same day resulted in a sweep for Tamatipat—the army/government party—for the elected seats in the assembly. The government-appointed half of the body consisted mainly of military officers. Pibun stayed on as prime minister but with reduced influence, sharing his power with Phao and Sarit. The troika, from 1952 to 1955, continued Pibun's anti-Chinese and anti-communist policies as political conditions in Southeast Asia became increasingly complex and unstable. The Thai government's wholehearted cooperation with the anti-communist governments of South Korea and South Vietnam, however, made it a major target of communist propaganda and infiltration and in 1953 the communists announced they had established an autonomous Thai government in southern China; its purpose was to encourage subversion and defection within Thailand.

The government's view that the major enemy of Thailand was the People's Republic of China led it to seek the protection of the United States. The result was the Southeast Asia Collective Defense Treaty of September 8, 1954—signed in Manila and therefore frequently referred to as the Manilia Pact—which created the Southeast Asia Treaty Organization (SEATO). The signatories were Thailand, the Philippines, Pakistan, France, Australia, New Zealand, the United Kingdom and the United States, and for the first time it extended the U.S. defense commitment to mainland Southeast Asia. SEATO headquarters were established in Bangkok and in 1955 its member nations were offered the use of Thai military bases. Already cordial U.S.-Thai relations became even closer and large amounts of U.S. economic and military assistance flowed into the country.

The Pibun government began to relax its strict internal policies as Thailand became increasingly prosperous, successful in containing internal communism, and the beneficiary of the support and protection of the West. Political parties were allowed to organize, a greater measure of local self government was condoned, and freer individual and media expression were permitted. Some 25 political parties contested the general elections of February 1957, with the result that the new Seri Manangkhasila Party of Pibun and Phao received only a bare majority; Sarit had disassociated himself from the elections which he described as "filthy." To mollify Sarit, Pibun appointed him commander in chief of the armed forces—and then suddenly declared a state of emergency.

Pibun was unable to reverse the political tide that had begun to favor Sarit and on September 17 Sarit displaced both Pibun and Phao in a bloodless coup. Pote Sarasin, then secretary general of SEATO, headed an interim government until the general elections of December which gave no single party a working parliamentary majority. Sarit therefore brought together a coalition of parties and factions—including leftists—under the umbrella National Socialist Party, and an interim government was formed in January 1958 by General Thanom Kittikachorn, Sarit's deputy, who served as prime minister while Sarit went to the United States for medical treatment. Upon Sarit's return in October Thanom voluntarily resigned in his favor.

Once he had come to power Sarit, in traditional Thai fashion, proceeded to outlaw political parties, suppress critics and close newspapers. In an important shift from the policy of the Pibun regime, however, Sarit worked closely with leaders of the Chinese associations, seeking assimilation of the Chinese community rather than its suppression. In January 1959 he placed in operation an interim constitution which called for an appointed assembly, with dual authority to legislate and to draft a permanent constitution—which became Thailand's eighth when it came into effect almost 10 years later.

Field Marshal Sarit formally became prime minister in February 1959 and remained in office until his death in October 1963. His years were marked by construction of major electrification and irrigation projects, inauguration of state operated enterprises, and encouragement of foreign investment. His anti-communist policies were directed against communist insurgents within the country and, in conjunction with the United States, Malaya and the Philippines, against the communist regime of North Vietnam and the communist factions in neighboring Laos and Kampuchea.

U.S. Presence   American air force personnel were originally stationed in Thailand as a consequence of the 1960 formal U.S.-Thai military assistance agreement that permitted United States aircraft to use Thai military and civilian airports. On March 6, 1962 U.S. Secretary of State Dean Rusk and Thai Foreign Minister Thanat agreed that the 1954 treaty which created SEATO also bound the United States to defend Thailand, with or without the concurrence of the other signatories.

The U.S. was soon called upon to make good its promises. In early May communist Pathet Lao and North Vietnamese troops in Laos routed the Royal Laotian Army, whose forces fled across the Mekong River into Thailand. The Thai government became alarmed at the potential communist threat on its northern border. The U.S. responded by agreeing to send substantial additional American air and ground forces. On May 17 a U.S. marine task force of 1,800 arrived for duty at Udorn in northeast Thailand, only 25 miles from the Laotian border. A reinforced battle group—air force units and an army engineer battalion—followed, increasing American military strength to more than 5,000. Within the week the United Kingdom, Australia and New Zealand, acting under the SEATO treaty, also dispatched small units to Thailand.

SEATO forces, including the American marines, were withdrawn later in 1962 following an agreement at the Geneva conference on the neutrality of Laos. However, an American military presence, mainly in the form of air force personnel, remained, since Thailand had agreed to the Laotian settlement only on the condition that the U.S. guaranteed Thai security.

In 1964, when the Laotian situation again appeared threatening and the war in Vietnam was increasing in magnitude, the Thai government allowed the U.S. to use Thai bases to prosecute the Vietnamese war, acknowledging the arrangement publicly three years later. By 1968 American military personnel in Thailand peaked at 48,000. Bangkok also served as the principal recreation and rehabilitation center for American forces in Vietnam.

U.S. President Nixon visited Bangkok in July 1969 as part of his effort to wind down American participation in the Vietnamese war and to advance the Nixon Doctrine that the primary responsibility for their security lay with the Asian countries themselves. Agreements followed which led to a staged removal of American troops from the country during the next year.

While the large American "invasion" hastened Thai material development because it brought substantial dollar funds into the country, it also brought inflation, the erosion of moral standards among the young and increased corruption in both government and business.

POLITICS AND ECONOMICS: 1968–1990

The period 1963–1968 had been one of relative political stability despite the war in Vietnam. General Thanom Kittikachorn, Sarit's trusted subordinate, peacefully succeeded to the premiership in December 1963 upon Sarit's death. He brought to the office a mild manner and a reputation for integrity. Through compromise, persuasion and coalition building, his government in its initial years hastened the transition from a government dominated by the military to one more responsible to the citizenry. He urged the Constitutent Assembly, which had been meeting since 1959, to produce a constitution as soon as possible, and he removed the controls on freedom of speech. He recognized that the traditional apolitical popular attitude—a product of the essential absence historically of social, political and economic tensions which could be exploited—was giving way in the 1960s to a demand for wider political participation and for responsible government.

Shortly after the new constitution was finally proclaimed in June 1968 political parties were again legalized, more than ten participating in the general elections the following February. As usual, parties were organized around personalities. Thanom's United Thai People's Party (UTPP) managed to maintain control of the government with the help of independents and Thanom was reappointed prime minister. The Democratic Party, transformed by erstwhile Prime Minister Seni Pramoj to reflect his more liberal views, won heavily in urban areas. The party's image appealed to basically the same voters as the Social Action Party of his brother Kukrit Pramoj, Bangkok's leading journalist and publisher.

The 1968 constitution provided for a bicameral National Assembly, with a Senate whose members were to be appointed by the king on recommendation of the government in power, and a popularly elected House of Representatives. The executive branch was headed by the chairman of the Council of Ministers, appointed by the king. Contrary to previous parliamentary practice, the ministers could *not* be members of either house. All executive, legislative and judicial power was to be exercised in the king's name. The constitution provided no procedure for removal of the prime minister nor did it grant express authority to the executive branch to dissolve the House of Representatives. These lacunae allowed the executive branch, acting in the name of the king, to exercise a broad range of powers in an emergency. The cordial relationship between king and government which had characterized the reign of King Bhumipol since 1951 continued under the new constitution. Moreover, despite the numerous constitutions and governments the king, in his role of legitimizer of each succeeding ruling group, effectively symbolized national unity.

Although legalization of political parties made it possible for more elements of the population to express themselves at the polls, the diffusion of power which followed was accompanied by a sharp upswing in the intensity of political jockeying within the elected chamber of the National Assembly and more particularly within the cabinet. Members of Thanom's UTPP in the House of Representatives repeatedly threatened defection, and Thanom's announcement that he wished to retire from politics in 1972 whetted the ambitions of younger cabinet members who began to compete with each other for control of ministries and departments and their budgets. Thai politics soon reverted to traditional and divisive cliques and factions operating within the Council of Ministers.

Alarmed at the growing internal threat to their control, Thanom and General Prapat Charustiara—minister of the interior, deputy prime minister and commander of the army—mounted a coup against their own government! The Revolutionary Council which they formed in

November 1971 terminated parliament, repudiated the 1968 constitution and outlawed political parties. The king acquiesced in the bloodless takeover which was practically unopposed. Now unhindered by recalcitrant ministers or contentious factions. Thanom and Prapat devoted full attention—but with minimal success—to budgetary and urban problems, anti-crime measures and the strengthening of the military. They promulgated an interim constitution in December 1972 which insured executive dominance and provided for an appointed legislature.

Student Uprising 1973 In Thailand, unlike in other parts of Southeast Asia, students had traditionally been apolitical. But student unrest and student potential for political action surfaced in 1968 when some 1,000 students from Thammasat University engaged in demonstrations to protest the government's decision to retain martial law which had been in effect since 1958. In November 1972, with tacit government support, they demonstrated against the import of Japanese products. In early 1973 students successfully protested a government decree which would have compromised the integrity of the nation's judiciary and in May that year student demonstrators protested against personal corruption among government officials. In June the National Student Center of Thailand (NSCT) conducted the largest demonstrations in Thailand's history to protest expulsion of nine Ramkhamhaeng University students for writing a satire on the decision of Thanom and Prapat to extend, arbitrarily, their terms in office. The nine students were reinstated and the rector of Ramkhamhaeng University resigned. By July the students were demanding a new constitution. Demonstrations continued throughout August and September.

On October 5, 1973 thirteen activists, including six students, were arrested for circulating leaflets calling for a new constitution. Some 400,000 students and their supporters massed at Democracy Monument in Bangkok on October 13, threatening violence if the detainees were not released. The "Constitution 13" were released, charges were dropped, and the government promised a new document within the year. The NSCT, led by moderate students, now sought to end the protests, but technical college students and other more radical elements refused to leave the streets. Early on October 14—the day of the "Great Tragedy"—violence began. It was characterized at first more by thrust and parry between the military and the demonstrators than by actual fighting. The king asked restraint of the people and compromise by all. Although the military and police were reluctant to use force, the violence escalated, partly as a result of lack of communication between the contestants, partly because of the use of force by riot police, and partly because of deliberate incitement of the crowds by radicals. When heavy weapons from tanks and helicopters were

reportedly employed by government forces, the demonstrators regrouped at Thammasat University and then rampaged through Bangkok, burning public buildings.

Some 65 persons died and almost 1,000 were injured before the
violence ceased. Prime Minister Thanom and Deputy Prime Minister
Prapat, no longer able to depend upon complete military and police
support, were forced to capitulate and went into exile. On October 15
the king asked Professor Sanya Dharmasakti, rector of Thammasat
University and his close adviser, to form a new government, the first
civilian government since that of Pridi in the immediate post-World
War II period. The king's initiative in nominating Sanya as prime
minister—a civilian and head of the university whose students were in
the forefront of the uprising—was perceived as a progressive, pro-
democratic stance which significantly enhanced his already great prestige. The students, surprised by the totality of their victory, were quick
to accept Sanya, emphasizing that their original aims were not the
overthrow of the government but rather the release of the "Constitution 13" and a new constitution.

King Bhumipol in December appointed 2,000 persons from all walks
of life to a convention which was called to elect a new National
Assembly. The king's action automatically dissolved the military-
dominated assembly of Thanom and constituted an unprecedented
entry by the king into the political arena.

The new assembly was charged with drafting another constitution
and with exercising legislative authority in the interim. The constitution, the ninth since 1932 and the first that had not been handed down
from above, was signed by the king on October 7, 1974. It provided a
familiar form: a bicameral legislature comprising an appointed Senate
and a 299-member elected House of Representatives. It required however that the prime minister be an elected member of the latter.

Seni and Kukrit Forty-two political parties contested the January
1975 elections. The centrist parties were Seni's Democratic Party and
the Social Action Party of his brother Kukrit. Since no party obtained
a majority 69-year-old Seni, whose party had garnered 72 seats, formed
a coalition based upon policies calling for the timed withdrawal of
remaining American forces in Thailand, repeal of anti-communist laws,
a popularly elected Senate, reduction of the voting age to 18, land
reform and the establishment of diplomatic relations with the People's
Republic of China. However Seni's program and cabinet were defeated
on a confidence vote less than a month later. His brother Kukrit, also
pledging to secure U.S. troop withdrawal and to normalize relations
with the People's Republic of China, was able to form a coalition of
the Thai Nation Party of Pibun, his own Social Action Party, and five
smaller parties. The social, economic and security problems he faced

were severe. By 1975 the student movement had polarized into extreme right and left wing elements; and the dramatic rise in world oil prices in 1974 had fueled inflation, raising the cost of energy, manufactured goods and imports. Moreover, within two days of taking office Kukrit was compelled to declare an emergency in 30 provinces to deal with a communist insurgency and by the end of August he was faced with the fact that Vietnam, Kampuchea and Laos had all become communist states. He was unable, however, to address these issues effectively because of the time and effort required to keep his fragile coalition intact. Therefore on January 12, 1976 he decided to dissolve the National Assembly, hoping that new elections would increase his slim parliamentary majority, and avoiding by two days a scheduled confidence vote. In almost one year parliament under his leadership had passed only six bills.

The April 4 elections were a victory for the centrists and rightists. Seni's Democratic Party again won the largest number of seats, followed by the conservatives. The socialist parties fared very badly, and Kukrit failed to win a seat. Seni again became prime minister but was unable to develop momentum toward the solution of economic and social problems or to deal effectively with the crisis created by the sudden return from exile in September of former prime minister Thanom.

Thanom's return evoked bitter memories of his 10-year authoritarian regime. Radical student elements exploited the general dissatisfaction over his return, as well as Seni's weak leadership in handling the problem. Following parliamentary attacks on his administration, Seni resigned on September 23. The following day he changed his mind and the king reappointed him prime minister. The government now endeavored to negotiate with Thanom who refused to leave the country. Coincidentally two left-wing activists were hanged by the police on the outskirts of Bangkok, and leftist students at Thammasat University responded by hanging in effigy two rightist students, causing the rightists to storm the campus. By October 5 the university was the scene of a rally by thousands of leftist students, urged on by elements of the Maoist-oriented and outlawed Communist Party of Thailand and by Soviet and Vietnamese agents. An equally large number of rightist vocational students and sympathizers, aided by military groups, opposed them. The two factions clashed in violent riots.

On October 6 armed police fought their way onto the campus to quell the student warfare. Forty-six students and police were killed and over 180 persons were injured; police arrested over 3,000 people. The same day a military coup overthrew the Seni government. Thailand's effort to develop a viable constitutional democracy thus came to an end on the very university campus where it had begun exactly three years previously. Moreover the students were now polarized into opposing ideological camps.

Thanin Seni was kept under arrest for 24 hours, martial law was imposed throughout the country and an Administrative Reform Council of 24 military personnel and an 18-member civilian advisory board were established. Admiral Sangad Chalayu, who initially headed the junta, requested the king to designate Supreme Court Justice Thanin Kraivichien as prime minister. A close confidant of the king, Thanin was staunchly anti-communist and was, the military reasoned, easily controllable because he lacked a political base. Sangad became defense minister—usually considered the premier cabinet post, with interior second—in Thanin's otherwise largely civilian cabinet which was made up of his friends. Tough anti-communist laws were immediately promulgated, and the government embarked once again on constitution-making. The new constitution, which was designed to strengthen the executive, designated the Administrative Reform Council, renamed the National Advisory Council, as an advisory body to the prime minister, with authority to control the prime minister's appointments to the cabinet and to the 340-member National Administrative Reform Assembly, which in turn, comprised a membership two-thirds military and one-third civilian. The council exercised primary authority, and political leaders from the previous government were specifically excluded from membership in it.

Nevertheless Thanin professed the goal of an elected legislature and complete parliamentary democracy within 12 years. The prime minister, in all too-traditional fashion, devoted his major energies to anti-corruption drives, tight restrictions on press and assembly, arrest of suspected political subversives, and to quelling an attempted coup by a dissident general in March 1977. Meanwhile, Thailand drifted in the throes of what has been described as "encapsulated authoritarianism," a political situation in which a powerful bureaucracy, motivated almost exclusively by self-interest, operates in a tightly controlled arena which outsiders cannot penetrate.[2]

Members of the National Advisory Council, led by General Kriangsak Chammanand, became impatient as early as June 1977 over Thanin's lack of progress in combating unemployment, unequal income distribution, inflation and communist terrorism, and his refusal to broaden and rearrange his cabinet. On October 20, therefore, the armed forces, led by Admiral Sangad who had brought Thanin to power, overthrew Thanin's civilian government, abolished the constitution and formed a new administration under a 23-man Revolutionary Council. In not unexpected terms Radio Thailand announced: "the revolutionary group has seized power at this time to improve the economic and security situations of the nation and to maintain the institutions of nation, religion and king."[3] Thanin's government had proved too repressive and narrow even for the military.

Kriangsak General Kriangsak was appointed prime minister— Thailand's 16th since 1932—on November 11 by the king, upon the recommendation of Sangad, chairman of the Revolutionary Council which now termed itself the Revolutionary Party. An interim constitution, Thailand's 12th, and announced the day previous, granted the prime minister wide "power to 'prevent, repress or suppress' actions which subvert the kingdom or the national economy or threaten public order and good morals, or which destroy national resources."[4] It mandated a permanent constitution in time for elections to be held not later than April 30, 1979. The 35-member committee formed to draft a new constitution included the two Pramoj brothers, Seni and Kukrit. The committee's draft became law in December 1978.

Kriangsak caught the public's fancy during his first weeks in office, displaying a folksy, approachable manner which endeared him to the trade union movement, traditionally not the friend of Thai governments. He lifted censorship, pleasing the highly articulate Bangkok press. Unlike his fantically anti-communist predecessor, the prime minister initiated moves toward the communist states of Vietnam, Kampuchea and Laos "to make friends of old enemies."[5] Kriangsak's overtures were a reaffirmation of traditional Thai foreign policy of "bending with the wind" and a recognition of the permanence of the communist presence in Indochina. Kriangsak also moved immediately to address social and economic problems. He revived a village development program initiated by Kukrit in 1975 but abolished by the Thanin government. He attempted to give meaningful direction to the Fourth Five Year Economic Plan (1977–1981) which heretofore had failed either to raise the farmers' income and productivity or provide a genuinely healthy climate for investment and business enterprise.

Under terms of the new constitution, which again provided that the prime minister need not be a member of parliament, general elections were held in April 1979. Martial law had been suspended in February and 38 parties contested the 301 seats in the House of Representatives. Kukrit's Social Action Party won the largest number (82) of seats, but Kriangsak was chosen by the House of Representatives and by the Senate (which he had hand picked and whose 225 members were appointed by the king on the same day as the election) to form a new government.

In spite of not having a political base of his own in parliament, Kriangsak proved adept in steering legislation through the House of Representatives during 1979, partly because he controlled the Senate and partly because his deft handling of the Kampuchean border crisis (discussed below) enhanced his prestige. But economic problems, precipitated by quantum leaps in the price of imported petroleum, proved intractable. While the economy grew at about 8 percent—aided by a favorable rice harvest, an expanding manufacturing sector and a 25 percent increase in exports—the balance of payments deficit became acute. By the end of 1979 one-third of Thailand's foreign exchange earnings—equal to approximately the total annual trade deficit—was being spent on oil imports.

In July Kriangsak raised retail petroleum prices 40 to 60 percent, provoking criticism from both business and labor; inflation rocketed to 15 percent. The government responded with the same devices employed in the western world; it raised both minimum wages and interest rates. But the income-expenditure gap of the masses remained unclosed. In October and November Kriangsak raised telephone and electricity rates—by 100 percent in some cases—to cover the higher cost of petroleum and to permit expansion of service, but exacerbating consumer distress. Meanwhile the tight money policy worked further havoc on business ventures. After consulting with the king, Kriangsak resigned on February 29, 1980, in the wake of widespread public criticism of his policies.

Prem On March 3, 1980, by secret ballot, General Prem Tinsulanonda, who had been army commander in chief and deputy minister of the interior in the former government, was elected premier by parliament. Kukrit obtained the second largest number of votes—80 compared to 399—and pledged his party's support to help Prem address the country's economic problems.

The economy steadily worsened, however, and the government temporized. It defused dissatisfaction over oil price rises by reducing prices of kerosene, diesel oil, and liquified petroleum gas and at the expense of contributions to the oil stabilization fund which had been set up to provide a cushion against further OPEC (Organization of Petroleum Exporting Countries) increases. The fund was soon exhausted and by 1981 the inevitable increases in the price of oil products and electricity beset the public anew. A Thai government study forecast that total bankruptcy would overtake Thailand within the next six years unless the economic structure of the country was drastically revised. Both the government study and a World Bank report cited Thailand's runaway foreign debt as the major contributing factor. The government study predicted foreign loans could increase from US$3.8 billion to US$26 billion by 1986 and repayments would absorb 25 percent of Thailand's export revenues. Severe fiscal retrenchment measures and greater agricultural production were suggested, by both the government and the World Bank studies, to bring the economy into a more manageable context.

Not economic pressures, however, but interparty conflict caused the fall of the first Prem government. On March 4, 1981 Deputy Premier Boonchu Rojanastien and eight other ministers of Kukrit's Social Action Party resigned; they were dissatisfied with the manner in which the prime minister handled a dispute between themselves and the conservative Thai Chart Party. Prem managed to put together a new coalition government of five parties which was sworn in by the king on March 12, exactly a year after his first coalition government. The second Prem 40-member cabinet showed a significant shift to the right. Another political crisis followed within a month.

In a pre-dawn move April 1, 1981 Deputy Army Commander in Chief Sant Chitpatima and a group of senior military officers seized power in Bangkok. Prem fled by helicopter with the monarch and the entire royal family to an army camp at Korat, 130 miles to the northeast. When the king's presence with, and therefore support of, Prem became known, the coup began to dissolve. The next day the rebels gave up without a fight and Prem's forces reentered Bangkok, taking possession of government buildings and military installations.

During the coup attempt the two feuding army factions held to the usual pattern of non-violence in military takeovers, although the deployment of opposing troops brought the parties closest to battle since the bombing of Prime Minister Pibun's boat in Bangkok harbor in 1951. The king's support of Prem involved him more directly in partisan politics than at any time previously, and reflected Bhumibol's developing concept of the role of the monarch as an active participant in the political process. In early May the king, on Prem's advice, granted amnesty to all the participants in the coup who had surrendered; General Sant, with Prem's acquiescence, fled to Burma, but was allowed to return in late June.

His cautious, non-partisan leadership and the support of the king reinforced Prem's standing with the armed forces as well as with the five major political parties that constituted his coalition. But political tensions began to emerge during 1982. Protest, accompanied by mass rallies, with students reemerging as an important pressure group, forced the government to rescind a decision to raise bus fares, to increase the minimum price paid to rice farmers, and to revoke a university rector's appointment. Meanwhile the two main parties within Prem's coalition—Social Action and Thai Chart—began to bicker openly. Events came to a climax in March–April 1983 when the military sought to extend the transitional powers in the current (1978) constitution.

On March 16 a joint session of parliament rejected two military-backed amendments that would have extended transitional powers of the appointed, military-dominated Senate. Under terms of the constitution the transitional clauses would expire April 21. The amendments sought to maintain the legislative powers of the Senate and to permit permanent civil servants, including military officers, to continue to hold cabinet posts. A third military-sponsored amendment pertaining to the transitional clauses, which would have required adherence to the prevailing electoral system of individual candidacies instead of a new party-slate system, was also defeated; the military had sought to keep parties weak by making it hard for any one party to obtain a majority.

Three days after the humiliating parliamentary defeat for the military, an unexpected royal decree dissolved the House of Representatives and set a general election for April 18—three days before the transitional clauses expired. The decree thus nullified the effect of the defeat of the third amendment, since elections held prior to April 21 would be conducted under the old, individual candidacies rule. The royal decree could hardly be interpreted as other than monarchical involvement in politics on the side of the military.

Nevertheless Prem's coalition parties swept the elections, winning 221 of 324 (expanded from 301) seats. At this point Prem startled the country by announcing he was retiring from politics, but quickly reconsidered in response to Kukrit's personal appeal to accept nomination for another four-year term. A four-party coalition emerged— Social Action, Democratic, National Democracy (of Kriangsak), and Thai Citizen. The coalition was inherently weak, however, because the Democratic and Social Action parties campaigned on the single issue of opposition to the army-backed constitutional amendments; the Thai Citizen and National Democracy parties were supportive of the military.

Another abortive coup September 9, 1985, led by 27 active-duty officers and implicating former prime minister Kriangsak Chammanand and three other retired generals, was quelled by loyalist military leaders within 10 hours. King Bhumipol apparently did not intervene.

The foregoing political actions underscore three features of contemporary Thai politics: 1) the persisting and determined efforts of the Thai military establishment to decide political succession, 2) the equally determined efforts of civilian politicians to reject the military's attempts to dictate to them, and 3) the frequent involvement of the monarch in partisan politics.

Kriangsak's involvement in the failed coup, his subsequent detention on sedition charges, and the collapse of his National Democracy party reduced the alliance to three major parties. The alliance prevailed nevertheless in the 1986 elections and Prem's fifth government was formed in August. The pragmatic Prem was faced with temporarily depressed world commodity prices, accompanied by lower farmer purchasing power, foreign exchange losses from currency devaluation in 1984, rising numbers of unemployed university graduates, and increasing migration from rural to urban areas. He persuaded parliament in 1986 to adopt belt-tightening measures to attract investment. The strategy was immediately successful. Within a year the industrial sector grew almost 10 percent, for the first time replacing the agricultural sector as the catalyst for growth. Prem also made use of King Bhumibol's sixtieth birthday in 1987 to propel tourism to major status. His "Visit Thailand Year" brought over three million visitors.

Although Prem managed to minimize factional rivalries, criticism of his governing style inevitably developed. Within the coalition the Social Action Party's veteran leader, Kukrit Pramoj, complained that the government's military-dominated Policy and Corrdinating Committee influenced coalition MPs to accept all government bills without challenge. In his capacity as Deputy Director General of the committee, General Chaovalit Yongchaiyut, Acting Supreme Commander and Commander-in-Chief of the Army, stunned both the government and the opposition in early 1987. He presented the radical view that political parties are inherently corrupt: ". . . his view was that government policies which served the interests of the people made a political system democratic rather than symbols of democracy such as political parties, the constitution and elections which, he said, sometimes destroy democracy."[6]

In April 1988 Prem, as formerly, chose parliamentary dissolution as the means to resolve an emerging political impasse; upon Prem's advice, King Bhumibol therefore dissolved the House of Representatives. Eight years of political stability had enabled Thailand to rise to star status among newly industrializing nations. But the experience had also unleashed a people's aspirations for more democratic political processes and Prem was criticized as a non-elected chief executive whose ties with the monarchy and the military establishment were no longer appropriate. The decade of the 1980s was also characterized by a rising, better educated and more prosperous urban middle class. Extra-parliamentary forces, i.e., more and broader political interest groups, had emerged to challenge the narrow roles of political parties which were traditionally confined to tactical maneuvers by individual leaders in parliament.

Prem, recognizing the emerging political climate, stepped aside as he had wished to do four years earlier, retiring as a public hero. In the ensuing general elections, July 24, 1988, the Thai Chart Party won a plurality of the now-357 seats in the House of Representatives, choosing its leader, Chatichai Choonhaven, to head a multi-party coalition government. Three other major parties—Democratic, Social Action and Rassadorn (Citizen)—joined.

Chatichai The first elected member of parliament to be chosen prime minister in more than a decade, and the 18th prime minister since the 1932 revolution, Chatichai won acclaim for his easy personal style and his government's quick and decisive actions. Chatichai's expansionist budget for fiscal 1989 departed markedly from the austerity budgets of the Prem years. It emphasized major infrastructural investment to support business and industry.

Chatichai's foreign policy initiatives were equally noteworthy. He forswore ideology for economic opportunity and proposed transforming Indochina "from a war zone to a trade zone." In June 1989 he called upon the United States to approve the participation of Indochina and Burma in the process of economic development upon settlement of Kampuchean and Burmese internal problems.

Drawing upon his diplomatic record of normalizing Sino-Thai relations when he was foreign minister in 1975, Chatichai surprised his ASEAN colleagues in early 1989 by informally inviting Kampuchea's Hun Sen—prime minister of the hitherto scorned Phnom Penh regime—to Bangkok. With Chatichai's blessing, Foreign Minister Siddhi Savetsila visited Vietnam, and in March Chatichai received Vietnamese Foreign Minister Nguyen Co Thach in Bangkok.

Chatichai appeared to be taking full advantage of Thailand's increasing regional importance in Southeast Asia to maximize the nation's political and economic influence in Indochina in anticipation of a political settlement of the Kampuchean issue. His strategy appeared to be three-dimensional: 1) assist the Khmer Rouge resistance to ensure that a solution in Kampuchea would preclude Vietnamese domination of a post-settlement government; 2) court the Hun Sen regime to persuade it to tolerate Khmer Rouge participation in Kampuchean politics; 3) at the same time reaffirm Thailand's traditional role in the non-communist world as the "front line" state against possible security threats from its communist neighbors, China and Vietnam.

The Thai strategy serves specific ends.

Support for the Khmer Rouge weakens Vietnam's role in Kampuchea, a stance reflecting the centuries-old rivalry between Thailand and Vietnam for influence over that state. Thailand supplies the Khmer Rouge with arms and simultaneously courts its enemies in Hanoi and Phnom Penh because a political settlement in Kampuchea, of whatever factional composition, is a necessity if the Indochina "war zone" is to be transformed into a "trade zone." Finally, an anti-communist posture practically guarantees continuing U.S. commitment to Thailand's security, as well as U.S. arms supply.

NATIONAL SECURITY PROBLEMS

American security assistance to Thailand wound down beginning in 1969. By June 1975, when the war in Vietnam ended with a communist victory, all American military installations had been closed and the American military presence had ended, except for advisers attached to the U.S. diplomatic mission. However continuing communist insurgency, the aggressive behavior of Vietnam toward Thailand, and the destabilizing impact of hundreds of thousands of refugees on Thailand's borders combined to create serious security problems, and Thailand turned again to the U.S. for military assistance.

Communist Activities   The communist movement in Thailand dates from the 1920s. In 1942 it coalesced to become the Communist Party of Thailand (CPT) under pro-Chinese leadership and with extensive external help. Although the CPT was outlawed in 1952, its armed guerrilla forces, called the Thai People's Liberation Army, developed into a formidable force. By 1965 insurgency had become a serious problem in the northeastern plateau region of Korat, in the northern tier of provinces facing Burma, and in the southern peninsula adjacent to Malaysia. The CPT grew steadily until 1979 when its guerrilla force reached a peak strength of 13,000. The split between China and Vietnam, and the subsequent alliance of Laos and Kampuchea with Vietnam, curtailed further growth of the movement and denied the pro-Chinese guerrillas their sanctuaries in the latter states and their supply route from China through Laos. At the same time the government became actively engaged in two major socio-economic-political programs to win the countryside: the Aw Paw Paw village voluntary self-development and protection program, and the People/Civil-Police-Military system (P/CPM) which attempted to integrate the efforts of the people with those of the government and beat the communists at their own game. The programs gained momentum as the government strengthened the rural infrastructure with new schools, roads, dams and communications facilities. The reforms undercut CPT efforts to recruit followers, efforts keyed to injustices that were disappearing. Meanwhile Premier Prem's emphasis upon forgiveness produced wholesale defections and lured back the radicalized student leaders and intellectuals who had fled to the jungles in 1976. It was estimated that by 1982 the government's anti-communist strategy had reduced CPT strength to little more than 5,000 guerrillas. Significantly, the counter-insurgency campaign contrasted sharply with the heavy reliance on military force and sweeping crackdowns that failed in Indochina.

Nevertheless, the CPT remained an internal security threat, especially in the south where government military drives continued to be mounted against CPT strongholds. Guerrilla operations in that region appeared to be directed by the Malaysian Communist Party (MCP) which exploited Muslim-Malay sentiments. Communist insurgency lessened in the late 1980s as the national economy improved. A significant communist faction surrendered in 1987 and another group announced it would cease fighting and dissolve by the end of August 1989 provided the Thai government would permit participants to settle unmolested on the Thai side of the border should they so desire. Adherents to other MCP components were described as willing to surrender under similar terms.[7]

Border Disputes Longstanding security problems exist at the convergence of the Thai-Laotian-Burmese frontiers, an area known as the "Golden Triangle." Opium produced from poppies, a major hill country crop, has traditionally been traded freely across the borders. Factories for production of the raw opium, markets for selling it and supply routes for distributing the drug proliferated in Thailand. Recognizing the seriousness of drug addiction and responding to international pressures, the Thai government, beginning in 1982, achieved partial short run success in its efforts to reduce the drug trade and to break up private armies of narcotics lords. Despite strong anti-drug measures the trade has continued, largely because of the prolonged Burmese insurgency.

A flow of refugees into Thailand began with the success of the communist forces in Indochina in mid-1975 and became a flood when the boat people, forced to flee Vietnam during the next three years, found first asylum along the Thai coast. In 1979 the Thai government— already burdened with 150,000 Lao, Hmong, Khmer and Vietnamese refugees—established border holding centers administered by the United Nations High Commissioner for Refugees (UNHCR) for the wave of people fleeing the "politics of starvation" practiced by the new Vietnamese-backed Heng Samrin regime in Kampuchea. By April 1980 there were 150,000 Khmer in the centers, most suffering from malnutrition, a condition significantly eased later in the year as a result of effective international food relief measures.

In July 1981 Thailand took action to discourage a further influx of boat people, now fleeing Vietnam for primarily economic reasons. The Thai announced that after August 15 new arrivals would not be resettled but would be forced to remain in camps indefinitely, without possibility of permanent resettlement in any country. The same policy was applied to Kampucheans and Laotians. According to Thai authorities the "humane deterrence" policy was effective. The UNHCR reported that during 1980 refugees arriving in Thailand numbered 113,867. The figure for 1982 had declined to 11,261 and continued to decline through 1984. Thailand, meanwhile, had become a participant in the 1979 Geneva Conference at which Southeast Asian nations had agreed to serve as countries of first asylum, conditional not on refugee status but on resettlement in third countries. (See Political Cohesion; Response To Refugee Problem, Chapter 12.)

The arrangement stabilized the refugee inflow until 1987 when the numbers increased dramatically—far beyond resettlement quotas— mainly due to desperate economic conditions in Vietnam. In January 1988 Thailand began to turn back or redirect some boat loads of Vietnamese. Others were permitted to land but the refugees were placed in new camps on the Kampuchean border where they had UNHCR protection but were denied access to consideration for resettlement. At the same time Thailand joined Malaysia in calling for a new international conference on the refugee problem.

The Vietnamese invasion of Kampuchea also resulted in the continued presence of Vietnamese troops on the Thai-Kampuchean border. These engaged in intermittent action against supporters of the Khmer Rouge government they had overthrown, and against rightist forces of the coalition government-in-exile.

Acting upon the not unreasonable conviction that the Thai were feeding and rearming Khmer Rouge refugees, and sending them back across the border, Vietnam, on June 24, 1980 invaded Thailand with some 2,000 men backed by tanks and artillery. Vietnamese troops overran three villages and several refugee centers. The fighting created still another wave of refugees and concerned international reaction. In a swift response the United States promised accelerated delivery of the U.S. military aid already in the pipeline, new military aid authorizations and emergency air delivery of guns, ammunition and howitzers. The Vietnamese troops soon retired to the Kampuchean side of the frontier. At the same time the United States noted that it regarded the 1954 SEATO defense treaty linking Thailand with the United States, Britain and other countries, as still in force, reaffirming the position in April 1981.

Thai-Vietnamese border warfare erupted anew in April 1983 during what became the annual spring Vietnamese military offensive against the Khmer Rouge guerrillas. Fighting spilled over the Thai border and the Thai air force attacked Vietnamese ground forces with fighter bombers. The Vietnamese retreated into Kampuchea and again the U.S. speeded up weaponry flow to Thailand. During fiscal year 1983 the U.S., as Thailand's major supplier, undertook to deliver US$66 million in arms and equipment.

A 1984 Vietnamese spring offensive caused Prime Minister Prem, during his state visit to the United States, to purchase an additional 40 M48 tanks and a number of F16 fighter aircraft. A December attack on Ampil, a major rightist rebel camp, resulted in a further flood of refugees across the border, a brief incursion into Thailand by Vietnamese troops, and a further indication of U.S. readiness to supply Thailand.

In 1987 a Thai-U.S. agreement established a war reserve stockpile, the Thai government purchased six additional F-16 warplanes from the United States and the U.S. reaffirmed its commitment to assist the Thai against any "Vietnamese threat." Thailand, in turn, reiterated the "need for a U.S. military presence in the region and the two nations continued to engage in annual joint military exercises."[8]

WHITHER THAILAND?

Having experienced remarkable gains in the decade of the 1980s, Thailand has, in effect, achieved newly industrialized country status (NIC), joining South Korea, Taiwan, Hong Kong and Singapore among Asian states which have reached the point at which the value of industrial output exceeds that of agriculture. Thailand squarely faced problems of the 1970s (balance of payments deficits, rising petroleum costs, inflation, consumer distress) by revamping its fiscal policies, by encouraging food production for export (Thailand is the fifth largest food exporter in the world, and the only one in Asia), and by a much greater emphasis on industrial manufacturing. Collapse of OPEC-controlled petroleum prices and the austere leadership of Prime Minister Prem were also important to the transformation.

In 1990 the nation enjoyed a prosperous economy founded upon a stable currency, a formidable export-oriented industrial sector and broad investor confidence. Led by Prime Minister Chatichai the nation is expanding its economic role by developing and modernizing its infrastructure. Moreover, Thailand's rich agricultural land, its success in assimilating its large Sino-Thai populace, and its strong civil service provide advantages other developing countries lack.

The Thai political elite, more often than not dominated by the military, continues to be reluctant to share power with the masses. Changes of government from one group of elitists to another, often through bloodless coup, has been the norm. But no successful coup has occurred since 1977 and governing coalitions are lasting longer. While Thai political parties have traditionally functioned mostly within unstable parliamentary factions, the emergence of broader, middle class, political interests groups suggests that mass-based parties could be in the offing.

For much of its modern history the Thai nation has been able to outmaneuver others. In the 18th and 19th centuries Thai kings repeatedly gained territory at the expense of their neighbors. Thailand escaped western colonialism, chose the winning side in WWI, and prospered from WWII even though it chose the losing side. Since then it continues to play a winning game. The Thai have defeated the communists within the country, won the respect and assistance of the West as a "frontline state" against communist expansion in the region, and are leading the Vietnamese and the Kampucheans toward resolution of their conflict.

FOOTNOTES

1. D. G. E. Hall, *A History of Southeast Asia* (London: Macmillan, 1961), p. 314.

2. See Robert F. Zimmerman, *Reflections on the Collapse of Democracy in Thailand* (Singapore: Institute of Southeast Asian Studies), 1978.

3. *Data Asia* (Manila: Press Foundation of Asia), 1977, p. 4942.

4. *Ibid.*, p. 4990.

5. George McArthur, "Thailand Has Honeymoon with Leader," *Los Angeles Times*, November 26, 1977.

6. See *Southeast Asian Affairs* (Singapore: Southeast Asian Studies), 1988, p. 275.

7. *Foreign Broadcast Information Service (FBIS)*, EA, June 26, 1989. 63–64.

8. *Southeast Asian Affairs, op. cit.*, p. 282.

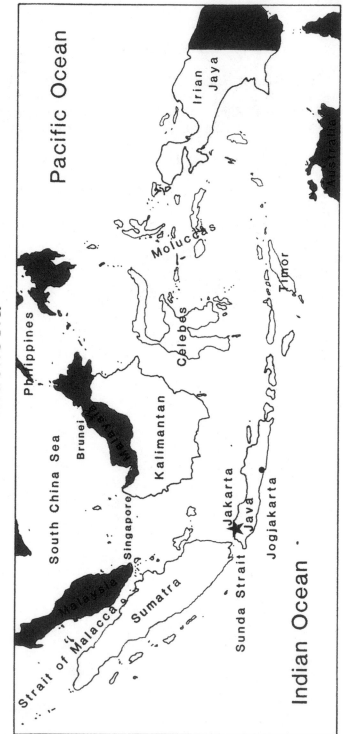

CHAPTER 10
INDONESIA

The importance of the Republic of Indonesia in the contemporary world is underlined by its dimensions. With a population of approximately 178,000,000 the state is the world's fifth most populous nation and contains 40 percent of the total population of Southeast Asia. The largest archipelago in the world, consisting of 13,677 islands, 6,044 of which are inhabited, Indonesia has a total land area slightly smaller than Alaska and California combined.

The islands which make up the Indonesian archipelago lie athwart the equator, between 6 degrees north and 11 degrees south, and extend over 3,000 miles east and west. They form a natural barrier between the Indian and Pacific oceans, and the straits between them have been strategically important from earliest times. The republic comprises the territory of the former Netherlands East Indies and Portuguese Timor. The five large islands—Sumatra, Java, Kalimantan (Indonesian Borneo), Sulawesi (Celebes) and Irian Jaya (Western New Guinea)—account for more than 90 percent of the land area and almost 94 percent of the population, with Java alone supporting one-half the latter.

The majority of the inhabitants are Deutero-Malay who drifted eastward from the southern Asian mainland beginning in the second milennium B.C. The insular aspect of Indonesia provided naturally discrete homelands for the slightly differing cultures. At the same time the sea provided a natural means of inter-island communication.

EARLY EMPIRES

By the first century A.D. river-mouth settlements along major sea routes had grown into small kingdoms founded upon waterborne commerce. Their rulers exercised control over the local movement of goods from and into the interior, and they sought to control neighboring river settlements as tributaries. Increasingly these kingdoms engaged in overseas trade as well, and some attempted to develop sea-based empires. At the same time small colonies of Indian merchants had settled at key points along major sea routes, and Indonesian commercial settlements sprang up in India—in Bengal and along the Coromandel Coast in the south.

Hindu culture spread rapidly throughout the archipelago. Hindu priests, preaching the Brahmanic cult of the supernatural powers of monarchy, were welcomed by Indonesian rulers who perceived that the concept of the god-king reinforced the magical powers they already claimed through animism. Indian learning in all fields was introduced and the use of the Sanskrit alphabet facilitated the transmission of religious, artistic, scientific, and political thought. Mahayana Buddhism, also imported from India, became temporarily dominant on Java and more permanently so on Sumatra. Unlike in India, Buddhism and Hindu-Brahmanism became mutually supportive court religions. The two monkhoods "came to form one elite group at courts revolving around deified kings who presented themselves now as Hindu gods, then reincarnations of the Buddha, if not both simultaneously."[1]

Srivijaya, first of the Indianized empires, emerged on the island of Sumatra as a direct result of interisland and overseas trade. By 650 A.D. it was an important naval and commercial power and remained so until the 13th century. The Hindu kingdom of Kalinga emerged in central Java in the 7th century, followed by the important Sailendra (Lords of the Mountain) dynasty in the latter half of the 8th. The success of the Sailendras was a result of the massive if brief infusion of Mahayana Buddhism into Java between 760 and 820. Borobudur and other Sailendra monuments mark a high point in Javanese culture and reflect advanced social and economic development.

The last great Javanese kingdom, the Hinduized Majapahit, rose in the valley of the Brantas River in 1293. Gaja Mada, who was chief minister and virtual ruler of Majapahit from 1331 until his death in 1364, pursued the imperialist aspirations epitomized by the term *nusantara* (other islands), as used by earlier rulers who envisaged the entire archipelago under Javanese rule. Gaja Mada is believed by some historians to have extended the Majapahit empire to include all of modern Indonesia plus part of the Malay peninsula. Recent scholarship, however, suggests that it was restricted to East Java, Madura and Bali. Whatever the case, Gaja Mada is probably the most respected person in Indonesian history and became a symbol of Indonesian, and specifically Javanese, nationalism in the modern period.

Impact of Islam   Islam was carried eastward during the period of Arab expansion under the aegis of the Abbasid caliphate in Baghdad (7th–8th centuries), but its movement into Southeast Asia was greatly accelerated after Turkish Muslims conquered and converted north India in the 11th and 12th centuries. The egalitarian aspects of the new religion appealed to the lower caste artisans and tradesmen, many of whom were already active in the spice-and-pepper trade with Southeast Asia. These new converts soon outpaced the Arabs in bringing Islam to the entrepots of northern Sumatra and to the new trading town of Malacca on the Malay peninsula. Merchants from Malacca in turn introduced the faith into northern Javanese coastal towns along the trade routes to the Moluccas (spice islands) and by 1450 the busy Javanese ports were coming under the control of Muslim *shahbandars* (rulers of ports). As in India, wholesale conversion took place. Just as the egalitarian aspects of Islam had captivated the northern Indians, Sufi mysticism, with its magician-healers, appealed to the Indonesians and "challenged traditional Shiva-Buddhist mystics on their own terms."[2]

16th and 17th Centuries Portugal was the first European nation to seek a foothold in Southeast Asia. Following its capture of Goa on the western coast of India in 1510, it quickly broke the Arab hold on Indian Ocean trade and simultaneously seized the Muslim-Malay entrepot of Malacca on the Malay peninsula. It sought to control Malacca's trade routes to the Moluccas whose nutmegs, mace and cloves—along with Sumatran and Javanese pepper—were the components of the highly lucrative European trade. The Portuguese were opposed by Islamic merchant-princes in the Moluccan states of Tidore and Ternate, and by the sultanate of Demak on Java, the most powerful realm after the eclipse of Majapahit. Opposition and competition were such that the Portuguese failed to dominate the spice trade, most of which remained in the hands of Malay, Javanese, Chinese and Indian merchants, but they were able to control the trading centers. By 1570, however, their hard won position in the Moluccas had weakened to the point that they lost all pretense of dominating the archipelago. After they lost Malacca to the Dutch in 1641 they were able to retain only the island of Timor.

The sultanate of Demak in north central Java, which had risen to prominence around the end of the 15th century under the patronage of Malacca, continued its rise to power after Malacca's capture by the Portuguese, reaching its peak around 1540. Demak, and its commercial dependency Bantam on the Strait of Sunda, controlled most of the Java trade, particularly in pepper. Bantam eventually turned on Demak, captured the port in 1588 and extended its influence throughout western Java and much of southern Sumatra. Another former dependency, Mataram to the south, declared its independence around the close of the 16th century and quickly extended its authority over most of interior central Java, creating an agriculturally-based land empire. Sultan Agaung (1613–1645) of Mataram subjugated most of east Java and Madura Island, but was unable to conquer western Java where the

Dutch, in their newly fortified coastal settlement of Batavia, successfully resisted his attack (1629). Although Mataram remained an important power for another half century it never again threatened western
Java and the Dutch began a period of significant success and expansion.

POLITICAL INDICATORS

1. Java and Sumatra have been bases of political power from earliest
   historic times.
2. The concept of *nusantara* (a pan-archipelagic empire), while espoused by Gaja Mada and earlier rulers, never existed in the sense
   of a politically centralized kingdom, but was to become a political
   goal of both the Dutch and independent Indonesia.
3. Mysticism is an essential component of Indonesian religious belief,
   and Sufi mysticism of Islam was compatible with the earlier Hindu-
   Buddhist beliefs, and so permitted the continuity of Indonesian
   culture.

NETHERLANDS EAST INDIA COMPANY

At the beginning of the 17th century England and Holland formed
companies to develop trade with the East Indies. The English East
India Company received a royal charter for this purpose in 1600 and a
similar but much stronger Vereenigde Oostindische Compagnie (VOC,
Netherlands East India Company) was chartered in 1602. The VOC
possessed 10 times the capital of its English counterpart, a reflection
of that nation's complete commitment.

The Dutch for many years had been distributors to northern Europe
of the spices brought to Portugal by the Portuguese. When Philip II of
Spain and Portugal denied Dutch traders access to the port of Lisbon
in 1594, the Dutch began to make agreements with native rulers in the
spice islands, arrangements which were designed both to oust the
Portuguese and to abort any English efforts to interfere with the
monopoly they hoped to develop. By the time the company was
organized, the Dutch had already established factories in the Moluccas, Java, Sumatra, and the Malay peninsula. The Portuguese, of
course, challenged the Dutch intrusion. Naval engagements between
the two ended with the decisive defeat of the Portuguese in 1602 and
the seizure by the Dutch of the Portuguese trading posts on Amboina
and other islands of the Moluccas. By 1609 the Dutch held most of the
spice islands, and their physical possession was buttressed by a truce
which legitimized their conquests over the Spanish and Portuguese
colonies in the Far East. At the same time the Dutch institutionalized

their authority by creating the position of Governor General of the Indies; he was expected to insure permanent possession of the spice islands, exert complete authority thereon, and see to the exclusion of all competitors.

In 1619 the new governor general, Jan Pieterszoon Coen, established headquarters for Dutch operations at the small west Java port of Jacatra and renamed it Batavia. Batavia was a swamp infested by wild animals that the Dutch transformed into a little Holland by means of Chinese immigrant labor. The new town controlled the Sunda Strait which meant that Dutch spice ships could sail their cargoes across the Indian Ocean directly from Java to Africa, assisted by the southern tradewinds. Batavia therefore increasingly displaced Malacca which was dependent upon the more northerly and seasonal monsoons. Traders from all countries were well received at the new entrepot as long as they submitted to Dutch trading rules and kept their vessels out of the spice-producing areas.

Coen defeated the English at sea in 1620 and in 1621 conquered the Banda Islands, ruthlessly exterminating much of the population. His justification for the outrage was that the Bandanese were delivering their produce to Tidore which was held by the Spanish. He divided up the cultivated lands of the Bandanese and assigned them to the company's employees to work with slave labor. This act inaugurated Dutch territorial acquisition and the Dutch became landlords as well as traders. Coen also forced the chiefs of Amboina and Ceram to recognize Dutch political authority. With the help of the Malay state of Johore, Malacca was successfully besieged and taken in 1641. The city was allowed to languish and the Portuguese were reduced to a minor role in Far Eastern trade. By the 1650s the Dutch had achieved naval superiority in Southeast Asia and by 1700 had taken control of most of Sumatra, the Celebes and all of Java.

The company prospered during the 17th century because it was interested in trade—not in religious proselytizing or political control. However the introduction of coffee, and the expansion of pepper, sugar, indigo and cotton cultivation to counteract the decline in the spice market in the early 18th century, presaged a shift from a trade empire to a political and territorial empire centered on Java.

Unlike the low bulk, high value spice crops, the new commodities were low in value and high in bulk and more extensive land areas were required for adequate production. The company therefore began to require quotas of these crops from local princes under an arrangement known as "contingents and forced deliveries," i.e., the Javanese were required to provide crop quotas (contingents) at Batavia-determined prices (forced deliveries). The princes, backed by the company, increased levies on their subjects and took a percentage for themselves before delivering their quotas. On estates developed by the company Dutch supervisors were appointed to oversee the planting and care of the plantations. These "coffee sergeants" were the first Europeans to come into regular and extended contact with the Javanese and they became the nucleus of the Netherlands Indies civil service.

The East India Company reached its zenith at the beginning of the 18th century, although the fact was not obvious for some decades. The company, which had originally sought to avoid territorial commitments, had become the heir to the Javanese kingdoms of Bantam and Mataram. But indirect rule through indigenous chiefs (regents) was an exercise in public administration for which it had little expertise, and administrative expenses multiplied rapidly. While the company was able to maintain a strong presence in Java, the Moluccas and the Celebes, it was unable to achieve a similar presence elsewhere, and Chinese, English and Buginese traders soon cut deeply into company profits. As its power waned and it was unable to control the shipping lanes, the seas of the entire archipelago became infested with pirates. Internally, the company was also vulnerable. Salaries of company officials were so low that they invited corruption and speculation, and the practice of paying high dividends to shareholders, regardless of the amount of cash on hand, emptied company coffers to the point that after 1782 no dividends could be paid. By 1789 the company's debt stood at 74 million *guilders* and the company was unable to borrow further on the open market.

At the same time Netherlands involvement in the Franco-British-American (American Revolutionary) War caused the British to cut communications between Holland and Batavia, and the Treaty of Paris which ended the war in 1784 gave British shipping free access to the Indies, thus breaking Dutch monopoly in the archipelago itself. The French revolutionary wars delivered the final blows to the company. Holland was occupied by France in 1795 and its king fled to England. There he issued orders placing the company's possessions in British custody to prevent their being seized by the French; the British promptly occupied all the East Indies except Java. In Holland the company dissolved and transferred its debts and possessions to the state on December 31, 1799, the date its charter expired.

Six years later Louis Bonaparte, Napoleon's brother, became King of Holland and sent as governor general to the Indies Wilhelm Daendels, who withdrew his forces from the outer islands and concentrated them in Java in anticipation of a British attack. He transformed the local sultans and regents into salaried state employees—an affront to their dignity—and centralized public administration in Batavia. Disregarding the traditional land tenure system by authorizing *taille* (harvesting) taxes and corvée labor, Daendels also expanded the areas of forced cultivation of coffee and cotton. Therefore when the British captured Batavia in 1811 the local princes greeted the invaders with relief.

The British seizure of Java was a punitive measure against Napoleon for the annexation of the Netherlands; it did not presage British sovereignty over the island, primarily because the British were not impressed with its economic value. However Thomas Stamford Raffles, a young servant of the English East India Company who was sent to administer Java and its dependencies, thought otherwise and aspired to add the island to the English company's "Asian empire." Raffles persuaded the Javanese princes to transfer the title and ancient rights of the Majapahit kings to the British governor general in India. He set up a system of residents, changing the pattern of indirect rule through regents to one of direct administration by Europeans, thus depriving the princes of more of their power. He also replaced the old and undesirable system of contingencies with a land tax as a single source of revenue. His theory was that all land belonged to the state and the cultivator or user—even though he possessed the land—should pay rent on it in accordance with its productive capacity. Raffles' action required the introduction into Java of a money economy, a complete land survey, and the keeping of rent rolls by village chiefs, few of whom could read or write. Yet, despite its problems and shortcomings, the Dutch retained the policy after Java was returned to them in 1816.

COLONIAL GOVERNMENT

The Dutch constitutions of 1814 and 1815 gave the crown the "exclusive" power to direct the administration of the East Indian colonies, and "the Government interpreted the term 'exclusive' to mean exclusive of the States General [parliament]."[3] Parliament acceded to this interpretation until the new constitution of 1848. Thus during the first half of the 19th century the king not only had unrestricted administrative power over the Indies, including the power of appointments, but he also determined policy.

Resumption of Dutch authority was difficult in the immediate postwar years. A number of outer islands (islands other than Java, the small inshore island of Madura, and Sumatra) were under actual Chinese control. Illicit spice-growing in the Moluccas was widespread. The Dutch could not keep out the British "country ships" from India, which distributed cotton cloth and opium throughout the islands, and Singapore was rapidly becoming a major entrepot, outstripping Batavia. Worst of all, the Indonesians harbored ideas of independence. Pacification measures thus became the first priority of the Dutch colonial administration.

From 1825 to 1830 the so-called Java War—a rebellion led by Diponegoro, a prince of the royal house of Jogjakarta and a hero to modern nationalists—cost the lives of 15,000 government troops and some 200,000 Javanese, mostly from famine and disease. After defeating the rebels the Dutch annexed territory from the sultanates of Jogjakarta and Surakarta (heirs to Mataram) to prevent a recurrence of the rebellion, but mollified the princes by modifying the direct rule instituted by Raffles, transferring certain substantive authority from the European residents to the Indonesian regents.

Culture System   The Java War and wars in Europe had emptied the Dutch treasury. Therefore Johannes van den Bosch was dispatched to Java in 1830 as governor general with the mission of increasing production of export crops by plunging the government directly into the business of agricultural production. While resembling in some aspects the old system of contingencies and forced deliveries, the new "culture system" was much broader. Under the former the regents were simply required to provide certain export crops as tribute. How production was organized and by whom was immaterial. Under the new system the Director of Cultures determined the crop in each instance, and the government was involved in every step of the process: raising the crop, harvesting it, transporting it and preparing it for export in Dutch vessels to be marketed by Dutch merchants through the Netherlands Trading Society (a giant monopoly) in Holland. Simultaneously, Dutch home industry was assured a closed market in the colonies.

This mercantilist system quickly turned Java into one huge state-run plantation, a development which required a tremendous expansion of public administration, and the Indonesian peasants became part-time serfs, since forced cultivation and forced labor on roads and irrigation works sometimes exceeded 200 days of a villager's year. The system fragmented the social structure because the Dutch exploited the authority and prestige of the traditional governing class, the *prijaji*, by giving them a share of the profits for following Dutch orders. Village headmen were also coopted into the system. In consequence Islamic teachers and their followers such as the *santri* (devout Muslims), who stood apart from the governing groups, became the foci of antigovernment views and symbols of a nascent nationalism.

The culture system was an enormous financial success. Within the first three years Batavia had a treasury surplus and funds were transferred to Holland to retire the national debt. In a 45-year period the Dutch treasury netted an income from Java of almost one billion *guilders*, and the Netherlands merchant fleet became the third largest in the world.

Liberal System   The constitution of the Netherlands was changed in 1848 to give the States General certain legislative—primarily financial—functions in regard to colonial affairs, and in 1854 the East Indian Government Act was enacted that called in vague terms for abolition of slavery, greater freedom of the press, education of the natives and their protection against the evils of forced labor and land usurpation. In 1860 publication of the powerful satiric novel on Dutch colonial life, *Max Havelaar*,[4] aroused the Dutch much as *Uncle Tom's Cabin* did the Americans. Slavery in the colonies was abolished that year, and in 1864 the East India Accounting Act was passed which required parliament to pass on the East Indian budget after 1868. However, power over the budget gave parliament power to question the minister of colonies on overseas administration. As a result the minister began not only to demand detailed reports from the governor general of the Indies but to give him equally detailed instructions. The unforeseen consequence was that the governor general, to protect himself, began to centralize administrative functions in his own office, a tendency that continued until 1916 and the creation of the Indonesian Volksraad (People's Council).

Concommitant with increased political centralization was economic decentralization as the Liberal Party—which espoused economic laissez faire—rose to power in the Netherlands and began to dismantle the culture system. Forced cultivation of pepper, cloves, nutmeg, indigo, tea, cinnamon, cochineal and tobacco was ended, but cultivation of sugar and coffee—the only remaining *profitable* cultures—was retained. In 1870 the Sugar Law provided for phasing out government control of sugar production in favor of private enterprise; coffee remained under government control until 1917 by which time Brazilian coffee had replaced the Java product in the world market.

An Agrarian law was also passed in 1870 that facilitated the acquisition, but not ownership, of land by foreign entrepreneurs and opened the way for a quantum expansion of private plantations. The transition of the economy of Indonesia from government monopoly to a free economy of private investment was called the "liberal system." During the period 1870 to 1920 it produced significant social and economic change in the archipelago. The new system tended further to break up village social cohesion. Laborers were recruited for jobs in distant places and worked for the faceless management of large commercial enterprises. They lost the commonality of village life but gained neither skills nor knowledge in compensation. Moreover, despite the humanitarian clauses of the Agrarian Law prohibiting non-Indonesian ownership of agricultural land, mounting indebtedness produced *non-indigenous control* of much peasant-owned land.

A number of factors spurred Dutch financial and territorial expansion in Indonesia. The age of steam navigation, and the opening of the Suez Canal in 1869, transformed sea-borne commerce, and condiment and beverage crops were gradually replaced by industrial raw materials as money earners. In consequence, in the last quarter of the 19th century the Dutch began to extend administrative control to Sumatra and the outer islands, and to increase the private investment in plantation crops thereon. Tobacco, rubber and palm oil estates on the eastern and western coasts of Sumatra, petroleum discoveries in south Sumatra, and plantation crops and mineral mining in the outer islands challenged the Java-based economy, and brought the entire archipelago into more direct economic relationship with the modern world.

In the process of expanding these crop areas the Dutch fought a long and bitter campaign against the guerrilla resistance of Acheh, the only remaining independent north Sumatran state. The war began in 1873 and final resistance ended only in 1908. Thus the last flicker of independence in the Netherlands Indies was extinguished at the very moment Indonesian nationalism—exemplified by the establishment of the Budi Utomo Association—began to take hold.

Ethical Policy   The population of Java was 28.4 million in 1900, including Europeans and Eurasians whose number increased as mines, plantations, commercial ventures, financial institutions, shipping, and government administration proliferated. However the annual increase in the amount of land under cultivation had fallen behind population increase; more people were cultivating proportionately less land. Additionally, export production did nothing to benefit the people and living standards remained stationary or even declined, dashing the hopes of Dutch business and manufacturing interests for a market in the Indies. In these circumstances voices for reform were heard, with lower ranking European members of the civil service siding with the Javanese against the planter class. Pressure developed in parliament to expand education and social services, humanitarians arguing that the Netherlands was in debt to all Indonesians for the immense profits the islands had provided to the Dutch.

In response to the agitation, a new "ethical policy" was adopted by the Netherlands government in 1901. It was primarily a welfare program, somewhat akin to contemporary international assistance and development projects. New government departments of health, public works and agriculture undertook sanitation and hygenic improvement, irrigation projects and agricultural extension services. Provisions for village banks and credit facilities were made in 1901, native industries were protected by law in 1903, inspection of labor conditions was mandated in 1904 and a Village Regulatory Act of 1906 brought Dutch colonial officials to villages to supervise programs designed to assist them. Despite opposition from the European business community in Indonesia, reluctance both at the Hague and in Batavia to decentralize, and failure to enforce much of the program, the ethical policy did bring about some improvements. These occurred mainly in the fields of education and agriculture. Schools increased in number dramatically, but much of the education was a superficial exposure to western learning. Smallholder rubber planting was accelerated and a doubling of the area under irrigation increased the rice crop. Nevertheless, a corresponding growth in population counterbalanced the improvement in food production.

A law of 1903, designed to decentralize administration, authorized formation of regional and city councils with strictly limited authority, and subsequently a modest amount of self government was granted to villages and regencies. In 1916 the Dutch parliament raised the council concept to the archipelago level by creating the Volksraad, conceived as a multi-ethnic consultative body to the governor general. Half its members were to be elected by local councils and half appointed by the governor general. However at its first meeting on May 18, 1918 the deputies were so disappointed over the Volksraad's lack of authority and non-representative character—over half the members were Europeans—that they declined to transmit a cable of appreciation to the queen.

POLITICAL INDICATORS: DUTCH RULE

1. The three hundred years of Dutch rule in Indonesia was the history of the rise, consolidation and expansion of an economic empire. From the beginning the Dutch viewed their Far Eastern territories as central to the economic viability of the Netherlands, and it is estimated that eventually one-fourth of the entire population of the nation was in some degree dependent upon the colony for its livelihood. Although the Dutch approach to the Indies shifted from that of a paternalistic company, interested only in profits, to that of a government, first mercantilist in philosophy, then laissez faire, it was at all times commerce oriented.
2. Authority was centralized and located at the Hague and in Batavia, with little concession to local self government. Where possible the Dutch coopted the princes and aristocracy—the natural leadership in Indonesian society—to rule for them in an indirect exercise of central power.
3. Throughout the period Java remained the center of Dutch power, with control of the outer islands dependent, as in the case of earlier empires, on control of the sea lanes. With the exception of the Moluccas, Celebes and part of Sumatra, the outer islands were brought under Dutch control only in the last half of the 19th century and then only in peripheral fashion.
4. The state had assumed a leading role in determining the direction

and often the specifics of economic development, predisposing the leaders of an independent Indonesia toward socialism and state planning.
5. Despite an expanding economy during most of these years, few of its benefits were realized by the rapidly increasing Indonesian population.

NATIONALISM AND POLITICAL PARTIES

The first rumblings of anti-colonial sentiment were heard when Marxism was introduced at Semarang, on Java's north coast, in 1903 by *Indos* (Eurasians) who felt threatened by the Dutch. Their leader, Douwes Dekker, grandnephew of the author of *Max Havelaar*, proclaimed an interracial Marxist socialist movement. His party so offended both Dutch and Islamic sensibilities that he and his associates were exiled in 1913. The banner of Marxism immediately reappeared among adherents of the National Indies Party which mirrored European socialism and which was also promptly suppressed. Thenceforth Eurasians identified with the Insulinde Party, western oriented and outside the mainstream of the nationalist movement, as the majority of the Eurasians apparently came to see their best chance lay in continued identification with the Dutch.

In 1908 the Budi Utomo (High Endeavor) association emerged as the first organized expression of indigenous dissatisfaction with the character of colonial rule. Reformist rather than independence minded, Buti Utomo was an upperclass Javanese organization, founded by Waidin Sudira Usada, which sought equality with the Dutch in education and official employment. Raden Adjeng Kartini, daughter of the Regent of Japara and founder with Usada of the Kartini schools for girls, influenced its formation. Buti Utomo appealed to Indonesian intellectuals, certain levels of officialdom, and to the aristocracy, but it was soon eclipsed by broader based nationalist organizations which advanced their ideas through the vehicle of Islam.

The Sareket Dagang Islam (Islamic Trading Union) was formed in 1911 as a protective association of batik merchants who feared Chinese competition. This organization of Muslim traders immediately attracted broad religious-nationalist support; it changed its name to Sareket Islam, dropping the term "trading" in 1912. Initially professing loyalty to Dutch rule, Sareket was soon exploiting the widely held resentment of the Sino-Dutch monopoly of commerce, as well as resentment over the perceived sellout by the Indonesian elite to the Dutch. Its religious orientation appealed to the Muslim faithful throughout the archipelago and within five years Sareket membership had skyrocketed to 800,000 and was accorded legal status by the governor general. With the rise within it of *santri* elements who were influenced by modern socialist interpretations of the Koran, Sareket Islam took on a religious reformist and socialist orientation.

Socialism was attractive to Indonesians. The aristocratic and western-educated elite, who had become bureaucrats rather than landholders or capitalists under the Dutch plantation system, endorsed the idea that economic matters should be regulated by the state. The peasantry was attracted to socialist principles because of the village tradition of communal obligation. The contest within Sareket Islam, therefore, was not between socialism and capitalism, but between Islamic and Marxist interpretations of socialist doctrine.

Hendrik Sneevliet, a Dutch communist, undertook to promote the latter by recruiting the gifted young Javanese Marxist, Semaun, as an intermediary. Highly intelligent and an able organizer, Semaun rose rapidly to a position of prominence within the party and began to influence its political philosophy. His chief protagonist for a number of years was Hadji Agus Salim, "who took special joy in demolishing communist opposition within Sareket Islam by pointing out that Mohammed had been preaching the principles of socialist economics 12 centuries before Marx was born."[5] Each side perceived that a complete break was inevitable and accordingly tried to position itself. The struggle reached a decisive point in 1921. At the Sixth National Congress that year the Islamic leaders began a move to expel the communists on the grounds that they were atheists, and decreed that no member of Sareket Islam could at the same time be a member of another political party. Forced from the party, the communists took with them a significant segment of labor and reemerged as the Partai Kommunis Indonesia (PKI, Communist Party of Indonesia). The PKI sought peasant and labor support and came to dominate the trade unions. It also won over a number of provincial branches of Sareket Islam, or founded rival *sarekets*. The PKI-organized railway strike of 1923 and the strike against the metal industry in 1925 were forcibly suppressed by the government, as were revolts in Java and Sumatra in 1926 and 1927. The government thereupon banished 1,300 activists to a concentration camp in western New Guinea and banned the party, marking the effective end of communist activity in the colonial period.

The Perserikatan Nasional Indonesia (PNI, Indonesian Nationalist Party) was formed in 1927, the outgrowth of the Indonesian Society in Holland. Unencumbered by ideological or religious baggage, and led by the genuinely charismatic Sukarno (who could be all things to all men and who has been described as "a living case study of the synthesis that is colonial nationalism"),[6] the PNI prospered. The party cooperated with other groups to develop a unified national political identity, making use of symbols (flag, anthem) and emphasizing use of the Indonesian language. However Sukarno overplayed his hand exactly as the communists had done. His speeches became more and more inflammatory until the government detained him and his lieutenants in late 1929 and imprisoned them until 1932. In 1933 Sukarno was arrested again and exiled to Sumatra.

Political initiative next passed to a moderate socialist party, the Indonesia Party, organized in 1932 by former pro-Marxist Sjahrir and Mohammed Hatta, both Sumatrans. Hatta, a brilliant young economist, tried unsuccessfully to unite the socialists and the nationalists. But when the PNI was outlawed, PNI members drifted into the Indonesia Party which in turn adopted the PNI program. Sareket Islam, meanwhile, had split into factions and lost its influence.

Dutch Response   The Dutch posture toward Indonesian nationalism hardened after 1930 for a variety of reasons. One, vastly increased agricultural production had attracted large numbers of Europeans to the colony, who after 20 years returned home on pensions; these temporary residents wanted closer ties with the Netherlands than had their predecessors. Two, communist uprisings and Sukarno's political agitation had given rise to the view among the Europeans that the native population should be ruled firmly, especially since the Netherlands could not survive economically in the absence of close association with the Indies. And, three, ironically, the world depression of 1930–1934 obliged the government to intervene at all levels of the economic process in order to save the Indonesian economy by combating unemployment and taking action to curtail cheap Japanese imports.

Non-governmental political activity was therefore increasingly suppressed. At the same time the government cautiously encouraged partisanship *within* the Volksraad on the condition that nationalists would change their tactics from non-cooperation to cooperation. Many of them did. And the government embarked upon a program "to kill home rule with kindness." A new system of provincial government was introduced to decentralize administration and to increase slightly the elected base for the Volksraad. Efforts were undertaken to extend higher education which culminated in the formation of the University of Batavia, now the University of Indonesia.

In 1936 the Volksraad requested that a conference be convened of representatives of the Netherlands and of the Netherlands Indies to plan gradual autonomy for the islands within the framework of the Dutch constitution. When three years later the minister of colonies at the Hague finally replied negatively to the request, the nationalists gathered forces. In May 1939 they formed the Indonesian Political Concentration (Cabungan Politik Indonesia) made up of seven nationalist parties, and passed a resolution in the Volksraad in February 1940 reiterating their request. At the same time they offered to cooperate with the Dutch in the face of the rising Japanese threat to Southeast Asia in return for some assurance of concessions, carefully avoiding any mention of independence.

World War II On May 10, 1940 Holland was invaded by German armies and was occupied four days later. In November the Dutch government-in-exile in London consented to formation of a commission to study limited autonomy for the islands; its report 13 months later was minimally responsive. The Political Concentration meanwhile formulated a specific program for internal autonomy: 1) adoption of the name "Indonesia," 2) universal adult suffrage, 3) a new chamber of elected people's representatives to serve as a lower house of a bicameral legislature, with the Volksraad functioning as the upper house, 4) greatly enhanced Indonesian representation in public administration, and 5) Indonesian representation on the Council of the Indies in Holland. In June 1941 Dutch authorities in exile in England agreed to a postwar conference to study the situation.

Dutch indecision and lack of forthrightness lowered Indonesian respect for the metropolitan power. When Dutch military forces in the archipelago were rapidly defeated by the invading Japanese in March 1942 the Dutch were further discredited. Expectations that the Japanese were coming as liberators, and their speedy release of Sukarno, Sjahrir and Hatta, generated an initial enthusiasm for the new occupiers. However, the harshness of Japanese rule, and the realization by the Indonesians that the occupation was a military operation whose main objective was to further the Japanese war effort, soon cost the Japanese the initial good will they had enjoyed. To regain public support the Japanese decided to woo nationalist leaders with hints of independence. Amir Sjarifuddin, Sjahrir and Adam Malik, who were engaged in resistance activities, refused to work with the occupying force; Sukarno and Hatta collaborated but maintained communication with the anti-Japanese underground.

Hatta's collaboration appears to have been in consequence of a genuine conviction—based upon his political experience as a socialist member of the Hague Assembly in the 1920s—that under the umbrella of collaboration he could do more for the Indonesian independence movement than otherwise. Sukarno's motivations are more suspect. One of Sukarno's biographers portrays him as basically an egoistic opportunist whose overriding urge was to play a major role in Indonesian affairs.[7] Nevertheless Sukarno's flamboyant oratory was to propel him to the forefront to such a degree that in 1945 he was the only candidate considered for the presidency of the new revolutionary Republic of Indonesia.

In return for helping the Japanese organize the economy, form a puppet political organization and recruit a volunteer Indonesian army, Hatta and Sukarno had at their disposal a massive communication system comprising radio and loudspeaker networks extending to the villages and to youth and military organizations. Contact was thus reestablished between the indigenous political elite and the people which had been essentially absent since the 1920s.

When the tide of war began to turn against them the Japanese, as they did elsewhere in Southeast Asia, made specific concessions toward independence. Shortly before surrendering they authorized an Independence Preparatory Committee under the chairmanship of Sukarno. But Sukarno and Hatta temporized. They were apparently fearful before the Japanese surrender of incurring the wrath of the Japanese; and after the surrender of jeopardizing their standing with the Allies. Militant youth groups, however, forced their hand, and on August 17, 1945 (Merdeka—Freedom Day), Sukarno unequivocally declared Indonesia's independence.

REPUBLIC OF INDONESIA

Sukarno became president and Hatta vice president of the newly formed Republic of Indonesia. A constitution was promulgated within a week, providing for a presidential form of government in a unitary state and containing, as a philosophic framework, five principles (*pancha sila*): belief in one God, a just and civilized humanity, nationalism, democracy and social justice. *Pancha sila* was to become an important symbol and rallying cry of the nonaligned nations in the 1950s and 1960s.

The method of selecting the president, vice president and the Madjelis Permusjawaratan Rakjat (MPR, People's Consultative Assembly), the supreme body with power to exercise the sovereignty of the people, was not specified in the constitution. It was decided that a Komite Nasional Indonesia Pusat (KNIP, Central Indonesian National Committee), appointed by the president and representatives of various social groups, would advise the president and his cabinet until election procedures could be worked out. The president, meanwhile, enjoyed broad powers.

The original Allied war plan had been for the Americans to occupy Indonesia, but the plan was abandoned and the British were assigned the operation. The sudden surrender of Japan found the British unprepared and unable to land forces until the end of September. When they arrived they dealt with, and sought the cooperation of, the Republic, thus affording it de facto legitimacy. However, the Dutch government representative, H. J. van Mook, who arrived the following week with plans for a federation of Indonesian states linked to the Kingdom of the Netherlands, refused to negotiate with Sukarno because he had been a collaborator. While the British strove to bring the Dutch and the Indonesians to the conference table, Indonesian military resistance against European reoccupation of the archipelago developed.

In the meantime political changes were taking place. Sukarno's power was curtailed when the KNIP was converted from a presidential advisory body to a legislative body, sharing lawmaking powers jointly with the president. It delegated this function to the Working Committee responsible to it. The powers of the president were further diluted when the Working Committee insisted that the cabinet be responsible to the KNIP rather than to the head of state.

Sukarno accepted the dimunition of power because of his political vulnerability. He was under attack by both the radical left and the pro-western moderates for his collaboration with the Japanese. He therefore dismissed his cabinet and invited Sjahrir to become prime minister, with the prerogative of choosing his own ministers. By this adroit action Sukarno: 1) saved his presidency, 2) eliminated his cabinet which had fallen increasingly under the influence of communist party leader Tan Malaka, 3) distanced himself from his critics who objected to his collaborationist image, and 4) paved the way for talks with the Dutch which had been held up because he, as head of government, had rejected in toto the Dutch plan of federation.[8]

Sjahrir vs Sjarifuddin   Sjahrir and Hatta began talks with the Dutch in November. They realized that compromise was essential since they were unable to control the revolution. Throughout Java and Sumatra radical religious and secular elements were overthrowing local rulers. Direct military confrontation between Netherlands forces and the ill-equipped forces of the republic would be disastrous. If the republic was to stay alive it needed to husband its human and political resources and negotiate.

Nevertheless Sjahrir proved no less intractable than Sukarno. In December 1945 he rejected the Dutch proposal that Indonesia be a partner in the Kingdom of the Netherlands, reasserting instead the demand for Dutch recognition of the Indonesian Republic, although the republic represented little more of Indonesia than Java and part of Sumatra. In early 1946 he turned down a Dutch proposal for a commonwealth and later a "compromise" for the Indonesian Republic to become a unit of a Federated Netherlands State. Meanwhile, beginning with pitched battles at Surabaya between reoccupying British troops and Indonesian units, a four-year war of resistance had commenced.

The republic was also rent by internal political dissension. The leftwing radicals, led by Malaka, adopted an uncompromising revolutionary stand and attempted a *coup d'état* in June 1946; they were supported by armed youth groups in many areas. Right-wing radicals,

led by pro-fascist Subardjo, were equally opposed to the parliamentary
democracy which Sjahrir represented. The communist PKI, with its
adherents scattered through various small organizations, was not a
significant force until several years later and initially supported the
government.

The Sjahrir regime successfully withstood the pressures and the
attempted coup, and by 1947 the principal parties active in political
persuasion were: 1) the PNI of Sukarno, 2) the Muslim Masjumi
(Council of Indonesian Muslim Associations), and 3) the Socialist Party
(PSI), the former Indonesia Party, whose moderate wing was led by
Sjahrir and the pro-communist faction by Sjarifuddin. A veritable flood
of splinter parties also began to emerge, partly in consequence of the
Dutch legacy of proportional representation and partly because they
were political units of the many armed groups that had formed during
the war.

In March 1947 Sjahrir signed the Linggadjati Agreement with the
Dutch which called for a federated Indonesia. Although the Working
Committee reluctantly agreed to the plan, controversy broke out over
Dutch insistence that the Netherlands government was sovereign
throughout the archipelago until the federation came into being. Sjahrir
was forced to resign in June and was replaced by Sjarifuddin who was
supported by a coalition of socialist, labor and communist elements.
In July the Dutch, tiring of the delay, issued an ultimatum and when it
was rejected launched their first "police action." By the time the
United Nations Security Council stopped them—through a ceasefire
ordered on August 5—they had retaken two-thirds of Java, and the
republican government was left in control of only its capital city,
Jogjakarta, and its environs.

A UN Committee of Good Offices brought the disputants together
aboard the United States warship *Renville,* and on January 17, 1948
the two again agreed to a United States of Indonesia, with provision
for plebiscites which would determine whether various island groups
would join the republic or some other part of the federation. Sovereignty would remain with the Netherlands until the Netherlands transferred it to the United States of Indonesia.

Sjarifuddin's left-wing ministry was unable to achieve acceptance of
the Renville Agreement by the Masjumi and the PNI, which unseated
him. Since neither of the latter desired to be associated with the
agreement, Sukarno appointed Hatta as premier in a cabinet responsible to the president as permitted by the constitution under such
circumstances. Hatta pulled his cabinet together in late January with
most of its members from the PNI and Masjumi, the very parties that
had been recalcitrant. Political battle lines between government and
anti-government factions quickly hardened, although their positions on

the agreement changed. The Masjumi and PNI now supported the Renville Agreement, while the left-wing groups responsible for signing it opposed it. In the meantime the Dutch set up states in the archipelago according to their federal plan and in March 1948 established an interim federal government which comprised all of Indonesia except the much-reduced republic.

Within the republic tensions continued to mount, with the communist party building strength and demanding that Indonesia take sides with the Soviet Union in the Cold War. Troops sympathetic to the PKI seized the city of Madiun in the fall and forced the party into revolt. Sukarno and Hatta rallied enough support to suppress the rebellion by December, and the bloody actions in this campaign resulted in the deaths of many of the leftist leaders, including Sjarifuddin. In consequence the PKI did not reemerge as a political force until 1952.

Dutch Reaction The Dutch took advantage of the leftist revolt—even though it had failed—asserting that the republic was in communist hands, and launched a second "police action" in December. The move followed months of recrimination by each side: the Dutch accused the republic of violating the truce produced by the Renville Agreement; the Indonesians asserted that the Dutch were trying to blockade them into surrender. The UN Good Offices Committee reported in July that the Indonesian complaints were substantially factual.

The Dutch military action resulted in the occupation of Jogjakarta, the republican capital, and the capture of Sukarno, Hatta and Sjahrir. It also inflamed the international community, particularly the Asian portion, and in January 1949 the UN Security Council called for release of the Indonesian leaders, restoration of the republican government, resumption of negotiations, and reconstitution of the Good Offices Committee into the more authoritative UN Commission for Indonesia. The Dutch quickly acquiesced in the face of adverse world opinion, the economic pressures against them, and their own unhappiness at the degree to which their behavior had discredited them in the international system. A strong initiative developed in Holland to achieve a settlement which would meet Indonesian national aspirations. In consequence the Round Table Conference at The Hague, August–November 1949, arranged for transfer of sovereignty over all of the Netherlands East Indies (except Western New Guinea) to a federally structured Indonesia, and on December 27, 1949 the United States of Indonesia came into being, a federation in which the republic was one of sixteen component states. The arrangement heavily overrepresented the outer island populations.

Almost immediately the republic moved to absorb the other states where most of the political leaders held their positions as legatees of Dutch power. Rebellions broke out in western Java and in the Dutch-

established state of East Indonesia (Celebes, Moluccas, Banda, Flores
and Bali). Republic troops were dispatched to various islands where
they freed political detainees sympathetic to their cause and encouraged merger with the republic. In the South Moluccas genuine popular
resistance to the unification movement produced an attempt to create
an independent Republic of the South Moluccas, which was suppressed
by the republican army. The Christian Ambonese population of the
South Moluccas had supplied much of the manpower for the Netherlands Indies army and was distrustful of republic rule; emigré Ambonese in the Netherlands have continued to agitate for an independent
Moluccas to the present, at times engaging in terrorism to underscore
their objective.

The UN Commission on Indonesia watched mutely as the federation
crumbled, and on August 17, 1950 the unitary Republic of Indonesia
was announced—five years to the day after the original declaration of
independence. A provisional constitution was promulgated which divided power among the president, the cabinet and a legislature, and
transformed the country into a unitary state based on parliamentary
democracy.

PARLIAMENTARY DEMOCRACY

With the inauguration of unitary government Hatta was replaced as
prime minister and again became vice president. Mohammed Natsir,
leader of the Masjumi Party, the largest party in the House of Representatives (Dewan Perwakilan), became prime minister after building a
coalition of nine parties. He was followed in rapid succession by
Sukiman in 1951 and Wilopo in 1952, both serving with a Masjumi-PNI
moderate coalition. During these early years of the 1950s ideological
division deepened between the Masjumi and the PNI-moderates who
had backed Hatta during the independence struggle; and the PNI-
radicals and the revitalized PKI communists under the new leadership
of Dipa Dipanegara Aidit. Both groups nevertheless identified with
Sukarno.

A crisis occurred in October 1952 when the government attempted
to reduce the size of the overly large armed forces. Army Chief of
Staff Colonel Abdul Haris Nasution, and the experienced western-
oriented officers, thoroughly supported the reform; *semangat* (fighting
spirit) officers, many of them former irregulars who had risen through
the ranks during the revolution, opposed it. Sukarno, already irritated
that the 1950 constitution reduced the president's role, and highly
conscious of his position as Supreme Commander of the Armed
Forces, sided with the jingoist *semangat* elements. Nasution faltered
and Sukarno carried the day. It was Sukarno's relationship with

semangat army officers which explains much of his subsequent dealings with the army.

The army crisis mortally wounded the Wilopo cabinet which fell in June 1953, and with it fell the hope for effective parliamentary democracy. The Natsir, Sukiman and Wilopo cabinets had failed to clear squatters from estates, reduce the size of the civil service, reduce the size of a swollen and expensive army, or make progress against the extremist Darul Islam (House of Islam) rebels whose guerrillas controlled large areas of western Java and the southern Celebes. Hatta and other moderates gradually lost ground to the radical nationalists in the parties and in the army, and especially to President Sukarno. The relatively pragmatic approach of these early years began to give way to what would become, according to one author, Sukarno's "gigantic circus performance," founded upon "a mixture of Javanistic and Marxist messianic expectations."[9]

The Wilopo ministry was succeeded by the first Ali Sastroamijojo cabinet (July 1953–July 1955), a coalition between the PNI and the Nahdatul Ulana (NU), the conservative Muslim Party. The PKI, now a burgeoning, powerful, monolithic organization on its way to becoming the world's largest communist party after those of the USSR and the People's Republic of China, supported the new government. During these years failure at home was obscured by popular foreign policy initiatives undertaken by Sukarno as head of state. These included effective exploitation of Dutch intransigence about transferring sovereignty in New Guinea, and hosting the widely publicized Bandung Conference of 1955 which popularzied the nonaligned movement. Sukarno's skillful exploitation of the issues foreshadowed his employment of outright foreign adventurism in subsequent years.

The army intervened to bring about the government's downfall in 1955 on charges of corruption, just as the country was preparing to go to the polls for the first time in Indonesian history. (Prior to this time governments were formed by political deals among parties which were based upon ideological, religious, ethnic, regional or personal relationships.) More than 100 parties contested the September election, 30 of whom won seats in the 260-seat House of Representatives. Proportional representation, borrowed from the Dutch, insured that no party could gain a majority, and the election from which so much had been expected pleased no one.

Sastroamijojo returned to head a cabinet comprising a coalition of the PNI, the Masjumi and the NU. The communists were specifically excluded from the government at the insistence of the Muslim parties, but the coalition was unable to tackle problems effectively because politics had become polarized. There was sharp disagreement whether Indonesia should be founded upon the specific principles of Islam or upon the nonspecific ideals of *pancha sila,* and the division between the Javanese and the remainder of the Indonesian peoples had widened. The PNI, the PKI and the NU were perceived as Java parties, each having obtained more than 85 percent of its vote on the central islands—Java, Sumatra and Madura; the Masjumi and the Socialists were considered parties of the outer islands.

The nation was also beset by disaffection and political assertiveness on the part of regional military commanders who openly defied the government and engaged in smuggling because, as they said,the unfavorable exchange rate made it impossible otherwise to care for their soldiers and their areas.

BUNG KARNO

For a decade in the mid 1950s and 1960s any analysis of Southeast Asian politics was likely to begin and end with reference to "Bung (brother) Karno," one of the great demagogues of the 20th century. He was Machiavellian, charismatic, chauvinistic, a great national unifier, and above all in western eyes, a great spoiler. He was an important influence on both regional and world politics.

In October 1956 President Sukarno began to speak of the failure of party government and of the desirability of "burying" parties. On November 10 at the opening session of the Constituent Assembly, elected the preceding year for the purpose of drawing up a new constitution, the president delivered a blistering attack on parliamentary democracy. Alarmed at the president's behavior, Hatta resigned from the vice presidency. Sukarno's proposed new political framework was termed guided democracy. He called for an all-party cabinet to include the communists, and a national council representative of all interests—peasants, workers, intellectuals, businessmen, the armed forces and the religious—which would operate on the basis of consensus, a concept indigenous to Malay village life. Parliament would funnel ideas to the all-party cabinet which would study them and send them on to the president.

Sukarno's proposals were anathema to residents of the outer islands who saw power being retained in the hands of the Javanese, and defiance of the central government spread during early 1957 to Sumatra, Sulawesi (Celebes) and Maluku (Moluccas). The regionalists called for restoration of the Sukarno-Hatta team with Hatta as prime minister; regional autonomy; greater power for the army; and government measures against the communists. Ignoring these pleas, Sukarno pushed his concept of guided democracy and temporarily declared martial law, taking the government into his own hands. And in order to divert the people's attention from Indonesia's economic condition, he encouraged xenophobic nationalism.

Working with the PKI which was not part of the then government, Sukarno targeted the Netherlands for his first attack. In retaliation for Dutch unwillingness to compromise on West Irian (Western New Guinea) the Indonesian government in February 1956 had unilaterally abrogated the statute which established the Netherlands-Indies Union created by The Hague Agreement of 1949. Special privileges of Dutch citizens in Indonesia were revoked and in August 1957 the government repudiated the 3 billion *guilder* debt to the Netherlands it had assumed upon transfer of sovereignty. These measures proved popular and gave Sukarno opportunities to stay in the international spotlight as well as to practice his oratory at home. Therefore, when Indonesia's fourth application to the UN for resumption of negotiations with the Dutch over West Irian failed, Sukarno looked on benignly as, beginning on December 3, 1957, workers began to take control of Dutch businesses and property. By December 13, when Army Chief of Staff Nasution instituted military control over it, the huge Dutch business establishment—consisting of estates, mines, banks, trading houses and shipping valued at US$1.5 billion—was in Indonesian hands. Most of the 46,000 Dutch still in Indonesia prepared to leave, 10,000 departing within the month. The Eurasian population also departed; they had elected to be Indonesian citizens, but found their social and economic position undermined by independence and destroyed by nationalization.

While the exodus of the Dutch and Indos produced economic chaos, in a public relations sense the action strengthened the hand of the government, accentuating the sense of unity at the expense of the dissident regionalists in the outer islands. It also provided opportunities for almost unlimited patronage.

However Hatta, as well as Masjumi leaders, were aghast at the economic consequences of the Dutch exodus. Some Masjumi leaders, and politicians of the Socialist Party (PSI) which was committed to liberal democracy, fled to Padang in western Sumatra and called for a new non-communist government headed by Hatta or the Sultan of Jogjakarta. When no response to their demands was forthcoming, they proclaimed the Revolutionary Government of the Republic of Indonesia on February 15, 1958. Rebellious military commanders in both central Sumatra and north Sulawesi, with the alleged assistance of the U.S. Central Intelligence Agency, supported this attempt to form a new government, but could not coordinate operations because of the 1,500 miles between them.

The Jakarta government launched an all-out invasion of Sumatra in March, and by early May had reduced the rebellion to guerrilla proportions. In June and July the north Sulawesi insurrection was put down in a more difficult campaign because the rebels there received air support from the Republic of China on Taiwan. Suppression of the rebellions strengthened Sukarno and the army; discredited Hatta, the Masjumi and the PSI; eliminated the regionalists; and pushed Indonesia from a nonaligned into a distinctly pro-communist foreign policy.

Relations with the United States deteriorated drastically from the cordiality that marked them at the time of independence. The Americans proved unresponsive in 1957 and again in 1958 to Foreign Minister Subandrio's request for US$700 million worth of arms; on the other hand the Soviet Union began to supply substantial amounts of economic and military aid. The U.S. proposal of May 14, 1958 to negotiate a ceasefire with the rebels was termed by Subandrio as "downright intervention," and two days later he called in USSR and PRC diplomats to discuss this and other "interventions" on the part of the British and the Chinese Nationalists. From this low point U.S.-Indonesian relations improved somewhat, with the U.S. agreeing in August to sell, for Indonesian *rupiahs,* some military goods and services. A military assistance group was established to administer the military sales program, which increased in 1959 and continued until Dutch-Indonesian armed conflict over West Irian commenced in 1962. But the U.S. did not regain its earlier influence.

New Ideology   In February 1959 the Constituent Assembly (in session since 1956) refused President Sukarno's proposal to revive the constitution of 1945 which would restore the president's strong authority. In July therefore Sukarno dissolved the assembly and illegally reactivated the 1945 constitution by decree. At the same time he took steps to personalize the government by establishing a new 10-member "inner cabinet" of which he was premier, Djuanda "first minister," and Nasution minister of security and defense. An "outer cabinet" of 29 deputy ministers was also formed.

The authority of parliament had already been vitiated by creation in 1957 of Sukarno's brain child, the National Council, which was supposed to act as a supreme advisory body, but which had proved to be entirely ineffective. In order to diminish further parliament's role, he replaced the National Council with a Supreme Advisory Council (that had communist members, but from which the Muslim Masjumi was excluded) and formed the National Planning Council which was mandated to draw up a plan for guided democracy.

Sukarno chose Freedom Day, August 17, 1959, to deliver a speech entitled "The Rediscovery of Our Revolution," in which he justified the return to the 1945 constitution and called for renewal of the revolution. The speech became the basis for a new state ideology known officially as MANIPOL-USDEK, from *Manifesto Politik* (Political Manifesto) and the first letters of its five major components: the constitution of 1945, Indonesian socialism, guided democracy, guided economy and national identity. Pointing to the traditional Indonesian concepts of *musjawarah* (search for consensus through discussion) and *mufakat* (consensus), Sukarno insisted that the communists should be included in the new system if the traditional concepts were to be meaningful. The acronym NASA-KOM—an abbreviation for *nasional-isme* (nationalism), *agama* (religion) and *kommunisme* (communism)—was devised to identify the main forces in the government.

Sukarno's moves to consolidate his position within the new framework continued apace. In September he gave himself power to appoint and remove regional governors. In January 1960 he assumed authority to dissolve any disloyal political party as well as to appoint and dismiss members of the Provisional People's Consultative Assembly (MPRS), the supreme sovereign body according to the 1945 constitution under which the state again operated. In March he dissolved the elected parliament, appointing in its stead a Mutual Assistance House of Representatives with strong communist and functional representation, and a new MPRS of 616 members. Elected bodies had disappeared from Indonesia and neither of the appointive bodies enjoyed real power. During the same months the Masjumi and the PSI were ordered to disband and all party activities were suspended in September. Newspapers critical of the regime were seized.

In the view of several leading scholars, what Sukarno sought to achieve was essentially power without responsibility.[10] He was unable fully to achieve the former, nor eventually, to avoid the latter. Under his new system he would continue to be restrained by the same forces that had always determined the limits of his action, namely the army general staff and the orthodox Muslims. Moreover he failed to develop specific plans or to take actions to achieve social or economic progress within the country. Instead, like frustrated political leaders throughout history, Sukarno turned increasingly to foreign adventurism to keep his ship of state afloat.

Foreign Affairs Sukarno was popular with the USSR for his anti-western posture, and that nation provided him with much of the US\$1.5 billion in foreign aid he needed, and awarded him the Lenin Peace Prize. Simultaneously Sukarno developed the Peking-Jakarta axis. He was the hero of the radicals at the 1961 Summit Conference of Non-Aligned Countries in Belgrade. Moreover, with the assistance of the United Nations and the U.S., who put pressure on the Dutch, he obtained de facto control of West Irian. However any hope that the West Irian victory would placate Sukarno were dashed when in 1963, with PKI support, he plunged the country into another foreign adventure which was to prove less successful.

The British in 1962 had suppressed an armed rebellion in Brunei

(Borneo), supported if not instigated by Indonesia. Its goal had been to abort plans to unite British Borneo (Brunei, Sarawak and Sabah) with Malaya as the Federation of Malaysia. In August 1963 Sukarno persuaded Philippine president Diosdado Macapagal and Malaysian prime minister Tunku Abdul Rahman to meet with him in Manila to discuss the issue of federation. The three formed MAPHILINDO (contraction of the names of the three nations) and agreed to ask the UN to survey Sarawak and Sabah to ascertain if there was general support for the projected Malaysian union. Abdul Rahman met in good faith. Macapagal had the ulterior motive of pursuing a Philippine claim to Sabah. Sukarno's aims were to obstruct Malaysia's formation, damage western interests in the region and perhaps to recreate the boundaries of the ancient Indonesian empires of Srivijaya and Maja-pahit which had extended to the Malay peninsula and the coastal areas of Borneo.

Neither Sukarno nor Macapagal would accept the results of the survey which were favorable to Malaysia's formation. When the fed-eration (minus Brunei) became a reality on September 16, 1963 Su-karno unleashed thousands of demonstrators who destroyed British property in Indonesia and molested British citizens; and Indonesian regular troops were soon attacking the borders of Sarawak and Sabah. Despite a brief ceasefire in January 1964, negotiated by the United States, fighting escalated. After the new nation of Malaysia was elected to a non-permanent seat on the UN Security Council in late 1964, Sukarno withdrew Indonesia from the United Nations. The USSR admonished him to reconsider, but the PRC applauded his audacity and thus strengthened the bonds that were being forged between Peking and Jakarta.

During this period of political adventurism inflation in Indonesia broke all records. In 1964 the consumer price index was 25 times higher than when "guided economy" began in 1959. The money supply quadrupled between 1961 and 1963 as war spending mounted, and as hotels and government buildings were constructed as showpieces. Western aid ceased, consumer shortages became endemic and exports declined. Meanwhile the headlong rush toward more symbols, slogans, acronyms (creation of which seems to be an Indonesian pastime) and actions to divert attention from the country's economic woes contin-ued. One effort was establishment of the Games for New Emerging Forces, in retaliation against the International Olympic Committee's suspension of Indonesia in 1963 for its treatment of Israeli and Tai-wanese athletes. Sukarno saw the New Emerging Forces (NEFOS), i.e. the extreme left-leaning nations of the nonaligned bloc and the communist countries, as permanently arrayed against their opposites, the Old Established Forces (OLDEFOS), who were portrayed as agents of neocolonialism, colonialism and imperialism (NEKOLIM). For example, the formation of Malaysia was attacked as a "NEKOLIM plot," and the UN was accused of displaying a "NEKOLIM attitude." Sukarno even planned a Conference of NEFOS for 1966 to rival the UN.

Fall of Sukarno   By 1963 Indonesia could parade its military might of Soviet-supplied cruisers and destroyers, long range bombers and missiles; it could show off its great stadia for games and rallies; construction had begun on the Freedom Mosque, scheduled to be the world's largest, and on a national monument to be higher than the Eiffel Tower and larger than Borobudur. At the same time the PKI was becoming a major force in the government. Aidit had become a minister without portfolio (1962) and PKI influence steadily increased at the cabinet level where Deputy Prime Minister and Foreign Minister Subandrio led the country further on a pro-communist course. The army, however, became ever more distrustful of the communists and moved quickly to prevent take-over by communist unions of the foreign-owned assets which had been sequestered in retaliation for their nations' support of Malaysia. The army, moreover, intensely resented PKI infiltration of the air force and marine corps, where it was exploiting the dissatisfaction of the younger officers over conditions of service. However, with three million regular members, a like number in its youth movement, and 20 million supporters in front organizations of women, workers, peasants, students and government officials, the PKI seemed destined to come to power.

President Sukarno's health had begun to fail in the same years that his dramatic actions made him a world figure. During his numerous trips abroad he sought medical help and increasingly turned to Peking for treatment. In early August 1965 he was seized by a serious attack of kidney stones. A PRC physician was rushed to his side by the top communist leaders, Aidit and Nyoto. The physician diagnosed severe but not yet fatal kidney poisoning. Alarmed that Sukarno's death or protracted illness might prompt anti-PKI generals to seize power and destroy the party, the communist leaders apparently decided to forestall such possibility by destroying their adversaries.

On the night of September 30, 1965 units of two divisions, some troops of the Jakarta garrison, a number of officers and men of the security battalion at Helim air base and about 2,000 communist troops who had been secretly trained at Helim, occupied key buildings in Jakarta and raided the homes of Minister of Defense Nasution and generals who had consistently taken a strong anti-PKI line. Air Marshal Omar Dhani, chief of the Indonesian Air Force and in charge of the air base, appears to have been the principal military leader. Three generals were murdered in their homes. Three others were taken to

Helim air base where they were slowly tortured to death by bands of hysterical girls and women of the Communist Women's Organization, and their mutilated bodies were thrown into an abandoned well at the base.

Nasution managed to escape his would-be executioners and was able to convince Sukarno, who had gone to Helim early in the morning of October 1, that the conspirators would not be able to sway the army to their cause; Sukarno certainly knew of the conspiracy and had probably given it his tacit approval, but had not committed himself. Meanwhile Major General Suharto, commander of the army's Strategic Reserve in Jakarta, acted quickly against the rebel commanders in the city. He persuaded them to surrender and moved on to Helim. The plot collapsed and the plotters were soon apprehended. Sukarno's admission "that he had gone to Helim of his own free will 'to be near an airplane if that should be necessary,' did the President irreparable damage."[11]

When the grisly details of the night's work became known, unbridled fury swept the country. PKI headquarters in Jakarta were destroyed and from their redoubt around Jogjakarta the communist leaders and their military supporters dug in for battle. All the communist units were defeated by mid-November. Disclosure of the atrocities they had committed against their local enemies in Jogjakarta further infuriated the populace and a bloodbath began. By December mobs led by Muslim organizations were killing communists and their sympathizers in eastern and central Java, Bali and Sumatra. When the army did nothing to prevent them the killings increased; within months some 200,000 to 500,000 persons had been slain.

Because of the close relationship between the PKI and the Peoples' Republic of China, and since many of the local party members were ethnically Chinese, large numbers of Chinese were killed or detained and deported, and the Chinese embassy and consulate were attacked. The Jakarta-Peking axis was completely broken. Extermination of the communists in Indonesia in 1965, the large scale human slaughter practiced by the Pol Pot regime in Kampuchea from 1975 to 1977 and the refugee exodus triggered by Vietnam during 1975–1980, rank among the most unsavory events in the postwar history of Southeast Asia.

The official Indonesian version of the September 30 action squarely blames the communists with plotting to overthrow the state. The unpublished "Cornell Report" by American researchers who carried out fieldwork on the matter, suggests that the revolt was the product of relatively junior army officers who were dissatisfied with service conditions and were ideologically opposed to the army's leadership.[12] According to the report, the PKI was only peripherally involved; most scholarly opinion does not accept the Cornell explanation. Sukarno himself attempted to minimize the plot and refused to condemn the communists, although he appointed Suharto chief of staff in response to army pressure. In February 1966 he reshaped his cabinet, dropping Nasution and retaining pro-communists, including Subandrio and Dhani. He then tried to ban the student organizations which had turned against him, but student agitation increased. With continuous demonstrations and threats from all sides, the country was rapidly falling into chaos. Finally on March 11 Sukarno was persuaded to confer upon Suharto extraordinary powers to restore order and manage the government.

Suharto immediately banned the PKI, arrested pro-communist ministers and set out to eliminate communist influence in the government. In June the MPRS, with Nasution presiding, stripped Sukarno of some of his titles, confirmed the special powers granted to Suharto in March, made provision for Suharto to be acting president should the president be incapacitated, and called for termination of the "confrontation" with Malaysia. Suharto announced a new cabinet in July 1966 which consigned Sukarno to the lesser presidential role he had had in the early 1950s. Actual authority now resided in Suharto as chief minister, Adam Malik as foreign minister and the sultan of Jogjakarta as minister of finance and economics.

Sukarno made several desperate efforts to escape eclipse. On Freedom Day 1966 he raised the old war cries of "crush Malaysia" and "shun the UN." In December he blandly called for the reintroduction of guided democracy. His talk fell on deaf ears. Meanwhile evidence that implicated Sukarno was introduced at the trials of Subandrio and Dhani—who had been dropped from the cabinet by Suharto and were on trial for the September 30 plot. Asked to explain his actions, Sukarno refused. On March 12, 1967 the MPRS decided to make Suharto acting president, allowing Sukarno, nominally, to remain in office. Sukarno retired to his place in Bogor and lived there, under guard, among his wives and ex-wives, discredited, rejected and increasingly ill, until he died from acute kidney poisoning on July 20, 1970. He was buried in an unmarked grave in East Java for fear that a conspicuous tomb in Jakarta would spark inflammatory passions or become a cult center. Suharto and his colleagues had moved with great skill. They had restrained the activists in the army and elsewhere who wanted to try Sukarno, cognizant that Sukarno had considerable support among the masses, especially in central Java, even in his disgrace.

SUHARTO AND THE NEW ORDER: 1967–1975

When Suharto was elected by the MPRS and sworn in as President of Indonesia on March 27, 1968, his "New Order" had already undone in a year's time major damage inflicted by Sukarno's old order. Indonesia's international debt which exceeded US$2.5 billion had been rescheduled; arrangements had been concluded for the country to resume its seat in the UN, the World Bank and the International Monetary Fund; and aid funds had begun to flow from western powers. Suharto placed first priority on continued economic reform. He appointed a "Development Cabinet" which emphasized economic pragmatism. Minister of Trade Sumitro Djojohadikusumo and a gifted group of his former students—young economists who had received advanced training at the University of California, Berkeley, and were to be known as the "Berkeley Mafia"—accomplished the economic turnaround. During the first Five Year Plan (Repelita I, 1969–1973), these young technocrats achieved an upsurge in the output of development industries (especially fertilizer, cement and agricultural and processing machinery), and industries whose products could supplant imports (textiles, paper, tires and chemicals). While state owned enterprises proliferated, a significant increase in investment from abroad also occurred.

Political Restructuring   Suharto's companion priority was adoption of a political formula which would be responsive to both public and private interests. Interest group representation in the decision making process and meaningful universal adult suffrage were deemed important. Although political parties were included in Suharto's perception of the political process—which lay somewhere between guided and western democracy—the party politics of 1950–1959 were not to be revived.

In point of fact what role to assign political parties created a dilemma since the MPRS at its March 1968 session had called for elections to a House of Representatives not later than July 1971. The government therefore directed the numerous splinter parties to resolve their differences and to consolidate. It urged creation of a new Muslim party as an umbrella for Muslim interests, and sponsored the Joint Secretariat of Functional Groups (GOLKAR), consisting of members of the armed forces, police, civil servants, teachers, workers and others, as an umbrella party to represent its own interests. The government made certain that GOLKAR would win the July 1971 elections by banning all political activity and discussion of the New Order at the village level. GOLKAR won 236 of the 360 elective seats; the other nine parties split the remaining 124.

To make certain the new House of Representatives would be malleable the government appointed to it another 100 members, mostly from the armed forces. At the same time the government increased pressure on the remaining political parties to consolidate, its goal being for the parties to form two major groups which, with GOLKAR, would constitute a three-party assembly. The four Muslim parties accommo-datingly formed the United Development Party; the remaining five independent parties, which included two Christian parties, became the Indonesian Democratic Party.

The People's Consultative Assembly (MPR)—which had dropped the word provisional—remained the nation's supreme policymaking body, with responsibility for selecting the president and vice president. Law fixed the membership at 920, half of whom were to be members of the House of Representatives and half appointed by the government. The appointed half was to comprise members elected by regional legislative councils; armed forces representatives; functional represen-tatives (e.g., lawyers, businessmen, unionists), and representatives of political parties. On March 12, 1973 Suharto delivered an account of his five-year stewardship to the MPR and, not surprisingly in view of the makeup of the MPR, was confirmed in office for a second five-year term. The sultan of Jogjakarta was chosen vice president.

Foreign Relations Suharto proved as adept in dealing with delicate international problems as with internal ones. In May 1963, when the administration of West Irian had been transferred from the Netherlands to Indonesia, the latter had promised to ascertain (before the end of 1969) whether that island's 700,000 inhabitants wished to be a part of the republic. Sukarno subsequently made it clear that he had no intention of honoring the conditions. Suharto thus found himself in a dilemma. On one hand the annexation of West Irian was a political imperative; to give it up was to risk being outflanked by the radical nationalists. On the other hand the need to comply at least nominally with its obligation to the UN was essential to Indonesia's credibility with much of the external world. Suharto announced that Indonesia would meet its obligations. The regime then indoctrinated selected chiefs and headmen in West Irian who voted overwhelmingly in August 1969 for continuation of union with Indonesia. A United Nations observer mission registered its reservations about the procedure, and leaders of the Free Papua Movement in West Irian garnered some international support, but Indonesia's action was accepted by the international community.

The political demise of Sukarno and the rise to power of Suharto had brought an immediate improvement in Indonesia's relations with its Southeast Asian neighbors. Suharto called off the confrontation with Malaysia and the by-now-independent Singapore, and renewed traditional trade and commercial relations with the latter. In response to an invitation from Malaysia, Thailand and the Philippines, Indonesia joined with those states and Singapore to form the Association of Southeast Asian Nations (ASEAN) on August 8, 1967. The purposes of ASEAN were to promote peace and stability in the region and to accelerate economic growth, social progress and cultural development. Jakarta was designated as headquarters of the Permanent Committee (now the Permanent Secretariat) and hosted the First Annual Ministerial Conference the following year. The largest member state geographically and numerically, and with oil resources essential to the area, Indonesia has played a major role in ASEAN affairs. It supported, in 1971, the Kuala Lumpur Charter of the ASEAN foreign ministers calling for Southeast Asia as a "zone of peace, freedom and neutrality." In 1974, in conjunction with the Philippines, it enunciated the "archipelago theory" at the Third International Conference of the Law of the Sea at Caracas, Venezuela, insisting on the right of archipelagic states to draw a perimeter around their outer islands and claim as territorial air, sea and seabed the space within the perimeter.

Relations with the PRC, however, remained cool. Political leaders continued to fear Chinese intervention in Indonesian affairs at the behest of PKI exiles in Peking; and local Chinese were seen as a potential fifth column. Moreover it was feared that full diplomatic relations with the PRC would create a political link between one of the region's strongest states and Indonesia's wealthy Chinese business community, to the detriment of the indigenous Malay.

Economic Repercussions   Under Repelita I (1969–1973), Indonesia's economic infrastructure was rehabilitated. Foreign investment was encouraged through incentives and guarantees and accounted for about 50 percent of resource input. Beginning in 1970 Indonesia's growth performance was higher than that of the Philippines and Thailand but lower than that of its other two ASEAN partners, Malaysia and Singapore. But while infusions of foreign capital produced a rapid increase, as much as tenfold, in the production of a wide range of products—textiles, auto parts, basic industrial goods and consumer items—much of the industrial development was capital intensive, resulting in a disappointingly small increase in employment. Only 200,000 new jobs were created between 1967 and 1976. Moreover, progress in the industrial sector was not matched in the agricultural sector. Rice production increased at an annual rate of more than six percent from 1968 to 1972 and then fell back to a two percent annual increase, failing to keep up with the growth of population and the demand due to rising incomes. In succeeding years the nation (traditionally a rice importer in any case) had to increase its imports up to two million tons. Although Suharto had restored financial stability in the wake of the Sukarno excesses, the rice crisis of 1972, the oil price rise of 1973–74 and the rapid acceleration of worldwide inflation reintroduced extreme price instability. In 1974 inflation reached 33 percent.

As the economic strains became evident student activists, intellectuals, and the press charged that foreign aid and foreign investment were not benefiting the Indonesian masses—who watched the wealthy grow richer while they became poorer. In August and October 1973 rioting broke out against Chinese rice brokers and middlemen. In early 1974 the students singled out Japanese businessmen as prime examples of how foreign investment was helping foreigners rather than Indonesians, and violently protested the state visit of Japanese Prime Minister Kakuei Tanaka. Eleven persons were killed and hundreds injured. The protests were seen as actually directed against government policies which allegedly "sold out" Indonesian resources to Japanese and other foreigners, and against high-living generals. Suharto was quick to take the cue. In late January 1974 he disbanded his inner circle of personal assistants who had come under student and press attack. In another high visibility move he removed the commander of Kopkamtib, the powerful military agency for domestic security and intelligence. The second Five Year Plan (Repelita II, 1974–1978) attempted to shift emphasis from capital intensive to labor intensive production, and from domestic consumer goods to export products, seeking to emulate the policies of Taiwan, Korea, Hong Kong and Singapore which had proved so successful. *Pribumi* (indigenous) entrepreneurship was encouraged, as in Malaysia, by discriminating in favor of *pribumi* business initiatives.

The likelihood of achieving the goals of Repelita II were dashed, however, when Pertamina, the huge state owned oil company (through which all foreign oil firms had to deal), showed signs of severe financial distress. Pertamina had grown to the point that it was providing 75 percent of the nation's foreign exchange earnings (US$7.4 billion in 1974), with the bulk of the money being plowed back into economic development. Pertamina's cash flow problems increased as crude oil exports lagged and the worldwide recession continued; the company began to miss loan repayments to foreign banks in February. At this point the government was forced to assume financial responsibility for the organization, which barely averted collapse in late 1975. Although Pertamina's debt was brought under control, foreign banks had to shelve projects which would have brought US$1 billion into the country, and the government was forced to borrow that amount to rebuild its currency reserves, and an additional US$450 million to pay off Pertamina's short-term paper.

Nusantara Revisited: East Timor Perhaps because of economic problems, Suharto's New Order proved no more immune to the temptation of adventurism in foreign affairs than the Sukarno regime. Following Portugal's decision in 1975 to give up sovereignty over East Timor, Suharto announced that, while Indonesia had no claim to the colony, it was concerned over alleged persecution of pro-Indonesian elements there. On August 10 the Democratic Union of Timor took over police and army headquarters at Deli, the capital, and demanded immediate independence; on August 16 Suharto announced that Timor would be welcome to integrate with Indonesia.

By September the Indonesian government was denying that its troops had entered East Timor to prevent a takeover by the left-wing Revolutionary Front for an Independent East Timor (known by its Portuguese abbreviation, Fretelin), one of three main factions engaged in a power struggle there. On December 5, while U.S. President Gerald R. Ford was visiting Suharto, the Indonesian government briefed foreign ambassadors on the "aggravated situation" in East Timor which the government termed a threat to Indonesia's national secur-ity—particularly the proclamation of independence by Fretelin. Two days later Indonesian sea and air forces invaded Timor and seized the capital.

Indonesia's ASEAN colleagues supported the action, the Malaysian press stressing that Indonesia's intervention would close a "festering wound." The U.S. and the Soviet Union both condemned the aggres-sion; Portugal broke diplomatic relations with Indonesia, and the UN General Assembly's Trusteeship Committee and the UN Security Council called for Indonesian withdrawal. Indonesia rejected the call as irrelevant and began a new offensive to expand its occupation. The contest between the UN and Indonesia over East Timor was waged over the next six months, but on July 12, 1976 East Timor was formally integrated into Indonesia.

Indonesian annexation of East Timor was expensive in both human and material terms. Some 60,000 persons were killed during the hostil-ities and it is estimated that 100,000 people—15 percent of the popula-tion—died, mostly of disease and starvation.

POLITICS: POST 1975

The principal political actors in Indonesia by 1976 were the military, whose power had always been strong; the Muslims, whose power had revived; and student movements which had little political base but whose rhetoric could be important. These forces, operating within and behind the political parties, contested the May 2, 1977 general elections for the House of Representatives which had come to the end of its six year term.

Some 64 million of the 70,772,015 registered voters participated. The government-backed GOLKAR (acronym for Golangan Karya) organi-zation of functional groups retained its overall majority in parliament with 39.75 million votes, the Muslim United Party received 18.74 million and the Democratic Party 5.5 million. The three parties divided the 360 parliamentary seats, as well as the thousands of regional and provincial legislative assembly seats, on a proportional basis. The final 100 seats of the 460-member body were filled by President Suharto's appointees from military and civil service functional groups, not affiliated with GOLKAR but who backed its policies. The new House of Representatives, the third since Indonesia gained independence, was installed October 1; members also automatically became members of the MPR.

Despite the elections and the new parliament, by early November mounting student discontent was expressing itself in demonstrations alleging that the heralded anti-corruption campaign was sparing certain top leaders, and questioning whether Suharto should be reelected by the MPR to a third term. The students also asserted that Suharto's developmental policies were contributing to the growing disparity in income; Muslim groups complained that Suharto was anti-Islam.

The armed forces, however, publicly pledged to support the president and to act firmly against those trying to foil his March 1978 reelection. In January four major Jakarta dailies were suppressed for the manner in which they covered anti-government student demonstrations. The government also cracked down on student activities, stopping the operation of student councils. When the government closed four more newspapers and banned anti-Suharto literature, the intellectuals reacted. Fourteen of them, led by crusading journalist Mochtar Lubis, sent a public letter of protest to the government. Even so, Gaja Mada University in Jogjakarta was closed in February, after the distribution of leaflets originating there which called for protest marches.

In addition to silencing the opposition Suharto sought to regain his popularity with the masses, and erase the drab image of the New Order, by reviving the memory of Sukarno whom the people had idolized. Therefore immediately before the presidential selection in March, he let it be known that Sukarno's grave would be rebuilt "as a token of thanks for his services to the nation." It was rebuilt in marble and precious stones, a suitably costly memorial.

Suharto's Third Term   Suharto was chosen president and the popular Adam Malik vice president by the MPR on March 23, 1978. The armed forces thus illustrated anew their special socio-political role. As the most disciplined and cohesive of all political groups, the armed forces had risen to political power primarily because of the weakness of civilian political organizations. Ever pragmatic, as well as distrustful of political groups which sought to promote an exclusive ideological or religious cause, the armed forces, and GOLKAR which they dominated, were so much stronger than opposition groups that the latter melted away. No party opposed giving Suharto a new mandate; stu-

dent, press, intellectual and religious opposition went no further than
the rhetoric stage.

Suharto's "third development cabinet," appointed March 29, retained the technocrats and other ministerial veterans in key economic
and political posts, indicating that no basic change in state policy was
contemplated. For the first time no opposition members were included
in the cabinet list. As part of a structural reorganization three "super
ministers," each with coordinating authority over other ministers,
were appointed. In April Suharto vacated the powerful post of national
security chief, assigning it to his chief of staff, Admiral Sudomo.

Suharto's reelection was followed by a quiescent period in internal
politics. Muslim political factions and the Democratic Party withdrew
to lick their wounds after their inability to mount effective opposition.
But the president's increasingly close identification with the West and
western-type institutions (e.g. the Inter-Governmental Group on Indonesia, a consortium of 14 donor nations headed by the U.S. and Japan;
the World Bank and the International Monetary Fund), again become
a focus of criticism by 1979. The ultra nationalists linked the continuing
growth of economic disparty within the society to the western-oriented
technocrats whose economic initiatives created entrepreneurship
mainly among the narrowly based urban elite. The popular and dramatic, albeit inefficient, socialist initiatives of the Sukarno years,
designed to reduce inequalities, were recalled with nostalgia.

Suharto sought to placate his critics by releasing thousands of *tapols*
(political prisoners), bringing to 29,283 the number released during the
years 1978–1980. On the other hand in March 1980 he reiterated "the
determination of the New Order to make a total correction of deviation
from *Pancasila* [sic] and the 1945 constitution."[13] By emphasizing
pancha sila, the secular national ideology, as the means to bring about
a just and prosperous society, the president rejected a religious framework for the country. And in the same extemporaneous speech,
seemingly contradicting *pancha sila* tenets, he casually added socialism, nationalism and religion (to communism and Sukarno's brand of
social ideology) as philosophies detrimental to the well being of the
state. He also indicated that the army might have to support GOLKAR
in the elections scheduled for 1982. Thus he gratuitously managed to
upset nearly all elements of society. Three weeks later he lashed out
at personal criticism of himself and his wife, again identifying support
for *pancha sila* with support for himself.

Responding on May 13, a group of 50 respected statesmen delivered
an "expression of concern" to parliament, pointing out that *pancha
sila* was intended as an ideology to unite, not divide, the nation. They
also feared the political implications of army intervention in politics
and in the possibility of Suharto seeking a fourth term as president.

The parliamentarians had not long to wait for a response. On November 1, 1981 GOLKAR officially named Suharto as its candidate to serve a fourth five-year term as president of Indonesia.

The elections to the House of Representatives were held in May 1982. Amid charges of election fraud and campaign violence GOLKAR received 64 percent of the vote. The Muslim United party and the Democratic Party both lost seats. On March 11, 1983 the 920-member People's Consultative Assembly (MPR, now shortened to People's Congress), composed of members of parliament plus regional delegates and functional groups, reelected the president.

Suharto—a continuum Emboldened by his national popularity. President Suharto further institutionalized his interpretation of the *pancha sila* concept during his fourth term. A 1985 law required the two opposition political parties—the Christian-cum-nationalist Democratic Party (PDI) and the Islamic-based United Development Party (PPP), as well as all government-approved "mass organizations"—to accept the ruling GOLKAR's highly secular version of *pancha sila* as their sole ideological basis. Correct ideology thus became a condition for *organized* political participation. The PDI and the PPP amended their charters accordingly, but the conservative Nahdatul Ulama (NU), the largest Muslim faction within the PPP, abandoned its association with the party.

The controversial Political Parties law of 1985 was apparently designed to separate religion from politics. But it was also perceived among Muslim and Christian groups as an effort to weaken, if not emasculate, Islam and, by inference, any entity which did not reflect the *pancha sila* line. A series of state trials against Muslim defendants for allegedly subversive activities did indeed ensue during 1985, suggesting that the authorities perceived and were reacting to a growing radicalization of Islamic populism in consequence of the restrictive political parties legislation.

Suharto's successful initiatives, in effect imposing consensus politics, had borne fruit by the time of the 1987 elections. Conflict over religious/ideological issues had diminished and popular interest had shifted to pressing social and economic concerns. Moreover, voting took place in 1987 in a passive political environment and thus was marked by minimal physical confrontation.

Indonesia's five general elections since 1945, scholars note, have been mainly contests for parliamentary seats through which the government maintains its legitimacy, rather than catalysts for change as in western cultures. GOLKAR, assisted by the effective voter recruiting capability of the very large, self interested bureaucracy, won an overwhelming 73 percent of the ballots in 1987 compared with 64 percent in 1982. The PPP's share, reflecting Suharto's effort to secularize politics at the expense of the Muslims, fell to less than 16 percent, compared with almost 28 percent in 1982. The PDI, representing the only secular alternative to GOLKAR, received some 11 percent, up from about 8 percent in 1982. The newly elected members of the House of Representatives joined their appointed colleagues as part of the MPR which reelected President Suharto to his fifth five year term in March 1988.

ECONOMY

Serious imbalances in growth among various economic sectors continued to be a problem under Repelita II. The percentage of the national income going to workers in the traditional sectors of the economy, especially agriculture, declined; that of the extractive dollar-denominated exports, which commanded higher output, higher returns, and higher wages for a relatively small labor force, increased. The skewed distribution of income in Java brought about a decline in the per capita consumption of all basic food staples. Rising food costs hit hardest the urban poor whose income goes mainly to purchase food and who cannot grow their own.

Repelita III (1979–1983) was designed to promote *pribumi* small scale industry, equalize income distribution, move families outside crowded Java and increase food production and non-oil exports. But the fundamental problem remained: how to shift the benefits of the dollar-denominated export superstructure—oil and other primary commodities—into rural development. The government in November 1978 had devalued the *rupiah* by 33.4 percent. In so doing it permitted the rise in foreign exchange assets to "spill over" into the domestic economy, increasing the money supply and, in consequence, the rate of inflation. The relative prices of tradeable goods (rubber, coffee, palm oil, textiles and electronics) fell because prices of non-tradeable goods (services, rents and land) rose rapidly. Within the context of these developments Repelita III was scarcely a success.

Recession and Recovery   The advent of Repelita IV (1984–1988)— emphasizing industrial and agricultural projects as well as improvement in infrastructure, social services and human resource development— coincided with the worldwide collapse of petroleum prices in the early 1980s. Oil and natural gas exports had until then provided 64 percent of government income and 70 percent of foreign exchange.

A number of steps were taken to compensate for the loss of revenue. The government embraced fiscal austerity by practically abandoning Repelita IV targets in favor of stimulating consumer spending. The *rupiah* was devalued by 31 percent in September 1986 to provide price incentives for a shift of resources into tradeable goods. The short term result was sustained capital flight, arrested only by sharply higher interest rates which peaked at over 40 percent but also discouraged investment. The government then turned with positive results to relaxing a portion (removing impediments on the shipping sector, for example) of the extensive government controls it had inherited from the Sukarno era. Foreign investors responded favorably, their commitments in 1988 doubling the US$900 million of the preceding two years. Domestic manufacturers benefited from removal of import controls which gave them access to cheaper materials and components. Finally, increases in foreign aid, which supplies more than one third of the government's budgeted spending, enabled Indonesia to continue to service its mounting total foreign public and private debt, estimated in 1988 by the World Bank to be US$50 billion. The Inter-Governmental Group on Indonesia consortium's pledge of US$4 billion in 1988, and Japan's agreement to extend US$2.3 billion in new aid the same year, helped Indonesia avoid debt rescheduling despite a rising debt-service ratio of 40 percent.

Repelita V, emphasizing mundane but essential measures, was inaugurated in April 1989. It called for tighter auditing procedures, bigger penalties for tax avoidance and expansion of the tax register. The petrochemicals industry was budgeted to receive US$4.5 billion in joint venture investment, to be provided mainly by foreigners (principally Dutch, British, Japanese and German), in order to establish a strong non-oil manufacturing export base. Indonesian partners in the venture were expected primarily to provide goodwill, i.e., high level political connections.

Population Planning   Each Repelita plan has emphasized programs to reduce the annual rate of population growth to two percent or lower. Achievement of that goal by 1983 was predicted through Repelita III programs based upon the national number of acceptors, family planning clinics and educational programs. Official Indonesian estimates before the October 1980 census put the population size at about 142 million and the annual growth rate at about two percent. But according to the census the actual population in October 1980 was 147,383,074, showing a growth rate of 2.34 percent annually from 1971 to 1980. At the end of 1984 the population had risen to 162 million.

An "intensified effort" during Repelita IV was more successful. The U.S.-based Population Reference Bureau reported in 1988 that, although the population had risen to 177.4 million by 1987, the average annual growth rate from 1980 through 1987 declined to 1.7 percent. In recognition of the success, President Suharto was honored with the United Nations Population award at a 1989 ceremony in New York.[14]

Indonesia's unique policy of reducing population pressures by transmigration, i.e., migration of people out of heavily populated Java and

Bali to the less populated outer islands, became the largest voluntary resettlement program in the world. Some 500,000 families were resettled during the period 1969–1989 with loan funds from the World Bank. On a per capita basis, however, transmigration is highly expensive when compared with providing incentives, such as easy credit for small farmers, to discourage flight to urban areas where population pressures are greatest.

FOREIGN POLICY

Indonesia's relations with her ASEAN neighbors strengthened after U.S. withdrawal from Vietnam and the communist victories in Indochina, as ASEAN nations sought to enhance their mutual security through regional cooperation. Indonesia supported the ASEAN position on Indochinese refugees both before and after the Bali conference of February 1979, and also stood firm with ASEAN in opposition to the seating of the Vietnamese-backed Kampuchean regime at international conferences and in the United Nations.

Indonesia's stance toward the People's Republic of China in the post-Vietnam War years has been marked by increasing complexity. Chronic Indonesian fear of Chinese regional hegemony is compounded by the presence of a large Chinese minority, disliked because it has resisted assimilation into Indonesian society and because the Chinese have traditionally dominated finance and commerce. The attempted coup in 1965, led by the Communist Party of Indonesia in which ethnic Chinese were numerous, caused Indonesia to suspend diplomatic relations with the PRC in 1967 on suspicion that the PKI had PRC backing. However the Vietnamese invasion of Kampuchea in 1978 and military occupation of that country in 1979, importantly affected Indonesian policy. All ASEAN partners were united in the conviction that Soviet-supported Vietnam had become the immediate threat to regional stability. In the absence of any indication that Vietnam would entertain a political settlement in Kampuchea, Indonesia appeared to modify its stance toward China.

Largest of the six ASEAN countries, Indonesia has increasingly asserted its influence within the ASEAN compact since 1985. Its foreign ministry became ASEAN's designated "interlocutor" with Vietnam over the Kampuchean issue. In 1987 Indonesia encouraged its five partners to embrace policies for achieving reconciliation with Indochina. A significant component of Jakarta's leadership strategy was to take advantage of the PRC's desire for reestablishment of Sino-Indonesian diplomatic relations. In tempering its stance toward China, Indonesia backed away from its annual demand for Chinese admission of involvement in the 1965 coup. In return the Chinese tolerated

Indonesian reconciliation initiatives which disfavored the Khmer Rouge, the PRC's principal candidate for assumption of power in Kampuchea. In 1989 Indonesia declined to criticize the PRC government for its forcible suppression of the student movement.

Within the two year period, 1988–89, Indonesia, employing informal discussions techniques, brought together for the first time at a "cocktail party" in Indonesia its ASEAN partners, all four of the divisive Kampuchean factions, and Vietnam. The several cocktail party meetings—later termed Joint Informal Meetings (JIM)—provided perfect settings for Indonesia to employ the traditional village procedure of discussion (*musjawarah*) to reach consensus (*mufakat*). Since voting was not required and the sessions were informal albeit heated, they served as catalysts for subsequent broader formal agendas. By mid-1989 progress toward a political settlement in Kampuchea was clearly evident, thanks in part to Indonesian diplomacy.

WHITHER INDONESIA?

Indonesia, the largest Islamic nation and the fifth most populous country in the world, achieved remarkable recovery from the shocks of the Sukarno years. The nation's political stability is ensured by a pragmatic and assertive authoritarian regime.

Authoritarian political organization has been a hallmark of Indonesia throughout its history and is likely to continue. Its current expression, as stated by President Suharto in describing *pancha sila,* is a democracy that does not involve voting, or draw upon "western liberalism" or "communist authoritarianism." Indonesia's parliament (House of Representatives) is an elected body with no effective leverage over a strong executive. The latter sets policy for the military, bureaucracy and technocrats who, working as a triumvirate, appear to be as effective a governing elite as exists in any nation in contemporary Southeast Asia.

The historic ideal of *nusantara,* an Indonesian empire which includes the outer islands, was achieved with acquisition of West Irian and East Timor. Territorial expansion has created a contemporary Indonesia far larger than the former Netherlands East Indies. Further physical expansion is unlikely because it would bring the nation into confrontation with its ASEAN partners, Malaysia and Brunei.

By reason of its numerous advantages—enormous physical size, large and productive labor force, strategic geographic location and abundant natural resources—Indonesia will undoubtedly continue to build its leadership role within ASEAN and in Southeast Asia. The major problem facing the nation is that of adjusting its state-controlled economy—a legacy of the colonial culture system when the Netherlands Indies resembled a vast state-run plantation—to meet contemporary challenges posed by the successes of economic decentralization elsewhere in Asia. The large, under-performing state enterprises which dominate the Indonesian economy are no match for the thriving entrepreneurial economies of neighboring Singapore and Thailand.

FOOTNOTES

1. John Bastin and Harry J. Benda, *A History of Modern Southeast Asia* (Englewood Cliffs, N.J.: Prentice-Hall, Inc., 1968), p. 10.

2. John F. Cady, *Southeast Asia, Its Historical Development* (New York: McGraw Hill Book Co., 1964), p. 153.

3. Amry Vandenbosch, *The Dutch East Indies* (Berkeley: University of California Press, 1944), p. 74.

4. Written by Douwes Dekker, a former Dutch colonial official, under the *nom de plume* "Multatuli," meaning "one who has suffered."

5. Jeanne S. Mintz, *Indonesia: A Profile* (Princeton: D. Van Nostrand Co., 1961), p. 65.

6. Lea E. Williams, *Southeast Asia: A History* (N.Y.: Oxford University Press, 1976), p . 175.

7. See C.L.M. Penders, *The Life and Times of Sukarno* (Rutherford, N.J.: Fairleigh Dickinson University Press, 1974).

8. See George McTurnan Kahin, *Nationalism and Revolution in Indonesia* (Ithaca: Cornell University Press, 1952), p. 148–69.

9. *Penders, op. cit.*, p. 198, 201.

10. Donald W. Fryer and James C. Jackson, *Indonesia* (Boulder, Colo.: Westview, 1977), p. 86.

11. *Ibid.*, p. 99.

12. *Penders, op. cit.*, p. 190.

13. *Asia Yearbook* (Hong Kong: Far Eastern Economic Review Ltd.), 1981, p. 185–86.

14. "1988 World Population Data Sheet," *Population Reference Bureau Inc.*, (Washington).

Philippines

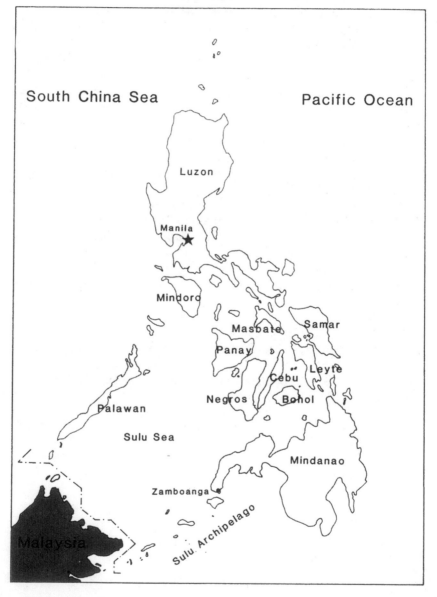

CHAPTER 11
PHILIPPINES

The Philippine archipelago comprises some 7,000 islands that extend 1,200 miles, from 22 degrees north latitude to within 5 degrees of the equator. The northernmost island is 65 miles southeast of Taiwan, and the southernmost 30 miles east of the tip of Borneo (Malaysia). The land surface is about one-sixth of the surrounding waters, straits and near-landlocked seas claimed by the present day Republic of the Philippines. Some 1,000 islands are fertile enough to support human habitation but only 11 are 1,000 or more miles square. Luzon, the northern anchor, accounts for more than one-third of the archipelago's total land area. Mindanao, second in size, forms the southern anchor. Between the two lie the eight major, but much smaller Visayas: Mindoro, Masbate, Samar, Panay, Leyte, Cebu, Bohol, and Negros. Palawan lies to the southwest as do the 800 islets of the Sulu subarchipelago.

The climate is tropical and monsoonal, and over much of its length the terrain is rugged and mountainous—especially along the eastern seaboard which faces thousands of miles of open Pacific Ocean, with a comparative absence of landfalls. However, the west coast, facing the South China sea, is dotted with bays and anchorages and was settled from earliest times.

The archipelago's earliest inhabitants were Negritos, pockets of whom survive today in mountainous parts of Luzon and elsewhere. They appear to have been pushed into the mountains by waves of Proto-Malay who began arriving by sea about 1500 B.C. These first Malay also became highlanders, interbreeding with the Negritos. Later migrations of Deutero-Malay from Borneo, the Moluccas and mainland Southeast Asia took place during the last 2,000 years. The Deutero-Malay, among whom the largest element are the Visayans of the central islands of the archipelago, came to constitute a majority of the inhabitants and developed a maritime-oriented culture. In a fundamental sense modern Indonesians, Malaysians and Filipinos are ethnic brothers.

PRE-SPANISH HISTORY

The Chinese traded with the Philippine islanders from the early centuries of the Christian era and in time developed more or less permanent merchant communities along the coasts. By the 12th century Chinese junks were bringing manufactures, including porcelain, to trade for pearls from Sulu, rare woods, cotton and medicinal plants. At the beginning of the Ming dynasty (1368–1644) the now permanent merchant communities were augmented by the presence of Chinese officials who were able to enforce an extraterritorial status for the Chinese settlements, and even to extract small amounts of tribute from the natives on the theory—soon abandoned—that the islands were tributaries of the Chinese empire. It is thus quite accurate to conclude that the Chinese have been an ingegral part of Philippine life for more than 1,000 years. Chinese blood is widespread among the modern Filipino population and ethnic Chinese-Filipinos are important in every aspect of national society.

Indian socio-religious influence on the archipelago derived from the Indianized Sumatran empire of Srivijaya which emerged as a powerful maritime nation in the second half of the 7th century, and from the Java-based empire of Majapahit in the 14th century. Both traded with and attempted to control parts of the archipelago. It was Islam, however, that produced the strongest and most lasting impact on the pre-Spanish inhabitants. Proceeding from Malacca through Sumatra and Java, Malay and Arab traders and evangelists established Islam in the Sulu islands by 1500, from thence it spread to the large island of Mindanao. The Muslims had the advantage of possessing firearms, a knowledge of science and warfare, more sophisticated art forms and a superior alphabet—all part of their Arabic heritage. By 1565 Islam had reached Luzon; only the arrival of the Spanish at the same time prevented Islamicization of the entire archipelago.

The lack of large settlements and centralized government distinguished the Philippines from the rest of the region at the time of European conquest, especially from mainland Southeast Asia, where large ethnic groups such as the Thai had migrated in sufficiently cohesive fashion that they were able to achieve and maintain a homogeneity of language and culture and develop a sense of national identity. By contrast, migration to the Philippines, with its hundreds of islands and thousands of miles of shoreline, was sporadic and by small groups of differing peoples. Except in the south where Muslim rajas ruled wide areas, few political units broader than the village *barangay* existed.

The *barangay*, the basic political unit of the pre-Spanish Philippines, was organized as an armed camp because security, from other tribal groups or from coastal pirates, was the foremost concern. Basically an enlarged family group, holding land in common and operating on communal principles, the *barangay* was led by an hereditary chief who, from Muslim times, was termed a *datu*. The *datu* was assisted by an elders' council which also judged criminal and civil infractions. The kinship orientation of the *barangay* was reinforced by religious practices which included ancestor worship. Behind the polytheism of spirit and ancestor worship, however, was a vague monotheism, a concept of a supreme being who was creator of the universe and who ruled all men, and a belief in an afterlife. These two ideas were to be a bridge between indigenous religion and the Christianity brought by the Spanish.

SPANISH CONQUEST AND RULE

Ferdinand Magellan, a Portuguese in the service of the Spanish throne, set foot on Samar Island March 16, 1521 after a long voyage across the Pacific in search of a western approach to the spice islands. Within a month he sailed west to Cebu where the local ruler and his chief subordinates accepted Christianity. Magellan was killed shortly thereafter when the Spaniards intervened in an inter-tribal skirmish. His essentially revictualing visit to the archipelago, however, subsequently became the basis for Spain's claim—by right of discovery—to the Philippines.

Spain and Portugal in 1529 signed the Treaty of Saragossa to delineate their respective spheres of interest among the new-found lands of the east. Although the San Lazaro Island Group, as the Philippines were initially named by Magellan, fell within the Portuguese sphere, the Spaniards, seeking access to the spice trade, mounted expeditions in 1526, 1527 and 1542 to establish a permanent colony there. None succeeded but in 1542 Ruy Lopez de Villalobos renamed the islands Las Filipinas in honor of Philip, the Spanish crown prince, and claimed them for Spain. Meanwhile Spanish desire for the Philippines increased. Voyages from Mexico to the archipelago confirmed the feasibility of trans-Pacific trade and, since Chinese ports were closed to Europeans, Spain perceived the islands as a point of transshipment of Chinese silks and Mexican silver. Moreover Philip, as Philip II, regarded the Philippines as fertile ground for the conversion of souls. He therefore commissioned a new expedition to the archipelago from New Spain (Mexico) in 1564 under the command of Admiral Miguel Lopez de Legaspi whom he also designated as governor of the territories he was to annex. With four ships and 400 men, including six priests, Legaspi reached Cebu in April 1565 where he established the first permanent Spanish settlement. His soldiers, meeting little resistance, extended Spanish dominion over the islands of Cebu, Leyte, Panay, Mindoro and central Luzon. In 1571 Legaspi transferred the administrative center of the colony to Manila, Luzon, taking possession of the town from resisting Muslims.

At the time Muslim influence in central and northern Luzon was superficial. Had Spanish penetration been attempted even a few decades later, it is doubtful that it would have succeeded. As it was, Muslim resistance in the south—a consequence partly of the strength of the indigenous rajas and of the cohesion generated by the religious-political commonality of Islam—proved too formidable for the Spanish.

Nature and Organization of Political Authority Unlike the Dutch and British, whose empires in Southeast Asia emerged from the activities of their East India trading companies, the Spanish from the beginning sought political control and territory in the cause of God and king. For governing the 500,000 Filipinos who had become their subjects the Spanish crown pieced together an administrative structure based upon Spanish civil law, institutions developed in New Spain, and traditional indigenous authority patterns. The indigenous *barangay* became the *visita,* later the barrio, the lowest administrative unit. The status of the *datu* was preserved by designating him *cabeza,* a hereditary position until 1786. *Cabezas* were charged with: 1) collecting an annual tax in the form of specie or goods, and levied as payment to the Spanish administration for services provided; 2) enforcing the *polo,* forced labor on public works; and 3) collecting the quotas of agricultural products and timber for compulsory sale to government supply stores, a form of extra-legal taxation. In return they were exempt from tribute and forced labor and were, as were the lower nobility in Spain, entitled to use the Spanish title "don."

The pueblo was a more extensive territorial unit than the barrio and the forerunner of the modern township. It consisted of a principal settlement to which the surrounding barrios were attached. The pueblo's chief magistrate, the *gobernadorcillo,* was appointed annually by the Spanish authorities from among popularly nominated candidates; it was the highest office to which a Filipino could aspire. The *gobernadorcillo* and other local officials, many elected, were responsible for enforcement of law in the villages and in the countryside. Tending to rotate the positions among themselves, they comprised an oligarchy which monopolized political office, and the system degenerated to caciquism, i.e., government by bosses who could dispense or withhold favors and who frequently indulged in graft. The legacy of caciquism, while affording extensive political experience at the local government level, helps explain the later tendency for Philippine political parties to coalesce around leaders rather than principles or issues.

From the provincial level upward the Spanish administrative system developed in Mexico was transferred in toto. By the end of the 16th century the archipelago was divided into 12 provinces, administered by Spanish officials who reported directly to Manila. They were responsible for military and judicial matters, maintenance of roads and public works, and assistance to missionaries. A few large pueblos, Manila foremost among them, were organized as cities and governed similarly. Unpacified areas were divided into districts and administered by politico-military officers.

The central government in Manila was headed by the crown-appointed governor general whose broad executive, military, judicial and religious powers included the conduct of foreign relations with Asian rulers—a latitude permitted because Spain was half a world distant. The Royal Audiencia, used in Spanish overseas dominions, combined the role of supreme court with executive authority and policy making. The *audiencia* protected the rights of the state against encroachment by the clergy and reviewed acts of government to safeguard the people. The *fiscal,* or crown attorney of the *audiencia,* was charged with defending the indigenous population without fee. The *audiencia* also insured that the unique *residencia* requirement was met. *Residencia* stipulated that the governor general and other principal officials must remain in the colony for a designated period following completion of their terms in office, to answer complaints and grievances arising from their service. In Manila the governor general chaired the *audiencia;* its members included four or more senior justices, an attorney general and other officials.

The government in Manila was accountable to the viceroy in New Spain. Authority over all Spanish colonies was delegated by the crown to the Royal Council of the Indies in Madrid. Although the number of Spaniards located outside Manila was minimal, the government established military garrisons at strategic points and managed to unify hundreds of island units—except in the Muslim areas of Mindanao, Palawan and the Sulu archipelago where the Moros (from Moors, the Muslims whom the Spanish had finally expelled from Spain in 1492) continued to repulse the Spanish for 250 years.

Several factors contributed to the stability of the political system. First, the indigenous rural upper class was coopted into the colonial establishment by the authorities and provided a vital link between Spanish administration and the village populations. Second, a landed aristocracy supportive of the regime evolved. Borrowing a device used in Mexico, the colonial administration divided the colony and the population into land areas *(encomiendas)* for the twin purposes of collecting tribute and protecting religious converts. The tracts usually comprised several barrios and were originally assigned for limited periods to religious orders, charitable groups (e.g., hospitals) and individual Spaniards (e.g., to military personnel in lieu of cash pensions). Extension of the grant periods was achieved by various subterfuges. And third, temporal authority was buttressed and paralleled by religious authority in the form of two clerical hierarchies, the secular priesthood and the orders.

The Spanish crown entrusted the missionary task of Christianizing the Filipinos to five powerful religious orders which quickly established themselves in the islands—Augustinians (1565), Discalced Franciscans (1578), Jesuits (1581), Dominicans (1587) and Augustinian Recollects (1606). In addition a hierarchy of secular clergy, headed by an archbishop, constituted the parish clergy in the established Christian communities. Of the two, the missionary clergy of the religious orders were the most crucial to Spanish control. Thus, for the overwhelming majority of Filipinos these priests were the fount of both spiritual and temporal authority, as well as the only persons to whom they could turn when harassed by the government's petty officials and tax gatherers.

External Affairs   From the beginning the Spanish colony of the Philippines was beset by threats from European and Asian powers with interests in the region. Legaspi had to fend off Portuguese attacks in 1568 and 1570, but Portuguese hostility ebbed after the political union of Portugal and Spain in 1580. In the meantime Chinese and Japanese harassment arose. Overshadowing these events was rising Spanish-Dutch competition. The Dutch, bent on trade expansion, began naval and land onslaughts to displace the Spaniards, both in Philippine waters and in the Moluccas where the Spanish, intervening from their base at Zamboanga on Mindanao, had come to the aid of the Portuguese. For some 50 years the Dutch supplied arms to the Moros, tried repeatedly to capture Manila and intercepted the Mexico-Manila galleons. Dutch hostility waned after the signing of the 1648 Treaty of Munster by Spain and the Netherlands, and Spanish garrisons were withdrawn both from the Moluccas and Zamboanga. The Dutch won the war of the spices, but the Spanish retained the Philippines. The colony thenceforth became increasingly isolated from the mainstream of competition among the European powers in the region, save for the 20-month occupation of Manila (1762–1764) by the British, a spinoff from the Seven Years War in Europe.

Internal Political Developments   Although historians are wont to characterize the first 200 years of the Spanish colonial period as "inert"—a time of slow social change—internal developments during that period provide important clues for understanding contemporary Philippine society.

While control over, and colonization of, the maritime areas of the northern and central portions of the archipelago had been achieved quickly and with minimum difficulty, further expansion and political integration were seriously impeded by the implacable opposition of the Moros of the south, by the resistance to assimilation of the mountain peoples of Luzon, and by periodic efforts of groups within the Christianized areas to overthrow Spanish hegemony.

Moro rejection of Hispanization was the most crucial and enduring threat to internal stability. The factors which unified the Moros against Spain were the traditional antagonism between the Crescent and the Cross, and the strength of the politico-religious-military authority embodied in the rajas and sultans, some of whom were powerful enough to gain international recognition. The Spanish were unable to break Moro resistance even though in 1637 and 1638, respectively, they captured the Moro citadel on Mindanao and Moro headquarters on the island of Jolo in the Sulu archipelagao. Instead for the next century Spain was reduced to founding coastal garrisons to protect the central Visayan Islands from constant Moro raids.

It was not until 1718 that Spain was able to reoccupy Zamboanga and 1744 that the sultan of Jolo agreed to permit Catholicism within his domains. However Spain's military prestige was so shattered by the British occupation of Manila two decades later that Moro depredations intensified for the remainder of the century. Modern arms and the steamship finally brought about acceptance of Spanish sovereignty by the sultan of Sulu in 1878 and pacification—but not assimilation—of the Moros began.

The hostility and alienation of the mountain people of Luzon was a similar problem. Military expeditions to pacify them repeatedly failed, primarily because the highlanders had been resisting intrusions by lowlanders for centuries. The Spanish were no different to them than previous encroachers. Although the prospect of significant gold deposits in the mountains was a powerful added incentive, the Spanish lacked the military personnel necessary to cope with the inhospitable mountain terrain. The colonial authorities therefore settled for a buffer zone, a neutral ground where limited trade took place, where lowland products of hogs, salt, iron and cloth were exchanged for gold, wax and cacao from the highlands. The Negritos, in isolated pockets, remained entirely outside the perimeters of Spanish influence.

In the settled areas five major revolts and a number of lesser outbreaks occurred from the mid-17th to mid-18th centuries. These were suppressed with relative ease because the cohesion of the rebels depended entirely on kinship and local paternalistic leadership. Although some of the leaders of these early revolts have since been elevated to the status of national heroes (in particular Diego Silang and his wife, "the Ilocano Joan of Arc"), in reality, "it took two hundred and fifty years of the *pax hispanica* before a Philippine national consciousness could become articulate."[1]

Clerical Politics The Papacy had specifically entrusted the administration of the new Church of the Indies to the Spanish crown, thus uniting church and state. The archbishop in Manila was second in authority only to the governor general. Although the interlocking relationship between church and state seemed ideal, it proved incapable of evolving a satisfactory division of authority between the clerical and civil hierarchies. At best the roles overlapped since, besides spreading Christianity, missionaries were the major vehicle for spreading Spanish sovereignty; at worst the civilian governors saw the ecclesiastics as usurping their powers. The authority of the archbishop reached its zenith in the early 18th century when for a period the clergy almost eclipsed the bureaucracy.

Intense as it was, the conflict between government and religious personnel was exceeded in its impact on Philippine politics by the continuing struggle within the religious community between the orders and the archbishop over the control of the country's parishes. Control of the spiritual life of the parishes, most of which were administered by the friars (orders), equated with temporal power. The civil authorities, recognizing that the maintenance of Spanish authority in the provinces depended upon the friars, acquiesced in 1776 to the de facto independence of the orders from the archbishopric.

In the meantime the controversy assumed greater political significance because the orders declined to extend ordination to Filipinos (except in rare cases) for fear of compromising their elite status; they viewed the Filipino as inferior. The problem came to a head following the expulsion of the Jesuits from the country in 1768, due to European politics rather than events in the Philippines. Parish vacancies were filled by the archbishop and governor general with Filipino secular priests. Unfortunately some of the seculars lacked the degree of literacy and training required for positions of authority. This action unleashed the fury of the friars and buttressed their rationalization that Filipinos were unsuited for the responsibilities of priesthood and authority. Soon the *status quo ante* was restored, with the friars returning to the parishes and the Filipino priests reduced to serving as their assistants. But the racist aspect that had been injected into the controversy became one of the driving forces of Filipino nationalism in the 19th century.

Economy In the early 17th century the Spanish lacked access to the spice trade and had few exportable agricultural or mineral products. Business thus was limited primarily to the exchange of silver from Mexico for luxury products from the East. Initially the galleon fleet (belonging to the crown) brought prosperity to Manila, but the trade flew in the face of mercantilist economic theory: silver was being drained from the Spanish American colonies to Asia, rather than being sent to Spain, and the flood of Chinese silks was adversely affecting the Spanish textile industry. However efforts by Spain to limit specie outflow and textile inflow were mainly unsuccessful. For their part the merchants, on whose financial health the colony increasingly depended, were subjected to great risks. Ships were lost to typhoons, English freebooters and the British navy, and British smuggling undermined the official trade monopoly. The colony was unable to pay its way and required an annual subsidy.

Attempts to reform the economy were initiated by Governor General Jose de Basco y Vargas in 1781. Agricultural production—that had been neglected during the heyday of the galleon trade—increased and export crops such as tobacco, indigo, cotton, sugar, hemp and copra were encouraged. As commercial export agriculture became a reality, the prospect of profit enormously enhanced the desirability of acquiring land. Eventually Filipinos and Mestizos (children of Chinese or Spanish fathers from whom they inherited business acumen, and Filipina mothers who afforded them ethnic legitimacy) acquired the bulk of the agricultural land. This new rural aristocracy far outnumbered, and far exceeded in their holdings, the Spanish landlords, among whom the ecclesiastical orders constituted the largest segment. The indigenous landholders became the leading families—subsequently termed *ilustrados*—amassing fortunes and eventually displacing the traditional leadership based upon heredity. They also developed and perpetuated a sharecropping system that increasingly forced Filipino peasants into permanent debt peonage.

Coincident with the new emphasis on agriculture, the government set up a tobacco monopoly and a trade monopoly (the Royal Company of the Philippines), both of which were immediately profitable. The Philippines became the largest tobacco producer in the East and the profits of the Royal Company were invested in other export commodities—spices, silk and sugar.

To expedite trade in these products the port of Manila was opened in 1789 to all ships trading in the Asian market. But the move was only marginally successful, as was an earlier effort to develop direct trade between Manila and Spain. Disintegration of Spain's American empire, which began in the first decade of the 19th century, precipitated the end of the galleon trade in the second, and the decline of Manila as an entrepot. The Royal Company became ineffective and was dissolved in 1834. Private trading was authorized—although strict anti-foreign laws remained in effect—and a new wave of commercially-oriented Spaniards succeeded in raising trading volumes for a brief period. British and American ships for the first time began to outnumber Chinese and

Spanish ships in Philippine ports. However the Treaty of Nanking in 1842 between China and Britain put an end to this brief upturn in trade. Under its terms five Chinese ports were opened to foreign shippers, eliminating any need to call at Manila. Trade therefore languished anew and only the profitable export of tobacco slowed the colony's drift toward insolvency.

POLITICAL INDICATORS

1. The geographical isolation of the Philippines—on the periphery of Southeast Asia—minimized contact between its people and the more advanced political cultures of the region during the pre-Hispanic era.
2. Absence of ethnic and cultural homogeneity facilitated the almost bloodless Spanish conquest of the northern and central Philippines, but a major struggle developed in the south between Christianity and Islam, reaching a stalemate and impeding assimilation ever since.
3. The church-state relationship, that conferred upon the missionaries of the religious orders the double task of religious and political proselytization, helped to make possible the conquest and assimilation of the Philippines and insured that that nation became the sole Christianized culture of East and Southeast Asia.
4. Geographical fragmentation and kinship politics tended to perpetuate decentralization. In consequence the Filipinos accumulated considerable experience in local government.
5. Spanish rule through indigenous chieftains and *gobernadorcillos* increased the incidence of caciquism (rule by bosses), a phenomenon that became a permanent feature of Filipino politics.
6. A Filipino rural upper class, frequently of Malay-Chinese ethnicity, arose with the introduction of private property, combining wealth and high status, and replacing the hereditary elite.
7. Because Spain was a loser in the competition among European powers for domination and influence in greater Asia, the Spanish Philippines remained isolated from mainstream international politics until the 19th century.
8. The colony's internal development was impeded by failure to assimilate the mountain peoples and the Moros, by frequent rebellions, by divisive clerical politics and originally by neglect of the agricultural economy, all problems that can be seen in various guises today.

ANTI-SPANISH NATIONALISM

Just as missionary education, offered in the Spanish language, established western culture more firmly in the Philippines than elsewhere in Southeast Asia, so too did it instill modern European nationalist ideas. Ironically the Philippines, the least unified region in pre-European Southeast Asia, became the first colony to rebel against the metropolitan power and demand national statehood.

The first stirring of Philippine nationalism can be traced to 1841 when Father Opolinario de la Cruz led the struggle of the indigenous clergy against the European friars, founding his own religious order, the Colorum, because he had been denied admission to a regular order. Anti-Spanish and anti-Mestizo, it included pre-Hispanic messianic values. Opolinario's unorthodoxy resulted in his being hunted down and killed by Spanish soldiers, thus becoming the first Filipino martyr. In protest the indigenous clergy in 1843 began a series of rebellions, often using the Colorum name. Their resentment against the racism of the regular orders was paralleled by the deep discontent among the landless peasants in Luzon who blamed their debt peonage on friar landlords. This popular reaction against Europeans, their institutions and practices, included resentment of European-educated Filipinos, the *ilustrado* class of prosperous leading families and landholders. In another rebellion, this time by soldiers at the Cavite arsenal near Manila in 1872, three Filipino priests, fathers Burgos, Gomez and Zamora, were executed and their names added to the growing list of nationalist priest-martyrs.

The major Philippine nationalist figure of the 19th and 20th centuries, however, was Jose Rizal-Mercado y Alonso (1861–1896). A Chinese-Spanish Mestizo educated in the Philippines, Rizal subsequently studied philosophy and medicine in Spain. His novel, *Noli Me Tangere* (Touch Me Not) of 1887 was a social commentary that quickly assumed political import. It was followed by *El Filibusterismo* (The Reign of Greed). Both were written and published abroad.

Although in Europe Rizal was associated with Marcelo H. del Pilar, founder of the Philippine separatist movement, he never espoused that philosophy. On his return to his homeland he founded instead a reformist society (La Liga Filipina). For this he was exiled by the colonial government to northern Mindanao. While there he was courted by revolutionary nationalists Andres Bonifacio and Emilio Jacinto who had organized the Katipunan, a society to overthrow the Spanish regime by force and unite all Filipinos into a national state. Rizal specifically disassociated himself from Katipunan objectives, but when the Katipunan insurrection erupted in August 1896, he was arrested, tried and executed for "rebellion, sedition and illegal association." His death on December 30, 1896 inflamed popular feelings.

The insurrection of August was precipitated by the fact that Katipunan plans (which included the murder of all Spaniards) had fallen into the hands of the authorities. When the government tried to arrest him, Bonifacio issued a call to revolt. Fighting erupted on the outskirts of Manila, and especially in the adjacent province of Cavite which became the center of the rebellion. The forces of Emilio Aguinaldo, a Cavite official turned military leader, were defeated by December. Nevertheless the following March the revolutionaries regrouped and established a revolutionary government to succeed the Katipunan. They chose Aguinaldo as president of the newly declared Philippine Republic, over Bonifacio who then attempted to form a government in opposition, but was captured, tried and executed by Aguinaldo's forces. In November 1897, in the tiny mountain town of Biaknabato in Bulukan Province to which they had been forced to retreat, the nationalists proclaimed a provisional constitution. Increasing military pressure, however, soon impelled Aguinaldo and his chief associates to agree to exile in Hong Kong in exchange for a general amnesty for their men and a cash payment. With 25 of his lieutenants Aguinaldo thereupon sailed for China at the end of December, and the remaining rebels surrendered to the Spanish. Neither side would wholly live up to its agreements.

AMERICAN ANNEXATION AND RULE

On February 15, 1898 the United States battleship *Maine* suffered a devastating on-board explosion while anchored at Havana, Cuba, a Spanish colony, also in revolt, half a world away. The vessel was destroyed and Spain was the suspected culprit. "Remember the *Maine*" became a battle cry. During the next two months the United States tried high-handedly to pressure Spain into granting Cuba independence. The Spanish answer was to declare war on the U.S. on April 24th. In retaliation the U.S. ordered Commodore George Dewey, commander of the U.S. Asiatic Squadron anchored in Hong Kong harbor, to destroy the Spanish fleet at Manila Bay. On May 1 Dewey entered the bay and sank or damaged the 12 Spanish war vessels found there. While awaiting arrival of the necessary American ground forces to attack the Spanish on land, he brought Aguinaldo back to Manila in an American ship, enlisted his help against the Spanish and supplied him with weapons.

Philippine nationalist fervor revived, with the Filipinos under the impression they were fighting for political freedom, although Dewey later insisted he had made no such promises. This time the rebels were joined by the heretofore cautious *ilustrados*. On June 12, 1898 the Filipinos proclaimed their independence in Cavite and on September 9 established a provisional capital at nearby Malolos where a revolutionary congress met to draft the first republican constitution in Asia. Under the terms of the Malolos Constitution, approved by the congress on November 29, an elected assembly would choose the president, thus subordinating the executive to the legislature. The constitution also provided for a permanent commission, chosen from among assembly delegates, to whom authority would be delegated when the assembly was not in session. Aguinaldo was chosen president by the assembly on December 23, and the constitution was promulgated January 21, 1899. On January 23 the second Republic of the Philippines was proclaimed.

The reinforcements Dewey had requested began to arrive in July 1898. In August the new Spanish governor general, Fermin Jaudenes, secretly arranged to surrender Manila to the Americans after a mock battle, rather than to the Filipino revolutionary forces surrounding the city. On the same day Madrid and Washington agreed to negotiate a peace settlement; President William McKinley's order directing cessation of military operations arrived in Manila three days after the city surrendered.

Aguinaldo's confidence in the Americans was justifiably shaken, although he complied with an American request to withdraw his forces beyond Manila's suburbs. Peace negotiations between Spain and the U.S. began in Paris in the fall, with the two nations signing the Treaty of Paris on December 10, 1898. The treaty ceded the Philippines, Guam and Puerto Rico to the United States in return for a payment to Spain of US$20 million. McKinley had concluded—as he said "with the help of divine guidance"—that the Filipinos were unfit for self government and that United States departure from the archipelago would invite indigenous misrule at best, or anarchy leading to European intervention at worst. McKinley's Benevolent Assimilation Proclamation of late December set forth an American trusteeship policy under which the islands would be occupied and a military government established, pending recommendations of a commission to determine their future status.

On February 4, 1899 hostilities broke out between the revolutionaries and the American forces and Aguinaldo issued a proclamation of war. On February 6 the U.S. Senate consented to the Treaty of Paris by a single vote margin. The American military thereupon began a full scale pacification campaign against the revolutionary government, capturing Malolos on March 31. In August American sovereignty was acknowledged in an agreement between the United States and the sultan of Jolo which neutralized the Muslim military threat for the time being.

However hostilities between the U.S. forces and the revolutionaries did not officially end until after Aguinaldo was captured on March 23, 1901—two years later. In the interim *ilustrado* and intellectual support for the revolution had largely evaporated. Apolinario Mabini, the passionate nationalist, had been gradually pushed to the sidelines of republican politics, his previously commanding influence being replaced by that of moderates who accepted the autonomy promise of the Americans. Aguinaldo himself took the oath of allegiance to the United States after his capture and received in return a U.S. pension.

Quelling the "Philippine Insurrection," however, required another four years of organized military operations and almost a decade of flushing out Filipino guerrillas. The Moros, in spite of the Jolo agreement, were even more difficult to pacify. Repeated military campaigns in the newly designated "Moro Province" were necessary, beginning under the military governorship of the province of General Leonard Wood in 1903 and lasting through that of General John J. Pershing in 1913.

Taft Era: 1900–1913   In April 1900 a five-man civilian commission headed by Judge William Howard Taft arrived in Manila empowered to act with executive authority in preparing the Philippines for the transition from military to civilian government. The commission succeeded the military government on July 4, 1901 and immediately began vigorous efforts to carry out proposals of the earlier Schurman Commission. The proposals called for the development of self government, land reform, better utilization of natural resources, recruitment of American specialists for chief administrative posts, and an extensive system of public instruction. At the same time the commission sought to adhere closely to President McKinley's instructions that "the measures adopted should be made to conform to their [Filipino] customs, their habits and even their prejudices."

In the Organic Act of 1902 the U.S. Congress set forth more specific political arrangements for the Philippines. The act guaranteed civil liberties, provided for a future national legislature and significantly strengthened the position of the commission, which as early as 1901 had three Filipino members. An American-type Supreme Court was devised and a Filipino became its first chief justice. The act also provided two non-voting seats in the U.S. Congress for the Philippines. Local elections were held under terms of the act in 1903 and elections to the legislature in 1907. Introduction of electoral and representative political forms spurred the organization of Philippine political groups and the Progressive Party quickly emerged as one whose goal was eventual independence within the American system; the faction which became the Nacionalista Party advocated immediate independence.

From the beginning the Taft Commission paid particular attention to education and public health. It took the initiative in providing universal free and secular education at the primary level by recruiting over 600 American teachers, 560 of whom arrived aboard the *S.S. Thomas* on August 21, 1901. Known henceforth as the Thomasites from their ship of passage, these teachers lived in towns and villages throughout the archipelago. Their pervasive influence was a major reason that English became the lingua franca of the islands and that the Filipinos were loyal to the United States during World War II.

An equally important contribution of the Taft years was the creation of a public health service—with a resultant dramatic improvement in health.[2] Taft also established uniform codes of law based upon Spanish civil law, at the same time respecting customary Moro law. He disestablished the church and purchased substantial amounts of church lands, and established the bureaus of agriculture, water, forest, education, printing and customs. Recalled to Washington to become secretary of war in 1904, he nevertheless, in effect, continued to govern the Philippines.

Taft was succeeded by fellow commissioner Luke E. Wright with whom he had worked closely during his years in Manila. Wright was the first American to have the title of governor general. During the tenure of James C. Smith (1906–1909), Taft's personal choice as governor general, an 80-member National Assembly came into being (1907) as the lower house of a bicameral legislature. The commission sat as the upper house. The governor general retained executive authority, and the commission became his cabinet, with several members, including a Filipino (1908), serving as heads of executive departments. The cabinet-upper house and the elected assembly could veto each other's legislative proposals. Taft journeyed to the Philippines to open the first session of the assembly (whose Speaker was Sergio Osmena), and committed the United States to eventual Philippine independence.

The basic pattern of economic relationship between the United States and the Philippines was determined by the Payne-Aldrich Act of 1909 which granted Philippine products privileged access to the American market on a quota basis, and assured United States exports to the Philippines of duty-free status. This hastened American investment in the Philippines in export industries—sugar, tobacco, lumber, vegetable oil and hemp. In 1913 the Underwood-Simmons Tariff Act equalized and intensified the relationship by abolishing quota limitations and all duties on Philippine exports to the United States. While the U.S.-Philippine free trade environment enormously benefited both American and Filipino companies, it also linked the Philippine economy so closely to the U.S. that other foreign markets were neglected. Economic dependence resulted, a phenomenon that has plagued the two nations' relationship ever since.

Harrison: 1913–1921   Francis Burton Harrison, who served as governor during the presidency of Woodrow Wilson, adopted a policy of accelerated Filipinization. Filipino membership on the commission was increased to a majority and the civil service list of Americans fell from 29 percent in 1913 to four percent by 1920. During Harrison's administration the important Jones Act of 1916 transformed the legislature into a genuine bicameral body. The commission as such was abolished, although a cabinet made up of department heads was retained. The governmental reorganization called for a Senate of 22 elected members, with two members appointed by the governor general to represent the minority peoples. The National Assembly became the House of Representatives; here seven seats were reserved for appointed minority representation. Supreme executive authority was retained by the governor general who could veto legislation, with ultimate veto power reserved for the United States Congress. The governor general and the chief justice continued to be appointed by the American president, with the advice of the U.S. Senate.

The Jones Act specifically reiterated the intention of the United States to recognize Philippine independence as soon as stable and representative government was established. In the interim it called for as extensive control as feasible by Filipinos of the conduct of domestic affairs. Harrison liberally interpreted the intent of the act. He reasoned that the ability of Filipinos to manage their own affairs could best be demonstrated by rapidly transferring responsibilities to them, despite the probability of an initial cost in efficiency arising from their inexperience. Thus Harrison gave the Senate a voice in approving all cabinet appointments, used his veto sparingly (five times in seven years) and permitted a significant degree of legislative oversight of the operations of the executive agencies. In 1918, at the urging of Speaker Osmena, he created an advisory Council of State—namely the cabinet plus the presiding officers of both legislative chambers.

Difficulties soon arose, however, in connection with the Philippine National Bank. Large unsecured loans made by the bank's new *ilustrado* directors went to cacique familes to build sugar mills rather than to industrial development, and some US$124 million was never repaid. The Manila Railroad Company, funded by the bank became insolvent. The malaise extended to the judiciary whose courts of first instance— devoid of trained Americans—amassed a backlog of 50,000 cases. Land distribution to the peasants on easy terms ceased because the cacique-dominated legislature abolished the land registration system, and only the large landowners prospered from the World War I demand for sugar, hemp, minerals and timber.

Republican Administrations   In 1921 the new Harding administration in Washington sent General Leonard Wood, former military governor of the Moro Province, and ex-governor general Cameron Forbes to investigate. Their commission of inquiry concluded that Harrison had exceeded the latitude intended by the Jones Act with his rapid Filipinization and that the attendant governmental "instability" clearly called for extended, rather than shortened, Filipino apprenticeship. Wood was appointed governor general (1921–1927) and proceeded to take a much narrower view of the prerogatives of the Philippine legislature than had his predecessor. He used his veto against legislative enactments 126 times in his six years. Already frustrated because the Jones Act provided no definite date for independence, Filipino political leaders reacted strongly against Wood's policies. Speaker of the House Manuel Roxas, President of the Senate Manuel Quezon and all Filipino department heads resigned in protest from the Council of State in 1923. Wood entrusted the duties of the latter to undersecretaries and military personnel. The disaffected Filipino leaders thereupon took their case to Washington, intensifying their already formidable lobbying.

Upon Wood's sudden death his successor Henry L. Stimson (1927–1929), a statesman and diplomat, proceeded with tact and caution and gradually won back the confidence of the Filipino leadership. He defined the governor general's role as that solely of an administrator, and declined to become involved in the question of independence. During Herbert Hoover's presidency (1929–1933), marked chiefly by worldwide depression, sympathy for the independence movement gained considerable headway in the United States, fueled primarily by economic considerations. The depression increased outcries of American sugar, vegetable oil and cordage producers against free entry of similar products from the Philippines; American trade unions complained of the inroads of Filipino immigrants in the American job market, and isolationists in congress and elsewhere demanded abandonment of American overseas security commitments. Filipino politicians saw their chance. In addition to the annual resolution of the Philippine legislature stating Philippine desire and capacity to be independent, Filipino lobbyists increased their activity in Washington. Beginning in 1929 when a Philippines independence resolution attached to a tariff act barely failed of passage, lobbyists successfully persuaded members of the U.S. Congress to introduce 11 proposals in four years calling for Philippine independence.

In 1932 Osmena and Roxas, heading a Philippine independence mission, achieved progress when congress for the first time set a date for Philippine independence. The Hare-Hawes-Cutting Act of that year—passed over President Hoover's veto—provided for independence after a 10-year transition period, with retention by the U.S. of military reservations in the islands, continuation of both American and Philippine trade preferences, and restrictions on Filipino immigration to the United States. Osmena and Roxas returned to Manila in triumph but quickly learned that Senate President Quezon refused to be up-staged. He broke with Osmena and rallied enough support against the provision for retention of military facilities to stall a vote on approval of the plan as the act required.

COMMONWEALTH

In June 1933 President Franklin Roosevelt appointed as governor general Frank Murphy, a strong advocate of independence. Murphy's excellent rapport with Quezon in Manila, and Senator Millard Tydings' persuasive political skill in Washington, produced the acceptable Tyd-ings-McDuffie (Philippines Independence) Act of 1934—termed a com-promise but actually almost a duplicate of the plan to which Quezon had objected. The Tydings-McDuffie Act provided for a Common-wealth of the Philippines, to be inaugurated July 4, 1936, which would be based upon a constitution that would be drafted by a 200-member popularly elected convention. The act required that the constitution create a republican form of government and contain a bill of rights. The American president retained authority to approve amendments to the constitution. Foreign affairs and defense continued to be U.S. prerogatives. The 300,000 acres of U.S. Army installations were to revert to the Philippines when complete independence was achieved and the question of American naval facilities was finessed, to be dealt with subsequently. At the conclusion of a 10-year transition period the independent Republic of the Philippines would be inaugurated—July 4, 1946.

A constitutional convention in Manila drew up a constitution that was ratified by a national plebescite May 14, 1935. The document closely followed the American model, providing for separate and balanced powers among the executive, legislative and judicial branches. Two unique features—a unicameral legislature and a single six year presidential term—were eliminated by amendment in 1940. Quezon and Osmena of the Nacionalista Party, their rift healed, were elected as president and vice president, respectively, in September, and the constitution became operative on November 15, 1935 by proclamation of President Roosevelt. Murphy became United States High Commissioner, moving his office from Malacanang Palace to make way for the new chief of state.

Quezon-Osmena Administration Politics in the Philippines from the year of the first elected Philippine assembly through World War II were dominated by Quezon and Osmena. Quezon, a Spanish-Malayan mestizo who combined "personal charm, arrogance and political skill,"[3] was a patrician of the landowning class—wealthy, a lawyer, a patriot, and an admirer of American ways—adjectives that might rightly describe a number of his political colleagues as well. He was the majority floor leader of the 1907 assembly, resident commissioner to the United States and president of the Philippine Senate. His politics centered in ceaseless campaigning for early independence and in negotiating with members of the U.S. Congress in pursuit of that goal. He was a good organizer, assumed responsibility easily and demonstrated high firmness of purpose. He was also known as a champion of the common man, the Philippine *pinoy*. Sergio Osmena, a Chinese-Malayan mestizo, combined personal integrity, patriotism and religious morality. Also of wealthy background, Osmena was an expert in parliamentary procedure, a skill arising from his extensive experience as speaker of the lower house. He proved adept at articulating the main themes of Filipino political demands.

The Quezon-Osmena administration, employing suddenly available monies from U.S.-refunded tax proceeds on sugar and coconut oil, embarked upon an extensive "social justice" program. The program was designed to reduce rural unrest which had its roots in peasant landlessness—a condition which had grown as large scale production for export had led to ever greater concentration of land in the hands of the few and the ever increasing tenancy of the many. Widespread landlessness, in turn, had provided radical reformers an issue to exploit.

Marxist political and economic thought reached the Philippines in the mid-1920s after a Filipino delegation attended a labor conference in Moscow at the invitation of the Soviet government. Upon its return, the Society of Workers of the Philippines was founded to agitate against landlords and debt peonage. The society was most active in central Luzon—the traditional center of peasant unrest. Thus it was at this time that the Philippine Communist Party (PKP) emerged. The party was outlawed in 1931, but membership grew during the decade as the movement was increasingly supported by intellectuals as well as peasants. Communist-organized assaults prompted some landlords to maintain private armies for protection. Unfortunately, the Quezon social program failed to reverse the trend and, disappointingly, the president began to centralize power in his own hands.

Paul V. McNutt (1936–1939), who succeeded Murphy as high commissioner soon after the Commonwealth was established, had doubts as to the wisdom of complete Philippine independence. He felt it would be a mistake for both countries on the grounds that their mutual economic and political interests would be better served if they were joined. The upsurge in the value of Philippine gold after devaluation of the American dollar may have influenced McNutt, but he was also concerned that full application of American tariffs might ruin the Philippine economy. He was also worried about the possible consequences of American withdrawal from Asia in view of the expansion of Japanese militarism. Quezon was equally concerned about the planned termination of the profitable customs union with the U.S. A Joint Preparatory Committee on Philippine Affairs (six Americans and six Filipinos) recommended in 1938 that tariff preferences for Philippine exports to the United States be extended beyond 1946 to 1960, but the proposal was not acted upon.

The last American high commissioner to the Philippines, Francis B. Sayre (1939–1942) was sent to prepare the Philippines for final independence. Instead he and much of Quezon's government were to flee the invading Japanese in early 1942; the peaceful evolution toward Philippine autonomy was shattered by war.

Japanese Occupation Japan's military and political expansion in China during the 1930s, and its goal of a greater East Asia Co-Prosperity Sphere, had long frightened the Commonwealth government. Quezon introduced compulsory military service early in his presidency and persuaded Major General Douglas MacArthur—who was sent as U.S. military adviser to organize the islands' defenses in 1935—to remain on as a field marshal in the Philippine commonwealth army after his retirement from the U.S. army at the end of 1937. In the meantime MacArthur began building a defense against expected Japanese attack. In 1941, as war clouds deepened, MacArthur was recalled to active duty in the U.S. army as commander of the U.S. Forces in the Far East, a force comprising U.S. army units in the Philippines and Philippine regular and reserve forces that were incorporated into the U.S. Army. On November 4 Quezon and Osmena were reelected.

The Japanese, operating from Taiwan, began bombing military objectives in the Philippines December 8, 1941 and on December 22—following several smaller landings—launched a full scale invasion of Luzon. MacArthur was forced to retreat along the Bataan Peninsula and he established a new headquarters on the fortified island of Corregidor, commanding the entrance to Manila Bay; Manila was declared an open city and surrendered to the Japanese on January 2, 1942.

On Corregidor, to which they had fled, Quezon and his cabinet were bitterly disappointed to learn of Roosevelt's decision to pursue the war in Europe before countering the Japanese occupation of Southeast Asia. They thereupon called for immediate independence and neutralization of the Philippines, to be followed by the "evacuation of all American and Japanese troops."[4] Sayre agreed, but to no avail. Sayre and the Philippine government were evacuated surreptitiously by submarine to Australia and eventually to the United States. MacArthur himself was ordered to Mindanao and later to Australia. The 30,000 Filipino and American defenders of Bataan surrendered April 9 and General Jonathan M. Wainwright and the 12,000 defenders of Corregidor on May 6. On May 7 the Japanese forced the Filipino and American prisoners to begin the notorious death march back to Manila and the internment camps; between 7,000 and 10,000 died en route.

Although Quezon and Osmena set up a government-in-exile in Washington, a number of Filipino political leaders in Manila, including members of Quezon's former cabinet, collaborated actively with the Japanese. Roxas, Speaker of the House of Representatives and Quezon's protégé, was initially captured by the Japanese and imprisoned, but subsequently emerged as a collaborationist and helped write the constitution for the Japanese-sponsored republic which was established on October 14, 1943. Senator Jose P. Laurel became president. He and other collaborators were motivated in part by the belief that they could soften Japanese rule and so benefit the people, and that Philippine nationalism could best be served by solidarity with fellow Asians; and in part by a desire to protect family and personal interests. Indeed, many of the Philippine elite accommodated to Japanese occupation, and some became millionaires helping the Japanese exploit Philippine mineral resources.[5]

The majority of the Filipinos, however, were not attracted to the Co-Prosperity Sphere. They gathered in the mountains and elsewhere in ever increasing numbers, along with remnants of the American and Philippine armed forces, waging unremitting resistance and engaging in sabotage and intelligence activities. Some 260,000 were in guerrilla units, and the underground was so extensive that the Japanese effectively controlled only 12 of the country's 48 provinces. In the Luzon rice bowl resistance tactics weakened the Japanese occupation to the point that left-wing peasant groups, led by communists and socialists, established local governments and successfully denied Japanese access to the rice harvest. The most important guerrilla movement in that area—the Hukbo ng Bayan Laban sa Hapon (People's Army to Fight the Japanese) or Hukbalahap and referred to as Huk—was well organized, copied the military tactics of Mao Tse-tung and controlled significant portions of central Luzon where the movement set up soviets.

Liberation of the Philippines in 1944–45 was almost as rapid as its earlier capture. General MacArthur made his famous return on October 20, 1944 when he landed at Leyte with four divisions of American troops and 650 ships. He was accompanied by Osmena who had succeeded to the presidency-in-exile upon the death of Quezon in

August. An American landing in strength on Luzon January 9, 1945 signaled the beginning of the battle for Manila. The city that had been spared throughout the war was leveled in the furious struggle before it fell to the Americans on February 23.

On the American return the Japanese-supported republic was repudiated and the Commonwealth reinstated, with Osmena as president. The immediate political issue was that of collaboration, rather than of nationalism and independence as in other states of Southeast Asia. A law of August 1945 authorized the government to set up a court to try traitors, but Roxas, the most prominent suspect, was a close prewar friend of MacArthur who defended him, as did much of the Manila elite. Subsequently elected president of the Senate, Roxas and his friends obstructed approval of Osmena's non-collaborationist appointees who might have made trouble for them. In consequence the Nacionalista Party was split on the issue. In the elections of April 1946 to select the first president and legislature of the about-to-be proclaimed Republic of the Philippines, Osmena, the official Nacionalista candidate (supported also by a coalition of liberals and Huks) was opposed by Roxas, supported by the wing of the Nacionalista Party that subsequently became the Liberal Party. The campaign was fought largely over the issues of collaboration, communism and change. The elite supported Roxas, whose vigor and comparative youth contrasted with Osmena's apparent inability to cope with the problems of rehabilitation and economic recovery. Roxas defeated Osmena by a margin of 200,000, and his close friend Elpidio Quirino was chosen vice president. In 1948 President Roxas proclaimed amnesty for all alleged collaborators.

REPUBLIC OF THE PHILIPPINES: 1946–1972

Roxas was inaugurated president of the Commonwealth, but on July 4, 1946 he became the first president of the Republic of the Philippines, a nation politically independent but tied to the United States economically and militarily.

On the eve of independence the U.S. Congress passed the Bell (Philippine Trade) Act. The Bell Act permitted free entry of Philippine products into the United States on a quota basis during an eight year transition period (1946–1954), after which a duty would be leveled that would increase at the rate of five percent a year until it reached the full amount of the American tariff in 1974. By the same token American products would be duty free during the transition period, and would be subject to a similarly increasing proportion of the Philippine tariff until full duty would be imposed in 1974. Americans would also enjoy "parity" with Filipinos to develop natural resources and to operate public utilities in the Philippines until the latter date. Philippine currency was pegged at two *pesos* to one dollar and its dollar convertibility was assured.

The Bell Act's provisions concerning American control of the exchange rate of the *peso,* the "parity" clause pertaining to U.S. citizens, and quota limitations on duty-free Philippine exports to the U.S. were quickly perceived by many Filipinos as infringements on their sovereignty. But Roxas had little choice since the war damage compensation promised in the Philippine Rehabilitation (Tydings) Act of 1946 was tied to Philippine acceptance of the Bell Act. The Roxas administration, supported by sugar interests, manipulated the Philippine Congress into accepting an amendment to the Philippine constitution which had reserved exploitation of natural resources to Filipino citizens. A popular referendum of March 1947 confirmed the amendment and an executive agreement with the United States placed the Bell Act provisions in effect.

In 1944 the U.S. Congress had passed a joint resolution to retain post-war military, naval and air bases in the Philippines, for the protection of both countries, and on March 14, 1947 a Military Bases Agreement was concluded by the two states which gave the U.S. a 99-year lease on 23 bases. A second agreement provided for American training and logistical assistance to the Philippine military establishment, including the Philippine Constabulary. These postwar economic and military accords were to form the basis for the relationships and the antagonisms between the two nations that continued through the decade of the 1980s.

As the elite consolidated their national power, the traditional local patron-client relationship was transformed into a nationwide system of political patronage which operated through the bureaucracy, political parties and individual political leaders. Since Filipinos differentiate little between the behavior and obligations required in family relationships and those pertaining to areas beyond the kinship group, and since the client-patron relationship has a reciprocal value (e.g., one's vote becomes a quid pro quo for special treatment), the personal character of political life raised the problem of corruption to major significance.

Politics were Manila-centered where the central government's politicians and bureaucrats could influence import licensing (steel, automobiles, machinery) as well as jobs. The elite reaped profits; the middle class functioned as lower level administrators and political brokers (under the *pakiusap* tradition a middleman is employed to approach a patronage-dispenser so that if negotiations fail all can easily be forgotten since the parties involved never met); and the masses suffered. The early years of the republic were thus clouded by an increasing gap between the rich and poor, a deterioration in the quality of life and an upsurge in rural unrest.

The roots of rural discontent—unsatisfactory landlord-tenant relationships, usury and ever increasing landlessness—were not addressed by the political leadership. The Huks exploited the situation and refused to surrender their arms which had been stockpiled during the war. Roxas declared them an illegal and seditious organization and sent Philippine Constabulary units against them, with the result that the movement was driven underground but not suppressed.

Roxas died suddenly of a heart attack in April 1948. The new president, Quirino, was a political unknown who had been elected vice president as Roxas' protégé. He embarked upon reform efforts— establishing a labor council and agricultural banks—but accomplished little before the 1949 elections. He was narrowly nominated by his own party to run against Nacionalista nominee Laurel, president of the Philippines during the Japanese occupation. The political contest was waged during a military campaign against the Huks and was marked by open violence and broad employment of government funds to support Quirino who won by a small margin. The election was universally considered to be extremely corrupt.

Quirino faced a sea of problems. Although domestic production by 1949 had reached 91 percent of the 1937 level, the slow recovery of exports and the cessation of special United States postwar dollar transfers had produced a foreign exchange crisis. The Huks had become so strong that they threatened Manila itself. Renouncing reform by constitutional means, they called for total overthrow of the government and merged with the PKP's Hukbong Mapagpalaya ng Bayan (People's Liberation Army). The army was demoralized and, worst of all, Filipinos had lost faith in the integrity of their government—only three years after independence.

Ramon Magsaysay   A drift toward complete governmental collapse was reversed in 1950. The government made a successful appeal for American financial assistance (which was furnished under terms of the Quirino-Foster agreement in return for specific Philippine actions regarding tax reform, exchange controls and minimum wages) and appointed Ramon Magsaysay, a former guerrilla leader, as secretary of defense with a free hand to deal with the security situation. Magsaysay's appointment was a tonic in itself. Large framed, dynamic, an ethnic Malay—the former congressman from central Luzon was perceived as a man of the people, a posture he maintained. In his campaign against the Huks he slept with his troops in the barrios, waded streams and fixed his own jeep. The army began to make progress against the Huks in the field, and in Manila on October 18, 1950 the government captured the entire communist politburo. This was the turning point and Magsaysay quickly ended the armed challenge.

Magsaysay simultaneously set out to restore the people's faith in their government. He used army equipment and personnel to clear land areas in Mindanao for the resettlement of large numbers of landless peasants from central Luzon, and he insured that the senatorial and provincial elections in 1951 were honest, employing the army, the ROTC and a private organization, the National Movement for Free Elections, to police the polls. His enormous popularity made him an attractive presidential possibility. In 1953 he broke with Quirino, resigning from the cabinet and the Liberal Party, and accepted the Nacionalista Party's offer of nomination—an easy transition since the two parties differed little in either platform or practice. Promising government for the people, Magsaysay took his campaign to the barrios and won the election by the largest number of votes cast for a candidate in the history of Philippine politics.

For the first time the hold of the elite on the political system was loosened because Magsaysay's vision encompassed a people rather than a social class. Largely independent of party, and spurred on by American advisers and young Philippine intellectuals, Magsaysay embarked upon serious agricultural reform. But the elite-controlled congress, which had adopted his program to purchase land for redistribution to peasants under pressure of his personal popularity, moved just as quickly to weaken and delay its implementation. Moreover, the president's penchant for personalization of government—preferring to solve problems himself and on the spot—was expensive and inefficient. Nevertheless, production rose 25 percent from 1954 to 1957. Agricultural credit was greatly expanded and legislation was enacted that discriminated in favor of Filipinos in the retail trades, domestic industries and import businesses, legislation intended for use primarily against the Chinese business community, but after 1965 applied to the American.

In 1955 Magsaysay negotiated a Revised United States–Philippine Trade (Laurel-Langley) Agreement that abolished U.S. authority to control the exchange rate of the *peso* and make parity rights reciprocal. It extended the length of time the important Philippine sugar quota would remain in effect, and lengthened the period for reduction of quotas on other products, as well as for the full application of customs tariffs on non-quota Philippine imports into the United States. Duty preferences for U.S. imports into the Philippines were to diminish more rapidly. Acceleration in application of Philippine tariffs on U.S. products quickly reduced the volume of American imports while Philippine trade with Asia, especially Japan, increased.

At the same time Magsaysay developed closer military/security relations with the United States. In the bilateral Mutual Defense Treaty of 1951 the two nations had recognized that an "armed attack in the Pacific Area on either of the two parties would be dangerous to its own peace and safety," and that they would act in accord to meet such dangers. The treaty was supplemented by the 1954 Pact of Manila that resulted in the formation of the U.S.-inspired Southeast Asia Treaty Organization (SEATO). President Magsaysay's political opponents, however, exploited his close relations with the United States in the name of nationalism, berating him specifically for his alleged inability to resolve jurisdictional and sovereignty problems arising from the American military bases.

Magsaysay was killed, along with a number of his advisers, in an airplane crash in a mountainous area near Cebu in March 1957, three years and four months after taking office. His death left a void. He was the first president of non-elitist background, an ethnic Malay, and honest in a milieu characterized by corruption. He is commemorated by the Ramon Magsaysay Award Foundation which annually honors men and women throughout Asia who have distinguished themselves in service to their fellow man.

New Nationalism The period from the death of Magsaysay to the declaration of martial law by Ferdinand Marcos in 1972 reflected an increasing detachment from the United States, a growing involvement in Southeast Asian affairs, and declining economic and physical security at home. Vice President Carlos P. Garcia (1957–1961), who succeeded to the presidency upon Magsaysay's death, operated within Magsaysay's shadow. He barely managed to win the Nacionalista Party's presidential nomination in 1957 and won the election with only 43 percent of the popular vote. For the first time the electorate chose as vice president a member of the opposition party, Diosdado Macapagal, who resembled Magsaysay in that he was also of humble origin and a populist. He accumulated more votes than the president.

Garcia emphasized a nationalism based on "Filipino first" and the attainment of "respectable independence." Under him the government adopted tough policies regarding overstaying Chinese and temporarily banned further entry of any Chinese. Settlement with the United States of most of the issues relating to the 1947 military bases agreement predictably proved infeasible, and the Philippines drew closer to its Asian neighbors, founding, with Malaysia and Thailand, the Association of Southeast Asia in 1961.

Macapagal won the presidency in the November 1961 election that pitted president against vice president. He campaigned to alleviate the condition of the common man, and as president inaugurated an agricultural leasehold system (to replace sharecroping) which established a fixed rent and protected tenants from eviction. But only 72,000 out of one million acres had in fact become leaseholds by the end of his term of office. He also encouraged the new and expansive nationalist spirit of the nation by changing Philippine Independence Day from July 4 to June 12, the day in 1898 when Aguinaldo had proclaimed independence, and he formally laid Philippine claim to the British colony of Sabah (on the island of Borneo) which was about to join the Federation of Malaysia. The Philippine claim to Sabah was based on much earlier rights of the sultan of Sulu whose territory was now part of the Philippines.

Nationalism was further fanned by a series of incidents involving jurisdiction over U.S. servicemen serving at Clark Air and Subic Bay Naval bases. Philippine politicians seized upon the incidents to suggest anew that foreign military bases compromised Philippine sovereignty, and misrepresentation and exaggeration of the incidents by the press produced anti-American demonstrations in 1965 and 1966. In spite of his exploitation of nationalism and his expressions of concern for the common man, Macapagal lost the 1965 presidential election to Senator Ferdinand E. Marcos. The decades-old problems of corruption and unachieved economic reforms impelled the electorate again to vote for change.

Ferdinand Marcos   Marcos, Senate president and erstwhile Liberal, now Nacionalista, had broken with Macapagal over economic and social goals. He entered office possessed of extraordinary qualifications: war heroism, a record of political invincibility, connections to the powerful Romualdez family in the Visayas through his beauteous wife Imelda, personal attractiveness and a bold vision of the future. He immediately attempted to resolve the increasingly acute problems of the economy and of general lawlessness and violent crime. To alleviate the former he devoted significant government resources to encouraging cultivation of the "miracle rice" strains being developed by the International Rice Research Institute located in the Philippines. He undertook a massive public works program, building roads, bridges, schools, health centers and irrigation facilities; he commenced, with his wife's help, a program of urban beautification. He also appointed many able technocrats to positions of responsibility in government.

Marcos took advantage of continuing outcries against the American military bases by obtaining U.S. agreement in 1966 to shorten the 99-year bases lease to 25 years from the date of the agreement. He nevertheless demonstrated ideological solidarity with the United States, supporting the U.S.-led military operations in Vietnam by sending a 2,000-man military unit to South Vietnam which remained there for over five years. Marcos' anti-communism at home, meanwhile, was directed against the new Communist Party of the Philippines (CPP), and its military arm, the New People's Army (NPA), which were established in 1968–69.[6] Tensions and malaise, however, persisted.

Nevertheless Marcos won the 1969 election with nearly 60 percent of the popular vote, and became the first president to be elected to a second term. He campaigned on his need for more time to bring to fruition his reform initiatives, including a proposal to change the 1935 constitution to make it more responsive to the nation's needs. But conditions deteriorated after the election rather than improved.

In January 1970 thousands of students clashed with the police, demanding reform and jobs. Inflation that had forced devaluation of the *peso* in 1969 continued. In 1971 Vice President Fernando Lopez, scion of a wealthy sugar and publishing family, publicly disassociated himself from Marcos who retaliated against the business elite in general, and the Lopez family and its extensive interests in particular. In reporting developments, the free and powerful Philippine press sank to new lows of irresponsibility, its organs competing with each other for the greatest degree of sensationalism.

On August 21 two explosions of fragmentation grenades at a Liberal Party rally in Manila killed 10 persons and wounded 90 others, including several prominent Liberal Party leaders. Although culpability was never established, Marcos blamed "Marxist-Leninist-Maoist" elements supported by a "foreign power" and suspended the writ of habeas corpus. Liberal Party Senator Benigno S. Aquino, Jr., a presidential hopeful, accused the president of using scare tactics to keep himself in power; Marcos replied that Aquino was a communist. Violence also erupted in the south. The Moro National Liberation Front (MNLF), formed in Malaysia in 1969 by Filipino Muslims, began a bloody campaign for independence that was financially supported by the radical Khaddafi regime of Libya.

In 1972 a whole series of calamities beset the government. Financial problems mounted, floods and droughts caused crop failures, the guerrilla activity of the NPA increased; and both the administration and its opponents became irresponsible in their accusations against one another. Marcos accused the Liberal Party of conspiring with the NPA and on September 21 he charged specifically that Aquino and NPA leader Jose Maria Sison were masterminds of the conspiracy.[7] On September 22, 1972 he proclaimed martial law throughout the Philippines in accordance with the authority vested in the president by the 1935 constitution in the event of rebellion.

MARCOS AND THE NEW SOCIETY: 1972–1986

Marcos claimed existence "throughout the land [of] a state of anarchy and lawlessness, chaos and disorder, turmoil and destruction of a magnitude equivalent to an actual war between the forces of our duly constituted government and the New People's Army and their satellite organizations."[8] Before the announcement of martial law was made some 20 prominent persons were arrested, including Aquino and nearly all the leading journalists. All newspapers and radio and television stations were seized and closed except for one pro-government daily paper, one television station, and four radio stations, two of them government owned.

The twin objectives emphasized by Marcos when he proclaimed martial law—restoration of law and order and transformation of social, economic and political institutions from what he termed the "old sick society" to the "New Society"—were essentially achieved during the next few years.[9] Almost immediately private armies of politicians were disarmed, price controls were imposed on basic foods, a purge of corrupt and inefficient bureaucrats and judges was undertaken and a sweeping national land reform program to favor small farmers was inaugurated. Tax procedures, banking laws and commodity marketing organizations were revamped. Crime was reduced sharply, corruption in public office was prosecuted and the economy improved. Manila remained calm and bloodshed was absent except for an assassination attack by a knife wielder that wounded Mrs. Marcos in December 1972. The seven faceted New Society Program announced in mid-November 1972—encompassing law and order, land tenure, labor, education, the economy, social services, and politics and government—was well received by the citizenry.

1973 Constitution Marcos spurred into action the Commission on Constitutional Reform which had been meeting under the chairmanship of former President Macapagal since early 1971. On November 29, 1972 a draft constitution was submitted which would create a parliamentary system of government to replace the presidential system. Articles in the document insured that all martial law orders and decrees would become part of the law of the land, and that Marcos would continue to govern. During the period of transition he would exercise the presidential powers vested in the president under the 1935 constitution, as well as the executive authority vested in the prime minister by the new constitution.

Marcos devised new political tools to legitimize his new legal order. First, he revived the ancient Malay political organization of the *barangay* as a form of citizen assembly; all citizens throughout the country were grouped into *barangays* to discuss national issues. Second, he announced a plebiscite-referendum procedure by which voters were asked simultaneously to ratify (by plebiscite) new governmental forms and to approve or disapprove (by referendum) public policy and/or Marcos' performance in office.

The first public discussion in the *barangays* was of the proposed constitution. Since Marcos initially encouraged free debate, an opposition emerged which was mainly opposed to the provisions of transition rule which gave Marcos both presidential and prime ministerial power. Marcos halted the discussions on January 7, fully reimposing martial law. The referendum submitted to the *barangays* consisted of 11 questions. According to Marcos the voters approved of the new constitution; disapproved of calling a plebiscite to ratify it; endorsed the continuation of martial law; and approved a delay in convening the interim national assembly which the constitution prescribed.[10] The constitution was declared in force January 17, 1973. Periodically thereafter Marcos, exercising what he termed "constitutional authoritarianism," invoked the plebiscite-referendum procedure to demonstrate his accountability to the nation.

A People's Revolutionary Congress, (Katipunan ng mga Barangay), consisting of some 5,000 *barangay* captains and mayors and governors, was formed in 1973 to "articulate the wishes of the people throughout the country as expressed in meetings of the citizen assemblies." In 1974 the *barangays* were institutionalized as the lowest political subdivisions, replacing the 42,000 barrios. Provincial, city and municipal boards or councils were renamed Sangguniang Bayans and their membership broadened to include *barangay* representatives. In September 1976 a Legislative Advisory Council, consisting of cabinet officers and members of the Katipunan's executive committee, was formed to assist the president in lawmaking.

By a plebiscite-referendum of October 16–17, 1976 the *barangays* ratified a series of constitutional amendments that authorized creation of an interim national assembly (the Batasang Pambansa) and designated the president to serve concurrently as prime minister, exercising all the powers of both offices and remaining in both positions after formation of the interim legislature. Continuation of martial law was also endorsed. A further referendum of December 17, 1977 reaffirmed the grant of extraordinary power to the president.

In preparation for the legislative elections it was announced that leaders of the Nacionalista and Liberal parties had formed the New Society Movement (Kilusang Bagong Lipunan, KBL), to promote political unity within the country. The KBL proved to be the umbrella under which electoral politics would be conducted.

The election of 165 representatives to the new interim legislature was held April 7, 1978 with the KBL winning the majority of seats, and on June 12 the Batasang Pambansa, the first legislative body in the Philippines in almost six years, was installed; President Marcos was sworn in as prime minister. The occasion ended 32 years of presidential government and introduced an experiment in parliamentary government; it coincided with the 80th anniversary of the proclamation of Philippine independence.

During its first year, however, the Batasang Pambansa displayed deliberative, rather than decision making, proclivities and in August 1979 the president created a three-man super cabinet which gave more authority back to the executive branch. The first local elections in seven years—for city and provincial officers—were held January 30, 1980. The KBL won an overwhelming 95 percent of the positions, but the election was disturbingly similar to Philippine elections under the "old society," and was marked by violence and alleged fraud.

Termination of Martial Law   After eight years and four months of martial law President Marcos lifted the decree on January 17, 1981 to set the stage for the 1984 elections to the regular Batasang Pambansa. The president retained, however, the powers to suspend habeas corpus and to use the armed forces in an emergency, but he emphasized that his political opponents were now entirely free to operate, even to publishing newspapers. A United Democratic Opposition (UNIDO), led by ex-President Macapagal, Senator Gerardo Roxas and Salvador H. Laurel, son of the former president, immediately issued a 30-page manifesto opposing: 1) foreign military bases in the Philippines, 2) the 1973 constitution because it was not a product of a free assembly, and 3) retention of the authority to reimpose martial law and to suspend the writ of habeas corpus without consent of the legislature.

The KBL on January 29, meanwhile, proposed important changes in the structure of government to combine both presidential and parliamentary forms. Whereas in the 1973 constitution the president was identified as the "symbolic head of state," and executive power was to be "exercised by the prime minister with the assistance of the cabinet," the KBL proposed the creation of a strong president to be popularly elected for a six year term beginning June 30, 1981. The prime minister would be nominated by the president, elected by the National Assembly and could be removed from office either by the president or by vote of the assembly. The proposals required extensive amendment of the constitution.

New Republic   Accordingly the government conducted a plebiscite April 7, 1981 in which the people were asked if they agreed to the proposed amendments to modify the parliamentary system by subordinating the authority of the prime minister to that of the president. The proposals won overwhelmingly. A June 16 election date was set and Marcos urged the UNIDO to band together and nominate a candidate to give the people a choice. The UNIDO, however, boycotted the election. Marcos, not surprisingly, won reelection, polling 88.2 percent of the votes cast.

Marcos was inaugurated as president for a new six year term June

30 before 1.5 million cheering Filipinos and U.S. Vice President George Bush. He proclaimed the birth of a New Republic, dedicated to national unity and to liberation of the Philippines from the residue of the centuries of Spanish colonialization and the half century of American rule. In seeking unity the president stated that no one can deliver the country from poverty, from ignorance and from misfortunes except the Filipinos themselves. On July 28 the Batasang Pambansa accepted the nomination by the president of Finance Minister Cesar Virata as prime minister.

The year 1982 found Marcos more firmly in control than ever. He felt free therefore to announce that for the first time in 25 years the Communist Party could operate if it used only peaceful tactics. In May, in the first nationwide local elections in 10 years, a large majority of the 28 million registered voters cast ballots to choose from among one million candidates for posts in the now 45,000 *barangays*. Violence and charges of corruption during the elections appeared not be exceed what had become the norm in electoral politics. The KBL won overwhelmingly.

Aquino Assassination   The main opposition to Marcos had coalesced in UNIDO, which had grown to include 14 political groups. Among these was the once-prominent Liberal Party whose secretary general was Benigno Aquino—convicted by a military court of murder and subversion and sentenced to death. He had been imprisoned in Manila from 1972 until 1980 when he was permitted to go to the United States for heart surgery. Instead of returning to the Philippines as he had promised, Aquino became a fellow at Harvard and the Massachusetts Institute of Technology, and the focal point of opposition to the president among the substantial Filipino community in the United States. His "self-exile" had also served to enhance further his popularity in the Philippines.

As the Liberal Party's leading figure, Aquino strongly endorsed in absentia a UNIDO June 1983 proposal calling upon the president to: 1) declare a general amnesty for all political offenders, 2) repeal the anti-subversion law, 3) abolish presidential power to make arrests, and 4) keep the military from participating in civilian affairs such as elections and court procedures. UNIDO's proposal of amnesty included members of the pro-communist New People's Army and the separatist Moro National Liberation Front which had long sought autonomy for the southern island of Mindanao.

In July Aquino announced his decision to return to the Philippines to persuade Marcos to restore democratic institutions. He reserved 20 seats aboard a flight to Manila for Sunday (a day when thousands would be free to greet him at the airport) August 21 for himself, his family, reporters and TV cameramen, although he had been warned by the Marcos regime not to return because his security could not be guaranteed.[11] When he stepped down from the airplane on his arrival in Manila he was shot at very close range. The alleged murderer was immediately killed by security personnel. The assassination triggered huge popular demonstrations and student riots, as for 10 days before burial his remains were transported from place to place for viewing by supporters. The Marcos government appeared for the first time to be in jeopardy. The matter became more complicated because the government seemed unable to explain the assassination other than to describe the murderer as a professional killer, giving rise to charges, nationally and internationally, of complicity by the regime. The credibility of the commission appointed by Marcos to investigate the crime was immediately challenged by Aquino's supporters, and demonstrations continued to rock the capital. President Reagan cancelled his proposed November trip to the Philippines.

Serious repercussions from the Aquino incident impelled Marcos to call for a plebiscite designed to shore up his popularity. On January 27, 1984 the voters approved: 1) restoration of the vice presidency to replace the 15-person Executive Committee; 2) election of National Assembly members by provinces, districts or cities rather than by larger regions, a change disadvantageous to the ruling and centrally directed KBL apparat; 3) granting of disposable public lands to qualified persons; and 4) requiring the state to engage in socialized planning. Following wide voter acceptance and recognizing that the UNIDO boycott of the 1981 presidential election had had little political impact, two Aquino factions (the Pilipino Democratic Party and Lakas ng Bayan, or Laban) led an opposition drive—soon joined by all moderate opposition groups—to contest vigorously the May 14 elections to the new, regular National Assembly of 200 members.

Anti-administration parties and independent candidates led by UNIDO's Laurel and former senator Ambrosio Padilla won 71, of the 183 elective seats, a much larger than expected showing. Marcos' legislative allies achieved firm control of the new body, however, because the president was constitutionally authorized to appoint 17 members. These, added to the KBL's 112 assembly winners, provided him the substantial majority of 129 to 71. Despite arguments of the new opposition members, Marcos retained the power to legislate by decree, stating that he considered such authority a legitimate tool against subversives and terrorists.

On October 23, 1984 Chairwoman Corazon Agrava of the commission to investigate the Aquino assassination released a report accusing an air force general and six soldiers of involvement in the murder. The following day the remaining four members released their report, charging that Chief of Staff General Fabian C. Ver, 24 other soldiers and a civilian were involved. The commission rejected unanimously the military's contention that Aquino was killed by a communist-hired gunman.[12] Marcos originally ordered that the seven persons implicated by the chairwoman stand trial but in January 1985 also charged Ver and the others with the murder of Aquino and the man once called his assassin.

Economy   During the decade 1970–1979 the Philippine economy grew at an average annual rate of approximately 6.5 percent, lowest of the ASEAN nations. Real economic growth dropped to 5.4 percent in 1980 and continued to decline through 1983. The worldwide oil price-rise shock of 1979 brought double digit inflation, an increase in already widespread poverty, and mounting external debt.

Disturbingly, a World Bank study completed in 1980 reported that Filipino wages, when adjusted for inflation, had declined sharply since the 1960s "in both urban and rural areas, in all regions, and practrically all occupations."[13] Filipino workers were the lowest paid among the ASEAN nations, and an estimated 40 to 50 percent of the population of around 49 million were living in poverty, with the number reaching as high as 70 percent in the least developed regions of the country. Needed, according to the report, was a reduction in the birthrate (which averaged a 2.8 percent increase throughout the 1970s and 1980s as estimated by the Population Reference Bureau), an increase in basic public services, increased development of rainfed agriculture, a more balanced regional development, and an acceleration of industrialization to provide job opportunities.

Security Problems   Besides major political and economic problems, the Marcos regime faced two ongoing security problems, the secessionist insurrection in the south and the NPA movement throughout the islands.

The independent Philippines has been scarcely more successful than the Spanish and the Americans in achieving political integration of the Muslims. The problem was exacerbated when the Philippine government reiterated an earlier claim to the Malaysian state of Sabah in 1968–69. This move led the Malaysian government to support the Moros and to assist in the formation of the Moro National Liberation Front (MNLF) by providing funds and training. Fighting broke out subsequently which quickly developed into a full fledged separatist rebellion. The Muslim position came to be supported by Islamic states outside the region, particularly by Libya. The Islamic Conference of Foreign Ministers in 1973 called for pressure on the Philippine government to end the violence, in the meantime establishing an aid fund for the MNLF. The Front reduced its demand from independence to autonomy, but the ceasefire agreement between government and MNLF representatives negotiated in Libya on December 23, 1976 fell apart due to differing interpretations of the term "autonomy." Marcos guaranteed MNLF representatives top positions in the assemblies and executive councils of autonomous regions, but Front leaders refused to cooperate. During 1978 as much as 60 percent of the Philippine armed forces was deployed against the rebels, and by 1981 the conflict had produced some 50,000 casualties. Nevertheless the government conducted elections in the southern regions in 1979 and 1982, with the KBL winning all the seats. Although the conflict is rooted in cultural, religious and ethnic differences, it is compounded by the influx into Mindanao of Christians from the north who were settled on new lands by the government, and by expanding multinationals and government-inspired agri-business concerns.

Physical contact between the Philippine army and the MNLF diminished by late 1981 but a new complexity was added as the Maoist-communist NPA began to cooperate with the MNLF against the Marcos regime. Formed in 1969, the NPA was almost decimated by the army after the proclamation of martial law in 1972. It was only saved because the army became preoccupied with the separatist movement. It thereupon gained strength, rising from 1,500 in 1973 to between 12,000 and 15,000 in late 1985, and operated in most parts of the country but was strongest on Samar, Mindanao and in northern Luzon, where it had superceded the former People's Liberation Army.

In late 1985 the growing NPA insurgency (operating without known foreign support), Marcos' precarious health, and further economic deterioration evoked official U.S. expressions of concern. Marcos replied on November 3 that he was "ready to call a snap election [in] perhaps three months or less" to let the Philippine people judge his "alleged ineptness."

Foreign Relations Philippine foreign relations under Marcos were characterized by: 1) alteration of trade and security relationships with the United States, 2) opening of diplomatic relations with socialist countries, and 3) close identification with the Association of Southeast Asian Nations (ASEAN) and with third world nations.

Two agreements were reached with the U.S. which dealt with basic points of contention—economic perquisites and jurisdiction over U.S. bases. The Laurel-Langley Agreement of 1955, which had set forth the economic relationship between the Philippines and the United States, expired July 3, 1974. Tariff preferences which each of the nations enjoyed in the markets of the other ended, as did parity for nationals of each country in the territory of the other. Six years of discussions were necessary before a new trade agreement emerged. The United States desired that American capital entering the Philippines should continue to be accorded "national treatment." The Philippines desired liberalization of the United States General System of Preferences for

major Philippine export commodities. The trade agreement reached by
the two nations on October 30, 1979 "expanded the accessibility of
Philippine products not only to the United States, but also to the
members of the General Agreement on Tariffs and Trade (GATT),
having been concluded within the framework of GATT's Multilateral
Trade Negotiation." The Philippines received duty preferences of
about 65 percent on 97 items; the U.S. obtained tariff reductions of
only 5.7 percent on 60 items. The agreement was a major U.S.
concession to the Philippines.[14]

The U.S.-Philippine Mutual Defense Treaty of 1951 remained in
force, as did the Manila Pact of 1954; these constituted a U.S. defense
commitment. A Military Assistance Agreement with the U.S. also
continued in effect. Substantial change occurred, however, with respect to the terms of the Military Bases Agreement. On January 7,
1979, after lengthy negotiations, the two nations agreed to six major
amendments to the 1947 provisions: 1) reaffirmation of Philippine
sovereignty over the six U.S.-operated bases (down from the earlier
23); 2) installation of Filipino commanders at the bases; 3) reduction
of the areas of U.S. use within the bases; 4) responsibility of Philippine
forces for defense of base perimeters; 5) assurance of unhampered
U.S. military operations within the bases, and 6) review of the agreement every five years. The bases lease extends to 1991.

The first five-year review took place in April–May 1983. In consequence the two nations signed an agreement in which the United States
pledged US$900 million (up from US$500 million) in aid and loans for
the five years beginning in October 1984.

Besides redefining its relationships with the United States the Philippines sought wider and stronger ties with other nations, including
communist states. Diplomatic relations were established for the first
time with the People's Republic of China in 1975 and, following the
1976 visit of Imelda Marcos to Moscow, with the Soviet Union. In 1976
recognition was also extended to newly unified Vietnam.

The Philippines became an active member of ASEAN, often initiating policy thrusts which were adopted by the other partners. However
its relations with Malaysia were uneven in consequence of the Philippine claim to Sabah which has never been completely renounced, and
of support of Malaysia for the secessionist movement in the southern
Philippines. In 1977, however, the two nations signed a border agreement designed to halt smuggling, piracy and drug traffic between the
two countries. The Philippines was also an articulate member of the
Group of 77—third world nations seeking a new international economic
order—and hosted the first Group of 77 Conference in Manila in 1976.

In 1977 Foreign Minister Romulo spelled out the continued goals of
Philippine foreign policy: 1) the establishment of greater contacts with

socialist and third world countries, 2) reexamination of traditional friendships, and 3) the enhancement of cooperation with friendly countries on the basis of "equality and justice." As the only country in Asia with a Christian orientation, the Philippines also sought to identify more with its non-Christian Asian neighbors and with the non-Christian members of the third world, in an attempt to shed its earlier image of a western enclave.

PEOPLE POWER REVOLUTION: THE AQUINO YEARS

The significant opposition to Marcos that had emerged in December 1985, comprising Laurel's UNIDO and a loose coalition—the Pilipino Democratic Party (PDP) and Laban ("Fight") with which Aquino had been associated—coalesced spontaneously around Corazon, Aquino's widow. Noting Mrs. Aquino's instant popularity, Laurel, who himself had presidential aspirations, agreed to an Aquino-Laurel ticket to oppose Marcos at the February 7 "snap election." By January 1986 Aquino's supporters had organized "People Power," a campaign of non-violent demonstrations and commercial boycotts which drew ever larger throngs. Marcos' reelection suddenly was viewed as uncertain, a psychological factor which Aquino's forces fully exploited.

Both sides claimed victory following the election which was monitored by members of the U.S. Congress. It was immediately challenged for gross irregularities, massive vote fraud, and government delay of announcement of the election returns until it could manipulate them in its favor. The Marcos-controlled National Assembly declared him the victor. Opposition meanwhile escalated to the level of huge popular demonstrations.

On February 23 Juan Ponce Enrile—administrator of martial law from 1972 to 1981, one-time minister of defense and a member of Marcos' cabinet for 21 years—resigned in protest of what he termed a blatant theft of the presidential election. Chief of Staff General Fidel V. Ramos resigned simultaneously, protesting years of corruption and politicization of the military.

The two men, and several hundred defecting troops, occupied two large military bases near Manila; they were joined by other military units. Catholic prelates supported their efforts to topple the government. During street battles in Manila February 24–25 between the breakaway soldiers and loyalist Marcos troops some 12 persons were killed and 25 seriously injured. As the crisis drew to a climax armored government forces, hitherto loyal to Marcos, declined to advance against the human street barricades that included housewives, children and Catholic nuns.

The U.S. government called for an orderly transfer of power, simultaneously stating its willingness to negotiate Marcos' safe passage to the U.S.

Marcos was sworn in for another six-year presidential term at Malacanang Palace February 25, while almost simultaneously Aquino was proclaimed president at a suburban Manila clubhouse. Marcos' inauguration provided him a future claim to the presidential office. Aquino solidified her own claim by appointing Vice President Laurel prime minister, Enrile defense minister and Ramos military chief of staff. Marcos capitulated the same day. After nightfall U.S. helicopters transported him and his family from the palace grounds to Clark Air Force Base and thence to Hawaii.

Aquino's Politics   Aquino immediately abolished the 1973 constitution and the National Assembly, replacing them with her own provisional government. By June she had released dozens of political prisoners, created a temporary constitution and appointed a commission to draft a permanent one. She replaced most of the 73 Philippine provincial governors and some 1,500 local mayors with her Pilipino Democratic Party-Laban supporters. Thus it was no surprise that candidates whom she favored won heavily in May 1987 elections for 24 Senate and 200 House of Representatives seats under terms of a new constitution which the voters had accepted at a February plebiscite. The year 1987 was also characterized by violence and threats to the government posed by military and right wing factions, the renewed insurgency of the communist-led NPA, and the continuing Muslim separatist movement expressed through the MNLF.

In 1988 embryo parties, spawned by multi-member districting as specified in the new constitution, appeared and disappeared as national politics appeared to revert toward the traditional two-party Filipino pattern. The umbrella Lakas ng Demokratikong Pilipinas (LDP) emerged from a union of Aquino's PDP and Laban. Another coalition was led by the reemerging Liberal Party of Senate President Jovito Salonga. Competing factional leaders within congress personalized the legislative process to the point that needed legislation was frequently delayed. The parties appeared to function principally as undisciplined groups which presidential aspirants could manipulate in anticipation of the 1992 presidential elections. Vice President Salvador Laurel, and now-Senate minority leader Juan Ponce Enrile, joined forces in May 1989 to resuscitate the 82-year-old Nacionalista Party of presidents Magsaysay and Marcos.

Within Aquino's disunited cabinet various policy initiatives arose, mainly from prominent personalities, who urged differing political agendas. Aquino, a political neophite, was soon criticized by the media as lacking leadership qualities despite her personal popularity. Nevertheless, in Philippine politics personalities continued to be more important than policies.

Economy   Real gross national product (GNP) had declined in 1984–85 as Marcos cut back on public spending to combat the world wide recession. Half of the country's financial institutions were in difficulty. The Development Bank of the Philippines, the Philippine National Bank and the Government Service Insurance System were in trouble from defaulted loans of Marcos' cronies. On President Aquino's assumption of power she faced a legacy of paying interest on a US$27.6 billion external debt amounting to 11 percent of GDP (gross domestic product), and a population nearing 60 million, nearly 70 percent of whom were living in poverty.

Nor was the year 1987 kind to the new Aquino administration, even though the exuberance accompanying her accession to the presidency stimulated the economy and produced a 4.6 percent GDP increase. A series of military-related coup attempts adversely affected domestic and foreign investment as well as tourism. Privatization of Marcos-created corporations and "authorities" engaged in traditionally private business (manufacturing, trade, transport, real estate, hotels) also took longer than expected.

Greater political stability in 1988 was accompanied by a GNP growth rate of 6.4 percent. Expansionist economic policies produced a real growth of 10 percent in industrial activity (e.g., semi conductors and garments) in contrast to declines in 1985–86. Negative factors included an inflation rate of 8.7 percent compared to 5.2 percent in 1987 and a debt service burden of US$3.1 billion. About 44 percent of central government revenue for 1988–89 was devoted to interest and principal payments. Quite obviously substantial external assistance was necessary.

Multilateral Assistance   The international community took steps during 1988–89 to assist the Philippines: 1) the World Bank approved a loan of US$300 million in June 1989, 2) a project—variously termed the Multilateral Assistance Initiative (MAI), or Philippine Assistance Program (PAP), or Mini Marshall Plan—was launched in July 1989 when the so-called Consultative Group of 19 countries and six multilateral institutions pledged assistance amounting to US$3.5 billion for the first of five years, and 3) the International Monetary Fund (IMF) agreed to provide credits to the Philippines in the amount of US$1.3 billion.

Each of the commitments was accompanied by conditions, qualifiers or assumptions. World Bank financing was subject to reform of Philippine banking laws. The MAI project was founded upon a debt-financed growth strategy (half of the funds coming from bilateral contributions and half from private sector loans). The debt service ratio (repayments and interest as a percentage of export revenue), the highest in Asia, would be only slightly reduced. Moreover IMF financing was subject to prior commitment by foreign commercial banks to provide new loans.

Land Reform   In 1988 the Aquino government adopted a land reform program as mandated by the new constitution. It departed from Marcos' land reform principle of "landlord compensation," based upon a land's productive value, namely, two and one half times the value of the annual harvest. The Aquino program utilized instead a "just compensation" formula based upon the "fair market value" of land, an obvious concession to landlords which permitted them artificially to inflate land prices. The Marcos program had alienated the landlord class and favored his cronies by affording them agricultural monopolies. In contrast, the Aquino program favored major landlords, who were her supporters in 1986 and which included her own and the Aquino family. Moreover, it was landlords who helped draft the land reform clauses in the 1987 constitution.

Foreign Relations   Assertive nationalism which characterized the Philippines beginning with President Garcia's declaration of "respectable independence" in 1957 intensified with the advent of "people power" government. It targeted Philippine-U.S. relations, especially the long standing issue of Philippine sovereignty vis-a-vis continuation of American-operated Clark Air Base and Subic Bay Naval Base. In October 1988 a lengthy and acrimonious second bilateral review of the Military Bases Agreement was concluded with further U.S. concessions. The Philippines received a pledge from the Reagan administration to seek congressional appropriation of US$962 million in military and economic aid to Manila for the final two years of the lease. After 1991 the Agreement could be terminated with one year's notice. While the review was underway the Philippine foreign minister, as part of an effort to justify raising the annual "rent" from US$180 to US$481 million, publicly asked his ASEAN counterparts to assess the regional utility of the bases. President Aquino further tweaked the American nose by pointing out that according to the constitution foreign bases can no longer be allowed after 1991 except under terms of a treaty approved by the Philippine Congress. Opinion research through 1989, however, suggested that a popular majority continued to support the presence of the American-operated military bases.

1989 Crisis   The Aquino government had quelled five coup attempts since succeeding to power in 1986. A sixth, and by far the bloodiest attempt, occurred December 1, 1989 when an organized military rebellion erupted. Led by mutinous senior officers, elite units of the 160,000-member armed forces took over military installations in the Manila area as well as in Cebu, 350 miles to the south. They also occupied buildings in the capital's fashionable financial district, turning the high rise structures into a concrete forest of shooting galleries.

In response to President Aquino's request, U.S. warplanes from Clark Air Base were deployed against—but did not fire upon—the rebels as a show of force. Secretary of State James A. Baker III justified the U.S. demonstration as an act to prevent overthrow of a freely elected government by means of "bullets and bayonets." After week-long fire fights between rebel and loyalist troops the rebellion was defeated. Its cost included the lives of 113 persons. Over 500 soldiers and/or civilians were wounded and property damages caused 10,000 persons to flee their homes.

The Aquino regime was severely shaken by the deep divisiveness within the armed forces which the rebellion revealed. Speculation immediately arose as to whether Aquino could remain in office until the 1992 election. She immediately took steps to limit the political damage to her administration. One initiative to achieve reconciliation was to permit most of the rebellious troops to return to their posts without penalty. A companion effort to defuse rising public perception of governmental inadequacies was Aquino's wholesale revamping of her cabinet.

WHITHER THE PHILIPPINES?

The problem of developing effective political institutions remains. The nation has a history of greater exposure to western style democracy than any other Southeast Asian nation. But its western-replicated political parties have failed to develop into cohesive entities that identify and articulate issues. Political parochialism and temporary coalitions organized in support of individual personalities have been the rule. Corazon Aquino was vaulted into office, not as a representative of a coherent political philosophy; on the contrary, she had had no political exposure or experience. The widow of an assassinated hero, she was a popular and attractive alternative to Marcos, another one-time hero who fell from grace and resorted to authoritarianism in a desperate effort to remain in power.

Lacking a true national leader—such as Magsaysay or Marcos—and with none on the horizon, the weak political parties try to outdo each other through attention getting tactics but continue to fail to address serious problems. The irresponsibility which ensues shows little sign of abating. As Muslim (MNLF) and communist (NPA) threats have lessened so have the catalysts for social reform and political change.

The U.S. bases will remain a matter of concern. Intense feelings aroused by Philippine nationalists will ensure extreme difficulty in negotiations concerning their continuing presence. The U.S. may decide an acrimonious relationship is not worth the price and decide to look elsewhere to reestablish defense facilities in the Western Pacific—Guam is closer to Tokyo, the core U.S. security interest, than is Clark Air Base.

Since donor nations and international financial institutions have commited new resources to assist the Philippines, a respectable economic growth rate can be expected. But income redistribution and genuine land reform are unlikely as long as the government is too weak to challenge the small elite that continues to control most of the economy as well as politics.

FOOTNOTES

1. John L. Phelan, *The Hispanization of the Philippines* (Madison: University of Wisconsin Press, 1959), p. 151.

2. See Carlos P. Romulo, *Mother American* (Garden City, N.Y.: Doubleday, 1943).

3. Jean Grassholtz, *Politics in the Philippines* (Boston: Little, Brown, 1964), p. 29.

4. Emily Hahn, *The Islands* (N.Y.: Coward, McCann and Geoghegan, 1981), p. 220.

5. Nena Vreeland, *et al. Area Handbook for the Philippines* (Washington, D.C.: Superintendent of Public Documents, 1976), p. 65.

6. The Philippine Communist Party (PKP) organized a military arm, the People's Liberation Army (*Hukbong Mapaglapaya ng Bayan-* HMB) from which emerged the Anti-Japanese Army, or *Hukbo ng Bayan Laban sa Hapon* (Hukbalahap). Magsaysay's defeat of the Huks in the mid-1950s, and Jose Maria Sison's failure in the 1960s to influence communist policy, impelled Sison to found a new Communist Party of the Philippines (CPP), December 26, 1968. On March 29, 1969 Sison and Bernabe Buscayno (Commander Dante), officially founded its military arm, the New People's Army (NPA).

7. Allegations substantiated by Bernabe Buscayno (Commander Dante) in interview, "Ex-Rebel 'Commander Danté Enlists in a New Revolution," *Los Angeles Times*, October 28, 1989, p. A18.

8. Vreeland, *et al., op., cit.,* p. 221.

9. *Ibid.,* p. 222.

10. For record of questions and votes see *Data for Decision* (Manila: Press Foundation of Asia), 1973, p. 448.

11. Eduardo Lachica, "Aquino Making Gamble With Return to Philippines," *Asian Wall Street Journal Weekly,* July 25, 1983.

12. *Facts on File,* October 26, 1984, p. 794.

13. "World Bank Report Casts Doubt on Effect of Aid to Philippines," *Wall Street Journal,* January 15, 1981.

14. *Data Asia* (Manila: Press Foundation of Asia), 1979, p. 6621.

CHAPTER 12
REGIONAL CHANGE

ASEAN

In July 1961 Malaya, the Philippines and Thailand announced their common intention to move toward modified economic integration by organizing the Association of Southeast Asia (ASA). Two years later another regional association, Maphilindo (from the first syllables of the founding states) was formed by Malaya, the Philippines and Indonesia. It was an attempt to resolve the political dispute among those nations over the proposed Federation of Malaysia and the incorporation into it of the Bornean states of Sabah and Sarawak, in spite of the countervailing claims to those states by the Philippines and Indonesia. Maphilindo disintegrated when the Federation came into effect September 1963, but ASA survived. Further political change produced a better environment for area cooperation. In 1965 Singapore seceded from Malaysia, reducing Indonesian President Sukarno's perception of Malaysia as an obstacle to his aspirations to regional leadership. In 1966 the Philippines agreed not to press its claim to Sabah. In 1967 Sukarno fell from power and was succeeded by the moderate government of Suharto, who dropped Sukarno's policy of confrontation against Singapore/Malaysia. Therefore when ASA invited Singapore and Indonesia to join the organization, they responded positively.

On August 8, 1967 the foreign ministers of the five founding nations declared the expansion of ASA into the Association of Southeast Asian Nations (ASEAN). (Brunei joined in January 1984 after it became fully independent.) The Declaration expressed ASEAN's intention to: 1) accelerate regional economic growth, social progress and cultural development, 2) promote regional peace and stability, 3) collaborate actively and afford mutual assistance in the economic, social, cultural, scientific, educational, technical and administrative spheres, 4) collaborate for more effective utilization of agriculture and industry, trade expansion, improvement of transportation and communications facilities, and raising of living standards, 5) promote Southeast Asian studies, and 6) cooperate with existing international organizations. The principal organs of ASEAN are the annual Conference of Foreign Ministers, the Standing Committee, and the biannual Conference of Economic Ministers. The secretariat is located in Jakarta and coordinates eight permanent committees.

The five states were unused to cooperation, having been more often at odds over border problems (boundary claims, smuggling, insurgency) and fishing and oil rights, than in agreement on regional political cooperation and economic development. During the period 1971–75, however, a distinct ASEAN political posture evolved. The ASEAN states, first individually and then collectively, consciously distanced themselves from the West, partly because lessened U.S. presence and influence in Vietnam foretold a communist victory there, and partly because they shared a psychological impulse to embarrass the West for perceived past injustices. In 1971 Indonesia and Malaysia declared that the straits of Malacca and Singapore were not international waterways, and in 1974 Indonesia and the Philippines, at the Third UN Conference on the Law of the Sea, claimed, under the rubric of "archipelagic principles," the immense seas within a perimeter drawn around the outermost islands of their respective archipelagos. In May 1975, in a direct challenge to then United States interests, the ASEAN foreign ministers formally approved the proposition that Southeast Asia should be recognized as a "zone of peace, freedom and neutrality." With the fall of the government of the Republic of Vietnam, the ASEAN states quickly and repeatedly extended the "hand of friendship" to the communist-dominated states of Indochina. Meanwhile member nations had forged political ties with the worldwide nonaligned movement that, beginning with the Lusaka Summit of 1970, raised economic issues to a par with decolonization. The ASEAN states were among vanguard nations calling for a new economic order. Their Manila Charter of 1976 demanded economic retribution for underdeveloped countries from the developed states and produced a Treaty of Amity and Cooperation for peaceful settlement of disputes.

Economic Cooperation In 1988 the total ASEAN population was estimated to be 315.2 million, and its combined gross domestic product (GDP), the money value of all goods and services produced within the nations, was about US$196 billion. The ASEAN community possesses a number of natural resources needed by an expanding global population as well as other advantages. These include: 1) domination in 1988 of world production of tropical hardwood, abaca fiber, natural rubber, tin, coconut products and palm oil; 2) possession, with the exception of Singapore, of significant energy resources such as petroleum (Indonesia, Malaysia, Brunei), natural gas (Indonesia, Malaysia, Brunei and Thailand), coal, hydroelectric and geothermal (Philippines); 3) presence of a large low-cost labor force which is high in quality and attractive to labor-intensive industries, and 4) a strong and aggressive private industrial sector which has been assigned a key developmental role.

With its identity and its political orientation established by 1975, ASEAN turned to the task of expanding economic development through increased cooperation among its members. The first steps toward economic integration were taken by the ASEAN economic ministers at their Kuala Lumpur meeting in March 1976. They agreed to give member states priority in the purchase of rice and crude oil during crises and to develop appropriate regional industrial projects. Decisions were originally made to build ammonia/urea fertilizer factories in Malaysia and Indonesia, a super phosphate chemical complex in the Philippines, a diesel engine factory in Singapore and a rock salt/soda ash project in Thailand. The Philippine project was eventually changed to a copper fabricating plant. The Singapore diesel project met with Philippine opposition and was dropped.

Only the Indonesian and Malaysian ASEAN Industrial Projects (AIP) were fully operational by 1988. They were primarily funded by Japan which also absorbed most of the output. AIP development lagged otherwise due to failures to achieve co-financing and defective planning.

Member nations' central banks inaugurated (1977) a "swap" arrangement establishing standby credits whereby each member would set aside US$20 million to assist others with liquidity problems. The funds were to be exchanged or "swapped" for domestic currency for limited periods of time. A Clearing Union for clearing trade transactions among ASEAN states was anticipated and private banks within ASEAN began experimenting in the exchange of officers and in assessing the feasibility of intra-ASEAN loans. The Asian Bankers' Council, formed in Singapore in 1976, looked to the establishment of a Bankers' Acceptance Market to finance short-term commercial paper, and an ASEAN Investors' Group was organized by Filipino investors. The Philippine Development Corporation changed its by-laws to enable it to lend to any ASEAN member. Regional communications by submarine cables and satellite were envisaged.

While decrying a worldwide trend toward economic protectionism, especially in the United States and Japan, the ASEAN states did not hesitate to develop producer associations designed to protect themselves. In 1972 Indonesia and Malaysia, producers of 60 percent of the world's pepper, had joined to form the Pepper Community. A price-regulating and production-controlling Southeast Asia Log Producers' Association comprised of Malaysia, Indonesia and the Philippines, and a Coconut Community also including those three countries, were announced in 1974. The Association of Natural Rubber Producing Countries was formed in 1976 to establish quotas and buffer stock, and a Federation of ASEAN Shippers' Councils was organized.

Member states signed a Basic Agreement on Establishment of ASEAN Preferential Trade Arrangements in February 1977. The Philippines, Thailand and Singapore proceeded with bilateral arrangements to lower tariffs by 10 percent on a number of products and to sell or buy at preferential rates in time of glut or shortage such basic commodities as rice, sugar and crude oil. Indonesia initially proved reluctant to embark upon trade liberalization, but all five foreign ministers signed an agreement in Manila in March 1977 to confirm and extend the emerging preferential trade arrangements. Appropriate officials were to meet every three months to identify further items for duty reduction. Seventy-one products were so identified by June; by 1988 the list had grown to nearly 19,000. By 1988, however, only two percent of total intra-ASEAN trade was covered by and beneficial to the preference system.

In 1981 the five nations signed a Basic Agreement on ASEAN Industrial Complementation (AIC) whereby each country agreed to produce components for designated regional products, including an ASEAN automobile, but by 1988 industrial complementarity was characterized as "moribund." An outgrowth of AIC was ASEAN Industrial Joint Ventures (AIJV), i.e. ventures involving private investors from at least two ASEAN countries who would obtain government support for their projects. The idea behind the latter was that agreement between two nations is easier to reach. Only one AIJV among 21 awaiting implementation had begun production by 1988.

The difficulties of economic integration are not surprising. The hurdles that must be overcome are numerous. For example: the length of the negotiations; finding markets both within ASEAN and externally; the reluctance of most of the associated states to share markets or to permit an outflow of capital needed at home to finance projects in another country; and finally the preference of Singapore, as an industrialized nation, for free trade.

Cooperation within ASEAN is evident in communications, finance and banking, and its food and agricultural resources constitute a common pool. But the ASEAN partners are competitors in the manufactured goods sector of the international market. In the words of a scholar who has observed the region closely: "ASEAN economic programs are *supplements* to national development priorities; for political reasons they cannot *supplant* them."[1]

Political Cohension ASEAN clearly achieved success in establishing itself as a regional political entity. But collective proclamations of foreign policy positions—declaring international straits as territorial waters; proclaiming Southeast Asia as a zone of peace, freedom and neutrality; and calling for new international economic, technological and information orders—are easy to make. Achievement of such policies is another matter. It is unrealistic to expect the United States or Japan to regard the Strait of Malacca as other than an international waterway, although they may abide by the safety regulations enunciated by the ASEAN ministers, or to accept an "archipelagic" concept for determining the extent of territorial seas. Every ASEAN foreign minister knows that an ASEAN-proclaimed "zone of neutrality" will not deter major powers from infringing upon that neutrality.

Political cohesion is both more than and different from the establishment of a political stance. Political cohesion to the point of taking joint action to attain specific, short term political goals was forced upon the ASEAN states in the late 1970s by their communist neighbors—Vietnam and China. The developments which compelled a unified ASEAN response were the Southeast Asian refugee crisis, the Chinese invasion of Vietnam and the Vietnamese military occupation of Kampuchea. All three affected ASEAN. ASEAN political cohesion and ASEAN security were perceived as two sides of the same coin.

ASEAN found itself in the late 1970s the unwilling recipient of a flood of refugees from the communist states of Vietnam, Laos and Kampuchea, and an actor in the regional conflict between the communist powers of Soviet-backed Vietnam and the PRC. The flow of refugees from the harsh communist regimes that had been installed in South Vietnam and Laos in 1975 and the genocidal policies of the Pol Pot regime of Kampuchea during the succeeding two years, was exacerbated by the flood of ethnic Chinese, who fled in the face of an aroused xenophobic Vietnamese nationalism. Besides fleeing west, many of the Chinese fled north into southern China.

Fearing Chinese retaliation over the ethnic Chinese exodus as well as an intensified Chinese bid for expanded regional leadership in Southeast Asia, Vietnam suddenly became the nation seeking a hand of friendship. In September–October 1978, therefore, Vietnamese Prime Minister Pham Van Dong undertook a tour of the ASEAN states, the first Vietnamese communist head of government to do so. In each country he sought to allay suspicions and signed joint agreements to seek peaceful solutions to problems, promising to cooperate in maintaining peace and stability in the region. Thus Vietnam's armed invasion of Kampuchea in December, two months after the promises were made, and the fall of the Khmer Rouge government of Pol Pot on January 7, 1979, caused a deep moral revulsion within ASEAN even though Pol Pot's brutal pro-Chinese regime was not loved. Vietnam's overt aggression united the ASEAN states.

At a special meeting quickly called in Bangkok the ASEAN foreign

ministers issued a strongly worded statement calling for "the immediate and total withdrawal of the foreign forces from Kampuchea." The
statement recalled the "Vietnamese pledge to ASEAN member countries to scrupulously respect each other's independence, sovereignty
and territorial integrity, and to cooperate in the maintenance of peace
and stability in the region." In a corollary statement devoted to the
refugee problem, the ministers noted that the influx of refugees had
already created severe economic, political, social and security problems, particularly in Thailand and Malaysia which were bearing the
brunt of the influx. They stressed that Vietnam should take appropriate
measures to tackle the problem at the source. They expressed the fear
that the Vietnamese invasion would precipitate another flow of refugees, increase the extent of Sino-Soviet conflict in the area, shatter
regional stability, deter peaceful economic development and aggravate
security problems with ASEAN states. They also recognized the
vulnerability of Thailand as a "front-line" state to overt Vietnamese
attack.[2]

While the foreign ministers were meeting in Bangkok the ASEAN
ambassadors to the United Nations successfully lobbied the Security
Council to reject a Soviet bid of January 12 for official recognition of
the Vietnamese-backed Kampuchean regime of Heng Samrin. They
remained unmoved by a Vietnamese statement the following day
alleging that the Vietnamese "unswervingly respect the principles
concerning our relations with other Southeast Asian countries as
enunciated in the joint statements signed between Premier Pham Van
Dong and the leaders of these countries."[3]

In February the Heng Samrin regime and Vietnam signed a 25-year
Treaty of Friendship and Cooperation. This treaty, plus a similar
earlier one between Vietnam and Laos, brought into de facto existence
an Indochinese federation founded upon communist ideology, under-
written and enforced by Vietnam and the Soviet Union, which realists
among ASEAN leaders had long feared.

The flight of ethnic Chinese from Vietnam and the overthrow of the
pro-Chinese Kampuchean regime led in February–March 1979 to the
PRC invasion of Vietnam. Describing the incursion as a "punishing
action," the PRC sought to curtail what it perceived as Soviet-backed
Vietnamese thrusts to control mainland Southeast Asia. In response to
the Chinese invasion the ASEAN partners, rather than risk projecting
a perception of panic by calling a formal summit, began a period of
intense informal interaction which significantly advanced their move
toward political unity. Between the special ministerial meeting in
Bangkok in January and the annual ministerial meeting scheduled for
June, the member states conferred continuously among themselves

and with the Burmese (the only non-bloc nation on mainland Southeast Asia), via "piece-meal" summits.

As a calculated conciliatory move ASEAN introduced a resolution at the UN calling for "all foreign troops" to leave Southeast Asia, thereby avoiding the need to mention Vietnam by name. The proposal was vetoed by the Soviet Union. After castigating ASEAN for "colluding with the Chinese reactionaries and other imperialist forces against Vietnam, Kampuchea and Laos," Hanoi adopted the tactic of endeavoring to split the coalition.[4] On the eve of the June ASEAN ministerial meeting the Vietnamese offered separate non-aggression treaties to each ASEAN member but did not offer to stem the refugee exodus. The effort failed.

At the Bali Foreign Ministers' Conference of June 28–30, 1979 Singapore Foreign Minister Sinnathamby Rajaratnam spoke in unexpectedly blunt and forceful terms against the Vietnamese conquest of Kampuchea and against what he perceived to be a calculated use of refugees to upset the stability of the non-communist nations of Southeast Asia and, indirectly, to work to the disadvantage of China. Describing the refugees as "human bombs" purposely loosed upon the ASEAN nations by the Vietnamese who knew "full well that almost all ASEAN nations have delicate problems with their Chinese minorities," he went on to say that if the flow were sustained long enough it would lead to racial unrest and bloodshed and "in no time, ASEAN prosperity, ASEAN stability and ASEAN cohesion would vanish into thin air . . . It then needs only a small twist to convert racial wars throughout Southeast Asia into a massive anti-Chinese movement."[5]

The conference expressed "support for the right of the Kampuchean people to determine their future by themselves," reiterated ASEAN's call for "the immediate and total withdrawal of the foreign forces from Kampuchean territory, and renewed its "firm support and solidarity with the government and people of Thailand." Then, taking their cue from Rajaratnam's remarks, the ministers focused on the refugees. They went on record as identifying Vietnam as the cause of the refugee problem and announced their intention of refusing to take any more displaced persons—and of expelling those in existing camps—if resettlement efforts by other countries were not increased.[6] Their seemingly callous stand sprang from genuine fear that the refugee problem was nearing an uncontrollable level.

By the spring of 1978 the influx of all categories of refugees—ethnic Chinese or other—had already seriously disrupted ASEAN societies. Some 160,000 displaced persons from Indochina had sought refuge in Thailand alone. The "boat people" from Vietnam had headed primarily for Malaysia and 42,000 of them were in Malaysian transit camps by November. By June 1979 the UN High Commissioner for Refugees estimated that over one million persons had fled from their Indochinese home countries, 550,000 of them to non-communist nations in Southeast Asia.

As early as December 1978 Malaysia, partly to gain world recognition of the gravity of the problem, refused to accept a shipload of refugees and used the occasion to accuse the United States, Australia and other developed countries of "selective acceptance" of the displaced persons, leaving Malaysia with "the crumbs."[7] During the following six months as a new wave of people flooded into the ASEAN countries from Kampuchea, the UN and the developed western countries geared up to handle the flow which showed no signs of abating. Nevertheless the ASEAN partners continued to bear the major burden.

The united stance of ASEAN at the ministerial conference at Bali met with an immediate response from western ministers—U.S. Secretary of State Cyrus R. Vance and the foreign ministers of Japan, Australia, New Zealand and Ireland (as representative of the EEC)— who met with the ASEAN ministers in the two days following. Vance affirmed that the U.S. was "committed morally and by treaty to support the ASEAN states. We have made this clear to all concerned— and directly to the Soviet Union and Vietnam." Vance also promised that the U.S. would accept "double the number of refugees, increasing the number to 168,000," to seek with the international community ways to alleviate the pressures on ASEAN, and to increase and accelerate military aid to individual ASEAN States.[8] Japan also agreed to double its contribution to refugee relief and called for an international conference on Kampuchea.

Three weeks later ASEAN took its complaint about the influx to the July 20–21 Geneva Conference, called to take action on the refugee problem. It was attended by 57 countries including China, the USSR and Vietnam. The assembled governments agreed to accept 233,000 of the 372,854 refugees in Southeast Asian camps of temporary asylum at the end of June. Indicative of the problems faced by ASEAN nations, the number had increased by 25,000 in the ensuing three weeks.

Kampuchean Problem   The refugee crisis and the continuing Vietnamese military occupation of Kampuchea served: 1) to reinforce ASEAN cohesion, 2) to effect an era of good relations between the bloc and the PRC, 3) to enhance the status and prestige of ASEAN as an international force, and 4) to link US-ASEAN foreign policy objectives in Southeast Asia.

In September 1979 the ASEAN partners began an offensive against the international acceptance of Vietnamese aggression by recognition of the Heng Samrin regime at the Summit Conference of Non-Aligned Nations in Havana. The offensive had two objectives: to prevent recognition of the regime in international forums, and to generate sufficient international political pressure to force the Vietnamese out of Kampuchea. The endeavor initially had little success, although Rajaratnam addressed the issue with incisive logic. He made clear that he held no brief for the "barbarous, oppressive and undemocratic" displaced government of Pol Pot, but he "decried the fact that the conference was being asked to expel Pol Pot's Kampuchean government 'on the ground that armed intervention by foreign forces has been successful.' " If we are willing to accept this incredible proposition he argued, "then let us resign ourselves to becoming mercenaries for the lucky power which has captured us."[9] Neither the Pol Pot representatives nor those of the Heng Samrin regime were seated.

The ASEAN offensive picked up momentum, however, when two months later the UN General Assembly voted by a two-to-one margin to allow the deposed Pol Pot regime to keep its seat in that body, as it did again in 1980 and 1981. An ASEAN-sponsored resolution seeking an international conference to resolve the Kampuchean conflict was approved by the UN General Assembly October 22, 1980 by a vote of 97 to 23, although the resolution was vigorously opposed by Vietnam, the Soviet Union and their allies. The resolution specified that the conference should negotiate an agreement on the total withdrawal of foreign troops from Kampuchea within a UN-specified time frame and with UN-supervised free elections. The ASEAN members subsequently prodded UN Secretary General Kurt Waldheim to convene the conference while simultaneously persuading all countries with interests in Kampuchea to support it. In January 1981 the PRC agreed to attend without prior partial withdrawal of Vietnamese troops from Kampuchea. Chinese agreement to attend insured that the conference would take place, although Vietnam and the Soviet Union announced their refusal to participate.

At the Meeting of the Islamic Foreign Ministers in Saudi Arabia that same month, Indonesia and Malaysia, the two Islamic members of ASEAN, condemned Vietnam and called for withdrawal of Vietnamese troops. The entire ASEAN group reiterated this position at the February conference of Foreign Ministers of Non-Aligned States in India. Vietnam and the Soviet Union, meanwhile, set out to portray the Kampuchean situation as purely regional in character. Thus they proposed a regional conference to be held among Vietnam, Laos, the Heng Samrin regime of Kampuchea and ASEAN—a tactic which would have taken the problem out of the UN framework and the context of the UN resolution. In this they were unsuccessful.

The UN Special Conference on Kampuchea met July 13–17, 1981 in New York. It was attended by 80 nations, but boycotted by Vietnam, the Soviets and most of their allies. The U.S. joined with ASEAN in

condemnation of Vietnam at the opening session, restating its refusal
to normalize relations with Vietnam until its troops were withdrawn
from Kampuchea, or to provide economic assistance "as long as
Vietnam continued to squander its scarce resources on aggression.[10]
ASEAN members presented a resolution calling for a ceasefire, withdrawal of all foreign forces and the disarming of all Kampucheans, plus
establishment of an interim administration until elections could create
a new government. The PRC opposed ASEAN's call for disarmament
of all Kampuchean factions, calling instead for the disarmament of
troops of the government of Heng Samrin only, nor did it favor an
interim government pending free elections. However, a French-spon-
sored compromise was accepted which called for "appropriate arrangements to ensure that armed Kampuchean factions will not be able
to prevent or disrupt the holding of free elections or intimidate or
coerce the population in the electoral process and to ensure that the
armed Kampuchean factions will respect the results of the free elections." The language adopted did not specifically call for general
disarmament, for an interim regime or for UN-supervised elections,
although the ASEAN members maintained that the principle of such
goals was retained. A committee was created upon ASEAN initiative,
composed of representatives of Japan, Malaysia, Nigeria, Senegal, Sri
Lanka and Sudan. Its mandate was to negotiate with the Vietnamese
for withdrawal of troops, dispatch of a UN peacekeeping force to
Kampuchea and holding elections. The mandate apparently died
aborning.

Although ASEAN's new found political cohesion transformed it into
an international force to be reckoned with and constituted its most
significant achievement, the partners also appear to have accepted the
PRC as the leading regional power in Southeast Asia, despite long held
concerns over China's support of indigenous communist parties. PRC
diplomacy was clearly directed toward maintaining and enhancing such
a position.

In September 1981 PRC and ASEAN interests coalesced further.
ASEAN had been seeking an anti-Vietnamese resistance movement
that would be broader than the despised Khmer Rouge. The PRC
obliged by involving deposed Prince Norodom Sihanouk, then residing
in Peking, in a widely publicized meeting in Singapore with Son Sann
(a conservative former Kampuchean prime minister) and Khieu Samphan (leader of the Khmer Rouge).

The three stated their willingness "to form a Coalition Government
of Democratic Kampuchea." The triumvirate demonstrated little in
common beyond a desire to overthrow the Vietnamese-dominated and
Soviet-supported Heng Samrin government. But the fact that the
meeting was held in Singapore, an ASEAN state, served to identify

ASEAN with Chinese policy, even though the ASEAN partners had repeatedly stated that their opposition to Heng Samrin did not in any manner imply support for the (Chinese-supported) deposed Khmer Rouge.

Although the display of unity of the Kampucheans was momentary and they separated within hours, the idea persisted because inclusion of non-communists in a resistance movement would make it respectable enough for ASEAN support. In February 1982 Sihanouk and Khieu Samphan were invited to Peking for further negotiations and on June 22, 1982 at Kuala Lumpur the leaders of the three factions signed the Declaration on the Formation of a Coalition Government of Democratic Kampuchea. Prince Sihanouk was designated president of the coalition government, Khieu Samphan vice president and the 72-year-old Son Sann premier. From the Chinese point of view the formation of the Coalition Government was a perfect capstone to the communique of the ASEAN foreign ministers, issued at the end of their semiannual conference in Singapore June 16, which had expressed "their continued support for the efforts toward the formation of a Kampuchean coalition government in the spirit and according to the intent of the joint statement issued in Singapore on September 4, 1981."[12] The Khmer Rouge, as one of the three parties in the coalition, thus achieved legitimacy, a Chinese objective, despite earlier ASEAN protestations to the contrary. As midwife to the birth of the Coalition Government ASEAN had become the vehicle through which legitimacy was conferred.

Changing Indochina Policy   China's tactics to influence ASEAN policy continued to bear fruit. Led by ASEAN, the United Nations in 1982 and every year through 1989 bestowed the Kampuchean seat on the Coalition Government as the heir to the Pol Pot regime. But cracks also began to appear in ASEAN's hard stance. In early 1984 former Thai premier Kriangsak led a delegation to Hanoi at the latter's invitation, as did the Malaysian foreign minister. Within a month, General Benny Murdani, commander of Indonesia's armed forces, followed their example. A new Vietnam connection had emerged.

By 1987 ASEAN members, almost casually, had begun to hedge on their professed trade embargo against Vietnam. Some spokespersons announced that the partners had agreed only to abstain from trade which fell under the ASEAN aid embargo, namely credits, transfer of technology and state-supported trade. The ASEAN partners, they said, "never decided to suspend normal trade and services, or other forms of business for profit."[13] Led by Indonesia, individual member ASEAN trade missions to and from Vietnam became common. Surprisingly Singapore, most vociferous among Hanoi's critics, by 1988

was second among non-communist nations in bilateral trade with
Vietnam.

Indonesia invented the term "cocktail party," later termed Joint
Informal Meeting, or JIM, to describe informal meetings it hosted in
1988 and 1989 among the Kampuchean adversaries. Vietnam's foreign
minister agreed to attend the August 1988 JIM, that nation's first
concession concerning the Kampuchean issue. Thailand's new prime
minister, Chatichai Choonhavan, introduced a Thai bid to manage the
ASEAN agenda. He invited Prime Minister Hun Sen, as leader of a
Kampuchean faction, rather than as premier, for talks in Bangkok. At
JIM II in February Thailand's by then "de facto recognition of the
Hun Sen regime was tacitly and partially adopted by ASEAN. . . . in
the non-consensus 'Consensual Statement' on Kampuchea."[14] Perhaps
(at least in part) in consequence of the talks, in April Vietnam announced it would withdraw its 26,000 troops remaining in Kampuchea
by the end of September 1989.

Subsequent bilateral talks between Prince Sihanouk—ASEAN's
candidate to lead a "peaceful, independent, and neutral Kampuchea"—and Hun Sen, were broadened to include the other two Kampuchean resistance factions. In consequence, a 19-nation peace conference was convened in Paris in mid-year to reconcile their opposing
views. Unfortunately the month-long (July-August) effort ended in
"total disharmony" despite efforts by the United States and other
major nations to effect reconciliation. The Kampuchean factions could
not agree 1) on the use of the term "genocide" to describe the behavior
of the previous Khmer government (in effect questioning the legitimacy
of the Vietnamese-sponsored Hun Sen regime), 2) whether the UN
should supervise national elections, 3) on arrangements for power
sharing among the factions within a transitional government, and 4) on
the status of an alleged 1,200,000 Vietnamese alleged to have migrated
to Kampuchea during the years of the conflict.

MAJOR POWER INTERVENTION

The generalization was advanced in the introduction to this volume
that the peoples of Southeast Asia (except Brunei) have encountered
severe problems as they sought to achieve political and economic
expectations at the close of the colonial era. It was posited further that
the post–1945 political history of the area is a record of experimenta-
tion and contest over what kind of political and economic order can
best fulfill national aspirations. The nations set out on their quest from
a base of similar experiences and problems. With the exception of
Thailand all experienced colonial rule, Japanese invasion and military
occupation, a struggle for independence, ethnic and religious tensions

and nationalistic fervor. All including Thailand suffered from unbalanced, ill-balanced or underdeveloped economies. In each (except Brunei) a strong communist movement arose as a fundamental challenge to the political institutions and economic orders which the departing colonial powers had attempted to implant.

As the colonial powers reluctantly withdrew from the region the new political entities embarked upon developmental paths strewn with hard lessons. Neither socialism nor capitalism proved to be panaceas for their economic ills. Internal diversity of language and culture inhibited national political integration as leaders realized that the people's strongest loyalties were not national. Western political institutions— parliaments, constitutions and courts—were ineffective because a developing political polarity between communists and non-communists, as well as the presence of deep ethnic and religious cleavages, precluded attainment of consensus necessary to enable them to transform expectations into reality.

As further suggested in the introduction, the decolonization of Southeast Asia at the close of World War II was a mutual objective of the United States and the Soviet Union. The United States, as leader of the western European and Atlantic world, wanted a Southeast Asia committed to the values of private property, individual rights, western parliamentary institutions and the preservation of an international system founded upon laws, economic institutions and relationships which would reflect such values. The edifice thus created would be undergirded by mutual security alliances.

The Soviets and their then junior partner, the People's Republic of China (PRC) sought to create in Southeast Asia a fundamentally different order, one founded upon socialist—i.e., centrally planned and/or non-market economies, collective property and collective rights—political systems, economic institutions and laws that would reflect these values. Their edifice would replace that which the colonial powers had previously set in place, and would be maintained and controlled through national communist parties which would loyally accept the leadership of the Communist Party of the USSR. The new political systems and economic orders of the Southeast Asian nations would be linked to the Soviet and Chinese economies and would be sustained and safeguarded by economic, political and military ties to the Soviet Union.

The first post-World War II decade, 1945–1955, was a see-saw period for the superpowers in Southeast Asia. Communist triumphs in Indochina at the expense of France and, indirectly, the entire West, were offset by serious American intervention in Indochina in the early 1950s, and by completion in 1955 of a system of American alliances designed to counter the communist movement in the region and bind the non-communist states more closely to the United States specifically, and to the West generally. A tripartite security treaty, the ANZUS Pact, was concluded upon American initiative in 1951, by Australia, New Zealand and the United States, committing the U.S. to defend the other two. The Southeast Asia Collective Defense Treaty (Pact of Manila) was agreed to in 1954 among mainly non-Southeast Asian states—the United States, the United Kingdom, France, Australia, New Zealand, Pakistan, the Philippines and Thailand—to deter both external aggression and internal subversion. A protocol to the Pact of Manila extended the protective umbrella of the defense treaty to Vietnam, Kampuchea and Laos. The Southeast Asia Treaty Organization (SEATO), a military-economic arrangement based on the defense treaty, was inaugurated in 1955. Although SEATO was subsequently disbanded, the Manila Pact remained operative in 1990. During the same period (1951) the United States concluded a bilateral security treaty with the Philippines. In effect, the United States was the principal ally of many of the Southeast Asian states until the end of the war in Vietnam.

Withdrawal of the United States from Southeast Asia after the signing of the Paris Agreement on Ending the War and Restoring Peace in Vietnam in 1973, was followed by the fall in 1975 of the anti-communist regimes in south Vietnam and Kampuchea. The successor communist governments in both of those states, as well as in Laos, immediately became prey to the competitive designs of the now two communist superpowers—the PRC and the Soviet Union.

Sino-Soviet Conflict In order to assess conflictiong interests in Southeast Asia, it is useful to retrace the development of the Sino-Soviet quarrel which began in 1956 after Krushchev denounced Stalin in a speech to the 20th Communist Party Congress. The speech was an implied indictment of communist party leaders everywhere and was so perceived by Chinese leader Mao Tse-tung. The quarrel flared openly beginning in 1960, and the Soviet elite began a determined effort to destroy China's credibility as the leader of the communist movement in Southeast Asia. Not only ideological rhetoric but massive military assistance began to flow to Hanoi to overshadow Chinese aid to the communist Democratic Republic of Vietnam for use in its struggle against the anti-communist Republic of Vietnam and the western powers. In the immediate post-Vietnam War years, the USSR made significant political gains. By 1977 it had become united communist Vietnam's most important military and economic supplier and military-political ally. Since the Vietnamese communists had by then reduced Laos to effective dependency, Laos was also a de facto ally of the Soviet Union. There is little doubt that the USSR hoped that the PRC would again be forced into junior partner status in the worldwide communist movement after the death of Mao in 1976, but these expectations were dashed when Teng Hsiao-ping succeeded to power.

From the Chinese point of view, not only did Soviet relations continue to be cool, relations with Vietnam deteriorated as that state came into conflict with the pro-Chinese communist regime of the Khmer Rouge in Kampuchea. The outbreak of a serious border war between the two nations in 1977 caused the Chinese to increase their support of the Khmer Rouge. Vietnam retaliated by persecuting its large Chinese minority so severely that they fled by the thousands, inaugurating the tragic saga of the "boat people." As the Vietnamese, with ever increasing Soviet financial, advisory and materiel support, prepared to overthrow the Khmer Rouge regime, the Chinese suspended all economic assistance to Hanoi. Ministerial level talks on refugees and border incidents between the two nations resolved nothing. At the same time Teng, a political as well as economic pragmatist, sought to find allies outside the communist world. In August 1978 the PRC concluded a Treaty of Peace and Friendship with Japan that included an "anti-hegemony" clause openly directed at the USSR. Teng also developed economic links with Europe leading to arms purchases and visited the United States in early 1979, a prelude to what many observers considered an emerging Sino-American de facto alliance against the Soviets. In November 1978 Vietnam and the Soviet Union had signed a 25-year friendship treaty which included a defense clause, and in mid-December the Chinese and Americans announced establishment of diplomatic relations, an announcement which was followed on Christmas day by the Vietnamese invasion of Kampuchea.

In retrospect it appears that in exchange for treaty assurance of Soviet protection, the Vietnamese undertook to invade Kampuchea in pursuance of the mutually desired objective of crushing Chinese political influence in Southeast Asia. It is also clear that the December 25 timing of the invasion was linked to the Sino-American announcement 10 days earlier. In short, the substantive Chinese-American rapprochement threatened the expensively won Soviet position in Southeast Asia, and its client, Vietnam, was entrusted with preventing such erosion by establishing a pro-Soviet regime in Kampuchea before the PRC-US rapprochement could have an effect on Southeast Asian politics.

With the overthrow of the Chinese backed Khmer Rouge government of Pol Pot and the establishment of the Vietnamese-Soviet backed regime of Heng Samrin, the PRC's worst fear had become a reality. Its status as the leader of the communist movement in Southeast Asia and its political influence in the region were compromised. On February 17, therefore, Chinese forces attacked along the entire Sino-Vietnamese border. They moved through "Friendship Pass" 12 miles toward the provincial capital of Lang Son which they overran on March 3. Teng and other Chinese leaders repeatedly stated that the military action was a limited one. On March 5 Vietnam announced a general mobilization. The same day the PRC announced that its military action had sufficiently "punished" Vietnam for its invasion of Kampuchea and that Chinese forces would be withdrawn. After Chinese troops had departed the two governments agreed to begin to negotiate their differences. The PRC had partially revived its credibility as the communist ally of the deposed Khmer Rouge, but according to Goh Keng Swee, Minister of Defense for Singapore, "the fact that Chinese armies did not venture further than a few miles inside the border was ample testimony to the credibility of the Soviet deterrence.[15]

Most observers conclude that the Soviet Union was the real winner in the events of 1978–79. First, by promoting the Vietnamese conquest of Kampuchea the Soviets insured deep Chinese hatred of the Hanoi regime, driving the latter further into the Soviet embrace, and precipitating the former into the essentially fruitless limited invasion of Vietnam. Second, the Soviets accurately concluded that since the military conflict was inconclusive, so too would be the subsequent Sino-Vietnamese negotiations, thus guaranteeing Chinese "pressure on the Vietnamese through a variety of means, including occasional military sorties, support of insurgent groups, and economic and military pressures designed to bleed the Vietnamese," which would insure the necessity of a continuing Soviet-Vietnames alliance.[16] And finally, Soviet use of Vietnamese bases was "likely to increase in gradual stages so that all concerned will get accustomed to the new naval presence. In this way, the Soviet Union will try to avoid unduly provoking Washington or Tokyo while gaining Vietnam as a military ally and developing access to its base facilities—achievements that will represent a major triumph of Soviet power against both China and the United States.[17] By 1985 Hanoi maintained some 250,000 troops along the Sino-Vietnamese border, tying down an equal number of Chinese soldiers. Border clashes, some involving battalion and regiment-size units, were frequent and Soviet naval and air forces were freely utilizing base facilities in Vietnam.

United States Reentry   United States involvement in Southeast Asia during the two years following the fall of the Republic of Vietnam (April 1975) was limited primarily to political and diplomatic confrontation with the new united Socialist Republic of Vietnam (SRV) and to adjusting to the increasingly independent foreign policy postures of its treaty allies, the Philippines and Thailand.

In 1975 and 1976 the U.S. blocked SRV entry into the United Nations. U.S. opposition to seating the SRV ceased in 1977 but continuing disagreement between the two states kept them far apart.

The SRV accused the United States of reneging on Nixon-Kissinger promises to assist in post-hostilities rebuilding of Vietnam and demanded reparations. The United States maintained that it was Hanoi that had reneged by its conquest of the Republic of Vietnam in violation of the Paris peace settlement of 1973. Hanoi initially refused to return American prisoners of war as agreed to in the peace settlement. The Vietnamese government also declined to search or account for American servicemen missing in action.

Events in 1978 ended all prospects for near term Vietnamese-American reconciliation. The tragic flotillas of "boat people" escaping harsh Vietnamese measures against the ethnic Chinese population, added to the earlier flood of political refugees, incensed Americans. President Jimmy Carter declined to accept a Vietnamese offer to drop the demand for reparations and establish diplomatic relations without conditions. The Vietnamese invasion of Kampuchea in December 1978 and the simultaneous Sino-American rapprochement were the final nails in the coffin. The former development was perceived by the United States as another example of communist perfidy, as well as an action which would create serious disequilibrium throughout Southeast Asia; the latter rekindled Vietnamese hostility toward the United States for allying itself in a practical sense with Vietnam's principal enemy, China.

In consequence of the events in Indochina the United States became increasingly concerned over the Soviet role in Southeast Asia. In 1980 Assistant Secretary of State Richard Holbrooke stated flatly that "our overall objectives are to reduce and eventually eliminate the Soviet military presence in Vietnam."[18] Believing that the Soviet force buildup—globally and in the Pacific—far exceeded any legitimate defense requirements, U.S. leadership saw Soviet aims in the region as: 1) neutralizing Japan in any conflict, 2) threatening Pacific sea lanes, and 3) utilizing Vietnamese air and naval facilities as a means of projecting Soviet military power and political influence throughout the region.

U.S. reentry into Southeast Asian regional affairs was via Thailand, which had been its most valuable regional ally during the war in Vietnam. Although in 1975 Thailand had unilaterally decided upon the closure of American bases there, subsequent events (serious communist guerrilla attacks in its northern and southern frontier areas, the flood of refugees from Kampuchea, and the fighting along its borders between the forces of Pol Pot and Heng Samrin) prompted the government to request and receive resumed military assistance, beginning in 1976. Citing the Pact of Manila, the Department of State in March 1980 announced renewed support of the United States for the security of Thailand.

In June 1980 some 2,000 Vietnamese troops crossed the border from Kampuchea into Thailand. Although they quickly withdrew, the U.S. expressed the opinion that a "Vietnamese attack on Thailand . . . could not take place without Soviet support," and nearly doubled its military sales to Thailand for fiscal year (FY) 1980 and 1981. In April 1981 the new administration of Ronald Reagan reiterated that under the terms of the Pact of Manila the government "considers that the United States is obliged to come to the assistance of Thailand." Moreover in 1981 the United States for the first time provided military assistance to all ASEAN partners. FY 1983 military assistance and sales to ASEAN states were approximately US$200 million, and the Reagan administration reassured ASEAN members that the United States remained committed to the defense of Southeast Asia.

Chinese leadership also sought to counter the Vietnamese thrust toward Thailand and repeatedly declared that it would defend that nation in the event of Vietnamese attack. Since the U.S. was the *de jure* and the PRC the *de facto* ally of Thailand, United States and PRC policies rather neatly coincided. Some observers considered that the convergence of Sino-American policy in Thailand and Indochina would be detrimental to long term U.S. interests in the region. They questioned the American policy of pressuring Vietnam—through political, diplomatic and economic actions—to make concessions concerning Kampuchea and to alter its relations with the Soviets. What was overlooked, they suggested, was that Vietnam perceived a grave threat from the 250,000 Chinese troops on its border. Hanoi's continuing occupation of Kampuchea, according to this scenario, was its only leverage to induce the Chinese to agree to pull back their soldiers and pledge not to use force against Vietnam. Viewed from this perspective the parallel Sino-U.S. policy toward Vietnam practically assured continued Vietnamese intransigence concerning Kampuchea, as well as continuing Soviet influence throughout Indochina, making the main U.S. policy objective of eliminating the Soviet presence in Vietnam unattainable.

In addition to political interests on mainland Southeast Asia, the United States had long term political, economic and strategic interests in the Philippines. The strong political relationship between the two countries dated back to the close of the 19th century when the Philippines was ceded to the U.S. by Spain. The islands were the ward of the United States for half a century and a "special relationship" between the two persisted until the Philippines endorsed the goals of the worldwide nonaligned movement in the 1970s. Even so, close political and economic ties remained. U.S. withdrawal from mainland Southeast Asia at the close of the war in Vietnam was not followed by U.S. military withdrawal from the Philippines. On the contrary, the

U.S.-Philippines Mutual Defense Treaty of 1951 remained fully opera-
tional and the Philippines became the southern anchor of American
strategic bases in the Western Pacific and Northeast Asia. The U.S.
Philippines Military Bases Agreement of March 14, 1947 (as amended
September 16, 1966) provided for American leasing of bases in the
Philippines until 1991.

To summarize, when the American military presence ended on
mainland Southeast Asia, security relationships in the region were
significantly altered. Both the Soviet Union and the United States
expanded naval and air units operating in the South China Sea. The
U.S. revived a specific commitment to the security of Thailand, and
provided military assistance to all of the ASEAN countries except
Brunei; the Soviet Union increased its military assistance to the
Indochinese states and developed the Vietnamese port at Camranh
Bay to naval base status. The United Kingdom withdrew its last forces
from Singapore in 1976, but maintained its security commitments,
together with Australia and New Zealand, to Malaysia and Singapore
under terms of the 1971 Five Power Defense Arrangement.

REFUGEES

A recurring phenomenon of major importance in the political history
of Southeast Asia is the displacement of large numbers of people from
their homelands. In the earliest instances, stronger or numerically
superior ethnic populations migrated into Southeast Asia from China,
and to a much lesser degree from India. Displacement in these instances was gradual and did not entail the hardship, privation and
mortality rates which accompanied subsequent displacement of persons in consequence of invasion and wars. In the course of the long
epic of the rise and fall of Southeast Asian empires, the antecedent
states of contemporary Vietnam, Kampuchea, Laos and Burma were
centers of human ebb and flow. In earliest historic times Kampuchea
was the heartland of empire, pushing its conquests into Laos, Vietnam
and Thailand. The Vietnamese repeatedly surged southward from the
Red River valley of Tongking, displacing the Cham and eventually
eradicating the state of Champa. In another series of expansionist
drives the Vietnamese moved against Kampuchea, pushing the peoples
of the Khmer empire westward to the frontiers of the rising Thai
state—where they were pushed eastward again by the Thai. Laos
experienced the same ebb and flow of Vietnamese, Thai and Burmese
invasions, accompanied by massive displacement of peoples. In the
west, the conflicts within Burma and between Burma and the rising
state of Thailand, resulted in a frequent flood of refugees into neighboring territories.

In the 20th century history has clearly repeated itself in Indochina, but with a new twist: displacement and mistreatment of nationals as a matter of national government policy. Some 900,000 Vietnamese fled from the north to the south when Vietnam was partitioned in 1954. Since the communist consolidation of Vietnam and conquest of Kampuchea and Laos in 1975, over 2.5 million persons have fled from these states. As many as one-third of them may have perished—succumbing to drowning at sea, murder, brutality, disease and starvation.

The postwar exodus from Vietnam was caused by three major factors: 1) fear in the south in 1975 of communist reprisals for having been associated with the previous government or with the U.S., 2) deliberate government effort, beginning in 1978, to rid the country of persons considered undesirable, especially Vietnamese of Chinese extraction, and 3) escalation of armed conflict in 1978–79 within the Indochinese states which reached crisis proportions with the Vietnamese invasion of Kampuchea in December 1978 and the Chinese punitive invasion of Vietnam in February 1979.

The exodus from Kampuchea had four basic causes: 1) the murder in 1975 of 100,000 persons associated with the former non-communist government, 2) the brutality and deprivation inflicted en masse upon the Khmer people by the Khmer Rouge regime of Pol Pot in its forced movement of persons from urban areas into the countryside, 3) the fighting during and following the Vietnamese invasion of Kampuchea, and 4) the famine conditions which developed in September 1979 and which were partly the consequences of deliberate government policy.

In Laos the campaign, begun in 1975 by the communist Pathet Lao government and Vietnamese forces to exterminate Hmong tribesmen who had cooperated with the previous Laotian government and the United States, resulted in a continuing flow of refugees into Thailand. City dwellers, villagers, lowland Lao, Black Thai, Khmer and other ethnic groups joined the exodus because of severe economic conditions and loss of personal freedoms.

In April 1975 over 135,000 Vietnamese sought refuge in the United States; they were persons who had worked with the U.S. government or the Thieu regime, or who had friends and relatives in the United States. By mid-1975, and continuing through late 1977, some 1,500 refugees per month fled Vietnam in small boats, mainly to Malaysian or Thai ports, most of them seeking eventual asylum in the West. A smaller number fled overland through Laos or Kampuchea to Thailand. Through 1977 the exodus consisted mainly of ethnic Vietnamese from the south.

Beginning in early 1978, as a consequence of deliberate government policy, Sino-Vietnamese from both the north and the south joined the outflow which rapidly increased. In the spring of 1978 alone, more than 160,000 Sino-Vietnamese fled overland into China from north Vietnam before the PRC sealed its land border in July; another 70,000 fled to China by sea. Many paid Vietnamese officials US$2,000 in gold to be allowed to leave on dangerously overcrowded freighters.

During the period July 1978–79 some 500,000 people fled south Vietnam, many losing their lives attempting to reach shelter, and a boat building industry flourished to facilitate their departure. Boat people continued to flee during the 1980s, although the numbers dropped substantially until 1987. The figures for Kampuchea were equally grim. Between 1975 and the end of 1980 some 400,000 Khmer fled the country. In 1975, despite the Pol Pot regime's strict control of population movements, 150,000 fled into Vietnam, and approximately 33,000 into Thailand. After the establishment of the Vietnamese-supported government of Heng Samrin in January 1979 about 110,000 of those who had gone to Vietnam returned, but an additional 100,000 sought refuge in Thailand. In June 1979 Thai troops forcibly returned 42,000 of them to Kampuchea, but famine conditions later in the year resulted in another exodus into Thailand. In Laos between 1975 and 1980 approximately 300,000, out of a population of 3 million, fled the country.[19] Four ASEAN states—Thailand, Malaysia, the Philippines and Indonesia—in descending order, were the countries of first asylum.

When the tide of refugees swelled to more than 60,000 per month in summer 1979 the ASEAN countries of first asylum refused to accept further arrivals and threatened to expel the 400,000 refugees already in holding areas and temporary camps should the crisis worsen. The governments cited three principal reasons for their policy stance: their fear of becoming involved in war, the impact of the refugees on their fragile internal ethnic balances and the severe economic pressures which the refugee influx had generated.

Thailand was the vulnerable "front line" state, with hundreds of thousands of Khmer refugees in the country, and with Khmer Rouge and non-communist guerrillas on the Thai border, facing the 70,000 Vietnamese troops nearby. Thailand feared armed conflict between the Vietnamese and the Khmer resistance forces would spread into Thailand and cause a new flood of refugees which would overwhelm available facilities. Malaysia, Indonesia and Singapore feared that the large number of ethnic Chinese who had fled from Vietnam would exacerbate traditional racial prejudice against the *nanyang* (overseas) Chinese. All of the first asylum countries feared unwanted political and economic consequences of the continued presence of refugees in camps where: 1) black markets fueled inflation, 2) ethnic hostility caused unrest among local inhabitants, and 3) distribution of free food and other benefits to refugees produced general resentment. Moreover, the presence of the refugees required additional funds for refugee-related security purposes.

Problems intensified in October 1979 when Vietnamese-Khmer Rouge fighting drove an additional 70,000 Khmer into Thailand in a 10-day period and the fighting threatened to spill over into that country. Bangkok and Hanoi traded harsh accusations with each other. At the critical moment the crisis was defused. Tension eased when in October coordinated relief efforts along the border and within Kampuchea by the UN Children's Fund (UNICEF) and the International Committee of the Red Cross commenced.

Throughout 1979 the western powers, the ASEAN states, the communist regimes in Vietnam and Kampuchea, and the PRC engaged in a four-way contest. By refusing to accept further refugees, and in cases mistreating them and threatening to expel them from the border camps, the ASEAN states were able to extract more bilateral and multilateral assistance for refugee aid. For their part, the western nations, acting through the UN High Commissioner for Refugees (UNHCR), pressured the ASEAN members to provide more first asylum facilities, as well as at least a token amount of permanent resettlement. The Vietnamese and the Heng Samrin regime, both clients of the USSR, used the crisis to intimidate Thailand, client both of the United States and China. The Chinese used the crisis to advance their objective of overturning the Heng Samrin regime through substantial arms deliveries to the Khmer Rouge guerrillas.

International Assistance Programs Beginning in July 1975 the UNHCR established an Indochinese refugee assistance program which provided funds to first asylum countries and to participatory voluntary agencies. By 1980 about US$400 million had been contributed, one-fourth of the amount coming from the United States. The international community's massive relief effort from mid-1979 through 1980 devoted US$400–450 million in additional funds to the program and the Soviet Union and Eastern bloc countries "may have contributed as much as US$200 million."[20]

The major countries of resettlement initiated a UN Conference on Refugees from Vietnam July 20–21, 1979, which was attended by 60 nations. The conference heightened global response to the problem, generated new permanent resettlement sites, and produced a Vietnamese promise to curtail "illegal departures" for a reasonable period of time. At the conference the United States agreed to accept 14,000 refugees each month through September 1980.

In the wake of the conference and at the urging of the western countries, the Red Cross and UNICEF began negotiations with the Heng Samrin government, as well as with the Khmer Rouge guerrillas, to reach agreement for transporting humanitarian relief to civilians within Kampuchea who were in danger of starvation. This was both a humanitarian gesture and to prevent a further exodus from that country. In October a small Red Cross/UNICEF office was opened in Phnom Penh and a daily airlift of 15 tons of food into the city began. At the same time food was dispensed across the Thai-Khmer border. Red Cross/UNICEF assumed the operation of border feeding stations and UNHCR coordinated the holding centers within Thailand. A Pledging Conference for Aid to Khmer People, convened by the UN in November in New York, was attended by 75 nations and produced US$210 million in cash and supplies to care for the 2.25 million people in need of immediate assistance in the area, and funds for the continuing UNHCR refugee program. The UNHCR-administered holding centers within Thailand continued to provide shelter, water, medical care and sanitation facilities. The thousands of Thai, who were displaced from their homes by the waves of refugees and the military incursions, were supported by international agencies and voluntary organizations and were helped in forming new communities.

The United States, followed by France, Canada, Australia, West Germany and the United Kingdom became the major permanent resettlement countries. The U.S. Refugee Assistance Act of 1980 institutionalized a "normal flow" of 50,000 per year for three years. By 1984 the U.S. had accepted 700,000 of the refugees and areas of Southern California had become Indochinese enclaves. Subsequently admission requirements were sharply tightened and lower quotas were established.

Between 1982 and 1986 the UNHCR refugee case load fell to fewer than 20,000 per year, a volume which could be accomodated despite reduced western resettlement quotas. But the boat people lost their priority as refugee crises developed elsewhere, e.g., 250,000 yearly arrivals in Europe from other third world countries.

Suddenly, and inexplicably, the Indochinese refugee inflow increased dramatically in 1987 and the delicate equilibrium between refugee inflow and resettlement outflow broke down. So called "compassion fatigue" emerged in Southeast Asian nations of first asylum. Thailand and Malaysia applied harsh deterrent measures. Refugee camps were closed and incidents of denial of landing rights and forced repatriation were reported although both nations denied any change in their policies of providing temporary shelter.

Thailand and Malaysia—joined by Hong Kong which had become a preferred haven—called for a Second International Conference on Indochinese Refugees. Seventy nations participated in the June 1989 meetings at Geneva where a Comprehensive Plan of Action was adopted. It endorsed screening procedures for distinguishing genuine refugees—including political prisoners newly released from "reeducation camps''—from "economic migrants," and further speed up of the orderly departure program. The latter was essentially a "family reunion" program administered by the UNHCR which had been adopted at the 1979 conference. In 1989 the U.S. quota for refugees from Southeast Asia was 50,000 annually.

POLITICAL CHANGE

Indochina The political climate in Southeast Asia was profoundly affected by the failure of orthodox Marxist/Leninist-based economies of the Soviet Union and Vietnam during the period 1975–1985. For the Soviet Union the years of Brezhnev and his two brief successors were periods of domestic stagnation and expansionist foreign policy. In 1985 Mikhail S. Gorbachev, General Secretary of the Communist Party and later conjointly President of the USSR, proposed a new two-track policy of *glasnost* (political openness) and *perestroika* (political, social and economic reform). Almost simultaneously the Communist Party of Vietnam changed direction. The Sixth Party Congress of 1986 chose leaders who, attributing Vietnam's failed economy to a "simplistic and unrealistic conception of socialism," initiated domestic reform and demonstrated flexibility in foreign policy.

Signaling a desire to reduce conflict in Indochina, the USSR also moved toward rapprochement with China, its long-time rival in the region. Vietnam responded by reducing its troop strength in Kampuchea and subsequently agreeing to remove all of its forces from that country by the end of 1990.

At the same time Vietnam and the United States modified their postures toward each other. By agreement in 1987 joint U.S.–Vietnamese teams commenced systematic on-site searches to recover remains of American servicemen missing-in-action (MIAs). The U.S. government endorsed private American humanitarian assistance to Vietnamese victims of the war, and the Vietnamese government resumed the orderly departure program to permit Vietnamese to join family members already in the United States.

Change occurred even more rapidly during 1989. In April Vietnam unilaterally declared that all Vietnamese troops remaining in Kampuchea would be withdrawn in September—a full year ahead of the time frame previously announced. This appeared to have been accomplished by September 26, but was not verified.

In May 1989 a Sino-Soviet summit in Peking, long sought by Gorbachev, was successful. Gorbachev and Chinese leader Teng Hsiaoping agreed on the necessity of a negotiated settlement in Kampuchea which would include participation of all four Kampuchean resistance factions. Accordingly France hosted a 19-nation Peace Conference on

Kampuchea in Paris during July–August 1989. Even though the conference ended in "total disharmony," a future accord is likely because the Soviets, the Chinese, the ASEAN partners, Vietnam and the larger international community all clearly desire a solution.

ASEAN ASEAN was established to achieve economic and social collaboration among its partners in order to "promote regional peace and stability," but efforts fell far short of expectations. Unforeseen ASEAN political cooperation suddenly developed in consequence of Vietnam's military subjugation of Kampuchea. The members' united opposition to Vietnamese expansionism was quickly applauded by most of the international community. The initiative also presented an opportunity for the organization to exert greater influence. ASEAN became a political bloc capable of influencing major powers in Asia, Europe and the western hemisphere.

As the impasse in Indochina persisted but did not intensify further, the perceived security threat to ASEAN members receded. Almost simultaneously, having weathered the mid-1980s recession, most ASEAN members' economies began to strengthen. Prosperity impelled a search for ever wider markets and the partners began informal relaxation, or reinterpretation, of trade and investment restrictions against Vietnam. Led by Thailand and Indonesia, representing respectively "continental" and "maritime" Southeast Asia, ASEAN is likely, in recognition of Vietnam's troop withdrawal from Kampuchea, to forgive past sins of aggression. Some Thai and Indonesian leaders have already expressed willingness to accept Vietnam as a member of ASEAN upon satisfactory resolution of the impasse over power sharing in Phnom Penh.

ASEAN remains wary of major power intervention in the region. The partners continue to lobby for international acceptance of their demand for a Zone of Peace, Freedom and Neutrality and a Southeast Asia Nuclear Weapons Free Zone—policies directed at the Soviet Union because of its military presence at Camranh Bay in Vietnam, and the United States for its presumed nuclear capability at bases in Japan and the Philippines. ASEAN nevertheless tolerates, even supports, an American forward presence in the Philippines or U.S. offshore military facilities elsewhere in the Pacific. The United States is a market for ASEAN agricultural, mineral and manufactured products, the source of official economic and military assistance to member states, and a guarantor of security in the broader sense.

ASEAN seeks further accomodation with China, a powerful border state and historically a threat to stability in Southeast Asia. Accomodation with the Soviet Union is also likely because of the Soviet presence in Indochina and the strategic interests of the USSR in the Western Pacific.

Regardless of the failure of the July–August 1989 Paris Peace Conference, ASEAN's insistence that all four Kampuchean factions be included in a transitional Phnom Penh government will probably prevail because of on-the-ground reality. Nevertheless resolution of the Indochinese refugee problem will continue to be a challenge.

Southeast Asia   Southeast Asia became a recognized regional entity only in recent years. Following an uncertain beginning (its boundaries were largely determined by the victorious allies in the aftermath of WWII), the region was immediately beset by political strife which impeded economic development. Yet it has achieved a transformation. By 1990 the non-communist nations of the Southeast Asian region enjoyed a more favorable growth rate than those of any other world region. Two Southeast Asian nations—Singapore and, more recently, Thailand—have reached Newly Industrialized Country (NIC) status.

Nations of the region have with some success addressed traditionally diverse ethnic and religious differences among their populations. Faced with continuous armed struggle in Indochina, Southeast Asian nations, themselves, have contributed significantly to efforts to resolve the conflict. They bid well to become ever more significant actors among the Pacific Rim states.

FOOTNOTES

1. Donald Crone, "The ASEAN summit of 1987: Searching for New Dynamism," *Southeast Asian Affairs*, 1988, p. 37.

2. *Data Asia* (Manila: Press Foundation of Asia), 1979, p. 5961.

3. *Ibid.*

4. Rodney Trasker, "Neutral But Not Neutral Enough," *Far Eastern Economic Review*, March 30, 1979.

5. "Mush and Steel at Bali, *Ibid.*

6. *Data Asia, op cit.*, p. 6345–46.

7. *Ibid.*, 1978, p. 5897.

8. "Statement of Secretary Vance to ASEAN Foreign Ministers," (Manila: U.S. International Communication Agency), July 3, 1979.

9. Robert Shaplen, "A Reporter At Large: Nonaligned Conference," *The New Yorker*, October 22, 1979, p. 163.

10. Quoted by Oswald Johnson, "Hanoi, Moscow Denounced at UN Talks on Cambodia," *Los Angeles Times*, July 14, 1981.

11. Don Shannon, "China, ASEAN Bloc OK Unified Approach for Cambodia Peace," *Los Angeles Times*, July 17, 1981.

12. Communique reproduced in the *Asia Record* (Palo Alto, Calif.: Asia-Pacific Affairs Associates) July 1982, p. 4.

13. *Foreign Broadcast Information Service*, November 5, p. 33.

14. Donald E. Weatherbee, "ASEAN After Cambodia: Reordering Southeast Asia," *Asian Update* (N.Y.: The Asia Society), June 1989.

15. Goh Keng Swee, "Vietnam and Big Power Rivalry," in Richard H. Solomon, ed., *Asian Security in the 1980s* (Santa Monica: Rand Corporation), 1979, p. 158.

16. *Ibid.*, p. 159.

17. *Ibid.*, p. 161.

18. "U.S. Position in the Pacific in 1980," *Current Policy* (Washington, D.C.: Department of State), No. 154, March 27, 1980.

19. All pre-1981 refugee figures are from Marjorie Niehous, "Indochinese Refugee Exodus: Causes, Impact, Prospects," *Issue Brief*, No. IB79079 (Washington, D.C.: Congressional Research Service), October 2, 1980.

20. "Khmer Relief," *GIST* (Washington, D.C.: Department of State), June 1981.

BIBLIOGRAPHY

ASEAN

Allen, Thomas W. *The ASEAN Report,* 2 Vols. Hong Kong: Dow Jones Publishing (Asia), 1980.

Anand, R. P. and Purification V. Quisumbing (eds.). *ASEAN: Identity, Development and Culture.* Honolulu: East West Center Press, 1981.

Costello, Michael A., Thomas R. Leinbach, and Richard Ulack. *Mobility and Employment in Urban Southeast Asia: Examples from Indonesia and the Philippines.* Boulder, Colo.: Westview Press, 1987.

Crome, Donald K. *The ASEAN States: Coping with Dependence.* New York: Praeger, 1983.

Fifield, Russell H. *National and Regional Interests in ASEAN.* Athens, Ohio: Ohio University Press, 1979.

Shee Poon Kim. *ASEAN.* Singapore: Nanyang University, 1976.

Siddayo, Corazon M. (ed.). *ASEAN and Multinational Corporations.* Brookfield, Vermont: Gower Publishing Co., 1978.

Simon, Sheldon W. *The ASEAN States and Regional Security.* Stanford: Hoover Institution Press, 1982.

Skully, Michael T. *ASEAN Regional Financial Cooperation.* Athens, Ohio: Ohio University Press, 1979.

Tangsubkul, Phiphat. *ASEAN and the Law of the Sea.* Brookfield, Vermont: Gower Publishing Co., 1982.

Viksnins, George J. *Financial Deepening in the ASEAN Countries.* Honolulu: Pacific Forum, 1980.

BRUNEI

Leifer, Michael, "Decolonization and International Status," *International Affairs* (London), Vol. 54, April 1978.

Runciman, Steven. *The White Rajahs: A History of Sarawak from 1841 to 1946.* Cambridge: Cambridge University Press, 1960.

Ryan, N. J. *A History of Malaysia and Singapore.* London: Oxford University Press, 1976.

Tarling, Nicholas. *Britain, the Brookes and Brunei.* Kuala Lumpur: Oxford University Press, 1971.

Wright, Leigh R. *Origins of British Borneo.* Hong Kong: Hong Kong University Press, 1970.

BURMA

Aung San. *The Political Legacy of Aung San* (compiled by and with an introductory essay by Josef Silverstein). Ithaca: Southeast Asia Program, Cornell University, 1972.

Cady, John F. *Contacts With Burma, 1935–1949: A Personal Account.* Athens, Ohio: Ohio University Press, 1982.

A History of Modern Burma. Ithaca: Cornell University Press, 1958.

Gyi, Maung Maung. *Burmese Political Values.* New York: Praeger, 1983.

Hall, D. G. E. *Burma.* New York: AMS Press, 1974.

Morse, Ronald A. (ed.) *et. al. Burma: A Study Guide.* Lanham, MD: University Press of America, 1988.

Pye, Lucian W. *Politics, Personality and Nation Building: Burma's Search for Identity.* Westport, Conn.: Greenwood Press, 1976.

Silverstein, Josef. *Burma: Military Rule and the Politics of Stagnation.* Ithaca: Cornell University Press, 1977.

Burmese Politics: The Dilemma of National Unity. New Brunswick, N.J.: Rutgers University Press, 1980.

Steinberg, David I. *Burma: A Socialist Nation of Southeast Asia.* Boulder, Colo.: Westview, 1982.

Burma's Road Toward Development: Growth and Ideology Under Military Rule. Boulder, Colo.: Westview, 1981.

Taylor, Robert H. *The State in Burma.* Honolulu: University of Hawaii Press, 1988.

INDONESIA

Brackman, Arnold C. *Indonesian Communism: A History.* Westport, Conn.: Greenwood Press, 1976.

Crouch, Harold A. *The Army and Politics in Indonesia.* Ithaca: Cornell University Press, 1978.

Emmerson, Donald K. *Indonesia's Elite: Political Culture and Cultural Politics.* Ithaca: Cornell University Press, 1976.

Fryer, Donald W. and James C. Jackson. *Indonesia.* London: E. Benn, 1977.

Jackson, Karl D. *Traditional Authority, Islam, and Rebellion: A Study of Indonesian Political Behavior.* Berkeley: University of California Press, 1980.

Legge, John David. *Indonesia.* Sydney: Prentice-Hall of Australia, 1977.

Lubis, Mochtar. *We Indonesians.* Honolulu: Southeast Asian Studies, University of Hawaii, 1979.

McDonald H. *Suharto's Indonesia.* Honolulu: University Press of Hawaii, 1981.

Penders, C. L. M. *The Life and Times of Sukarno.* Kuala Lumpur: Oxford University Press, 1974.

Ricklefs, M. C. *A History of Modern Indonesia, c. 1300 to the Present.* Bloomington, Ind.: Indiana University Press, 1981.

Simon, Sheldon W. *The Broken Triangle: Peking, Djakarta and the PKI.* Baltimore: John Hopkins University Press, 1969.

Sutherland, Heather. *The Making of a Bureaucratic Elite.* Exeter, N.H.: Heineman, 1980.

Vittachi, Tarzie. *The Fall of Sukarno.* London: Mayflower-Dell, 1967.

Vlekke, Bernard Hubertus Maria. *Nusantara: A History of the East Indian Archipelago.* New York: Arno Press, 1977.

Weinstein, Franklin B. *Indonesian Foreign Policy and the Dilemma of Dependence: From Sukarno to Soeharto.* Ithaca: Cornell University Press, 1976.

Wild, Colin and Peter Carey (eds). *Born in Fire: The Indonesian Struggle for Independence (An Anthology).* Athens: Ohio University Press/Swallow Press, 1988.

KAMPUCHEA

Ablin, David A. and Marlowe Hood (eds.). *The Cambodian Agony.* Armonk, N.Y.: M. E. Sharpe, 1987.

Barron, John and Anthony Paul. *Murder of a Gentle Land.* New York: Reader's Digest Press, 1977.

Chandler, David P. *A History of Cambodia.* Boulder, Colo.: Westview, 1983.

Herz, M. F. *A Short History of Cambodia: From the Days of Angkor to the Present.* New York: Praeger, 1958.

Hildebrand, George C. *Cambodia: Starvation and Revolution.* New York: Monthly Review Press, 1976.

Khieu Samphan. *Cambodia's Economy and Industrial Development.* Ithaca: Southeast Asia Program, Cornell University, 1979.

Kiernan, Ben and Chanthou Boua. *Peasants and Politics in Kampuchea, 1942–1981.* Armonk, N.Y.: M. E. Sharpe, 1982.

Kulke, Hermann. *The Devaraja Cult.* Ithaca: Southeast Asia Program, Cornell University, 1978.

Mason, Linda and Roger Brown. *Rice, Rivalry and Politics: Managing Cambodian Relief.* South Bend, Ind.: University of Notre Dame Press, 1983.

Norodom Sihanouk Varman. *War and Hope: The Case for Cambodia.* New York: Pantheon Books, 1980.

Osborne, Milton E. *Before Kampuchea: Preludes to Tragedy.* Boston: G. Allen & Unwin, 1979.

Pradhan, Prakash Chandra. *Foreign Policy of Kampuchea*. Atlantic Highlands, N.J.: Humanities Press, 1983.

Shawcross, William. *Sideshow: Kissinger, Nixon and the Destruction of Cambodia*. New York: Simon and Schuster, 1979.

Simon, Sheldon W. *War and Politics in Cambodia. A Communications Analysis*. Durham, N.C.: Duke University Press, 1974.

LAOS

Dommen, Arthur J. *Conflict in Laos: The Politics of Neutralization*. New York: Praeger, 1971.

Fall, Bernard B. *Anatomy of a Crisis: The Laotian Crisis of 1960–1961*. Garden City, N.Y.: Doubleday, 1969.

Langer, Paul Fritz. *Revolution in Laos: The North Vietnamese and the Pathet Lao*. Santa Monica, Calif.: Rand Corporation, 1969.

Manich Jusmai, M. L. *History of Laos*. Bangkok: Chalermnit, 1967.

Sisouk Na Champassak. *Storm Over Laos: A Contemporary History*. New York: Praeger, 1961.

Stuart, Fox (ed.). *Contemporary Laos: Studies in the Politics and Society of the Lao People's Republic*. New York: St. Martin's Press, 1982.

Toye, Hugh. *Laos: Buffer State or Battleground*. London: Oxford University Press, 1968.

Whitaker, Donald P. *Laos, A Country Study*. Washington, D.C.: Foreign Area Studies, American University, 1979.

MALAYSIA

Emerson, Rupert. *A Study of Direct and Indirect Rule*. Kuala Lumpur: University of Malaya Press, 1964.

Enloe, Cynthia H. *Multi-Ethnic Politics: The Case of Malaysia*. Berkeley: Center for South and Southeast Asia Studies, University of California, 1970.

Funston, John. *Malay Politics in Malaysia*. Exeter, N.H.: Heineman, 1981.

Gullick, John. *Malaysia: Economic Expansion and National Unity*. Boulder, Colo.: Westview, 1981.

Means, Gordon Paul. *Malaysian Politics*. London: Hodder and Stoughton, 1976.

Milne, Robert Stephen and Diane K. Mauzy, *Politics and Government in Malaysia*. Vancouver: University of British Columbia Press, 1978.

Musolf, Lloyd D. *Malaysia's Parliamentary System*. Boulder, Colo.: Westview, 1979.

Roff, William R. *The Origins of Malay Nationalism*. New Haven: Yale University Press, 1967.

Tilman, Robert O. *In Quest of Unity: The Centralization Theme in Malaysian Federal-State Relations, 1957–75*. Singapore: Institute of Southeast Asian Studies, 1976.

Van der Kroef, Justus Maria. *Communism in Malaysia and Singapore*. The Hague: Martinus Nijhoff, 1967.

Vasil, R. K. *Ethnic Politics in Malaysia*. New Delhi: Radiant, 1980.

Von Vorys, Karl. *Democracy Without Consensus: Communalism and Political Stability in Malaysia*. Princeton: Princeton University Press, 1975.

Zakaria, Haji Ahmad (ed.). *Government and Politics of Malaysia*. Singapore: Institute of Southeast Asian Studies, 1987.

PHILIPPINES

Agoncillo, Teodora A. *A Short History of the Philippines*. New York: Mentor, 1969.

Berry, William E., Jr. *U.S. Bases in the Philippines: The Evolution of the Special Relationship*. Boulder, Colo.: Westview Press, 1989.

Bresnan, John (ed.). *Crisis in the Philippines: The Marcos Era and Beyond*. The Asia Society. Princeton: Princeton University Press, 1986.

De Los Santos, Epifiano. *The Revolutionists: Aguinaldo, Bonifacio, Jacinto*. Manila: National Historical Commission, 1973.

George, T. J. S. *Revolt in Mindanao: The Rise of Islam in Philippine Politics*. Kuala Lumpur: Oxford University Press, 1980.

Gregor, James A. and Virgilio Aganon. *The Philippine Bases: U.S. Security at Risk*. Lanham, MD: University Press of America, 1987.

Karnow, Stanley. *In Our Image: A History of United States Involvement in the Philippines*. New York: Random House, 1989.

Kerkvliet, Benedict J. *The Huk Rebellion: A Study of Peasant Revolt in the Philippines*. Berkeley: University of California Press, 1977.

Kessler, Richard J. *Rebellion and Repression in the Philippines*. New Haven: Yale University Press, 1989.

Petillo, Carol Morris, *Douglas MacArthur: The Philippine Years*. Bloomington, Ind.: Indiana University Press, 1981.

Phelan, John L. *The Hispanization of the Philippines*. Madison: University of Wisconsin Press, 1959.

Romulo, Carlos Pena. *I See the Philippines Rise*. New York: AMS Press, 1975.

Rosenberg, David A. (ed.). *Marcos and Martial Law in the Philippines*. Ithaca: Cornell University Press, 1979.

Steinberg, David J. *The Philippines: A Singular and Plural Place*. Boulder, Colo.: Westview, 1982.

Wurfel, David. *A Precarious Democracy: The Aquino Era in the Philippines*. Boulder, Colo.: Westview Press, 1989.

SINGAPORE

Barber, Noel. *The Singapore Story: From Raffles to Lee Kuan Yew*. London: Fontana, 1978.

Bedlington, Stanley S. *Malaysia and Singapore: The Building of New States*. Ithaca: Cornell University Press, 1978.

Bellows, Thomas, J. *The People's Action Party of Singapore*. New Haven: Southeast Asia Studies, Yale University, 1970.

Busch, Peter A. *Legitimacy and Ethnicity: A Case Study of Singapore*. Lexington, Mass.: Lexington Books, 1974.

Chan Heng Chee. *The Dynamics of One Party Dominance: The PAP at the Grass-Roots*. Singapore University Press, 1976.

Josey, Alex. *Lee Kuan Yew: The Struggle for Singapore*. Sydney: Angus & Robertson, 1974.

Marshall, David. *Singapore's Struggle for Nationhood, 1945–59*. Singapore: University Education Press, 1971.

Nair, C. V. Devan (ed.). *Socialism That Works . . . the Singapore Way*. Singapore: Federal Publications, 1976.

Trocki, Carl A. *Prince of Pirates: The Temenggongs and the Development of Johor and Singapore, 1784–1885*. Singapore: Singapore University Press, 1979.

Turnbull, Constance Mary. *A History of Singapore, 1819–1975*. Kuala Lumpur: Oxford University Press, 1977.

Yeo Kim Wah. *Political Development in Singapore, 1945–55*. Singapore: Singapore University Press, 1973.

SOUTHEAST ASIA

Allen, Sir Richard H. S. *A Short Introduction to the History and Politics of Southeast Asia*. New York: Oxford University Press, 1970.

Benda, Harry J. *Continuity and Change in Southeast Asia*. New Haven: Yale University Southeast Asia Studies, 1972.

Cady, John F. *Postwar Southeast Asia*. Athens, Ohio: Ohio University Press, 1974.

    Southeast Asia: Its Historical Development. New York: McGraw-Hill, 1964.

Coedes, Georges. *The Indianized States of Southeast Asia*. Honolulu: East West Center Press, 1968.

Dobby, Ernest H. G. *Southeast Asia*. London: University of London Press, 1973.

Hall, D. G. E. *A History of South-East Asia* (4th ed.). New York: St. Martin's Press, 1981.

Lewis, John P. *Asian Development: The Role of Development Assistance*. Lanham, MD: University Press of America, 1987.

McVey, Ruth T. (ed.) *Southeast Asian Transitions: Approaches Through Social History*. New Haven: Yale University Press, 1978.

Mehden, Fred R. von der. *Southeast Asia 1930–1970: The Legacy of Colonialism and Nationalism*. New York: W. W. Norton, 1974.

Osborne, Milton. *Southeast Asia: An Introductory History*. Sydney: George Allen & Unwin, 1979.

Pluvier, Jan. *Southeast Asia from Colonialism to Independence*. Kuala Lumpur: Oxford University Press, 1974.

Raymond, Wayne and Kent Mulliner (eds.). *Southeast Asia, An Emerging Center of World Influence?* Athens, Ohio: Ohio University Press, 1977.

Snitwongse, Kusuma and Sukhumbhand Paribatra (eds.). *Durable Stability in Southeast Asia*. Singapore: Institute of Southeast Asian Studies, 1987.

Steinberg, David Joel (ed.). *In Search of Southeast Asia: A Modern History* (Rev. ed.) Honolulu: University of Hawaii Press, 1987.

Tarling, Nicholas. *A Concise History of South-East Asia*. New York: Praeger, 1966.

Tate, D. J. M. *The Making of Modern Southeast Asia, 2 vols.* London: Oxford University Press, 1971.

Williams, Lea E. *Southeast Asia: A History*. New York: Oxford University Press, 1976.

THAILAND

Ayal, Eliezer B. (ed.). *The Study of Thailand*. Athens, Ohio: Ohio University Center for International Studies, 1978.

Bowring, Sir John. *The Kingdom and People of Siam: With a Narrative of the Mission to That Country in 1855*. New York: AMS Press, 1975.

Bradley, William, *et al*. *Thailand, Domino by Default?* Athens, Ohio: Ohio University Press, 1978.

Bunbongkarm, Suchit. *The Military in Thai Politics, 1981–86*. Singapore: Institute of Southeast Asian Studies, 1987.

Bunge, Frederica M. *Thailand: A Country Study*. Washington, D.C.: American University Foreign Area Studies, 1980.

Darling, Frank C. and Ann Darling. *Thailand: The Modern Kingdom*. Singapore: Asia Pacific Press, 1971.

Elliott, David L. *Thailand: Origins of Military Rule*. London: Zed Press, 1978.

Haas, David F. *Interaction in the Thai Bureaucracy*. Boulder, Colo: Westview, 1979.

Ishii, Yoneo. *Thailand: A Rice-Growing Society*. Honolulu: University Press of Hawaii, 1978.

Jha, Ganganath. *Foreign Policy of Thailand*. New Delhi: Radiant, 1979.

Lissak, Moshe. *Military Roles in Modernization: Civil-Military Relations in Thailand and Burma*. Beverly Hills, Calif.: Sage Publications, 1976.

Marks, Thomas A. *Thailand, the Threatened Kingdom*. London: Institute for the Study of Conflict, 1980.

Morrell, David and Chaianan Samudvanija. *Political Conflict in Thailand: Reform, Reaction, Revolution*. Cambridge, Mass.: Oelgeschlager, Gunn and Hain, 1981.

Neher, Clark D. *The Dynamics of Politics and Administration in Rural Thailand*. Athens, Ohio: Ohio University, Center for International Studies, 1974.

(ed.). *Modern Thai Politics: From Village to Nation*. Cambridge, Mass.: Schenkman, 1976.

Ramsay, Ansil and Wiwat Mungkandi (eds.). *Thailand-U.S. Relations: Changing Political, Strategic and Economic Factors*. Research Papers and Policy Studies 23. Berkeley: University of California, Institute of East Asian Studies, 1988.

Riggs, Fred W. *Thailand: The Modernization of a Bureaucratic Polity*. Honolulu: East West Center Press, 1966.

Siffin, William J. *The Thai Bureaucracy: Institutional Change and Development*. Westport, Conn.: Greenwood Press, 1975.

Somsakdi Xuto (ed.). *Government and Politics of Thailand*. Singapore: Institute of Southeast Asian Studies, 1987.

VIETNAM

Buttinger, Joseph. *Vietnam: The Unforgettable Tragedy*. New York: Horizon Press, 1977.

Charlton, Michael and Anthony Moncrieff. *Many Reasons Why: The American Involvement in Vietnam*. New York: Hill and Wang, 1978.

Duiker, William J. *Vietnam: A Nation in Revolution*. Boulder, Colo.: Westview, 1983.

Elliott, David W. P. (ed.). *The Third Indochina Conflict*. Boulder, Colo.: Westview, 1981.

Ellsberg, Daniel. *Papers on the War*. New York: Simon & Schuster, 1972.

Herring, George C. *America's Longest War: The United States and Vietnam*. New York: Wiley, 1979.

Karnow, Stanley. *Vietnam: A History*. New York: Viking, 1983.

Kattenburg, Paul M. *The Vietnam Trauma in American Foreign Policy, 1945–1975*. New Brunswick, N.J.: Transaction Books, 1980.

Lansdale, Edward Geary. *In The Midst of Wars: An American's Mission to Southeast Asia.* New York: Harper & Row, 1972.

Lewy, Guenter. *America in Vietnam.* Oxford: Oxford University Press, 1978.

Long, Nguyen, with Harry H. Kendall. *After Saigon Fell: Daily Life under the Vietnamese Communists.* Berkeley: Institute of East Asian Studies, 1981.

Marr, David G. and Christine P. White (eds.) *Postwar Vietnam: Dilemmas in Socialist Development.* Ithaca: Cornell University Press, 1988.

McAlister, John T. and Paul Mus. *The Vietnamese and Their Revolution.* New York: Harper & Row, 1970.

Our President: Ho Chi Minh. Hanoi: Foreign Languages Publishing House, 1970.

Outline History of the Vietnam Workers' Party. Hanoi, Foreign Language Publishing House, 1976.

Pike, Douglas Eugene. *The Viet-Cong Strategy of Terror.* Cambridge, Mass.: M.I.T. Press, 1970.

   Vietnam and the Soviet Union: Anatomy of an Alliance. Boulder, Colo.: Westview Press, 1987.

Podhoretz, Norman. *Why We Were in Vietnam.* New York: Simon and Schuster, 1982.

Poole, Peter A. *Eight Presidents and Indochina.* Huntington, N.Y.: R. E. Krieger, 1978.

Rotter, Andrew J. *The Path to Vietnam: Origins of the American Commitment to Southeast Asia:* Ithaca: Cornell University Press, 1988.

Sheehan, Neil, *et al. The Pentagon Papers.* New York: Bantam, 1971.

   A Bright Shining Lie: John Paul Vann and America in Vietnam. New York: Random House, 1988.

Taylor, Keith W. *The Birth of Vietnam.* Berkeley: University of California Press, 1983.

Turley, William S. *Vietnamese Communism in Comparative Perspective.* Boulder, Colo.: Westview, 1981.

Turner, Robert F. *Vietnamese Communism,* Its Origins and Development. Stanford: Hoover Institution Press, 1975.

Vickerman, Andrew. *The Fate of the Peasantry: Premature Transition to Socialism in the Democratic Republic of Vietnam.* New Haven: Yale Center for International and Area Studies, 1987.

INDEX

Abdul Rahman, Tunku, 159, 163, 165, 167, 183

Abdul Razak, 163, 165, 166

Aguinaldo, Emilio, 338, 339–340, 353

Alaungpaya, 10, 214

Angkor, 10, 16; Kampuchea, 71–74, 76, 84, 88, 90; Laos 106; Thailand, 245, 246, 247. *See also* Kampuchea

Anglo-Burmese Wars, 215, 216–218

Annam, 10, 15–24 *passim,* 29, 31, 74, 75, 110, 111. *See also* Vietnam

Anti Fascist People's Freedom League (AFPFL), 226, 227, 230–231

ANZUK (Five Power Defense Arrangement), 168, 184, 193, 207, 389

ANZUS (Triparte Agreement), 375, 384

Aquino, Benigno, 354, 355, 358–360

Aquino, Corazon, 363–368

Arakan, 211–218 *passim,* 228, 233. *See also* Burma

Archipelagic Theory, 169–170, 314, 356, 363, 372, 375

Association of Southeast Asia, 162, 352, 371

Association of Southeast Asian Nations (ASEAN), 371–382, 395–396; archipelagic theory, 372, 375; Association of Southeast Asia, 371; Brunei as member, 207, 371, 372; Burma, 237; Chinese as ethnic problem, 375–377; economic assets, 372–373, 395; economic integration, 373–374; Indochina policy changes, 381–382; Indochinese refugees, 375–382, 388, 391, 392; Indonesia as member, 313–314, 316, 322–323, 371–382 *passim,* 395; Japan, 373, 375, 378, 380; Joint Informal Meetings (JIM), 382; Kampuchea, 95–104 *passim,* 375–382, 395–396; Laos, 375; Malaysia as member, 162, 168, 170, 371–382; Manila Charter (1976), 372; Maphilindo, 371–372; nonaligned bloc, 372, 378–379; organization of, 371, 395; PRC, 375–381 *passim,* 392, 395; Philippines as member, 361, 362, 364, 366, 371–382 *passim,* 395; political cohesion, 374–378, 393; population, 372; Rajaratnam, Sinnathamby, 377, 379; Singapore as member, 187, 192, 193, 371, 373–382, 395; SEA Nuclear Weapons Free Zone, 395; Thailand as member, 275, 371–382 *passim,* 393, 395; USSR, 376, 378, 379, 393; UN organizations, 378, 380, 392; UN Special Conference on Kampuchea (1981), 379–380; US, 372, 373, 375, 378, 382, 388, 389, 395; Vietnam, 59–60, 64, 372, 375, 395; zone of peace freedom and neutrality, 372, 375, 395